T0367942

Other Books

Confessions of a Hippie, Always searching for love

Love and Loathing in the Islands, Searching for Gauguin

LOVE AND REDEMPTION IN THE TROPICS,

MISSING GAUGUIN

ADRIANA BARDOLINO

LOVE AND REDEMPTION IN THE TROPICS, MISSING GAUGUIN

iUniverse books may be ordered through booksellers or by contacting:

iUniverse
1663 Liberty Drive
Bloomington, IN 47403
www.iuniverse.com
844-349-9409

ISBN: 978-1-6632-5371-2 (sc)
ISBN: 978-1-6632-5370-5 (e)

Library of Congress Control Number: 2023911558

Print information available on the last page.

iUniverse rev. date: 11/30/2023

CONTENTS

PREFACE

Adriana finds getting older sometimes poses more questions about life than answers. The time frame of this third book in the memoir series encompasses 1981 to 2001, a twenty-year period. Adriana embarks on a new life with her boyfriend in Florida. They plan to marry and live happily ever after in the Sunshine State. After having lived on the remote, laid-back, tropical island of Maui, they find adjusting to life on the mainland difficult. Their daily existence dangles at the edge of a precipice, fraught with one obstacle after another. The universe doesn't seem to be cooperating with their plans and dreams. Adriana begins to miss her life in Hawaii where everything flowed easily and naturally. She and her partner fall on hard financial times, and life becomes a struggle. They find out why islanders refer to the mainland as the *Madland*.

Adriana's journey as a woman approaching her forties and fifties is quite different than when she was a young woman in her twenties and thirties in books one and two. Her youth was a time when she threw herself into love and relationships with total abandon. Her life was erratic, and she colored it all through a romantic lens.

In her forties she begins to resurrect her dreams after being lost in transition for a long time. Crises in love, friendships, and family, change her, and force her into a reluctant, perhaps belated, adulthood. Through all of life's turmoil art is her center, her stability, her happy place. Unfortunate life events rob her creativity, and she even loses Gauguin (her art), which disappears into a black hole.

When Adriana reaches her fifties, she is forced by circumstances to question her life choices. She desires peace and security over turbulence and uncertainty. She experiences great emotional losses and betrayals along the way, and is swallowed up by darkness. She wonders if light and happiness will ever return. She misses and longs for her life in Gauguin.

Adriana strives to learn to love herself, and to forgive her past mistakes. She seeks redemption. Adventures in new lands help her to get out of familiar ruts and traps. As the year 2000 approaches new horizons appear. Will Adriana reconnect with Gauguin?

Adriana manages to find humor in just about any situation, even during times of tragedy and great personal loss. She never loses her lust for life or the desire for a connection with the opposite sex. She still experiences life through an artistic, sensual, and at times, ethereal lens. She continues to have hope, even when she is hurtling through space with planet earth spinning out of her reach.

As you travel along her journey, she will make you laugh and cry right along with her. I hope you enjoy Adriana's ongoing saga, and perhaps gain some insights into your own life—present, past, and future.

American writer James Baldwin said, "But people cannot unhappily, invent their mooring posts, their lovers, and their friends, any more than they can invent their parents. Life gives these and also takes them away. The great difficulty is to say yes to life."

If tragedy does not ensnare a man, if affliction does not agitate him, if love does not lay him down in the cradle of dreams, then his life is like a blank white page in the book of existence.

—Khalil Gibran, *The Broken Wings*

November 14, 1995, Maui, Hawaii

I heard moans in longing tones, and shouts, "Ma, Ma, Ma." The voice was familiar. It was my voice. I sat up in bed trying to focus because she was fading away.

He shook me. "What? What's wrong?"

"It was my mother standing on the sidewalk in front of the first house we lived in."

"You were dreaming."

"No. It was real; it was her. She was holding her arms out wanting to embrace me."

"What did she say?"

"She didn't say anything. She was smiling at me. Then she put her hands together like she was going to pray. She always did that when she was happy about something. For the first time in my life I felt that she was finally pleased with me."

He put his arms around me, and I began to cry.

"It's only natural. You've been through so much over the past few months, but you're home now."

I stopped crying. We lay back down, and I nuzzled my head in the crook of his shoulder while he rubbed my arm with tenderness. Soon we both fell back to sleep.

CHAPTER 1
LOST IN THE EVERGLADES

The miracle of the light pours over the green and brown expanse of saw grass and of water, shining and slow-moving below, the grass and water that is the meaning and the central fact of the Everglades of Florida. It is a river of grass.

—Marjorie Stoneman Douglas

Pelicans on Biscayne Bay

November 24, 1981, Miami, Florida

It was Thanksgiving Day. My partner Derick Ellis and I were at Ross and Laura Grant's apartment in Miami. We'd only been in Florida for a few days, and I was already missing Hawaii. Ross's mom was visiting from Brooklyn, and we spent much of the day preparing for the feast. There would be no tomato-and-mayonnaise sandwiches on white bread that day. The turkey was in the oven, and all the trimmings were on top of the stove. It was all copacetic and festive. I gazed at Derick and Ross on the terrace. They seemed to buddy up like they'd been altar boys together when they were kids. Even in all my happiness at the time, it worried me.

I turned my attention to Laura who was mashing potatoes in a large pot on the stove with lots of butter. She swept the short dark hair away from her face and asked me if I'd seen the royal wedding of Lady Diana to the prince of England. I remarked that I'd seen most of it. It was broadcast on Maui live from London, so we tuned in to watch the event in the middle of the night. Regina Rinaldi and I stayed up to watch the spectacle, but the TV cable went out near the end. This often happened in the islands in those early days. You'd be watching a program and the trade winds would kick up and knock out the cable at the last crucial fifteen minutes of the show. You never found out who the murderer was, or what happened at the end of a story. Regina and I marveled at the romantic fairytale gown Lady Di wore. It was an ornate mass of silk and taffeta tufts with antique lace, her tulle veil of twenty-five feet trailing behind her. All that was missing was the pumpkin coach driven by mice.

I walked out to the terrace with the Tanqueray and tonic I was nursing. Derick put his arm around me. We gazed out over the glistening water in the bay. I had a momentary thought of how different this horizon was from Maui. He smiled at me, kissed me tenderly on the lips, and the thought evaporated in the humid Miami air. I was adjusting to life on the mainland.

"It's nice, huh?" Derick said.

"Yes, Ross and Laura sure have a nice place."

"He won't let us down. It will all work out okay," he said.

"I know that. I'm just not used to depending on other people."

"He's your friend. You said he's like a brother to you. Don't you have faith in him?"

"He lent me a few thousand dollars for our move. There will be a price to pay," I said.

"Now you're talking crazy," Derick said, with an innocent expression, tousling his wild, wavy blond hair. "We'll pay him back."

"Rebel's in the dog kennel. We have to get our own place soon."

"We just got here," Derick said. I could tell by his tone that he was slightly annoyed with me. "Give him a chance to do what he promised."

Ross walked back out to the terrace with a joint and passed it to Derick. It was a breezy day, and his dark curly hair was blowing. He had a pensive look on his face, his brown eyes narrowing, and he still hadn't shaved off his beard. The three of us stood out there for a while passing the joint back and forth saying nothing. My friend Star Green's words rolled around in my brain: *"There will be a price. Everything in life has a price."* I left them and walked inside to help Laura and Ross's mom set the food on the dining room table. I gazed at the guys on the terrace laughing and joking around. My sweetheart and my old commune brother. I smiled, my heart melting and lifting.

> The cost of a thing is the amount of what I call life which is required to be exchanged for it, immediately or in the long run.
>
> —Henry David Thoreau

A few days after Thanksgiving the four of us went out on Ross's boat. The boat flew, barely touching the water as it glided past Stiltsville in Biscayne Bay. I gazed at the horizon. There wasn't a hill or a mountain in sight. I fantasized living in one of those wooden houses on the bay, picturing Derick fishing off the side with Rebel sitting next to him. It was so good to be on the water again. I loved the mountains, but I always preferred living by the sea. Ross slowed the boat down as we approached a dock in front of a restaurant, which I thought was a unique way to arrive. I remember having stone crab for lunch; Derick and Ross had grouper fingers, and Laura had a salade Niçoise. We laughed and talked over drinks, and I felt as if I was living the high life. We continued to be suspended in a vacation bubble for days, forever floating above the endless spans of water.

Stiltsville

Our former roommates from Maui, Dante and Regina Rinaldi, stopped in Florida on their way to New Jersey from Hawaii. They were staying at a motel in Miami. They came to Ross's place, and we hung out by the pool. I swore I could smell Maui on Regina's clothing. We took them fishing the next day. We reminisced about the wonderful and crazy times the four of us had living together in the house we shared on Nanu Street in Lahaina. Regina told me they had their dog, Honey Girl, with them. They'd snuck her into the motel room. I mentioned that I was determined to get our own place before Christmas, and that we would be picking Rebel up from the dog kennel very soon. I felt Derick's eyes on me when I made that comment, and not in a good way. It was fun to reconnect with them, but when they left I felt a longing for our life on Maui. Everything there was filled with familiarity, and life was natural and good. I hoped we hadn't made a grave mistake moving to Florida. Here, I felt as if I was in a strange Madland, the future filled with uncertainty.

Derick and I had our own bedroom and bathroom in Ross's apartment which afforded us privacy. We were still in the dreamy phase of our relationship. I missed Rebel, and it troubled me that Derick never mentioned him; after all, wasn't Rebel actually Derick's dog? Evenings were spent sitting around a large wrap-around couch in the corner of the living room watching TV. Ross Grant liked to watch pornography, and there were nights when I sat there uncomfortably watching porn and snorting cocaine. I thought, *As if Derick needs any encouragement in the sex department!* I didn't like how the films rendered me sexually aroused without any emotional or human connection. And for God's sake, who comes up with that crazy music while people are doing freaky stuff in front of a camera and floodlights? I kept my mouth shut because the guys seemed to like it. In a private moment I asked Derick if he liked watching porn.

"Not really," he said, with a guilty smile, probably sensing I didn't, and saying what I wanted to hear.

I was washing Derick's aloha shirts by hand in the bathroom sink, when Ross happened to walk by. He stood in the doorway staring at me with disapproval.

"What the hell are you doing? We do have a washer and dryer," he said.

"I know, but the shirts will last longer if washed by hand."

Ross stood there shaking his head, and I recalled his comment about my having a working-class mentality. I felt momentarily embarrassed, but I wasn't going to change my habits according to how someone else saw me.

"Do you guys have an ironing board?" I asked.

"If that's what you want, I'll have Laura get it for you," Ross said, visibly annoyed.

This was the routine for our first couple of weeks back on the mainland. I heard no business talk from Ross, and to be honest I was afraid to ask. When Derick and I were alone I brought up the topic.

"Has Ross said anything to you about looking for a retail space?"

"No, but he's taking me on a run with him tonight. I was going to mention it to you."

"Be careful. I don't know what he's up to, but that's not what we came here for."

"Relax, it's no biggie. Besides, we need the money," Derick said.

The guys never returned that night, and I began to wonder what the hell I'd gotten us into. Laura and I watched TV and talked, but my mind was preoccupied. The following day they returned mid-afternoon, and I felt a sigh of relief. When we were together I felt safe and protected, and knew everything would be all right. When apart I felt fearful and anxious. Once inside the bedroom with the door closed, Derick turned to me.

"Miss me?" he asked, with a boyish expression.

"You know it," I said, pouting.

He had a hot, melty expression on his face. "Wanna do it?"

I can't remember anyone else who made me feel the way I did right then. He filled my senses with love, sensuality, sex, and a little fear—always a little fear. He began to undress me slowly, watching my facial expressions. He stared at me as he took off his pants and T-shirt. I enjoyed watching him undress. He was my man, and it thrilled me. Soon we were tangled in that web of sex and emotion, and all seemed right with the world.

We had been in Miami for about three weeks, and although we were having fun I felt a sense of urgency to get our own place. Derick seemed very comfortable with Ross at the helm, but I didn't like it. I flashed on something one of the women on the old commune had said to me: "Ross moves people around like pieces on a chessboard." That same day when I went down to the pool I saw a guy with a dog on the elevator, and realized that Ross lied about dogs not being allowed in the building. His deception pissed me off.

One evening, the four of us were sitting on the couch in the living room watching a new cop show called *Hill Street Blues*. We were talking and laughing during the commercials, when Ross shared a horrific tale.

"Some guys I was dealing with came here one night and tied me and Laura up. Scared the shit out of us," he said.

"What the hell do you mean Ross? Why would they tie you and Laura up?" I asked.

"I owed the guy money. But it wasn't the first time we had a sketchy night like that."

I gazed at Laura who was laughing, but I could tell she was uncomfortable. I wasn't liking what I was hearing. Derick took my hand and stroked it while shaking his head and laughing. I didn't see anything funny about it. Just then, a helicopter appeared outside the apartment building and hovered outside the windows. Fear came over me with an awful thought—that the apartment was being watched? Ross ignored my bewildered expression.

When we went to bed that night, I waited until after we made love to talk to Derick. I didn't want to kill the sex vibe, because I knew he was going to tell me I was being negative.

"Derick, I'm beginning to feel uncomfortable here."

"Did that crazy story scare you?" he said, shaking his head and snickering.

"Not just that story, but the helicopter hovering around the building like that. What if they're watching this apartment?"

"Calm down tiger. Do you think I'd let anything happen to you?"

"Derick, I want to get our own place. Don't you?"

"Of course I do. Everything will happen in time."

"Besides, I miss Rebel. Don't you miss him? You never talk about him."

"Yeah, I miss him, but he's safe. Now let's not be hasty."

"I want to be in our own place for Christmas," I said.

"I'd like that too, but what do you think Ross will say?"

"I really don't care what he thinks," I said, annoyed that Derick seemed to take Ross's side.

Derick frowned reaching for his cigarettes, lit one up, and took a drag. There was a long silence. Now I was wide awake, so I flipped the radio on. Kim Carnes was singing her new song "Bette Davis Eyes." I soon relaxed a bit, put my leg over Derick's body and nuzzled my face in his neck.

"Don't be mad at me," I said.

"I'm not mad at you. I just think you're always too quick to do things."

"Yeah, that's me, but I know Ross better than you do. He can be very manipulate. And when did you start smoking Winstons?"

"I just wanted to try a different brand. Ross gave me some money for the run we did the other day. We do need the money," he said.

Suddenly, I realized what Ross's real motivation was in wining and dining us with that trip to Canada for his honeymoon last summer, and I felt anger. He was grooming us to be part of his marijuana business. I saw how he was using Derick, and God only knew what he had in mind for me. I closed my eyes as Derick stamped out his cigarette in the ashtray. He reached for me, and I hugged him. I played with his hair in the dark and kissed him slowly on the lips.

"I love you Derick."

"I love you too tiger."

It was an exceptionally beautiful day, so Derick borrowed Ross's car and we drove across a bridge and onto one of the Florida Keys. The air flowing through the windows was balmy and sweet. "Hold on Tight" by ELO was playing on the car radio. It reminded me that I needed to hold on to my dreams. I reached my hand to the back of Derick's neck and played with his hair, which was almost long enough now to make a pony tail. I watched a satisfied smile break out on his face.

He pulled the car off the road and parked. We got out and walked toward the water. I sat on the sand while Derick looked for small flat rocks to skim across the surface. I watched the rocks hop and disappear in the water.

The Florida landscape was nothing like the landscape of Maui. Instead of the vast ocean and neighboring islands, I stared at the Miami skyline in the distance, with highways, overpasses, and bridges. I felt sad and missed Hawaii terribly. When Derick turned to look at me, I smiled at him, hiding my feelings. I sat there knowing I was lost somewhere in the Everglades, and I wasn't even sure where the Everglades were.

It was getting close to Christmas. I bought a Miami newspaper and began searching for apartments. I didn't say anything until I found a condo apartment in Coconut Grove that looked promising. It was only a fifteen-minute drive from Ross and Laura's place. I told Derick about it, and I sensed trepidation in the look on his face. Once I got an idea in my head it was hard to stop me. I convinced him to have a look at it. We were all sitting around the dining room table eating breakfast, when I announced that I'd found an apartment in Coconut Grove. The only thing heard was the clanking of silverware dropping and coffee mugs hitting the table.

Ross shook his head. "I told you that you guys could stay here as long as you want."

"Our dog Rebel is sitting in a kennel, and it's been over three weeks," I said.

"Things take time to put together," Ross said. "Besides, right now is not a good time to go into business."

"Ross, that's why Derick and I sold everything and came to Florida. Why didn't you say this before we left Maui?" Now I was really angry. I saw that Ross had a scheme in mind, not a plan.

"Adriana, I had the best of intentions," Ross said.

"Derick and I are going to see the apartment today," I said, ending the conversation.

That afternoon Derick borrowed Ross's car and took me to see the apartment. It was a small condo complex on West Pelican Drive with ten apartments. We walked up a flight of stairs, and the owner was waiting for us at number 10. The number 10 was repetitive in my life, so this was significant. The apartment was modern and partly furnished, which was good, since we had nothing. There were two outside terraces, one off the living room, and one off the bedroom upstairs. As I was checking out the half-bath downstairs the owner asked us if it met our expectations.

Derick said, "It's really nice." But I could tell he had reservations as to how we were going to pay for it.

I signed the lease without as much as a second thought, and the owner and I shook hands. He told us we could move in any time, which made me happy. I had an inkling that Derick didn't see our situation the way I did, but I knew if we stayed there much longer, Derick would be seduced by easy money, and Ross and I would become enemies.

On the ride back to Ross and Laura's apartment there was a deafening silence I didn't understand. I jabbered away about how I wanted to decorate the apartment, and how great it was that there was a supermarket, a drug store, and a department store, only a block away across the boulevard. Derick said nothing. "I'll be so happy to see Rebel again," I said.

Derick stared straight ahead, his hands gripped on the steering wheel. I could only imagine what was going through his mind because he wasn't sharing his thoughts.

The next day I packed my suitcase, and over breakfast I mentioned how close the new apartment was to their place. There were conciliatory nods all around. Derick borrowed Ross's car again, loaded the TV and the box I'd packed from Maui, and we drove to the dog kennel to pick up Rebel. I was feeling elated as we drove to the new apartment—that is, until Derick basically dumped me and Rebel off like we were baggage, saying that Ross had something for him to do that night. In all my excitement I didn't noticed that Derick didn't have his suitcase. I was dumbfounded, but didn't stop him from walking out the door.

After he left I sat on the floor in the empty apartment with Rebel next to me feeling somewhat lost and abandoned. Derick didn't return that night, and I wondered if I had done something reckless. I plugged in the television to gain some semblance of normalcy. Rebel was staring at me when I said out loud, "We're lost somewhere in the Everglades, wherever the hell that is." Rebel tilted his head to the side sympathetically. He stood up and put his paw on my knee. That's when I began to cry.

By the next day, I'd calmed down a bit. After taking Rebel for a walk I cruised over to the small shopping center to buy groceries. Luckily everything was within walking distance because we didn't have a vehicle. Coffee and dog food were numbers one and two on my list. When I got back to the apartment I unpacked the coffee pot and made coffee. I toasted a Thomas' English muffin, one of the unavailable food items in Hawaii at that time. I fed Rebel and put the TV on, which seemed to be my only company with voices, and I unpacked the rest of the box. I wondered where Derick was, and what Ross had him doing. I figured Derick was angry with me, thinking I was screwing things up with Ross, and deviating from the grand plan. It never dawned on me at the time that I was emasculating Derick in some way. Derick probably figured he needed money and was going to do whatever Ross had lined up for him. Right then, all I wanted was to feel Derick's arms around me. I needed some reassurance that we were okay, that moving from Hawaii to Florida wasn't a big mistake—one that I had initiated on a promise, a wing and a prayer.

It was going on day three, and I was getting a little scared. Was Derick ever coming home? I took a stroll into the heart of Coconut Grove, which was only about eight blocks from the apartment. It was a trendy area with high-end boutiques and quaint outside cafés. I liked the area but found myself walking through a sketchy neighborhood to get there. I wasn't sure what kind of work I'd be able to find, but I had enough money for a few months. It was the first time in years I was without a car. I took a bus to the unemployment office to file a claim. Benefits wouldn't begin for a few weeks because they would be generated from the state of Hawaii. I came home and sat at the dining room table and began making to-do lists to keep my mind occupied. Every time I thought of Derick I would choke up, but I stopped myself from crying. I had to have some faith in him, and in our relationship.

On the fourth evening, there was a knock at the door. I heard Derick call out, "Adriana, open up; it's me." I opened the door and Derick was standing there with his suitcase. I threw my arms around his neck. He picked me up, carried me up the stairs, and tossed me on the bed.

"Where the hell have you been?" I asked.

"Ross told me not to say where I was going."

"But Derick, not even to call me. I thought you were angry with me, that maybe you weren't ever coming home."

"Now you're talking some crazy shit. Come here tiger, I want to make love to you."

He pulled his face away from mine and stared at me. His expression dissolved into mush, and his eyes watered. His eyes were a golden hazel that almost matched the highlights in his hair. There was always a wildness in them. Maybe that's what attracted me to him from the very beginning. I was so in love with him. I thought of the Charlotte Bronte quote from *Jane Eyre*: "You—you strange—you almost unearthly thing!—I love as my own flesh."

He got up off the bed and began to undress while watching me. I pulled my dress up to reveal I wasn't wearing underwear.

"Oh God. It's been a few days," he said.

He got on top of me and thrust it in. It was over pretty quick. He played with my breasts and sucked on the nipples. I began to squirm under him.

"Stop, it's not fair," I said, in a pouty tone.

"I want you to come too," he said, softly.

I pushed his head lower on my body and he got the message, pulling my legs apart and putting his head between them. The last few days were running through my brain, and I couldn't get past a certain point. Derick was hard again. He pulled himself up and thrust it in.

He whispered in my ear, "Forget everything. Just think about this."

My entire body throbbed in waves of pleasure.

Derick chuckled a little when we were done.

"I told you, if there's one thing I'm good at," he said, with a satisfied look on his face.

In the morning I left Derick asleep in bed and went downstairs. Rebel was up waiting at the front door while I set up the coffee pot. He'd stare at the door until I took him for a walk. I noticed a different car in our parking space as I walked down the stairs to the street. *Is someone parked in our spot?* I wondered. I didn't see Ross's car parked anywhere along the street. There was a yard on the side of the building on Pelican Drive, so I didn't have to walk far to find a place for Rebel to do his business.

Derick was up and outside on the terrace smoking a Winston when I got back. Unlike Ross's apartment our terraces overlooked a highway, not the bay. I walked up behind him and put my arms around him. He turned his face to kiss me.

"Derick, I think someone is parked in our space."

"It's my car," he said.

"Your car?" I asked, dumbfounded.

"Yeah, I made enough money on that run I did for Ross to buy a decent car."

I didn't quite know what to think or how to feel. I decided to not pick apart the situation, and to trust Derick's instincts. I knew he was doing what he could to make some money for us.

"Wanna go for a ride?" he said.

"We'll find a beach on one of the keys and let Rebel go swimming. He'll love that."

"I'll give him a bath downstairs with the hose when we get back," Derick said.

As soon as Derick reached for Rebel's leash, the dog got all excited, knowing he was going somewhere. The dog knew exactly what B-E-A-C-H and O-U-T meant. I put a towel on the back seat of the car so Rebel wouldn't mess it up with sand. I circled the car, which was a dull gold color, and immediately flashed on my parents' gold Oldsmobile, but there was no Virgin Mary on the dashboard. It was an older-model Chrysler sedan, but it was clean inside and out. I felt warm and mushy on the inside as we drove off. The fear about Derick leaving me, and the disappointment of the past few weeks slipped away. I reached over and played with Derick's hair to assure him that I was still very much in love with him.

We found a deserted stretch of beach on the first key, and he pulled the car off the road. As soon as I opened the door Rebel ran straight to the water's edge. The dog stood there barking at the waves, his brindle coat shining in the sun. Derick picked up a stick, threw it out into the water, and Rebel swam out to fetch it. I sat on the sand watching them play that game for a while. I finally felt relaxed and envisioned things were going to be all right.

On the way home we stopped at a local store and picked up a small fake Christmas tree with lights and all. Derick set it on the corner of the kitchen counter. That evening we sat at the dining room table and ate dinner.

"Feels homey," Derick said.

"Yes, but I miss the smell of pine."

"They're selling Christmas trees in front of Zayre's at the shopping center."

"I don't think we should spend money on a tree. Besides, it's already Christmas."

Derick looked disappointed.

On Christmas Eve, while Derick was asleep I walked across the boulevard to the shopping center. I spotted a group of guys selling evergreens. I gave them a sob story about not having enough money to buy a tree, but if I could just have some discarded branches to make my house smell nice. ... They told me to take as many as I wanted, so I took as much as I could carry. When I got back to the apartment I entwined them along the railing of the staircase going up to the bedroom. I didn't see Rebel, so I walked upstairs and saw him lying on the floor next to the bed. I sat on the bed waking Derick.

"I'll make you breakfast, whatever you want," I said.

"You know what I want," he said, with a sleepy but melty expression.

I kissed Derick. "After we have breakfast," I insisted.

Derick rubbed his eyes, sat up and reached for me, but I slipped away and went downstairs.

"I'll have bacon and eggs with an English muffin," he yelled down after me.

I was getting the plates out of the kitchen cabinet when Derick hopped down the staircase. I watched a big grin slowly break out on his face.

"Smells good in here. When did you do this?"

"While you were asleep."

"Tiger, now it really smells like Christmas."

He walked into the kitchen, put his arms around me and gave me a peck on my cheek. I felt the peace of the Christmas season as we sat together and ate breakfast.

"Ross and Laura want us to come to their place tomorrow for Christmas Day dinner," he said. Derick removed his gaze from my face when he realized I wasn't responding.

I took a sip of coffee and set my fork down. "We should go. It will be nice, although we don't have gifts to bring."

"They know that. I doubt they're expecting gifts from us," he said.

"I don't want to get on the wrong track with Ross. He's always been a brother to me."

"You two just have different mindsets."

"Yeah, let's go to their place tomorrow. We can stop at a bakery and bring a dessert."

With that, Derick got up and turned off the television. "Let's go upstairs," he said.

He took my hand and I followed him up the stairs. We spent that first Christmas Eve together with Rebel in our new apartment. I didn't care that we had very little money and no gifts to share, because we had each other.

I had my reservations about Ross's true intentions, but decided to give him a chance to follow through on setting his wife and me up in a clothing business. He had a lot of idle cash. He'd presented this offer to me many times while I was living in Hawaii. We did discuss it at the table over Christmas Day Dinner. Ross suggested that Laura and I get things rolling by bringing my hand-painted clothing to a trade show scheduled for February at the Miami Beach Convention Center. It would be all my hand-painted designs. I didn't understand how Laura's being a former model contributed anything. The money end of the business I figured. But at that point, I was willing to try anything to get something going.

New Year's Eve came and went without any fanfare. We had no money to go out to a club and celebrate. I watched the ball drop in New York City's Times Square on TV, and marveled at how I'd lived there for the first twenty years of my life, yet somehow managed to miss that event.

After the holidays I ordered three dozen white sweatshirts and five dozen T-shirts from the warehouse in Atlanta, with which I already had an account. My mission was to paint a few dozen sweatshirts for the February trade show. The painted T-shirts I'd box up and send to the two stores I had in California, and the two in Hawaii. Laura came up with a great name for our sweatshirt company, Saucy Sweats. She had something to contribute after all.

The dining room table was the only surface in the apartment available to use for painting. I covered it with newspaper and set a large jar of water on top with my brushes and tubes of acrylic paints off to the side. As soon as I began mixing colors with water on the plate, and dipped the paintbrush in, I felt my whole being take flight with the familiarity of the process. I had a few tailored white-cotton shirts I'd picked up at Zayre's, and began to paint fashion figures. I set them to dry outside on the railing of the terrace. When the paint was dry, I used a fine-point permanent marker for definition and detail.

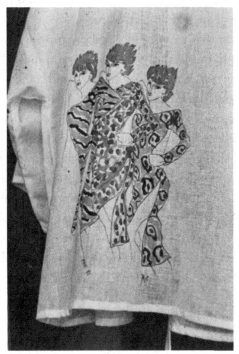

Fashion figures on tailored shirt

Before leaving Maui, I'd packed a trunk with linens and clothing, and had it sent to Ross Grant's apartment. When it finally arrived, Derick drove to Ross's to pick it up. Once the trunk was empty we placed it in front of the sectional couch to use as a coffee table. I remember that sectional couch. It was a hideous, brown, furry thing, but adequate and comfy. I unpacked a large tapestry from the trunk to use as a wall hanging behind the bed upstairs. I was glad I had kept the pillowcases stenciled with a lion's head, which were a gift for Derick's birthday, he being a Leo. I was aware of how Leos enjoyed being worshiped, but I wasn't that type. As time went by we added more furniture. I rummaged around the secondhand shops in town for lamps, end tables, and art pieces to hang on the walls. A home began to take shape.

Derick made friends with a California transplant who lived across the street on West Pelican Drive. He had a female black lab named Oreo, so Rebel gained a companion. Luke Skinner was a young surfer-type dude with curly blond locks, who liked to wear board shorts and aloha shirts. Derick spent many evenings at Luke's place when I was painting T-shirts, or watching a movie he had no interest in.

I was watching that new late-night show starring David Letterman. Rebel had to go out, but Derick wasn't home yet. I didn't like walking the dog late at night by myself. He wasn't neutered and could be hard to handle if we ran into another male dog. I reluctantly got Rebel's leash and took him downstairs. I saw a guy sitting in a parked car on the street watching me. I could tell he was jacking off, but I pretended I didn't notice. When I turned to walk back up to the apartment the guy followed us up the stairs. I made it inside and locked the door in the nick of time, but he began banging on the door. I called Luke Skinner's place and told Derick what had happened. Derick mumbled something that sounded like a curse and slammed the phone down. I rushed out to the terrace to see what he was going to do. A few minutes later I saw Derick walking down the center of West Pelican Drive carrying a wrench, with a menacing expression on his face.

He got right in the guy's face and said, "You bothering my girl?"

The guy ran to his car and locked himself inside.

Derick walked to the guy's car, "Open the fucking window pervert! I want to talk to you." When the guy refused, Derick broke the window with the wrench. I could hear the glass shatter from the terrace. The guy started the engine and sped away. That was the night I realized that, just like Dorothy, I wasn't in Kansas anymore, and Maui was light-years away.

CHAPTER 2

TALK IS CHEAP

The lack of money is the root of all evil.
—Mark Twain

Coconut Grove is a groovy little town a bit south of Miami. I enjoyed cruising around the streets, and wandering in and out of the boutiques on Commodore Plaza, the main drag. I entered an interesting boutique called Ava's, and felt that old fashion-world vibe. I loved the unique clothing and spent some time combing through the racks. The showroom was empty so I was free to explore. Walking past an open door to a tiny office I saw a woman sitting at a desk. She had very long dark hair and wore a black dress. She turned to look up at me. I noticed she had a very pale complexion, and her lips were covered in a deep shade of brown. My first impression was Lily Munster on that old TV show *The Munsters*. A bottle of Stolichnaya sat next to a tall water glass. She filled the glass about two-thirds full of vodka, stood up, and walked into the showroom.

"How can I help you?" she asked. She had a deep voice in a heavy Russian accent. Her thick black eye makeup was mesmerizing.

"I love the clothing in the shop. Are you the owner?" I asked.

"You could say that," she answered, taking a sip of vodka.

"It's been a while since I even thought about fashion. I was a fashion designer and illustrator in Manhattan at one time."

"I try to keep the boutique up-to-date with the latest trends," she said, eyeing me up and down.

"I feel an affinity to the shop," I said.

"That's a coincidence because I am looking for someone to work in the boutique."

"I just moved to Florida from Hawaii and I'd love to work here."

"If you would be satisfied with part-time," she said, taking another sip.

"I have my own hand-painted clothing business, so part-time works for me."

"Well, that's really what I had in mind. I need free days to go on buying trips." She walked back into the office with her hips swaying, signaling me to follow. I was watching Lily Munster walk toward that creepy house on Mockingbird Lane. She looked at me and said, "My name is Ava Budeev."

"Any relation to the famous scientist Andrey Budeev?"

"It's possible, somewhere in my family tree, but unlikely." She eyed the glass of vodka, then set it down. I could tell she fought with herself not to take another swig.

"I'm Adriana Bardolino."

"Ah, you're Italian," she said.

"My father is from Sicily. Some don't consider that part of Italy."

"The Sicilians are a strange mixture of people—Spanish, Italian, and Arab," she said.

"Well, Italians are a mixture of people. During the height of the Roman Empire, Rome was like New York City. People came from all over the world to live and work in Rome."

"That's true. Perhaps that is why I find Italian men so attractive. Well Adriana, why don't you come in on Monday morning, and I will go over the inventory with you?"

"I look forward to that."

I walked out of the boutique in a good mood, relieved that six months after landing in Florida I finally had a job, albeit part-time. I strolled along the sidewalk cafés and sat in one. I ordered a café au lait and a croissant with Camembert cheese. I thought that a glass of wine was in order to celebrate; then again it wasn't even noon, and I felt slightly tipsy just watching Ava drink straight Russian vodka.

When I arrived back at the apartment on West Pelican Drive, Derick was reclining on the couch watching television; Rebel was on the floor next to him. He briefly smiled up at me, then went on watching TV—the news coverage of the space shuttle *Columbia*. He looked scorching hot lying there, and desire welled up in me. He was wearing a pink golf shirt and utility jeans, the kind that have loops and deep pockets for various tools. He was barefoot with one leg on the floor close to the dog. I walked over and lay on top of him. He smiled at me and gave me a soft kiss on the lips.

"You've been gone a long time," he said.

"I was walking around the Grove. You know I like to do that."

"Anything new there?"

"I found a part-time job in a boutique."

Derick stared at me. "Really? What about the hand-painted T-shirts?"

"Oh, I'll still do that, but it's not enough money."

"Every job I've encountered pays about half what I was making in Hawaii," he said. I see guys standing on street corners waiting for day work. Trucks pick them up. That fucking Ross throws me a few bones once in a while. I don't like it, but I need the money."

"I feel foolish for believing in him," I said.

"Adriana, it's not your fault."

"I know, but it doesn't help how I feel. I'm responsible for us being in this mess."

"Come here tiger. Stop talking like that. We'll get through this if we stick together."

"That new movie *ET* is playing in town. Why don't we go see it? It'll take our minds off other things."

He gazed at me, his downhearted expression turning into a half smile. I slid off Derick and lay down next to him. He put his arm around me and I slipped mine over his chest. I wondered if I'd caused a rift between Derick and Ross, or if something had happened between them. They seemed so tight when we first arrived. I felt guilty about everything, and my anger toward Ross Grant grew with each passing day.

An old family scandal came to mind. My mother Vita owned a dress factory in the Bronx with her brother Victor. He was what one would call a silent partner. He put up the money for the initial investment, and my mother did all the work in the factory. Victor was there at the end of every week with his hand out to collect half the profits, despite his having nothing to do with the everyday running of the business. As time went by, my mother hired an accountant who subsequently found large sums of money unaccounted for. Upon further investigation it came to light that Victor's wife, my aunt, was skimming money off the business while she was the bookkeeper. My mother realized that she'd been used and betrayed by her own brother. Victor claimed he had no idea what his wife was doing. I had a hard time believing that, but my mother forgave him. "He's my brother," she said. I hoped I could be as forgiving as she was in regard to my familial relationship with Ross Grant.

I enjoyed my days at Ava's Boutique—well, at the beginning. I marveled at how this woman drank vodka all day long. I never saw her eat anything. Perhaps it helped her deal with a lifetime she wanted to forget about back in Russia.

Hannah Klein, one of the former owners of the Crafty Mermaid where I'd worked in Lahaina, Maui, was in Miami visiting friends. I told her to meet me at Ava's, and that we would have lunch in the Grove to catch up. We sat in a sidewalk café drinking bloody Marys and eating fried grouper fingers. We laughed and talked, and for a short while I felt like we were having lunch somewhere in Lahaina. She was still with her husband, the guy without a chin. I laughed heartily as she told me how she made him grow his beard back. She was telling me all about what was going on back on Maui. I confessed to her that I missed the islands. Suddenly my jovial mood turned somber. I missed my life on Maui, my job at the Crafty Mermaid, and all the friends I'd left behind. As much as I loved Derick, I knew that someday I wanted to go back to Hawaii. I doubted that Derick shared my desire. He hadn't lived on Maui as long as I had, and didn't have the same attachment to the island.

"What's wrong Adriana?" Hannah asked.

"I miss Maui so much."

"It's so nice here. Sunny and bright, beaches and palm trees as far as the eye can see. And you are closer to your family."

"Hannah, I can almost smell Maui on you," I said, taking her hand.

"Sorry we had to close the Crafty Mermaid. I miss it too. Have you talked to Annie?"

"Yes, I called her as soon as we got the phone hooked up in the apartment."

"I'm flying to California tomorrow to see my family, then back to Maui," she said.

"Well, I have to get back to Ava's. I'm glad we got together while you were here."

We hugged and kissed goodbye. She walked away from me, turned, smiled and shouted, "Aloha!" My heart broke in a million pieces.

Oddly enough, the phone rang in the middle of that very night waking us both up. Luckily the extension phone was on my side of the bed. I picked up the receiver and heard Dominick French's voice, my former lover on Maui before I met Derick. He began jabbering away as if it were the middle of the afternoon. I hung the phone up quickly, then took the receiver off the hook, intending to avoid another call.

"Who was that?" Derick asked.

"Wrong number," I said. I didn't like lying to him, but it seemed like the best thing to do at the time. I figured Annie Hughes (my Maui mom) must have given Demo my phone number. I had confessed to Annie how sketchy things were when we first landed in Florida, and how right she was in warning me about my friend Ross's business offer. "Talk is cheap," she had said, and she was so right. That night signaled the return of sporadic phone calls from Dominick French.

Flights to New York were cheap, $99 each way, so I decided to visit my parents. I also wanted to be there for my cousin Jenny's wedding. Derick didn't come with me. It would have been the cost of a second plane ticket, not to mention spending money for both of us, and we couldn't afford it. He said he'd be concentrating on getting out from under Ross's wing; he was determined to find steady work.

I hadn't written in my journals in a long time. I packed them in my suitcase with the intention of hiding them somewhere in my parents' apartment. I wasn't looking forward to another wedding, and getting a grilling from my family as to when Derick and I were getting married. My life seemed to have more twists and turns than the Bronx River Parkway.

Jenny's wedding reception was a lovely affair, about an hour north of the city at Ronnie's in Englewood, New York. My cousin Gia Ferrari and I were enjoying a private moment at a pop-up table with our drinks. She told me a story about one of our girlfriends from the old neighborhood in the Bronx. Our friend Fran was going through a rough time. Fran had become very depressed. She was struggling with the realization that she was gay, and had genuine concerns as to how her family would react. When her parents became aware that she was entertaining thoughts of suicide, they had her committed to a mental institution. She lost her memory for a while from shock treatments.

A few days after the wedding Gia and I went to see Fran in the institution. She was very aloof but knew who we were. It was difficult to act cheerful in the face of what she was going through. I felt helpless and sad. One of the nurses told us that Fran had developed the habit of taking her blanket and sleeping outside on the grounds under the trees at night. It was something a child would do for attention, for strokes. It only resulted in bad strokes, driving her family crazy with worry. There were times in my own life when I was in a deep hole of depression, but I had my art to stabilize me and lift my spirits. Like Friedrich Nietzsche said, "We have art in order to not die of the truth."

I was only in New York for two weeks, and was happy to get back to to Derick and Rebel. While I was gone Derick found work in a warehouse about forty minutes north of Miami. He told me about two of his coworkers from Trinidad and Tobago. They played cricket and taught Derick the game. Soon, he was playing cricket with them on weekends. I enjoyed going to the cricket matches. It all seemed so British! I knew these two guys were married, but I never saw their wives.

Derick came home from work one evening and told me the guys from Trinidad had invited us to their house for a meal after the cricket match on the Saturday coming up. I was looking forward to meeting the women who were attached to these two men. When the game was over that Saturday, we followed them to their house, which the two couples shared. The women were in the kitchen cooking when we arrived. I had a hard time understanding them because the little bit of English they spoke was unintelligible. I thought that was strange, since both husbands spoke English perfectly. I wondered if they'd married these two women, sight unseen, and brought them to Florida from Trinidad. While the guys were horsing around in the yard, I hung out in the kitchen with the wives. They were stirring some sort of stew in a pot on the stove. It reeked of curry and East Indian spices. I watched the women make dough by hand, first kneading it, then pulling off pieces and flattening them into round Frisbee-like disks. They toasted them on a large griddle, twirling them with their hands over the flames of the gas stove.

I asked them what was in the pot.

"Gut," one of the women said.

"Gut?" I asked, not knowing whose guts were in the pot. I detested organ meats and innards of any kind.

When it was time to eat the guys came in from the yard and we all stood around the kitchen while the women dished the food onto plates. There weren't enough chairs for all of us to sit down, so the women sat at the table and the men stood up holding their plates. The two couples from Trinidad scooped up the stew with the flat bread in their fingers. Derick and I followed suit, since we weren't given forks. I ate with trepidation, not knowing what it was, while Derick scarfed it down gladly. I fantasized us all sitting in a circle on the carpeted floor of a tent in the desert somewhere, eating like nomads. After I was finished, I set my plate in the sink, smiled, and remarked that it was very good. The wives nodded at me in appreciation.

One of the guys from Trinidad said, "So glad you enjoyed it. We eat goat all the time."

Derick and I glanced at each other but didn't react. He and I had a good laugh on the drive home, agreeing that it tasted like chicken.

1982 was flying high like a pelican being chased by an alligator. Each day was consumed with one financial struggle after another. I wanted to quit my job at Ava's, but just couldn't afford to. She was difficult for much of the time. Well, there was the vodka. Miami is a very international city, and at times it felt like living in a foreign country. There was a large Cuban population which is understandable, Cuba being only ninety miles south of Key West. I'd often stop at a street stand for a *bullet* (a tiny cup of Cuban espresso, very strong and very sweet).

I met an older Cuban woman in a café on Commodore Plaza, and we became friendly. We made a habit of meeting often for afternoon happy hour drinks. Her name was Carmen Lopez. She was a tiny woman with short red hair and a squeaky high-pitched voice. She always dressed well and had a sophisticated air about her. She was the bookkeeper and manager of a French restaurant in the Grove, L'Oiseau ("The Bird") du Paris. It was a funky place on a wide boulevard around the corner from Commodore Plaza. There was also a downstairs café with outside tables and a small kitchen. Café L'Oiseau served breakfast and lunch. The popular upstairs restaurant served traditional French cuisine. Carmen told me that the owner, Claude Canet, brought the chef with him from France, a guy named Vincent Delon, whom everyone affectionately called Vin.

While Carmen and I were having lunch one afternoon in the downstairs café, I happened to mention that my only sources of income were a part-time job at Ava's Boutique, and my hand-painted clothing business. The only stranger I came across was the UPS man who picked up my boxes of painted garments to send to Hawaii and California, and even he wasn't a stranger anymore.

Carmen laughed, her tiny body shaking. No voice ever escaped her mouth when she laughed, just little short gasps. She smacked her hand on the table and said, "You should come to work in the café. We need another waitress."

"Carmen, I don't know the first thing about being a waitress."

"You can work part-time behind the bar in the upstairs restaurant."

"I know even less about bartending."

"Honey, we serve only beer and wine. Everything's in bottles. It will be a breeze."

"I'll think on it," I said, wondering how Derick would react to me bartending.

"You need to get out there and meet new people," she said.

We clinked our drinks together, and I saw new opportunities on the horizon.

Café L'Oiseau

I quit my job at Ava's and began bartending at the upstairs French restaurant, L'Oiseau du Paris. I familiarized myself with the collection of wines and imported bottled beers in the cooler. At the corner of the bar was a large fake bird in a cage hanging from the ceiling. A tiny window at the end of the bar opened to the kitchen. The chef spoke English with a heavy French accent. He was a very happy guy but had a hot temper. The waiters were all foreign—two from France, one from Chile, and another from Argentina. The bus boys and dishwashers were from Haiti, another large demographic in Miami. There often were arguments and fights in the kitchen. Top dog in the kitchen, besides the chef, was the head dishwasher, Ricardeau St. Laurent, who liked to be called Ricky . He ordered around everyone below him in rank. Even the piped-in music couldn't cover up the yelling at times.

I laugh when I think back to my first Saturday night behind the bar. It started off all right, but as soon as eight o'clock rolled around the place was packed with reservations, and I was overwhelmed. I uncorked bottles of wine as fast as I could, handing off glasses and bottles at a phenomenal pace. Waiters stood in front of me holding their trays and barking orders at me. I somehow survived the night. Toward the end, Vin, the chef, slid a freshly made strawberry-and-whipped-cream marvel between layers of delicate pastry through the kitchen window. I sat there eating a fresh Napoleon and sipping a glass of white wine, while I closed out the register and tallied the evening's tickets. I had racked up a lot of tips, and had a smile from ear to ear as I washed the dirty glassware.

Derick reacted the way I thought he would. He didn't like the idea of me bartending. He often made a point of picking me up after work eyeing the waiters in a way that said, "Don't even entertain a thought about her." The waiters were hot, especially the one from Argentina. Derick spent many nights home alone when I worked the night shift. He wasn't the type to bitch about things he didn't like, but his disdain would ooze out in other ways.

"I went fishing off that pier today with Luke. I took you there once."

"Yeah, I remember that place. Did you catch anything?" I asked.

"Just a small fry, so I threw it back."

"Thanks for making dinner. It was a busy lunch at the restaurant, and I didn't have time to eat."

"There are girls on the pier offering blow jobs to the guys fishing."
I stared at him. "Really? That's just crazy."
"But I wouldn't do that."
"I smiled at him, not wanting to show that it bothered me.

He had a purpose in telling me, or he would have kept that tidbit to himself. We had a good relationship and I trusted him. Yet I'd been told that men will be men, so a woman always has an underlying uneasiness regarding that sort of thing.

I reached my bare foot under the table and rested it on his crotch moving it back and forth until I felt him get hard. He stared at me, his face breaking out in a grin. "Let's go upstairs," I said. We left the remains of dinner on the table, and he followed me up the stairs.

I received an unexpected call from Laura Grant. She claimed we weren't spending enough time together, and she wanted to take me to lunch. I knew there was no such thing as a free lunch, but I agreed to go anyway. She picked me up on West Pelican Drive, briefly stopping in the condo to see what furniture we'd collected over the past months. We drove to Joe's Stone Crab for a seafood lunch and a few drinks. I felt estranged. The last time we spent time together was when we did that trade show at the Miami Beach Convention Center.

"We should spend more time together," Laura said.

I didn't answer. I was downing Tanqueray and tonics like an athlete drinking water after running a marathon to gloss over my feeling distant, and to drown my disappointment in the failure of our original plan—the very reason Derick and I had moved to Florida---Opening a store together on Miami Beach. I didn't feel it was her fault that her husband, my commune brother, upturned our lives in Hawaii on a promise, and each day in Florida was a financial struggle for us. Walking out of the restaurant Laura told me she wanted to take me to her church service.

"I'm Catholic, perhaps not a practicing one right now, but still."

"I want to share with you the way I was raised in the South. I know you are going to love the experience," she insisted.

How bad could it possibly be? I thought. Besides, I was thoroughly inebriated, which would dull any pain I might have to endure.

When we arrived at the auditorium it was packed, and I could hear Holy Roller music. The preacher was an old rock'n'roll singer whose name escapes me. The sermon started off nice enough. I got into the music and felt the spirit—well, there was also all the gin I'd had.

The preacher yelled to the flock, "Someone here has hate in their heart!" The music got louder, the chorus of singers piped up, and I was totally overcome. "The Lord is our salvation. It's time to repent!" he shouted. "Are you ready for redemption?" His outstretched hands pointed at the crowd. The music raised to a crescendo. The singers began stomping their feet and waving their arms in the air. They would answer in loud tones, "Lord, forgive me. I testify!"

I began to cry, tears rolling down my face. Yes, I had hate in my heart for Ross Grant, but you can't hate someone you never loved. There is a thin line between those two emotions. Laura was crying too. She reached her arms out and we hugged each other.

On the car ride back to the apartment I didn't say what I was feeling. I guess I wasn't ready for redemption. When we arrived on West Pelican Drive I simply gave her a kiss on the cheek, and thanked her for sharing.

"Don't be a stranger," she called out, as she drove away.

I walked up the stairs and unlocked the door. I heard Rebel barking so I knew Derick wasn't home yet. I was relieved because I was holding so much guilt inside, and I wanted to cry it all out before he came home. Inwardly, I resented the fact that Derick was still hanging out with Ross, despite everything that went down.

A few days later Ross Grant telephoned. He said he wanted to talk to me, that he had a business opportunity I'd be interested in. I had the feeling that Laura had prodded him in some way. I had no idea what was on his mind or how our meeting would go. I needed to get some things off my chest. I drove to their apartment on the bay. I walked to the elevator wondering how I was going to feel when I saw him. I knocked on the door. As soon as Ross opened the door he put his arm around my shoulder in a brotherly way, walking me into the dining room. My anger with him seemed to dissipate. Ross took a couple of Heinekens from the refrigerator and sat down at the table with me. Laura was nowhere around. The conversation began warmly enough, but then got down to the nitty-gritty.

"Ross, what the hell happened to the plan of me and Laura opening a store together?"

At first he was silent. Then he said, "Adriana, weren't we giving it some time? I told you, it's not a good time to start a business."

My intuition told me he was hiding something from me. Maybe there was an issue between Ross and Derick that made him change his mind, and it had nothing whatsoever to do with me.

"We're struggling financially. Derick tells me he's making half the money here than he made in Hawaii. He's not the type to grumble, but I can tell he feels defeated."

"I'm not a psychiatrist," Ross said, coldly.

"You know what I mean. Derick feels emasculated, and I'm not sure how long before it begins to affect our relationship."

"I'm not a relationship coach either," he said.

I stared at Ross; he was smiling and taking all of this way too lightly.

"Ross, you were the one who came to Hawaii with the offer—and more than once over the past few years, I might add. We turned our lives upside down to come here."

"I'll tell ya what," Ross said. "I have a proposition for you."

My mood lifted slightly. "What do you have in mind?"

"I have a bunch of cash that needs to get deposited in my bank account in Europe. You'd be perfect for this job."

"What sort of job are we talking about?" I asked.

"I'll pay you $14,000 to take my cash to Europe. I'll pay for your flight and hotel. Laura will strap the money to your body under your clothes, hiding it really well. We'll be on the same flight sitting in the front area of the plane. When the plane lands you and Laura will find a ladies' room, and she'll retrieve the cash. Then we'll take it to the bank while you wait at the hotel."

I sat there in a state of shock, my blood boiling. I saw red and couldn't even speak. I rose out of the chair and walked toward the front door.

"Where are you going?" he called after me. "Adriana, its easy money."

I turned around and said, "Strap that cash to your wife, and then go fuck yourself!"

I walked out the door, slamming it behind me. Ross Grant wasn't my brother anymore. Being stabbed in the back didn't hurt as much as knowing who was holding the knife.

I walked to the car in a daze, filled with rage. I played that whole scenario over and over in my head—how he had made offers to me over the years. How he had wined and dined us, taking Derick and me along on their honeymoon to Canada last summer. I saw the whole intricate scheme he'd cooked up, and how he had planned to use us. I couldn't believe how blind I was. I had to calm myself down before going home, so I went to Café L'Oiseau. I walked into the outside café, and Carmen sat me at an out-of-the-way table. The waiters were cleaning up after lunch, and setting the upstairs for the dinner shift. Carmen brought me a glass of white wine without asking, and sat down with me.

"I can get you a café au lait if you prefer," she said, in her high-pitched voice.

"No, the wine is perfect," I said.

"You have the look of someone who just lost her best friend."

"I guess in a way I have," I said numbly, my voice a monotone.

An older woman walked into the café and straight to our table.

"Eleanor!" Carmen shouted. The woman sat down at the table with us. Carmen signaled one of the waiters to bring another glass of white wine. They exchanged pleasantries, then Carmen said, "Adriana, this is my very good friend Eleanor Gold."

"Hi, Eleanor. I'm Adriana Bardolino. It's nice to meet you."

"Nice to meet you as well," she said. "What is it you do?"

"I have a hand-painted clothing business, and I bartend upstairs."

"I'll bet its fun working here," she said.

"Oh, it's a barrel of monkeys, especially on a Saturday night."

"More like a birdcage filled with crazy birds," Carmen said, between snorts of laughter.

"I have a unique clothing store about a mile from here. Why don't you come by and bring some samples of your painted garments? They might work in my store," Eleanor said.

"I will do that. I live near here and can keep your store stocked."

"Here is my business card," she said, handing it to me. "Please do come by."

"Well, ladies, I should get home. I've been gone all day," I said.

I got up from the table leaving the two women engaged in friendly conversation. I felt as if I was meant to stop at the café that afternoon, as if God had a hand in it.

Derick was at the stove cooking something when I got home. Rebel greeted me with a nose nuzzle and a tail wag. I hugged Derick, watching him stir whatever it was he was cooking. Just being at home with them made me feel warm all over, and the drama and sadness of that day soon faded.

"You were gone all day?" Derick asked.

"Ross said he had a business proposition for me. I mentioned it to you this morning."

"You've been at his place all this time?"

"No, when I left Ross's apartment I stopped at the café."

"What did Ross have to say?"

"Let me tell you first about a woman I met at the café," I said. "She has a clothing store about a mile down the road from the restaurant, and she wants me to bring her some painted T-shirts. Maybe she'll carry them in her store."

"That's cool," Derick said. I sensed a negative undertone, that he saw me forging ahead of him with income possibilities. He probably also sensed I was changing the subject.

We sat down at the table for supper, and really, I was avoiding telling Derick what went down at Ross's apartment. Rebel was sitting on the floor between us praying for scraps. After we ate in silence for a bit, Derick began to interrogate me about my meeting with Ross, expecting to hear something positive. I calmly told him how Ross had approached me with what he figured would be a windfall for us—that he would pad my body with cash and send me to Europe on a flight to sneak his money through customs. Of course he and Laura would be sitting in first class, in case I should get arrested.

Derick stopped eating, set his fork down, and sat there with the craziest look on his face. "You didn't agree to that, did you?"

"I might be stupid at times, but I'm not dumb! I told him to strap the cash to his wife."

"What did Ross say?"

"He didn't say anything. Did anything happen between you two guys?" I asked.

"No!" Derick said, with a blank look on his face.

"I was so pissed off, all I saw was red. At some point I told him to go fuck himself."

"That son of a bitch," Derick said, standing up and reaching for the car keys.

"Derick, no, don't go over there, please."

"I want to punch that fucker's lights out for treating you like that. No fucking respect."

"Derick, I don't ever want to see him again. I don't want to cry, so please let's stop talking about it. I just want to forget the whole thing."

Derick tossed the car keys back on the counter and sat down. He stared off into space, as if he'd just witnessed someone kick me senseless. His eyes narrowed, and his pupils shrank to two tiny golden beads. The right side of his face with the scar twitched. He could be a little scary when he was angry. I am sure Ross found Derick less than compliant, and he wasn't used to people not following his lead. He wasn't in Ross' orbit of old friends, so maybe he didn't trust Derick, but the way things went down was bad. My old friend from the commune was right about Ross. He was playing us, and had planned to move us around like pawns on a chessboard.

Fall arrived, but there was very little change in the muggy weather. Epcot Center had recently opened. The letters stand for Experimental Prototype Community of Tomorrow, and boy was our life in Florida an experiment.

Luke and Derick already had their costumes for Halloween. There was a big event at a bowling alley in the neighborhood. Everyone was expected to come in costume. Derick dressed as a gangster. He peered through trendy sunglasses, wore a white suit jacket, black shirt, and slicked-back hair with lots of product. Derick looked tough, mean, and very hot. I was the gangster's moll. I wore a slinky black dress and red high heels. Luke Skinner was dressed as Luke Skywalker. As soon as we walked into the bowling alley, we noticed only a few bowlers in costume. They were all sitting at the bar, which was like that crazy-creature bar in *Star Wars*.

Luke should fit right in with the rest of the creatures, I thought. I felt out of place and out of sorts. Derick drank an exorbitant amount of alcohol that night. He had been drinking a lot recently. Luke drove home. I closed my eyes while the guys jabbered away about their bowling scores. For me, nothing about that night jelled, and I missed all the Halloweens I'd spent on Maui. I rebuffed Derick's advances for sex when we got home that night. A drunk making love to me was a big turn off.

Michael Jackson's *Thriller* album came out that November. A local department store, Burdines, was giving a big discount on electronics for opening a store account. I'd never had a credit card before. I purchased a stacked stereo system, which Derick hooked up in the living room. When I had the house to myself, I loved listening to music while painting T-shirts. My hand-painted clothing business was expanding. Even though checks from the stores were intermittent, art was keeping me sane. Painting took the place of writing and scribbling in my journals. Pablo Picasso said, "Painting is just another way of keeping a diary."

As I was walking home from L'Oiseau du Paris, two kids on bicycles tried snatching my purse right off my shoulder. Luckily, I saw them coming and held my purse tight enough so they couldn't snag it.

Derick was already home and making dinner when I walked in. He had a strange look on his face when he greeted me. I began telling him about the guys trying to rob my purse, but he interrupted me.

"You had a phone call from Hawaii. Dominick French!"

I played dumb. "Oh God," I said. "Annie must have given him my phone number."

Derick stared at me, "Demo didn't say anything, but he wants you to call him."

"I'm not going to call him," I protested.

Derick wasn't a stupid guy, and I could tell he knew I was hiding something. "You're not still talking to him behind my back are you?"

"No, I haven't spoken to him since way before we left Maui."

"The guy is calling you for a reason," Derick said, with a serious expression.

"Don't blow a stupid phone call out of proportion. It wasn't me who called him."

"Maybe not, but it's obvious he thinks he still has a chance with you."

"I don't want him. How can I ever convince you of that?"

Derick turned off the burner on the stove, grabbed Rebel's leash, and walked toward the front door. "I think I'll take Rebel for a long walk; clear my head," he said, slamming the door behind him.

The ghost of Dominick French, my former lover, was a nagging thorn in Derick's side.

I bought a plane ticket to New York to spend Christmas with my parents. They were getting up there in years—my mom was in her sixties and my dad in his seventies. Derick didn't want to go. He had a steady job and didn't want to take the chance of losing it. He said that he didn't mind if I went without him. It never dawned on me that I could be driving a wedge between us. That Christmas would be the first holiday we'd spent apart in the three years we'd been together. We'd had a number of arguments about money—or the lack of it—and maybe subconsciously I was escaping. Our lives had been dangling at the edge of a cliff ever since we left Hawaii.

Men want to be a hero, and life didn't seem to be offering Derick any opportunities to wear a blue Superman bodysuit with the big red S on the front. When the plane took off, I felt strangely free and released from my everyday struggles. At the time, running away from it all seemed to be what the doctor ordered. Well, for me. An excerpt from a book I'd read—*A Room of One's Own* by Virginia Woolf—popped into my head:

> Life for both sexes, and I look at them shouldering their way along the pavement- is arduous, difficult, and a perpetual struggle. It calls for gigantic courage and strength. More than anything, perhaps, creatures of illusion that we are it calls for confidence in oneself.

CHAPTER 3

MIAMI HEAT

August in Florida is God's way of reminding us who's in
charge.

—Blaize Clement, American writer

Derick and I were in a good place when I returned from New York. We
spent New Year's Eve at home ushering in 1983. We seemed to appreciate
each other again. It's easy to take your partner for granted when you
see that person every single day. I felt renewed love and sensed the same
from him.

I was making dinner while Derick watched television. He walked in
the kitchen and stood against the counter watching me. "What's up?" I
asked, noticing his gaze.

"Don't you think it's time we got engaged?" he asked.

I put the spoon down, thinking back to the first Christmas we were
together in the house on Nanu Street behind the sugar mill in Lahaina.
He'd surprised me with that beautiful diamond and ruby ring. Our love
affair was so intense during those first two years on Maui.

"Derick!" I said, pleasantly surprised. I was filled with emotion

"I mean, how many of our friends have we witnessed getting married?"

"Derick, yes," I said, my eyes tearing.

"I don't have money for a ring right now, but—"

"Derick, I don't need an engagement ring to know you love me."

We held each other, and I felt us melt into one person. Then he kissed
me very sweetly and rubbed my shoulder.

"I love you so much. I can't imagine life without you," I said.

He hugged me. "I feel like we're together even when we're apart."

"That's how I feel too, like we were meant for each other."

At first I thought he was going to carry me upstairs to the bedroom, rip
my clothes off, and fuck my brains out like in a Hollywood movie. Instead
we sat at the table eating dinner as if it were an ordinary day. Every once in

a while I'd stop and stare at him. The feeling was inexplicable. I wondered if sex was going to be different, if it would become a more down-to-earth obligatory act between partners. Later that evening my fears were laid to rest. We made love as passionately as we always had. I thought of that line from *Lady Chatterley's Lover* by D. H. Lawrence: "It's terrible once you've got a man in your blood."

The next day I called my mother in the Bronx to tell her the news. She was overjoyed. Well, I was thirty-seven years old.

Derick befriended a new guy while I was in New York. He lived in a private house on a side street off Pelican Drive. Jimmy Joe Riley was a very quirky guy. He must have been in his late forties at the time. He told us he grew up in the Carolinas but moved to Florida in his twenties. Jimmy Joe was not a good-looking guy, but he had a warm personality. He always sported a worn-out camouflage army cap; I supposed it was a remnant from his time in the service. He bought his house with a VA loan, and bragged that it was paid off. He collected antique glass bottles, two of which I still have displayed in my China cabinet, along with other treasures. He had an impressive collection of guns and antiques. While in his house, I was reminded that Florida *is* the South. People tend to forget that because of all the northern transplants that end up in the Sunshine State when they retire or get tired of frigid winters. We hung out at his house often, and I loved investigating the various nooks and crannies while Jimmy Joe and Derick talked and drank beer. They'd get pretty smashed at times, and I was thankful we were close enough to walk home.

Jimmy Joe did mentor Derick like an older brother. Derick never talked about his father or his childhood, only to mention that his father left when he was very young, that he'd gotten a few good beatings, and that there was no great love between them. His mother was on marriage two. When we visited them in Washington State I got the impression that he wasn't close with his stepfather either. Derick was drinking a lot, despite knowing how much I detested it. It was chipping away at my sensibilities, and I found excuses when he wanted to make love to me in his inebriated states. After all our time together I thought he'd figure that out about me, but his stubborn nature ignored it.

On Valentine's Day I worked the day shift at the upstairs restaurant, L'Oiseau du Paris. We were offering a glass of pink champagne, called a Kir

Royale, with lunch. Chambord, the black raspberry liqueur, sure improved the champagne to my taste buds. There weren't many couples at the tables holding hands and gazing into each other's eyes that afternoon, mostly friends or business associates. On my walk home through Coconut Grove I stopped to watch some of the artists paint. There was a particular Haitian artist's work that I really liked. His name was Rony, and his art touched something in my soul. I especially liked a black-and-white painting he did of ships in a storm landing on a tropical island. I'd admired it a few times. Rony came up to me as I was eyeing his painting yet again.

"I can see you like my painting. I'll give you a special price."

"It makes me feel something I can't quite put my finger on."

"I want you to have it. You appreciate the black-and-white. Most people want color. I know you want it," he said.

I took the tips I'd made that day and handed the money to Rony.

"Bless you," he said. "I hope my painting brings you joy."

Looking back, I suppose it visualized a subconscious wish to be on a boat going back to Maui. These days, Rony's painting hangs in my home office.

I walked home with the painting under my arm, praying that a thug wouldn't rifle it away from me.

When I got home I looked for a place to hang it. Rebel followed me around the apartment as I held the painting up to the wall in various places until I found the perfect spot. I got Rebel's leash and took him for a short walk. I picked up the mail while I was downstairs, opening a few letters on my way up. There were two envelopes with cards and cash from two of my aunts, congratulating me and Derick on our engagement, as well as a couple of utility bills. I went into the kitchen to start dinner and noticed a large envelope sitting on the counter. It was a beautiful valentine card from Derick. The words were so beautiful. It spoke of how great distances couldn't keep me from his heart. The last line read, "Love keeps us together, and I'm so in love with you." I stood there crying over a silly card, but the sentiment said it all and meant so much to me. I've saved that card all these years.

My friend Carmen Lopez hired a guy as the beverage manager for L'Oiseau du Paris, as well as the downstairs sidewalk café. I walked in the office and sat down at the manager's request. I had a good feeling about him immediately. He said that he just wanted to go over the new wine list with me. He was short and fairly good-looking, with dark hair and a neatly trimmed beard. One of the waiters told me he was gay, but he didn't give off a swishy vibe.

"You're talking to the wrong person. I don't know the first thing about wine," I said.

"So you just pour it in the glasses?" he asked, laughing.

"Maybe you need someone with more experience upstairs."

"Don't be silly. You're doing a wonderful job. Besides, all the waiters like you. I'm not hiring anyone else. You're the one for the bar upstairs." He pointed his index finger back and forth between the two of us, as if measuring the distance. "Can't you feel it?" he asked.

"Feel what?"

"The connection between us?"

I immediately felt at ease because of his outgoing, friendly nature. Leon Roberts and I would become the best of friends, and L'Oiseau du Paris was only the beginning.

That Saturday night I walked into the restaurant in time for our evening employee meal. Vin, the chef, always had the whole staff sit down at a large table in the dining room to eat together before we opened to the public. It was where he familiarized us with the specials du jour, and let us know if we were out of anything on the regular menu. These group staff meals put us in a family mode, and helped us all work together as a team. Vin, who was sitting next to me, whispered in my ear that he was making a fresh Napoleon for dessert, and would save a large piece for me.

Carmen informed me that we had a lot of reservations. I lined up all the wine openers in a row at the waiters' station, and made sure I had enough clean glasses, and a good selection of beers in the cooler.

Leon sat at the bar and asked me to pour him a glass of the new red wine he'd ordered. "You should know the character of a wine if you are offering it to patrons seated at your bar," he said, holding the glass out for me to have a taste.

As the night wore on I was lost in the weeds of orders, and tending to the few patrons sitting at my bar. Claude Canet, the owner, walked in with his girlfriend Brenda. She always dressed provocatively, but that night her outfit was over the top. She had on a crochet chemise, through which everyone could see the outline of her breasts, and if she moved a certain way you could see the nipples. The waiters were drooling, and Claude seemed proud. Claude Canet was much older than Brenda, but he was a very handsome man, well-spoken with a French accent. One would call him European suave.

One of the waiters ran to the bar, breathless. "There's big trouble in the kitchen." He looked slightly roughed up.

"What's going on?" I asked.

I peered through the little window that opened to the kitchen and saw Ricky, the head Haitian dishwasher, running around threatening the chef with a large kitchen knife. They were both yelling in French. They were speaking so fast that even with the three years of French I'd taken, I had no idea what they were fighting about. I noticed that the French baguettes on the floor, still in their white paper sleeves, were getting stepped on. Claude held steady with Brenda at the bar so as not to alert diners that anything out of the ordinary was happening in the kitchen. I peered through the window again to see a bunch of waiters struggling to get the knife away from Ricky, and attempting to calm the chef and the situation. The thumping of bodies bouncing off the wall could be felt at the bar, but the diners at tables seemed oblivious to the war going on behind the scenes.

Soon there was silence. A moment later a few waiters emerged from the kitchen straightening their aprons and smoothing their hair. They walked into the dining room carrying baskets of neatly sliced French bread, which I assumed were the same baguettes that had been trampled underfoot during the scuffle. I watched them place the bread baskets with small ramekins of butter on the tables, as if nothing had happened. Claude glanced at me with a sigh of relief. He left Brenda sitting at the bar while he walked through the dining room schmoozing patrons at the tables. I was left peering at Brenda's nipples through the crocheted chemise while attempting to make small talk.

That weekend, Jimmy Joe Riley took Derick and me to the drag races. The three of us sat in the front seat of his pickup, which had a gun rack in the back. I'd been to hot rod races as a teenager growing up in the Bronx, but these were not jalopies; these racing machines were technical marvels. They achieved such high speeds that they needed parachutes to slow them down at the end of each race. After the races were over, we went back to Jimmy Joe's house. He fetched a bottle of Kentucky bourbon whiskey out of a cabinet and set three shot glasses on the table. After we did a few rounds he took out a plastic bag filled with cocaine. I smiled at the thought. It had been so long, and we certainly didn't have money for such an expensive drug. We talked, drank, and snorted coke until the wee hours of the morning. Derick remained alert, the cocaine not letting the liquor overtake him.

We walked home through the balmy night air in a magical mood. Before locking up for the night Derick took Rebel for a brief walk. I knew what was on Derick's mind the minute he came back. We walked up the stairs to the bedroom holding hands. I got undressed and lay on the bed. Derick stood at the foot of the bed like a frozen statue staring at my nude body. After he came to his senses he began taking off his clothes.

"Stand there a moment. I want to look at you," I said.

He gazed at me shyly, as if I was sizing him up to draw him like a model in one of my life-drawing classes.

I was drawing—in my brain—the splendor of his body, paying special attention to the sun tattoo on his chest, so I'd remember it always. "Come here," I said.

He got on top of me and climbed inside of me. I wanted to remember every moment and feeling until I climaxed. I had flashbacks of that night for days afterward.

> I loved him very much—more than I could trust myself
> to say—more than words had power to express.
> —Charlotte Bronte, *Jane Eyre*

That May, the artist Christo surrounded eleven Biscayne islands with pink plastic as an environmental statement. The pink plastic remained there for two weeks. Leon, his boyfriend Flavio, me, and Dorian the hairdresser, took a scenic boat ride around the islands to get the full effect of the image from the water. It was quite impressive and must have been a feat to set up. The three of us had lunch and Cuba Libres at Monty Trainer's, hoping Jimmy Buffet would make a surprise appearance.

Derick wasn't home from work when Leon dropped me off. I threw myself on the couch and passed out. The phone woke me up. It was Dominick French.

"When are you coming back to Maui?" he asked.

"I don't have any immediate plans," I said.

"You still with Scaramouche?"

"Stop that, or I'll hang up the phone. We're engaged now."

There was dead silence on the other end of the phone line.

"What could you possibly have in common with that guy?" he asked.

"We love each other for starters."

"What kinds of things do you do in the Sunshine State?" Demo asked.

"Movies, bowling, drag races, fishing—it's Florida!"

"Oh brother, that sounds boring," he said.

"Okay, lots of screwing." Just then I heard a key in the front door. "I have to go," I said, hanging up the phone.

Derick walked through the front door in a good mood. He approached the couch, leaned down and gave me a kiss. He flipped the stereo on, and the radio station was playing that new song by the Police, "Every Breath You Take." I felt a little guilty that whole evening and wondered if I should tell Derick that Demo had called. But things were going so well between us; I didn't want to say or do anything to disrupt the harmony.

There were some awesome thunder-boomers in Florida during the rainy season, which begins in May and ends in October. I was home alone watching coverage of the *Challenger* rocket with Sally Ride, the first woman to go into space. I looked out at the sky from the terrace and could see it getting really dark. Bolts of lightning streaked the sky, followed by loud thunder-boomers that shook the building. Florida thunderstorms always sounded like God bowling in the sky. I didn't see Rebel, so I went looking for him. I found him crouched in the large walk-in closet in the bedroom upstairs. He was terrified; his body shaking violently from his head to his paws. I sat on the floor inside the closet and put my arms around him, but still he trembled. That closet was Rebel's refuge, his hiding place every time we had a thunderstorm. In time that closet became a hiding place for other things.

In the summer the humid air coated my skin with moisture. Summer in Miami was oppressively hot and muggy. I guess Annie Hughes was right when she warned me that Florida could be swampy. We had air conditioning in the apartment, but as soon as you opened the front door to the street, it was like walking into a bathroom after someone had taken a hot, steamy shower.

On the days I had no work, I'd get my paints out and work on T-shirts and sweatshirts. Being inside with the air conditioning blasting on those unbearably hot afternoons was the place to be. I flipped the stereo on and listened to an old Nina Simone album. I painted with joy to one of my favorite blues songs, "I Want a Little Sugar in My Bowl." I thought of how my relationship with Derick never diminished my creative side. He complemented my quirky, artistic side with his down-to-earth raw, wild side. The day flew by, and before I knew it the sun was going down. I retrieved the dried painted garments from the railing of the terrace and laid them carefully over a chair. I would finish them the next day. I had ordered sweatshirt and skirt sets from the warehouse in Atlanta, and was using a new technique of hand sewing beads and pearls on for definition. When they were complete, I would photograph them. I kept photos of all my designs in an album.

Sweatshirt skirt set

I was in the process of doing that when Derick came home. "I thought we'd go to Jimmy Joe's later."

"Your hair is all wet," I said.

"Yeah, the sky started dumping when I got out of the car."

"It's a good thing I got my shirts in from the terrace before the sky opened up. I need you to model a sweatshirt for me. I want guys to know they're not just for women."

He chuckled a little. "My shirt is soaked anyway," he said, taking it off.

I handed him a sleeveless, somewhat masculine sweatshirt painted with sailboats. He slipped it on, his muscular arms with tattoos adding to the effect.

"Now lie down on the couch," I said.

He smiled up at me shyly and chuckled like a little boy.

"Stop laughing! I need to snap the photo," I said.

I felt Jell-O in the pit of my stomach looking at his face, and got lost in his hazel eyes. I was overwhelmed with love and desire for him. I lay on top of him, kissing him, and began to tease him. We made love right there on that hideous furry brown couch.

I'd worked the day shift at L'Oiseau. I got home early, walked Rebel, and started dinner. Derick had called me at the restaurant to let me know he was going somewhere with Luke Skinner. Dinner time came and went and I ate alone. I watched TV for a while and walked the dog again but still no Derick. There was a sturdy knock at the door. I wondered why Derick wasn't using his key. I opened the door. Standing in the doorway was a policeman.

"Ma'am, I gave out one too many DUIs today, so I'm just bringing this guy home," the cop said.

I noticed Derick hiding behind him like a little boy who was afraid he was going to get a licking. He seemed more afraid of what my reaction would be than he was of the cop.

"He'll show you where we left the car. You can pick it up tomorrow. Consider yourself lucky."

The cop turned around and walked down the stairs. Derick was standing against the railing on the outside landing attempting to steady himself. He staggered through the door past me, and straight upstairs to the bedroom. "I don't want to hear anything," he said, slurring.

I decided to not tangle with him while he was drunk. I had no idea what the hell had happened that night. Luke wasn't with him, so I figured Derick stayed at a bar somewhere after Luke left and got plastered. Drinking was definitely an issue in his life, and it was beginning to affect how I felt about our relationship.

The next few days were filled with work, and there was no talk about the DUI he'd escaped. I'd hoped he took it as a lesson and realized how lucky he was. He could have lost his driver's license, or gotten tossed in jail. I didn't have to tell him any of that; he knew what jail was like. He'd spent two years in one before I met him. Derick wasn't a fun guy when he drank. He became belligerent and sloppy, and got himself into bad situations. It was a while after that incident before we were affectionate, and I rebuffed his sexual advances. A serious conversation seemed like a losing proposition, unless I was willing to threaten Derick with ultimatums. I got the feeling that wouldn't go over well with his stubborn nature. My friend Leon Roberts always said that Derick Ellis was the nicest guy—when he was sober.

Leon, Flavio, Derick, and I went to a Medieval Renaissance Fair at Crandon Gardens. Leon had a live-in boyfriend, a Latin guy named Flavio, who he often affectionately referred to as Flavia. Derick and Flavio strolled over to the beverage tent to get us drinks. Leon and I sat on a bench, talking.

"I was once a jockey for the Trotters when I lived in North Carolina. Now I'm too old and weigh too much to do that," Leon said.

"I've never been to a horse race."

"I'll take you sometime, perhaps for a big race, or when a famous horse is running."

"I'd love to go with you. I know it will be exciting."

"What do you think of the new waiter from Italy—Paolo?"

"He's pretty hot!" I said.

"Adriana, I was in the bathroom the same time as he was. His thing is the size of a baby's arm."

I began to laugh hysterically. "You'd better not tell that to Flavio. Did I ever tell you about Demosthenes, the Greek guy I had a tryst with when I worked in the fur market in Manhattan? He took me to a Greek restaurant on Ninth Avenue. We ate moussaka, drank Ouzo, and watched the belly dancers. I got drunk and ended up at his apartment. He had the biggest dick I'd ever seen."

"You'd better not tell Derick that story," Leon said, laughing.

"I'd be insane to."

"You know, I was married once."

"You were Lee?" I sometimes liked to call him that.

"To a woman. We're still friends, and her kids are like my kids."

We stopped talking when the guys came back with our drinks.

When we'd had enough of medieval times, we drove to Monty Trainer's for lunch, and laughed the rest of the afternoon away. Flavio was younger than Leon, but they seemed to have a good relationship. Besides, who was I to talk about age differences? Derick was younger than me. We did a lot of socializing with Leon and Flavio, even spending our holidays together. Leon Roberts was my constant companion when Derick wasn't around. We spoke on the phone every day, even if we knew we'd be working together later on.

That September my cousin Angie married her long-time boyfriend, Asher. The wedding was to take place in a little church in their town of Truro, Massachusetts, right outside of Cape Cod. Derick was coming with me; he'd been there before when we were on vacation from Hawaii. Angie's wedding was glorious. She arrived at the church in a horse-drawn carriage with her father. Their dog was the ring bearer, and had his own bed adorned with ribbons and flowers at the edge of the tent. Derick and I were staying at a bed-and-breakfast in a room next to my parents. It was nice to have a change of scene from Miami. The whole day was festive and beautiful. Derick looked smashing in the new gray suit he'd purchased in New York before we drove to the Cape. I often teased him, calling him a dandy, because he knew how to dress. Looking back at photographs from that day, I realized I wore the same dress to my cousin Angela's wedding that I wore to Haku's wedding in Hana, Maui. A dress I'd worn when I first met Derick. You'd think I'd have had the presence of mind to treat myself to a hot new dress, knowing how fussy he was about his appearance.

The day was moving along swimmingly—until Derick began knocking back drinks like a tennis pro chugging Gatorade. I pulled him aside, caressing his arm, and begged him to please not get trashed in front of my family. Of course, once I said that it just gave him license to continue. He acted as if I was his mother telling her naughty child to behave, and perhaps I was. I was so embarrassed I went back to the hotel room early, leaving Derick playing cards with my uncles tossing curses left and right, and acting stupid. The one time I pleaded with him to be mindful, he couldn't. He disappointed me, and I felt let down.

Derick stumbled into the room and crashed on the bed, waking me up like a dragon in a fairytale shooting breath of alcoholic fire. He reached his hand to touch me, but I was pissed off and made myself as stiff as a board. "Okay, if you want to be like that," he said, slurring. Next thing I knew he was snoring.

The rest of our vacation was great, and I don't know why that night bothered me so much. I guess it was his having no consideration for my feelings, even after I begged him not to get drunk. I would have never done something like that to embarrass him in front of his family. I questioned if he had respect for me. The thought haunted me for weeks after we were back in Florida.

My mother called to tell me that there was an earthquake at the foot of the Adirondack Mountains after we left the East Coast. What I didn't realize at the time was that there was an earthquake building inside of me.

My friend Suki Rosmond was getting married. I took a short trip to California to attend the wedding. Derick couldn't get the time off from work. I wanted to see her shop, Whimseys, where she carried my hand-painted clothing. Whimseys was full of quirky items like vintage posters, hand crafted jewelry, and Betty Boop memorabilia. I stayed with Suki and her soon-to-be husband. Her house was an eclectic marvel. She kept coffee beans in the freezer and ground them right before the brewing process. I never knew anyone that fussy about their coffee.

The wedding was a Jewish ceremony. Star Green, who was Jewish, was her maid of honor. I watched from the sidelines. I was thankful that the three of us women—the three musketeers—were still connected. I purchased a beautiful lamp in her little shop of oddities. It was patterned after the planet Saturn, a large white globe with red glass rings around it. When I got back to Florida I displayed it on top of our stacked stereo system.

That Halloween Leon Roberts had a Pink Coffin party at his house. There was an actual pink coffin in the corner of the living room. Leon had friends in the funeral business. Lying in the coffin was a mannequin, which Dorian the hairdresser made up to look like the actress Loni Anderson. While Leon and his boyfriend Flavio were setting up for the party, some guys happened to pass by their yard. They were musicians in a local rock band who offered to play at the party if they could participate in the festivities. The whole night was wild and crazy. As the band rocked out, a mummy dragged his rags through the crowd of costumed party-goers. Everyone we knew was there, and some we didn't. There were lots of drugs in the bathrooms, and the liquor was flowing. I noticed a taut expression on Derick's face that whole evening. I imagined he'd done a lot of cocaine.

I was dressed as Princess Poo-Poo-Ly (has plenty Pa-Pa-Ya) and Derick would pick flowers off my lei and toss them saying, "And she loves to give it away." Of course, I was no Teresa Brewer, but it was very funny. Derick was dressed as an Amtrak ticket agent. I have no idea where he got that plaid polyester jacket, the paisley tie, or the official Amtrak hat. Probably at the This'n'That Thrift Shop. We had a fantastic time! Best of all, we were invited to Thanksgiving dinner in someone's backyard in the Grove. I don't remember much about the dinner except that Derick volunteered to carve the turkey.

I worked a night shift at the restaurant and got home after midnight. As soon as I walked through the front door Rebel was standing there wanting to go out. I hated walking him late at night, but Derick was sound asleep upstairs and I didn't want to wake him. A guy had a pack of dogs that he walked around the neighborhood without leashes. I'd never seen them out that late at night, so I figured it was safe to take Rebel downstairs. I was waiting for Rebel to finish his business in the yard, when out of nowhere, there they were—a pack of snarling, barking dogs of different sizes and breeds. It was too late to drag Rebel away. They were on us like starving wolves on a sick deer. They attacked Rebel with no mercy, and the owner of the dogs was doing nothing to stop them. I began screaming, 'Help!' at the top of my lungs. I was afraid to get too near the fray because they might go for me. Derick must have heard the barking, yelping, and my screaming. I looked up, and thank God, he was standing there.

"Derick, they're gonna kill Rebel," I shouted.

"Get your damn dogs off my dog," Derick yelled at the owner.

The guy just stared at him with a blank expression, like he didn't care and had no intention of stopping the fight. Derick grabbed the front of the guy's jacket and threw him on top of the pack of dogs, which by now were a tangled scrambling mess. The guy stood up a little stunned and backed off. He whistled, rounding up his dogs, and walked down the street. Derick yelled after him, "And pick another fucking street to walk down!" Derick scooped up Rebel who was shaking and bleeding; we didn't know from where. When we got back to the apartment he rinsed him off in the bathtub, which revealed numerous bites and a gash on his neck. His thick collar had saved his life. The next day we took him to the vet to get stitched up. After that incident, Derick usually walked Rebel late at night. I saw that guy from time to time walking along West Pelican Drive with one of his dogs on a leash, but never again on our side of the street.

I flew to Maui for ten days, calling it a business trip, and ignoring Derick's objections. I couldn't help missing the island the way I did. Derick didn't seem to miss it at all. I told him it was good business sense to reconnect with the stores that were selling my hand-painted clothing on Front Street in Lahaina. We both knew, deep down, that the stores were not why I was going to Hawaii. Perhaps he feared I was going to reconnect with my former boyfriend, Dominick French. I didn't realize it at the time that I was driving that wedge deeper and deeper between us. I ignored his insecurities, brushing them off as silly, and thought only about what made me happy. I suppose Maui filled a place in me that was empty. Our life in Florida bore only a small resemblance to our life on Maui. I needed to recharge my batteries, and what better place than Hawaii?

As soon as I stepped off the plane in Honolulu, I was overcome with the scent of the air—the sweetness of it coming off the trade winds. As my connecting flight circled Maui and descended, I saw Haleakala Crater, waterfalls, and fields of sugar cane and pineapple. *This is where I belong,* I thought, and I choked up with emotion. That was the affect Maui had on me. Annie Hughes, my Maui mom, picked me up at Kahului Airport. She hadn't changed a bit; her long gray hair blowing in the trades. We hugged and kissed as she put a plumeria lei around my neck. The familiar aroma tickled my nose and brought back a million memories.

"So how's life in the swamp?" she asked, as we drove over the *Pali.*

"It's different for sure," I said.

"How's Hot Stuff?"

"He's fine, still a dandy, still hot."

"I'm taking you straight to the Yacht Club," she said.

"I can't wait to see everyone."

"Demo is so excited to see you. We'll go to the Mission Bar on Saturday night."

"He's called me a few times in Florida."

"I gave him your phone number," she said.

I was a little curious as to how I would feel when I saw Dominick French.

Annie parked the car in her yard. I was staying at her place while on Maui. I carried my suitcase upstairs while she waited for me at the bottom of the steps. She was still very round and fat despite the numerous diets she'd been on. We walked down Front Street, arm in arm, catching up on our time apart. Walking along the seawall listening to the waves break on the shore as the sun was setting, was like looking at a favorite painting in a museum one returns to see again and again. We pushed through the swinging doors of the Yacht Club and moseyed up to the bar. Tim Kork was waiting. He had saved us two barstools. I was soaking it all in because I knew that in less than ten days, I'd be back in the madland. People were buying me drinks left and right, some of which I sluffed off to the bartender, who spilled them out when no one was looking. Bully was sitting on the opposite side of the bar. He winked at me and lifted his glass, toasting my return.

Annie and I spent the next day on Kaanapali Beach. The ocean was rejuvenating, and we had lunch in one of the outside hotel cafés. I visited the two stores on Front Street that were selling my hand-painted T-shirts. I was filled with pride to see my designs displayed. I borrowed Annie's station wagon and drove to Kihei to see my long-time friend Loretta Perino. She'd been living on that side of the island ever since she broke up with Derick's bestie Carter. Derick never spoke about Carter, even when I pried him for information. Loretta told me that her parents were lending her money for a down payment on a house. She'd been going out with a local *haoule* (non-Hawaiian) guy, and told me she hadn't seen Carter in a long time. It was all so familiar and wonderful.

On Saturday night, Annie and I drifted into the Missionaries Hotel. Just walking on that street and up the steps of the hotel caused my stomach to drop about ten feet. I thought of how in love I'd been with Dominick French at one time, and what a crazy roller coaster ride that had been. When she and I walked into the Mission Bar in the back, Demo caught sight of us and stopped playing the piano. He pointed his finger at me, stamped his foot, and sang my favorite song, "Exactly Like You." I was swept up in the moment, or was it the past? I wasn't sure. On his break Demo sat at our table. I still felt a magical connection as I gazed at the musical notes along his arm. He grabbed and held my hand and wouldn't let it go. We sat there staring and smiling at each other. What I felt wasn't love at all; it was the whole magical experience of my first two years living on Maui, a life I sorely missed. Annie Hughes and Dominick French were a big part of it.

My ten days on Maui flew by in a flash, but when I left, I knew I'd be back some day. On the plane ride back to Florida, I considered where my life had been, but wasn't sure where it was going. I thought of my relationship with Derick, how it was when we lived in Hawaii, and how it was in Florida. I loved Derick and wanted to marry him, but even after our years together I had reservations. I guess everyone does when they are contemplating marriage. That concept of forever always troubled me. It was something that I felt deep down inside wasn't possible. I feared that if he stopped loving me, or I stopped loving him, I'd be lost. We all know it's a bad idea to look outside of ourselves for happiness, but when your life is so entwined with another person's, that's the reality. As the plane was landing at Miami International Airport, I knew he'd be waiting for me at the gate. I had to get myself together. As soon as I saw Derick's face, my concerns faded into the Miami heat.

During those first few weeks I was home, Derick and I spent a lot of time together. I guess that old adage is true—absence makes the heart grow fonder. We took Rebel to the beach, and the dog played in the waves. Derick took me to his favorite fishing pier. I didn't see any trashy women hanging around offering blow jobs, although we didn't stay very long. Derick didn't catch anything, so he lost interest.

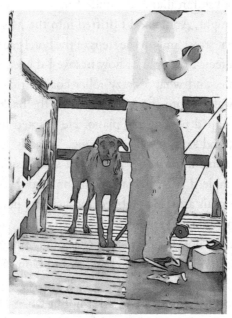

Derick and Rebel on pier

When we got home I cooked Rebel some chopped meat and rice, which I always mixed with his Kal Kan. The dog would sit next to me staring up at the frying pan. He knew I was cooking it for him. I'd offer him a little taste, which he'd take off the fork so delicately with his teeth. Rebel was a big dog, but he was my little boy, like a son to me. He followed me around the apartment, and wherever I was, whatever I was doing, the dog would lie at my feet. I had the feeling Derick was jealous that the dog became closer to me over the years we were together. Jimmy Joe Riley liked to tease me if he was at our apartment. I'd ask him to take the dog for a walk, and he'd say, "That's not a dog." I suppose he was inferring that Rebel was a wuss always lying at his mommy's feet.

We had a big Christmas at our house that year. Derick dragged that little fake Christmas tree out of the walk-in closet, and placed it on the corner of the kitchen counter. I bummed pine branches from the guys selling evergreens at the shopping center. The year 1983 had come in with a bang but was going out with a whimper.

I walked in the apartment after working the night shift at L'Oiseau du Paris. I found Derick and Rebel asleep on the couch. A feeling of complete love enveloped me, almost too much to bear. They were my *everything*, and I never thought anything could ever change the way we were, or the way I felt. I decided to stop taking my birth control pills.

Oscar Wilde said, "The mystery of love is greater than the mystery of death."

CHAPTER 4

TAINTED LOVE

Everything a man does secretly in the darkness of night
will be clearly revealed in daylight. Words intended in
privacy will become unexpectedly common conversation.
Deeds which we hide today in the corner of our lodgings
will be shouted on every street corner tomorrow.
—Khalil Gibran, *The Broken Wings*

The year 1984 was filled with questions and predictions from George
Orwell's novel *1984*, which he wrote in 1949—a cautionary tale
regarding Big Brother and totalitarianism. Everyone was waiting to
see if any of his predictions would come to fruition. Drug kingpins and
cocaine cowboys took over and changed the culture of Miami. I went to
the movies to see *Scarface*, starring Al Pacino. It visualized everything
I saw happening around me as a sad reality. So many were getting rich
off selling drugs, and too many were succumbing to states of madness
and drug-induced euphoria. It touched many of us, including our
household.

Derick had recently cut his hair, and he looked even more attractive
in a traditional haircut. It still had some length to it, with beautiful soft
waves of cocoa and blond. The scar on his face melting from my sight into
oblivion. I was feeling jealous of him. He hadn't given me any reason not
to trust him, but I'd heard that when people cut their hair it means they
are ready for a change in their lives. This made me insecure.

Leon, Flavio, Dorian the hairdresser, and I, spent an afternoon at
Vizcaya. It resembled a Venetian palace from the 1700s at the edge of the
water, where I sat imagining myself in another time. It actually was the
former winter home of James Deering, a wealthy farming manufacturer.
The interior had an extensive art collection. There were ten acres of formal
gardens, a native forest, and a mangrove shoreline. Florida has some

wonderful historical treasures. After Vizcaya we drove to Coral Gables and had lunch at my favorite Cuban restaurant on Calle Ocho, La Carreta. Fried plantains, pulled pork, and black beans were on the menu, followed by a strong, sweet, Cuban espresso.

Later on at Leon's house, Dorian insisted on doing something different with my hair. I entrusted my tresses to the professional. Leon made us drinks, and I let Dorian work his magic. When Dorian went to the kitchen to get a glass of water, Leon whispered in my ear, "I don't want to alarm you, but your head looks like it's covered in black shoe polish!"

After Dorian washed the dye out, I stood in front of the mirror. A sickening feeling came over me. One of my most attractive features, my hair, was ruined.

Leon dropped me off on West Pelican Drive. Rebel stared at me, tilting his head from side to side, as if trying to decode the fiasco on my head. Derick snickered and commented, "It's not that bad!" But I could tell by the expression on his face that he was just placating me. For me, it was the beginning of insecurities about my image and my age.

That spring Derick and I took a short trip to New York to visit my family. The weather was temperate, not hot and steamy like it was in Florida. We drove up to Cape Cod with my parents. Derick drove at speeds that scared even the Virgin Mary on the dashboard. We brought two boxes of Italian pastries from a popular bakery in the Bronx. My cousins took us to the ocean to see the sand dunes. We stopped to have lunch in Province Town which reminded us so much of Lahaina. We were all talking and laughing in the car on our way back to Truro. When we got back to their house we found two large empty pastry boxes on the kitchen counter. Their two dogs had eaten every last morsel. We laughed about it, but my cousins were livid.

Vita was so pleased that we were finally engaged, and seemed totally smitten with Derick. She told me in private that she thought Derick was so handsome with his short haircut. "He used to look like a wild man with that mop of long, wavy blond hair," she said. She gave him a beautiful eighteen-karat gold, filigree, antique cross on a thick rope chain, imported from Italy. "I'll give it to you now since you won't be here in August for your birthday. Derick seemed sincerely touched.

When we got back to Miami we drove straight to the kennel to pick up Rebel, who was overjoyed to be sprung from doggie prison. Derick and I seemed to be in a good place, although I was the only one working. Derick had been let go from his previous job, and was doing odd jobs. One of those jobs was cleaning a nightclub after hours. He'd come home with the craziest things people left behind in their inebriated states. Unclaimed property, after a reasonable amount of time, could be claimed by the cleaners who found it. That was how I came by a fourteen-karat gold filigree band. It was so tiny, he slipped it on my pinky finger.

Derick eventually found a job loading planes for a cargo company. He was up at 4:00 a.m. every morning. Rebel would creep up the stairs as soon as he heard the shower running. The dog would jump up on the bed with me, and lay his head on Derick's pillow. When the shower stopped the dog would jump off the bed and run downstairs. Derick would come out of the bathroom and hear me laughing in bed.

"What the hell is so funny at this ungodly hour?" he'd ask, as he put his pants on.

Was the dog smarter than Derick gave him credit for? I found myself feeling guilty that Derick had to work such a strenuous job leaving the house in the middle of the night. Imagine feeling guilty that your man, your partner, had to work hard.

We were invited to a barbeque at his new boss's house. We sat in their backyard for hours. While we were waiting for dessert, Derick handed me his boss's grandchild, who I held in my lap for a while. Derick stared at me with love and longing as I bounced the infant on my knee. I knew what he was thinking, and I was feeling something similar. Things were finally looking up financially for Derick. He traded in his old Chrysler sedan for a dark-green Chevy pickup truck.

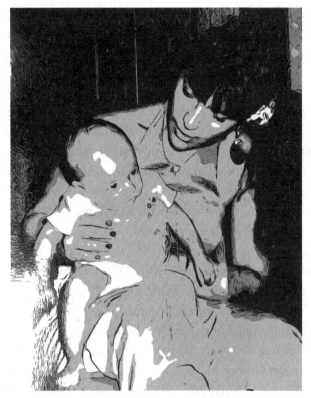

Me with the boss's grandchild

Derick and I had a day off together, and he got it in his head to drive to Alligator Alley where he'd heard the fishing was great. I would have preferred an air boat ride in Fort Lauderdale. It was a very long drive. Derick fished while Rebel splashed around in the canal. I watched them both, my feelings bouncing back and forth between soppy emotion and total boredom. Out of the corner of my eye I saw a large gator swimming toward Rebel.

"Derick, there's an alligator going after Rebel!"

"The gator's looking for lunch," Derick shouted, scooping the dog out of the canal.

Derick locked Rebel in the cab of the truck. The dog couldn't figure out why he was being punished. The alligator hung around eyeing the shore, as Rebel's smell lingered in the air and water. Derick made us stay there until he caught something. Fishing wasn't my thing, but it did give me joy to see how pleased Derick was with the good-sized fish he eventually caught. I took a photo of Derick holding the fish and smiling at the camera. He had the expression of a proud little boy. When we got home, he gutted, cleaned, and cooked it for dinner. I was filled with admiration.

There was a new guy on the scene I didn't care for, a Cuban guy named Ricardo. Everyone called him Rico. There was something about him that rubbed me the wrong way. Derick seemed to change around Rico, even his demeanor and facial expression looked different. At first I couldn't imagine what was going on with him, but as time passed, I assumed they were doing a lot of cocaine. I was honest with Derick regarding my impression of Rico, but he said I was being paranoid.

A bunch of us drove to Key West in Derick's new green pickup. We stopped for gas, which was up to $1.10 a gallon. I was riding in the back bed of the truck with Jimmy Joe Riley, Luke Skinner, and Rebel. I could hear Derick and Rico arguing about something. They hopped in the cab of the truck, still squabbling. Four hours later we arrived in the famous and unique town of Key West. It's the farthest tip on the Florida peninsula jutting out in the Gulf of Mexico. We walked for about an hour through the streets, past pastel buildings and conch shells in store windows. Then we loaded back in the truck and headed straight back to Miami. I was famished after that long drive, and wanted to have lunch somewhere. I thought we'd visit the Ernest Hemingway house, which had been turned into a museum, and maybe have a drink in the famous bar, Sloppy Joe's, where Hemingway hung out in his heyday. Everything Derick did with Ricardo had an urgency to it. Call it paranoia or woman's intuition, but I sensed undercurrents at play which rendered me uneasy.

That spring, Eartha Kitt had a new disco song that topped the charts, "Where Is My Man?" Leon and Flavio took me to the famous gay bar, the Seagull, on Miami Beach, where she was appearing. I think she was even on an episode of the popular TV show *Miami Vice* that same year. We had a great time boogying the afternoon away. I tried talking to Leon about what was going on with Derick, but he stopped me in my tracks with a hand gesture, like he didn't want to talk about it.

I didn't push the issue. It never dawned on me at the time that Leon and Flavio might have been engaged in the same drug practices, and were avoiding drawing attention to the subject. When they dropped me off on West Pelican Drive, I needed to examine exactly what the undercurrent was that I was sensing in my partner.

Derick's friend Rico was married to a woman who already had two children by another man. They were an odd couple—she was big and tall, and he was short and slight. The other thing was they never smiled.

Rico took us to a party at someone's house. We parked across the street from a large compound with a cement wall encircling it. I didn't like the vibe there at all. I felt as if we were in a big-time drug dealer's compound. We had Rebel with us. Everyone was very cliquish, speaking only Spanish. I sat alone at a picnic table in their yard feeling somewhat isolated, while Derick schmoozed with Rico and the other guys at the barbeque. The men had been drinking all day. I noticed the crowd of guys forming a pack, weaving back and forth in unison, like tuna in a large fish net.

A gunshot rang out, and I imagined that was the reason why all the men were writhing together trying to get hold of the gun. I grabbed Rebel's leash and jumped on top of the picnic table. I tossed him over the cement wall onto the ground outside, and climbed over the wall which was not very high. I ran across the street where a crowd of neighbors had gathered. Someone must have called the police after hearing the gunshot. I stood there among the crowd as if I was just a curious spectator.

Within a few minutes about half a dozen police cars arrived on the scene surrounding the house. I watched a task force in riot gear march in single file behind the cement wall with assault weapons drawn. I waited to see what was going to happen. I saw cops walk the men from the party, one by one, outside to the sidewalk. They were told to kneel on the ground with their hands raised behind their heads. Derick was among them. I was totally freaked out, and figured they were all getting arrested. I remained among the crowd that had gathered across the street, watching that frightening scene, feeling detached.

Eventually, the cops let them all go since no one was injured, and I assumed the gun was registered. Derick frantically twisted his head this way and that searching for me.

"Derick, I'm over here!" I shouted.

He walked across the street when he spotted me and Rebel. The neighbors that had gathered to watch the spectacle looked at me with suspicion as they began to disburse.

"I was looking everywhere for you," Derick said.

"When I heard a gunshot I felt the need to escape."

"You weren't worried about me?" he asked.

"I guess I went into some kind of survival mode," I answered, guiltily.

"Let's get out of here," Derick said, and we hopped in the truck.

"Derick, I don't like these people you're hanging around with. I think they're trouble."

Derick ignored my comment, blathering away about how lucky he was not to get arrested, and that the night could have turned out much worse. He became quiet when he noticed I wasn't responding to anything he was saying. I stared out the window with a blank expression. My mind was replaying a story my aunt Camille had told me. She was a young woman riding in the back seat of a friend's car with her three small children. She felt the car lurch forward, and the brakes ceased to work. The car began to roll out of control. Without a conscious thought she jumped out of the moving car leaving her three children in the back seat. She had blushed and giggled as she told the story. It was exactly the way I reacted, a kind of involuntary self-preservation.

I wasn't sure what I was feeling in the car that night sitting next to Derick, but it wasn't good. I was getting the impression that Derick was attracted to, and comfortable in, the criminal element. I certainly was not. Perhaps I was seeing a future I didn't see myself in.

Derick was definitely different in some way, and I suspected he'd replaced drinking with hard drugs. He'd developed a negative attitude with me that he'd never had before. I'd react with my New York sarcasm which didn't help the situation. He'd often come home, open the refrigerator, stand there and stare inside with his hand braced at the top, as if expecting his favorite foods to magically appear.

"There's nothing in here I want to eat," he'd say.

"If you'd buy some groceries—the ones you like—there would be," I'd answer.

He'd toss me an annoyed look and say that he was going out to get something to eat. He'd shut the refrigerator door and leave the apartment. I wouldn't see him until the wee hours of the morning, sometimes not until the next morning. I had the feeling he was hanging around with a pack of drug dealers, doing a lot of cocaine, and who knows what else.

My period was very late, and I was queasy. I thought I might be pregnant—the sacred mingling of blood between a man and a woman. When I looked at Derick I was filled with love, and when he touched me we were the same flesh. At least that's how I used to feel. I wanted to tell him the news and have it be a joyous occasion; instead, all I could think was *who is going to support me and a baby?* I was killing myself working as many shifts as I could in the restaurant, and had my hand-painted clothing business. I didn't see any money coming from Derick, even when he worked. What the hell was he doing with his money? He mentioned something about a beautiful gold bracelet he saw that he was getting me for my birthday. My birthday came and went, and I never saw the bracelet. Did he give it to someone else? Like in the movie *Love Actually*, where a woman finds a beautiful necklace in a gift box in her husband's dresser, but on Christmas Day when she opens the gift from her husband, it's a Joni Mitchell CD. At that moment she realizes he gave the necklace to another woman.

I imagined he was spending his money on drugs and drinking in bars with his friends, but I refused to accept the possibility that maybe he was spending it on another woman. He certainly wasn't spending any of it on me, the dog, or our home. A couple of months back he had told me he was walking to the Grove, and a thug ripped that beautiful antique gold cross my mother had given him right off his neck. I'd had purse snatching attempts while walking that same route, so at the time I believed him. After not receiving the bracelet I couldn't help but think he'd made up the story about the cross being stolen. Perhaps he sold it, and used that money to buy drugs. I hated thinking that way about him.

I was feeling more than morning sickness and knew something was wrong. I was so nauseated all of the time that the only relief was lying on my stomach. I couldn't work anymore; I couldn't even walk around without feeling dizzy. I saw a doctor who confirmed that, indeed, I was pregnant.

When Derick walked through the front door that evening, I blurted it out. "Derick, I'm pregnant. I've wanted to tell you but you're never around."

"Adriana," he said, momentarily softening his expression and hugging me.

"Something's not right," I said.

"What do you mean?"

"It doesn't feel normal. Something is wrong. I told you I was pregnant before, and I know what it should feel like."

I saw a mixture of emotions on his face.

"You don't want to have the baby?" he asked.

"I don't know, Derick."

He'd disappear at night with Rico, and come home with dark circles under his eyes. One night I waited up to talk to him.

"Derick, I can't work as sick as I feel. I'm going to have an abortion."

"If it's what you want to do, I can't stop you," he said.

I went alone to the clinic for the procedure. When I came out of the anesthetic the doctor sat on the bed and held my hand.

"I don't want to know what it was," I said, crying.

"You never would have carried that baby to term," the doctor said.

"What do you mean?"

"The placenta was full of blood, so not enough nourishment was going to the baby. Do you work a strenuous job?" he asked.

"No, but I'm on my feet a lot, and there's stress."

"Well, eventually you would have lost this baby," he said, patting my hand. "Better you didn't go any further with the pregnancy, or you might have been hospitalized with a miscarriage at a later stage."

After I rested for a while, I got dressed and took a cab home. Staring out the window as we drove along my mind flew back to a similar situation. It was when I lived on a commune and told my then partner Romeo I was pregnant, and that I was getting an abortion. Perhaps those were different circumstances, but Romeo was supportive whether he liked my decision or not, and was with me every step of the way. But today, I was going through this alone. When Derick came home that night I told him what the doctor had said. He stared at me as if I'd made up a story.

"Derick, we can still have a baby."

"Maybe you don't really want a baby," he said, in an accusatory tone.

I didn't answer him. Perhaps I felt guilt, and thought there might be some truth in what he was saying. We went through weeks of disconnectedness. Derick took his displeasure out on Rebel. I'd hear him yell at the dog to get off the bed, and once he even hit him with his leash. I heard the dog yelp and saw him cower. Then he'd look at me as if the dog's actions were my fault. I suppose he was right in a way, but Rebel was going to sleep there when we weren't home anyway.

Being a Cancer, the sign ruled by the moon, I could be moody at times. I had a tendency to retreat, like a crab, when things weren't going my way. I began to distance myself. I told Derick that maybe we needed some time apart. He claimed he didn't want us to separate, yet his actions showed me otherwise.

Pushing a man away when I was disappointed in a relationship was my pattern, like a self-sabotage. Sometimes we'd argue and Derick would pack his clothes in a suitcase and attempt to leave. He'd drape Rebel's leash over the suitcase as if to say, "If I go Rebel's coming with me." I'd cry and run upstairs. Derick would soften and wouldn't leave. It was my father leaving all over again. Childhood traumas remain with us forever. Derick had one foot out the door and the other one on slippery ground. I didn't want to let him go. It had always been his reaction to adversity, even when we lived in Hawaii he walked out on me a couple of times after squabbles. I began taking my birth control pills again.

A couple of months passed, and we seemed to drift back together, but things were on shaky ground, as if our apartment complex was built over a sinkhole.

Derick liked Prince's song "Little Red Corvette." If it was playing on the radio he'd sing along with the lyrics. He'd quote parts of the song directly at me: "I wonder if I've got enough class." The one that really irked me was when he'd stare at me and sing, "All the jockeys that were there before me." Was he feeling inadequate? Was he putting me down by bringing up my past, and the guys who came before him? It sure felt like it.

I awoke one morning as Derick was emerging from the walk-in closet in our bedroom. He went straight into the bathroom and stayed there for a long time. I didn't think much of it, until he emerged from the bathroom wanting to have sex right away. He stood at the foot of the bed looking down at me, not in a tender way, but with the look of a wild animal. It wasn't the first time I'd seen that look on his face. He seemed edgy and was sweating. He got on top of me and fucked me hard. I'm not saying it wasn't hot, but it definitely wasn't loving.

When we were finished he stood up and stared down at me. "I know what I'm good at," he said. He got dressed and went downstairs.

What the hell is this all about? I wondered. *Perhaps a show of power?* Sometimes men use sex as power over a woman, even a willing woman.

After Derick left the apartment I tore that walk-in closet apart. I looked in every jacket pocket, duffel bag, hatbox, and suitcase, until I found what I was looking for—a needle, a spoon, and a small rock of cocaine. When he came home that afternoon I was waiting for him like one of those ugly witches waiting to cast an evil spell. Perhaps my reaction was harsh. After all, wasn't my boyfriend Romeo, on the commune, a heroin addict? So why was this discovery so egregious? I imagine it was because this was a more serious relationship, and the fact that he was hiding it from me.

"What's this?" I asked, holding out the needle and spoon.

Derick stood there frozen, as if he'd been caught with the murder weapon in a crime drama. Without a word, he did an about-face and left the apartment.

> Recklessness is almost a man's revenge on his woman. He
> fears he is not valued, so he will risk destroying himself to
> deprive her altogether.
> —D. H. Lawrence

I slept downstairs that night to avoid having sex with him. He refused to talk about anything that was going on. We went for days with minimal communication. If I was upstairs, he'd sleep downstairs on the couch.

I called my mother in the Bronx. I didn't tell her exactly what was going on, but I told her that Derick and I were arguing a lot, and that I was punishing him by not giving him sex.

I heard my mother tsk and say, "Adriana, that doesn't work with a man. Derick's a young guy. If you don't give him sex he'll find it somewhere else." Never did I think she'd be right. Derick and I went on this way for a while, drifting in and out of a state of love.

Buck Morgan was a friend of Derick's I actually liked. He was an all-American type, tall, blond, and a bit stocky. One afternoon on our way to pick up Derick, he took me to the stables where he tended someone's horses. I enjoyed watching him brush the horses down and feed them.

One of the horses had a new colt. I watched the mother and baby together and was overcome with emotion. I began to cry. Buck turned toward me. At first he seemed uncomfortable. He flipped his short, straight, blond hair to the side revealing sympathetic blue eyes. Even though he was Derick's friend, woman's intuition told me he had a thing for me.

"Adriana, what's wrong?"

"Something terrible is happening between me and Derick, and we can't seem to turn it around."

At first, he didn't know what to say, so he continued brushing the colt. "I know Derick loves you. Maybe he doesn't show it enough."

"He used to. Derick professes his love for me, but actions speak louder than words! I know that's just a cliché, but he doesn't act like he loves me anymore. Instead he does things to test my love for him."

"We men often don't know what a woman really wants."

"I feel like he's doing too many drugs and they're changing him."

"Adriana, you and I just did some coke together before we drove to the stables."

"I know, but he's shooting it up. That's not recreational anymore."

Buck stared at me. "You know guys don't talk about things."

"We've been together for almost five years. We were planning on getting married. If he can't talk to me now, when will he?"

"Give him some time to come to his senses. I don't think he realizes what he has."

"Buck, I don't want to feel this unhappy five years from now. I love Derick, but some of the things he's doing, and the people he's hanging around with—I just don't know where this is going."

Buck put his arm around me and motioned for me to pet the colt. I walked into the stall with mother and baby. I patted the dam on her nose, and began to stroke her colt. I realized that I felt anger about the abortion, as if it was all Derick's fault. If I hadn't been working so hard to support us, the pregnancy might not have been in jeopardy. I didn't feel I could depend on him to take care of me and a baby. A woman needs to feel secure.

Buck stroked both horses and smiled at me. "Life can be pretty uncomplicated if we let it," he said.

We stepped out of the stall, he closed the gate, and we left the barn. As we walked to his truck my mood lifted slightly. We were on our way to meet Derick.

I flew to New York for my father's birthday. Perhaps I was escaping my situation, but I needed to be around my family. On the plane ride I pictured an out-of-control train barreling over a set of rails that couldn't stop or switch tracks. That was how I saw Derick and me—two people who loved each other, but somehow hopped on the wrong train and couldn't get off.

While I was in New York I got together with old friends and saw my aunts and uncles. My mother and I spent an evening at her sister's house, my aunt Camille. We were all playing cards, talking, and laughing.

"So when are you and Derick getting married?" Aunt Camille asked.

There was a deafening silence and everyone stared at me waiting for a response. I hesitated a bit too long.

"I'm not really sure," I answered.

"Adriana, don't you love him? We all do," Aunt Camille said.

In that moment, I realized that as much as I loved Derick, I wasn't sure about marrying him anymore. I always seemed to be waiting for another shoe to drop, something else to deal with, more disappointments. That is how my perception of our relationship deteriorated.

Once back home in Miami my evenings were filled with work at L'Oiseau du Paris, and most days painting garments. I expanded to hooded sweatshirts and pant sets for the California stores. I was experimenting with thick acrylic paints on fabric. I felt normal and happy when I painted. Derick and I were still cohabitating, but the marriage topic faded.

Hooded sweatshirt and pant set

I came downstairs one morning to make the coffee and found Derick asleep on the couch. He must have come home in the middle of the night. I walked into the living room as I waited for the coffee to brew. I took solace in listening to the trickle of the coffee pot. I stared down at him wondering where he'd been, and where we went wrong.

His wallet had fallen off the trunk we used as a coffee table and was laying on the floor. I bent down to put it back on the trunk and noticed a photo next to it—a photo of Derick sitting on a chair with a blonde woman sitting on his lap. She had a big smile on her face. I can't explain the feeling in the pit of my stomach. Instead of angry eyes ready to explode, I felt a combination of jealousy, helplessness, and betrayal, but mostly sadness. Wasn't I partly responsible? Hadn't I pushed him away sexually? I remembered my mother saying, "Adriana, you give a man enough rope and he'll hang himself."

It crossed my mind that he wanted me to see the photo to make me jealous. I slipped it back in his wallet, quietly walked back to the kitchen, poured myself a cup of coffee and went upstairs. I guess, inwardly, I hoped it was just a playful photo someone took of him with a girl who was flirting with him, but why would he carry such a photo in his wallet? I couldn't accept that he might be involved with, and making love to, someone else.

Later that day I was in the kitchen washing dishes when the phone rang. Derick rushed to pick it up. His conversation was muffled. He announced that he had to meet a friend at the shopping center, someone who owed him money. He left the apartment soon after. I waited a few minutes then followed him. I stood on the corner and strained my eyes across the boulevard to see who he was meeting. It was a woman standing in front of the drugstore. I walked back to the apartment wondering if he was picking up drugs, or just meeting her. I didn't question him when he returned. Perhaps I didn't want to know.

I was surprised when Derick announced that his mother Ellen was coming for a visit. I had only met her once before, when Derick and I were on vacation and we stopped in Washington State on our way home to Hawaii. I was happy to see her, but wondered what the purpose of her visit was. She never visited us during the two years we lived in Hawaii. I hoped perhaps she could talk some sense into her son.

"I want to talk to you alone," Ellen said.

"Do you want to go for a ride?" I asked.

Derick interrupted, "The keys to the truck are on the counter."

Something about the way he said that made me wonder if her visit was his idea.

We walked downstairs, neither one of us saying anything. We hopped into Derick's green pickup. I turned the ignition over, and we drove around for a while engaging in small talk. Then she spit it out.

"I came here to find out why this woman"—she meant me—"is dragging her feet to the altar!"

"Ellen, there are so many things going on."

"Derick told me that you want to break up. I thought you loved my son. You're engaged; you were going to get married. What happened?"

"Ellen, we've done nothing but argue lately." I was avoiding getting into the heavy stuff, not knowing how much I should tell her.

"Couples argue. It's normal, but that will pass," she said. She kept pressuring me, not being satisfied with any of my answers, so I exploded.

"You want to know the truth? Be prepared to hear it."

"My son and I haven't been close since he was in jail. I do know how stubborn he is."

"Ellen, this is way beyond stubborn."

"Derick told me you had an abortion."

Hearing that, I got angry, and against my better judgement I let it rip! "Did he mention that I would have lost the baby anyway?"

"No, he didn't say that. He said that you didn't want to have a baby with him."

"Ellen, Derick spends his money on drinking in bars with his friends, and never has any money for me, his dog, or the house. We don't do things together anymore. He even forgot my birthday. He's doing a lot of drugs, shooting up cocaine, and now I think he's screwing another woman."

"Just like a man to dip his wick," Ellen said, with a chuckle.

I stared at her, not seeing the humor in it.

"I have to ask myself how much more can I take in the name of love."

"I don't want to go against my son. We're just beginning to have a relationship again."

"I understand. You wanted to know, so I told you. I didn't sugarcoat anything."

When we got back to West Pelican Drive, she and I walked upstairs together. Derick and I kept up a somewhat amorous show during her visit. I felt guilty about telling her everything. I wondered if she ever discussed any of it with her son, although I doubted it. After she flew back to Washington State, nothing improved between Derick and me. I definitely wasn't an innocent participant in the downfall of our relationship, and I regret that.

I can't remember the exact time frame—probably blocked out those last painful months—but it was sometime in the fall of 1985 when it all came tumbling down. Every time I heard the song "Tainted Love" by Soft Cell, I'd think of Derick and our relationship.

I had worked the late shift at the restaurant and got home about 1:00 a.m. Derick was already asleep upstairs, so I slept on the couch in the living room. In the morning I needed to get into the walk-in closet upstairs. I was working a back-to-back at the restaurant. I tiptoed upstairs trying not to wake him. I saw his wallet on the nightstand, and something told me to go through it. I found a receipt from a motel. I totally freaked out and became enraged. I woke him up out of a dead sleep waving the receipt in his face like a mad woman. The past months' events coming to a head like a nasty, pus-filled boil popping.

"What's this? A receipt from a motel? I screeched. "So you are fucking someone else."

He lay on top of the covers fully dressed staring up at me, figuring he was dealing with a crazed woman. He jumped off the bed and stood with his back against the wall. He said nothing, just stared at me with a blank expression.

I went ballistic. I ran toward him like Medusa with eyes on fire and snakes wriggling and hissing from the top of my head. I started punching him and yelling, "I hate you! I hate you! I hate you!"

Derick put up with that for a few seconds. Then he grabbed me by the shirt and held me up against the wall. "I never hit you, so don't you ever hit me," he said, his voice cracking.

I stood there after he released me, knowing he could really hurt me if he wanted to. I couldn't even cry.

He ran down the stairs and out the front door. He was gone all day, and didn't come home that night.

The next morning, I took my cup of coffee and walked around the apartment like a zombie. I went into the walk-in closet upstairs and mindlessly began shoving all his clothes and personal items into his suitcase and duffel bag. I got some boxes from the supermarket and filled them with items I thought belonged to him. I set them in a row downstairs along the staircase. It was obvious that he didn't have much invested in our life together if everything he possessed fit in a number of boxes. I didn't know where he stayed that previous night, and wasn't sure when he was coming home. I didn't care. I was done!

The phone rang later that day. It was Derick. "I'm coming to get my stuff," he said, in a stern voice.

"It's already packed and ready for you. I left it stacked beside the staircase, so come and get it." I hung up the phone before he had a chance to say anything else.

I ran upstairs to the bedroom when I heard his truck pull in, not wanting Medusa to make an encore appearance. He loaded the boxes and suitcase in his truck without a word. When I heard the truck drive off I walked downstairs slowly. Rebel was standing there looking at me, not wagging his tail. *He left Rebel!* He must have been so miserable and incensed with me, that he didn't even care if he left his dog. Then I thought maybe he couldn't take the dog with him where he was going. Maybe he left Rebel because he knew I loved him so much, and he wanted to do that one last thing out of love and kindness. I didn't know.

I sat on the floor with Rebel just like the very first day we moved into the apartment and Derick dumped me and Rebel off like we were baggage. I began to cry—a good cry. I walked in the kitchen and saw a note on the counter. I read the note—it was the first time Derick had expressed any real thoughts or feelings in a very long time—it said that he didn't know what to say. He felt like he made me sad instead of happy. He didn't want to separate but felt that was what I wanted, and he had no power to change that. He said he couldn't seem to get on the right track. He knew he loved me but didn't know how to show me. He ended the note simply, "Please don't hate me, Derick."

I cried and wailed at the kitchen counter like a baby who'd been left on the doorstep of a church in the middle of winter with nothing but a rattle. That was the dramatic end to my engagement to Derick Ellis. He'd left no way to contact him, so I knew he was moving on with his life without me. I wondered how something that began so beautiful and loving could end so ugly and hateful. Only God knows the answer.

> Yet, it is more powerful, that nostalgia, that I can only write this a few sentences at a time. Nothing is more powerful than this nihilism, an angry readiness to throw everything overboard, a willingness, a longing to become part of dissolution.
> —Doris Lessing, *The Golden Notebook*

CHAPTER 5

VITAL SIGNS

Rambling thoughts:
Endless feelings of despair. Did he really care? No more laughter, no more lust, just tears of loneliness. Questions about tomorrow because where is yesterday? I loved you then. I miss you now.

In January of 1986, the space shuttle *Challenger* exploded in mid-air. I was at home painting T-shirts, and watching the launch on TV. I remember the smiles on the faces of the astronauts as they walked to the rocket in their cumbersome spacesuits. A little over a minute after takeoff, the *Challenger* exploded. The horror on the faces of their family members watching from the stands at the launch site, was hard to forget. They hugged each other rocking back and forth in grief. As awful as it was, I was glued to the television.

The Epiphany, January 6, was the day to take down the Christmas decorations, except I never put them up. I stared at that fake Christmas tree in the walk-in closet upstairs, and refused to take it out. I thought about flying to New York, but I didn't want to face my family and deal with all of their questions as to what the hell happened between me and Derick.

I was sitting alone in the apartment on West Pelican Drive; Rebel was lying on the bed upstairs. The dog could do that now that Derick wasn't around to chastise him. I wasn't exactly depressed, just existing in a sort of alternate universe. After I got over the initial shock of it all, I felt relief—the relief of not having to go through the stress, bickering, disconnectedness, and trauma of each day. Then my thoughts were replaced with so much more. I was watching an old movie on TV, and the female character said, "Do you think I ever cared if you had a million dollars in your pocket or nothing?"

My mind drifted … *That's how I felt about us. Just the way we were was rich. The last time I saw you, all I felt was anger, frustration, and betrayal. We let it slip away, that something special between two people. I know I played my part. I'd cry for the way we were, but I'm drained of feelings. Perhaps it wasn't you I hated, but what happened to us. In time, I hope we can forgive each other.*

My deep thoughts were interrupted by a knock at the door. I peered through the peephole and saw Rico standing there. I opened the door and motioned for him to come in.

"How are you doing?" he asked.

"I'm all right. Is Derick okay?"

"I guess so, but he doesn't say much." I wondered if Derick had sent him to feel me out, to see if maybe I was in a forgiving mood. Then he said, "You know she refused to see Derick until he cut his hair. Didn't want anything to do with him looking like a hippie."

"That's interesting," I said.

"She's married. It's a fucked-up situation."

Two cheaters doing drugs and licking each other's wounds—and other things, I thought.

I let Rico talk for a while, even though my mind went blank. He was telling me things I didn't want to hear. *To what end?* I wondered. I realized that what my intuition had been telling me all along was right. Derick must have been seeing this woman for a while. Like the saying goes, if you think your man is cheating, he is!

Rico said he had things to do and left. I stood there in a daze for a while, steeping in that awful feeling of betrayal. They say that women leave for their own peace, but a man leaves for another woman."

Luckily the phone rang interrupting my own pity party.

It was Leon Roberts. "Let's go to the Barnacle House."

"What's that?" I asked.

"It's an old house turned into a museum, right in Coconut Grove. You'll love it. It will take your mind off other things ."

"OK. I need time to shower and get ready. I've been in a funk."

"I'll give you an hour. I'll swing by and pick you up."

"I'll be ready in an hour," I said, hanging up the phone.

I walked Rebel and thought of how protective the dog had become of me after Derick left. If a man came to visit, even a close friend, he'd growl and follow the guy warily through the apartment until they passed some sort of doggie inspection.

I didn't feel like eating anything that morning. I walked upstairs to take a shower and passed the walk-in closet. Derick's side was empty, and I felt a flash of loss. I turned on the shower and let the water run over my body enveloping me with a temporary sense of normalcy. The mundane daily routines help get us through a bad time.

Leon Roberts

Leon beeped the horn, and I went downstairs.

With Derick gone the fact that I was without transportation grated on me. I was making decent money at the restaurant. and from the sale of my painted clothing, so I began saving for a car.

"Lee, thanks for thinking of me, and taking care of my well-being."

He took my hand and squeezed it. "You know I'm here for you."

"You've been such a good friend to me. I don't want to even think—"

"Stop it. Don't say anything else. What are friends for if not times like this?"

With each block we passed my mood lifted. When we arrived at the Barnacle House, I couldn't believe that this treasure was right in Coconut Grove tucked away in a forest, hidden from the water by mangroves. The noise of traffic and the chatter of people was obscured by the remoteness of the park that surrounded the house. Walking along the path we could hear bamboo creak. Upon entering the old house the intense Florida heat was replaced with a pleasant coolness. The interior was built in the round with special rafter windows that moved the hot air up and out of the building. I had no idea that such a place was right across the boulevard from Café L'Oiseau.

After we left the Barnacle House, Leon drove to the dry cleaners to pick up his shirts and took me with him. I guess he didn't want to leave me alone with my thoughts. We had lunch at a trendy new restaurant on Miami Beach. We spied street vendors along Collins Avenue and strolled along the beach walk looking at kiosks filled with artwork and jewelry. The afternoon heat was oppressive. Then he took me to the Seagull, which had an afternoon tea dance. We hung out there for hours and he made sure I got trashed.

We stopped at a service station for gas on the way back to Coconut Grove. I went to the restroom while Leon went to the window to pay. When I came out Leon was standing next to the car with his hands on his hips.

He shouted, "Some thug just stole my shirts right out of the back seat!"

"Lee, no! Are you kidding me?"

"For fuck's sake," he said. Then he began to laugh. "Maybe God thinks I really don't need that stuff."

"Never a dull moment," I said, as we drove away.

By the time Leon dropped me off at the apartment it was after dark. He watched me walk up the stairs until I was safely inside. Of course, I still had to walk Rebel, but I let Leon fulfill his brotherly role.

Months passed, and my life was in a general state of malaise. I was home alone, sitting on that hideous brown furry couch, the same couch Derick and I had made love on so many times. My mind was rehashing everything. I was watching *Miami Vice* on the television. I was concentrating on how hot Don Johnson was when the phone rang. I picked up the receiver, but there was silence on the other end. Then I heard a click. I couldn't help but think it was Derick, although I thought he was too damn stubborn to call me. My mind drifted from the TV, and I was hearing Freddie Fender singing "Wasted Days and Wasted Nights" in my head.

I wondered where Derick had gone when he left me, and what he was doing right at that moment. I became obsessed with the thought. *Maybe he's lonely and depressed. Maybe he's at a bar drinking and laughing with a friend.* Regardless, I still loved him, even after everything that had happened. I wanted to kiss him and touch him, and even more profound, I wanted him to touch me.

Maybe he thinks I'm with someone else. Maybe he doesn't think of me at all. Maybe he's with that woman, fucking her brains out right now. Maybe I should just forget about him. Maybe he's not good for me. Maybe I'm not good for him. Maybe it's as simple as he was the sun, and I was the moon.

It was a busy Saturday night at L'Oiseau du Paris. I was setting up the bar. Leon checked the coolers to make sure I was well stocked for the evening.

I received a call from the owner, Claude Canet. "How is everything?" he asked.

"All the tables are reserved for dinner. When will you be in?"

"I'm stuck in Fort Lauderdale with Brenda. We have a flat."

"Well, don't worry Claude. Everything's under control."

"Just wanted you to let everyone know that I will be late."

I hung up the phone and finished setting up the bar.

Claude Canet didn't make an appearance in the restaurant that night; in fact we never saw him again. There had been rumors about money problems, but none of us paid attention to hearsay. Two days later Leon and I, along with a couple of the waiters from the restaurant, went to Claude's house. We found the door unlocked, the house deserted, and all the closets empty. When we reported back to Carmen Lopez at the restaurant, she suggested that he probably had fled back to France, as he owed back taxes to the US government. She was his bookkeeper, so she should have known something was brewing.

It had been two weeks since any of us had been paid. I vividly remember the night she told Vincent Delon that Claude had flown the coop. Vin took a broom and began busting the glassware in the bar. "He hasn't paid me in six months!" he yelled. "I've been working on promises." Then Vin sat at a table, put his head in his hands and cried.

Carmen touched his shoulder attempting to comfort him. We were all stymied at the awful turn of events.

We sat at the big table and one of the waiters opened a bottle of wine. Vin said in his heavy French accent, "Fuck him. We will eat and drink on Claude Canet tonight."

We were discussing the situation when a food delivery arrived in the kitchen. Ricky was turning the delivery away.

"No, stop!" I shouted. "Take the delivery. I have an idea." I walked to the bar, took some cash out of the register and paid the delivery guy. Then I said, "This is what we will do. We will open tonight like nothing happened. When patrons call to make reservations, we will tell them that we are changing banks and cannot accept credit cards, only cash. At the end of each night we will split the proceeds until we pay ourselves what we are owed."

I saw smiles slowly appear on everyone's face.

Leon said, "What a fucking great idea!"

Carmen Lopez liked the sound of it as well. She planned on finding out how much back taxes Claude Canet owed, pay them, and put the restaurant in her name. It was a crazy idea but it worked. Each day we paid for the food deliveries in cash. After closing we'd all gather at the bar where I'd divvy up the night's proceeds. I'd hand everyone a share, with the largest portion going to Vin, since he was owed the most money. This went on for a while until one day, we came to work and found the gated courtyard to the upstairs restaurant locked with chains and a padlock. Carmen eventually paid Claude Canet's back taxes, but she only kept the downstairs café opened, and just a few of us remained with Café L'Oiseau.

The Miami heat was frying my brain. The steamy air coming off the Gulf of Mexico filled my nostrils with swampy odors. The café was a challenge on hot afternoons, and the money was nothing compared to what I'd been making upstairs in L'Oiseau du Paris. Vincent Delon had gone back to France after the French restaurant closed. Leon Roberts was bartending at a local sports club. Carmen was running Café L'Oiseau, and I was waitressing.

Carmen hired a woman named Virginia—Ginny, for short—as the cook. Most of the hot dishes were microwaved, and there were soups and salads on the menu. Ginny was a crazy redhead. She was getting over an affair with a guy and found herself pregnant. She decided to keep the baby. She came up with some unique menu items for the café. She drank a lot of beer, telling us that it was good for producing breast milk, but I had the feeling that she just liked drinking beer. She was getting bigger every day and looked ready to pop.

A new waitress came on the scene, Janet Prescott, whom we just called Jan. She had sandy blonde hair and hazel eyes, almost the same color eyes as Derick's. Janet and Flavio worked together as dock masters at the Merrill Steven's Marina. They'd seen cigar boats and yachts belonging to famous people dock there. Flavio told me they had a name for the guys they figured were smugglers; they were called *cha-cha boys*.

Jan lived on a houseboat docked off the mangroves of the Barnacle House. She'd take a shortcut through the forest across the boulevard, past the private grounds of the Barnacle House where she left her dinghy tied up, until one day a cop caught her.

"I see makeshift empty rafts drifting toward shore once in a while," she said.

"Really Jan?"

"Yeah, and I have to wonder if there are dead bodies in the ocean somewhere. You know, people trying to get to Florida from Cuba."

Neither Jan nor Ginny liked Carmen, and they constantly bitched about her. I stood at the espresso machine chatting with Jan. She laughed and told me she had plans for Carmen when she showed up at the café. These days Carmen Lopez usually drifted in around noon with some friends, bragging about how she owned the place now, and that Claude Canet keeps calling from France wanting his restaurant back. Carmen would sit at a table for hours drinking wine and yakking with her trendy friends.

There were a few diners having lunch outside when Carmen waltzed in alone. She sat at one of Jan's tables. We always split up the room.

"Bring me a café au lait and a croissant," Carmen squeaked, in her high-pitched voice.

Jan walked to the back where I was standing at the espresso machine. "I'll make the espresso; you steam the milk," I said.

Jan smiled a devious smile. I handed her the cup of espresso and watched her spit in it before adding the steamed milk. She calmly walked to Carmen's table and set the cup down.

I rolled my eyes. It wasn't the first time I'd seen her do that.

"Jan, I need some butter for the croissant," Carmen squeaked.

I wondered what Jan could possibly do to the butter before bringing it to the table.

There was a delivery of crusty French baguettes. Jan sliced off a couple of chunks and slathered them with butter for our morning coffee.

"There's a girl I let stay on my houseboat once in a while."

"A friend of yours?" I asked.

"Not really. I think she's homeless. She doesn't even use the dinghy, just swims out to the houseboat."

I looked at Jan and smiled when I heard Carmen ask her for a wedge of brie.

We were constantly scheming ways to get more money out of the café. The head waiter was a friend of Carmen's, a Cuban guy appropriately named Cuba Montez. We all liked him, and he never gave us any flack. Carmen did not want to pay for a cook. "After all, a cook is not a chef!" she'd say. Her method was to pay Ginny out of our tips. If two waiters were working, we were to pool our tips and give a third to the cook as a salary at the end of each shift. So Cuba Montez developed *the system.* If a large table came in for lunch or dinner, and they paid cash, we pocketed the money to compensate. I suppose it was stealing, but at the time we saw it as leveling the playing field.

I was cleaning one of the outside tables in the café toward the end of my shift. Jan was blabbing away about the time she fished an Eastern Airlines floatation cushion out of the water that had been bobbing against her houseboat.

"I called Eastern Airlines about it, and two agents in suits and ties showed up at the houseboat to retrieve it," she squawked.

I was about to say something when I happened to look up and notice a familiar figure across the boulevard; it was Derick Ellis. He was walking slowly, carrying a brown-paper lunch bag. I stared at the state the man was in—a dejected state. I was overcome with emotion and attempted to yell out, "Derick," but no voice came out. I was frozen. The figure got smaller and smaller while I watched him disappear down the boulevard. Then I realized that the man had long hair, like Derick had when I first met him in Hawaii. It wasn't him at all.

That spring, the Soviet nuclear reactor in Chernobyl exploded blanketing Europe with radiation.

The café was going through cooks like they were being deported back to their countries of origin. Ginny was out having her baby. None of the new applicants understood not being paid a salary. They didn't stay very long—unless they stayed long enough to be inducted into the system!

My mother came to stay with me for a month. It was so good to have her there. She fell in love with Rebel, and he fell in love with her. I discovered the dog liked lasagna with sausage and meatballs. I took my mother to Gulfstream Race Track for a day out in the fresh air. She complained that there was too much air and it tired her out!

My mother and I had an honest discussion about men.

"You always blamed me for the problems between your father and me," she said.

"Well, you always complained that Daddy was unmotivated, and that you had to pay for everything."

"Adriana, money isn't everything in life. You should know that by now."

"I do. It just seemed to be one of your big gripes with Daddy."

"When your father and I first got married he cheated on me with a prostitute and gave me a venereal disease. I was just a bride. How do you think that made me feel?"

"Why did you never tell me this?"

"I didn't want you to see your father in a different light. Adriana, he was no angel."

"Why did you stay with him if you weren't happy?"

"People just didn't get divorced in those days. You stayed together and made it work."

"Yeah, well, guys today always have one foot out the door."

"Adriana, you made mistakes too. Don't just blame them."

"I know that now. I suppose that's why I'm still single. Maybe I deserve to be alone."

"Adriana, don't sell yourself short. The right one will come along."

After my mother went back to New York I felt lonely again, and began to wonder if I was meant to be alone. I figured my therapist Joan was right about my having an Alone script. I played my favorite Nina Simone album and listened to "Blues for Mama." I sat on the couch feeling sorry for myself. I wasn't sure that marriage was for everyone. I was convinced that to stay married you had to give up a lot of yourself, compromise your dreams, overlook betrayals, and put up with a lot of shit.

I flew to Hawaii for four days over Halloween—that is how much I missed Maui. Those four days gave me enough of a Maui fix to last for a while. At that point I knew I wanted to live there again. I just didn't know when or how that would be possible. One of my old paramours, Blake Middleton, had recently written me a letter telling me he'd moved to Maui from California. He and I were an item back in the early seventies when I was living in San Francisco, after the commune broke up. We got together while I was on the island. He encouraged me to move back to Maui. It was nice to reconnect with him. Blake and I have remained friends through the years.

Annie and I showed up at the Missionaries Hotel in costume. I caught sight of Dominick French at the piano as we walked into the back-room Mission Bar. Demo gazed at me sentimentally and played my favorite song. I felt like Ingrid Bergman walking into Rick's Café in the movie *Casablanca*. On his break Demo sat at our table. Annie got up and disappeared; I imagined to give us time alone to talk.

"Are you back to stay?" he asked.

"Just here for Halloween."

"Where's Scaramouche?" Demo asked.

"I really don't know. We broke our engagement and he walked out on me."

"From what Annie told me, he went from a king to a clown!"

"That's harsh. Let's just say he disappointed me in a million ways."

"I'm getting jaded on my gig here at the Mission. It's a big world out there, and I'm thinking of moving on to new horizons."

"I get it. I'm planning to get out there and do some traveling myself," I said.

Demo let go of my hand. There was still an air of magic surrounding him as he got up and sat at the piano. I was happy to see him, but had no desire to resurrect a relationship.

Since I was only in Hawaii for a few days, Leon checked in on Rebel, fed and walked him, and hung out with him for a few hours each day.

When I arrived back in Florida, I took a taxi from the airport to West Pelican Drive. I walked up the steps and into the apartment, set my suitcase down, and felt the weight of sadness and loss overtake me. I was just going through the motions of a life, but I felt as if I wasn't really living it anymore.

1986 passed like a car racing down I-95, and before long it was the holidays again. We had a big Thanksgiving on West Pelican Drive. Leon Roberts came with Flavio, and Janet Prescott came with her husband. We ate, drank, and played cards. There was a crazy discussion about mad cow disease that was ripping through England. Cows were convulsing, toppling over, and dropping dead .

We laughed about my male friends having to walk through the front door with their arms in the air, as if someone was holding a gun to their heads. Once Rebel followed them around and got a few pets, they were able to pass his doggie test and could relax. He did bite the landlord once, and I was lucky the guy didn't sue me.

I spent that Christmas in the Bronx with my family. Slowly I came out of the dark, dead space in which I'd been dwelling, and began displaying vital signs.

In the spring of 1987 a new guy was hired as the cook at Café L'Oiseau. He and his girlfriend had recently arrived in Florida from England. They were both very young and attractive; they seemed like the perfect couple. Jules Buckingham was tall with short, spiky blond hair, and a small silver earring in his left ear. His eyes were robin's-egg blue, and he had a sensual face. He was quite tanned from the Florida sun. He reminded me of the Swedish actor Dolph Lundgren, only not as chiseled. He possessed all the exuberance of youth. Jules was sweet, warm, thoughtful, and sincere. He fit right in with our group, and we wasted no time in inducting him into the system. Jules and I became friends and often did things together outside of work.

Leon took me aside to pump me for information about Jules Buckingham. "So what do you think of this hot British transplant?"

"Just what you said Lee—he's definitely hot."

"You going after this one Adriana? He seems smitten with you."

"Lee, he has a girlfriend. She came over from England with him."

"They don't seem that happy together."

"The last thing I need to do is get involved in someone else's problems."

"Still Adriana, the guy is chill-worthy."

"Oh, I've noticed. He's pretty young though."

"Since when has that ever stopped you? Just sayin'!"

Jan interrupted, "Remember, life's a big buffet, so sample it all."

After a day shift working with Jules at the café, he suggested we have a drink in one of the cafés on Commodore Plaza. We sat down together hashing over the crazy things that happened in Café L'Oiseau during the lunch rush, and how we had run out of so many items on the menu.

"I had to create new dishes," he said, as I swooned over his British accent.

"Jules, you were very inventive today."

"I worked in a restaurant in London called the Circus, and that happened all the time."

"I haven't seen your girlfriend around for a while."

"We haven't been getting along lately."

"Sorry Jules. You guys make such a cute couple."

"Looks can be deceiving," he said, his robin's-egg–blue eyes captivating me.

"I've been alone for a while now. It's been strange," I said.

"I have to get out of that place we share. She's trying to cat thrash me."

"What? I don't understand what that even means."

"I think in America you call it pussy whipped."

"Jules you're so funny," I said, laughing.

"It's not really funny anymore."

Being around Jules was stimulating. Perhaps it was the innocence of his youth. One felt excitement about everything. He was awakening things in me I hadn't felt in a while. I was flattered that he found me attractive.

"Jules, come live with me. Rebel is used to you. You can have the bedroom upstairs."

"Really? I'll split the rent with you. Do you think it could work?"

"We can try. There's really only one day a week we work the day shift together, so we'll each have plenty of alone time at home."

"I'd like to try," he said, with more than a friendly interest.

> The ease of his manner freed me from painful restraint;
> the friendly frankness, as correct as cordial, with which
> he treated me, drew me to him.
> —Charlotte Bronte, *Jane Eyre*

And that's how Jules Buckingham came to live with me in apartment 10 on West Pelican Drive. Jules had a Ninja motorcycle that he referred to as the Assassin. It was nice having a mode of transportation again, and I loved riding on the back of that thing. His girlfriend showed up at my door looking for him. I told her he was at the café. She walked around the apartment sizing up the situation. I put her mind at ease letting her know that I rented him the upstairs bedroom, and I was sleeping downstairs. I'd gotten a single bed and moved the furry brown couch in front of the sliding glass doors that opened to the terrace.

She scoped out the living room suspiciously, like a private eye. She looked up the staircase, but I let her know by opening the front door that she was not going upstairs. I wanted to tell her how lucky she was, but it was obvious she already knew. After she left I sort of felt sorry for her. I knew exactly how it felt to leave your home, go to a new place where everything is unfamiliar, and then get dumped. I imagined she'd probably head back to England—sooner rather than later.

With Jules paying half the rent, I was able to save quite a bit of money. I wanted to buy a car, but had no way to get to the car lots. I did have Leon Roberts take me to a few car dealerships, but now I had Jules Buckingham and the Assassin. I learned to loathe used car salesmen. They were overbearing, and I always felt like they had me tied to a chair and were about to torture me. Jules rode me to a car dealership where I had been a few times before, and I was glad he was with me. The salesman had a contract in front of me, probably picturing a big commission when I signed. I squirmed in the chair as if I was being interrogated by the KGB, yet I had nothing to confess.

Jules said, "Adriana, let's go. You don't have to sign anything." He took my arm and coaxed me out of the chair, to which I seemed to be glued. He put his arm around me and walked me out of the showroom. As soon as I climbed on the back of the Ninja and felt the engine turn over, I was released from the evil spell.

> "No" I shouted. "Why, we haven't done anything yet." My legs felt rubbery. I gripped the desk and sagged toward her as she held out the envelope and refused to accept it. The woman's face was changing. Swelling, pulsing. Horrible green jowls and fangs jutting out, the face of a moray eel. Deadly poison. I lunged backward into my attorney who gripped my arm and took the note. "I'll handle this" he said to the moray woman. "My name is Doctor Gonzo" … The woman shrugged as he led me away.
> —Hunter S. Thompson, *Fear and Loathing in Las Vegas*

Leon Roberts often took me to a gay bar not far from our neighborhood called Uncle Charley's. They had the best dance music around. If I had to use the restroom Leon would accompany me and stand guard in front of the stall. Crazy shit happened in those restrooms.

We were standing at the bar drinking, when the song "Run to You" by Bryan Adams was playing. Leon noticed my expression change. He regarded me with intense interest. I told him it was nothing, just a passing thought. He ordered me another Cuba Libre.

I flashed back to the morning I found that photo of Derick with a woman sitting on his lap. I pictured them screwing, him kissing her the way he'd kissed me. I pictured him running to her every time I turned him away. I took another few sips of my Cuba Libre. I was glad when the song ended. "Goodbye to You" by Scandal blasted through the sound system. Leon led me to the dance floor. I danced and shook it all out.

Leon said, "This is a great place to drop acid."

I snapped my head back and laughed agreeing, although I knew my psychedelic days were over. I always came out of Uncle Charley's into the humid night air in a great mood.

> In a town full of bedrock crazies, nobody even notices an acid freak. We struggled through the crowded lobby and found two bar stools at the bar. My attorney ordered two Cuba Libres with beer and mescal on the side.
> —Hunter S. Thompson, *Fear and Loathing in Las Vegas*

I found a new car dealership and was happy with the salesman I was working with. I told him exactly what kind of SUV I was looking for, the color I wanted, and how much I could afford. Unlike the other dealerships who kept showing me cars that were well out of my price range, this guy worked with me. I never once felt like his hostage.

It had been about six months of searching for the car I wanted. I did get close a couple of times, but in the end I walked away. On a September morning in 1987 I received a call from the salesman I'd been working with. He said, "I think I found your car." I sensed something was different in his tone and felt a positive vibe.

Jules and I were both off from the café that day, so he whisked me away on the back of the Assassin, and we sped to the dealership. When we reached the lot I couldn't find the salesman, and began combing the lot with my eyes. I saw a gray SUV with a sign in the window with my name. It was a gray Jeep Cherokee Chief with black racing stripes. My heart was pumping out of my chest as I circled it.

Jules smiled. "Like it?"

"Jules, I love it. It's exactly what I wanted."

"Let's take it for a spin."

When the salesman caught sight of me he walked our way. The three of us got in the Cherokee Chief, and as soon as I drove it off the lot I knew it was my car. I signed the papers that very day. The car was only a year old, almost new. I handed Jules the second set of keys to bring home with him. He jumped on the Ninja and sped away yelling, "Buy the ticket, take the ride!" Jules Buckingham was a Hunter S. Thompson fan as well, although the quote didn't sound quite right in his British accent.

I shook my head and giggled. I drove along the highway in a dream. I cranked up the AC and flipped on the radio. I cruised down I-95 to the Latin sounds of Pete Rodrigues' "I like it Like That." I stopped at a supermarket on the way home to buy groceries. As soon as I parked and was walking toward the entrance, I felt something wasn't right. That's when I realized I had locked the keys in the car. I looked for a public phone and called the house.

"Jules, I locked the keys in the car."

He laughed. "You haven't even had the car for an hour."

"I know. Thank God, I gave you the second set."

"Where are you?"

"I'm at Publix, the one we always go to."

"I'll be there in a few," he said, still laughing.

I leaned against the Cherokee Chief feeling very relieved and laughing at myself.

That Halloween, Jules and I met Leon at Uncle Charley's. It was a last-minute decision. We didn't even wear costumes. Leon was waiting outside the club. When he saw us pull up in the Cherokee Chief he waved his arms and shouted, "That's such a butch car!"

The music was loud as the three of us walked through a crowd of people standing at the entrance. I couldn't help but think of that Hunter S. Thompson quote, "This is bat country." We fought our way to the bar and ordered drinks. There were five male bartenders dressed as Disney characters twirling drinks behind the bar. We ordered drinks from Goofy, and the three of us laughed up a storm. Leon had a crazy idea of creating a video will, besides the legal written contract directive used when someone dies.

"I'm telling you—you make a videotape that your family has to play upon your death at the reading of the will. You can tell everyone what you really think of them, and what you're *not* leaving them, and why," Leon said.

Jules and I lit up with laughter as Leon ordered us more drinks from Snow White.

When Jules went to use the restroom Leon turned to me. "Adriana, anything happen between you two yet? You know, do the wild thing!"

"No, not really."

"Adriana, just the way he looks at you … I'm a guy—a little swishy maybe, but still a guy—and I can tell he likes you that way."

"Really Lee? You think so?"

"I do. What the hell are you waiting for?"

"I don't know."

"Screw the pants off that guy already. What do you have to lose?"

I was just about to say something when Jules approached and reached for his drink. Leon was right; I was picking up on something happening between us, and I liked it. Of course, the gin I was drinking was increasing my libido. I was definitely hot for Jules, and now I was picking up on the sex vibe coming from him. Leon stood between us, watching us gaze at each other, with a silly smile on his face. He winked at me with an encouraging nod at one point.

A few hours in Uncle Charley's was quite enough, even on Halloween. Jules handed Tinker Bell a wad of cash for their tip jar, and the three of us walked out into the humid night air. Leon rushed to his car waving at us. I figured he was meeting someone. Jules and I got in the Cherokee and drove home. As soon as we walked up the stairs and I unlocked the door, I knew something was going to happen. Jules took Rebel for a walk. When they came back, he locked the door and walked toward me. He switched off the light and put his arms around me. He guided me down on the daybed in the living room. In the dark I pictured his robin's-egg–blue eyes as I unbuttoned his shirt. He kissed me for a while, as if he was uncertain about how far he should go. I took off my clothes, and Jules slipped his pants off. He made love to me, and it was a beautiful thing. I wasn't in love, but it felt good to be part of the human race again—well, in the biblical sense.

The next morning we both felt a little awkward. We had fallen asleep downstairs on the daybed. Jules walked Rebel, and I made coffee.

We drove the Cherokee Chief to the first key and went swimming. I watched Jules play in the water with Rebel. He was really something to look at, what a woman would call *eye candy*. I was always attracted to beautiful men; perhaps it was the artist in me that forever searched for visual beauty. I flashed on an amusing memory of Ross Grant teasing me about my choice in men. He'd said, "All your boyfriends are Chippendales." I laughed at the memory until I felt sadness at our not being friends anymore.

Funny how life has its twists and turns, and how we can lose important people. When we got home, I gave Rebel a bath with the hose while Jules went upstairs to make dinner.

With Jules Buckingham living with me I was able to take another trip back to Hawaii. I stayed with Annie Hughes. I borrowed her car and drove to Kihei to visit my friend Loretta Perino. I told her all about the gruesome end to my engagement to Derick Ellis, and that he had walked out on me for the last time.

"Adriana, didn't Derick walk out on you a couple of times when we lived on Nanu Street in Lahaina?"

"Yeah, every time we had an argument, usually about Dominick French."

"Adriana, I don't think he has the capacity to deal with adversity."

"I think he was screwing another woman, although he would never admit it."

"You know how guys are. They'd rather turn their attention to a different woman than work on what's gone wrong in the relationship with the woman they already have. As if the new one is going to put up with their bullshit."

"He always had a hard time saying what was on his mind. I guess he expected me to just know."

Loretta said, "Funny, a weird thing happened recently. I woke up one morning to find Carter, aka Cotton, camped in his van at the end of this cul-de-sac. He never knocked on my door or tried to contact me. I hadn't seen or talked to him since we broke up years ago."

"I wonder if he still keeps in touch with Derick. After all they were besties," I said.

"Adriana, Cotton once told me they jumped parole and escaped to Hawaii together, right before we met them. Maybe this happened for the best. If you would have married Derick, he probably would have done this again and again, and you would have been miserable."

"You're probably right. Maybe I would have had a lifetime of heartaches with him."

While on Maui, Annie and I spent a few nights at the Missionaries Hotel listening to Dominick French at the piano bar. I was glad he and I were still friends, but I winced at the memory of those 2:00 a.m. rambling phone calls. I was glad those days were over. Demo was on a health kick. He'd stopped drinking, swam a mile every day, and was a mere slip of his former self. He told me he was planning to sell his house and buy land on a remote island somewhere in the South Pacific.

I left Maui in a state of limbo. My heart resided there still. I missed the person I was there, and my life on the island. Annie Hughes assured me that if I moved back to Maui I could stay with her until I was settled. I told her that I was working toward that goal, but I wasn't quite ready. Thinking back, perhaps subconsciously I was hoping Derick Ellis would contact me.

When Annie dropped me off at the airport in Kahului, she waved and yelled, "Have fun back in the madland, but don't forget where you belong."

Rebel and Jules were happy to see me back in Miami. He brought me up-to-date on what had happened while I was in the islands, and what was going on at Café L'Oiseau.

"I washed the Cherokee and gave Rebel a bath yesterday, after I took him for a run at the first key," he said.

"Jules thank you so much for taking care of him. He likes you so much."

"I've always wanted a dog, but now I see how much work and responsibility they are."

"Well, anything worth having or loving warrants a lot of attention."

He smiled, nodding in agreement.

He let me know that Carmen Lopez intended to work me to death over the next two weeks to make up for my time off. That was fine with me. I wanted my time occupied so I didn't dwell on any of my deeper concerns.

"We should go to bed early tonight because she has us both on the day shift, and you're opening in the morning,."

I made a face. "Oh great!"

I got through the next week like a programmed robot. I thought about nothing in particular, just put one foot in front of the other. Janet Prescott and I worked a few shifts together and had some good laughs. Ginny came by with her new baby in a stroller. She sat at a table and asked for a beer, even though she looked like she'd already been drinking, because her face was as red as a beet.

"Adriana, I ran into Ramon the other day," Jan said.

Ramon, who was from Chile, had been one of the waiters in the upstairs French restaurant. He was gay and looked a lot older than his age. He had fair skin and dark hair but was balding. Ramon was very dramatic, almost theatrical when he spoke, whether it was about someone he'd met at a bar, or the vegetables he'd purchased at the supermarket. He would lift his eyebrows, bug out his eyes, and display all sorts of facial contortions to make a point. Everything was a major drama to Ramon.

Jan said, "Ramon and I went to one of those street stands on Twenty-Seventh Avenue for a colada. Boy, was I glad I was holding a Styrofoam cup filled to the brim with espresso. We started off laughing, but then his demeanor changed, and the conversation went to a very dark place. I have no idea why he even chose to tell me."

"Jan, what did Ramon tell you?"

"He met this guy at Uncle Charley's and they hit it off, so after drinks he invited the guy back to his apartment. That's when it all turned ugly."

"Jan, what the hell happened?"

"Ramon said that after sex the guy took out a knife, leaned over, and slit his throat!"

"Jan, no!"

"Yeah, even pulled the neck of his T-shirt down to show me the scar."

"Holy shit!

"I didn't know what to say. I just hugged him and told him I was glad he was alive."

"Knowing the way Ramon talks, I can just picture him telling the story."

"I know I'll have a hard time forgetting it," she said.

A group of trendy young people came into the café at the very end of my night shift. They sat down and ordered the works—dinner, a bottle of wine, our famous key lime pie for dessert, and espressos. This would be a big ticket. It was my table, so when they paid cash I nodded at Cuba Montez who nodded back approvingly. We thought nothing of it when we split the cash from that entire table, tip and all—three ways with Jules in the kitchen.

The next day, I was at home drinking my morning coffee when the phone rang. It was Carmen Lopez.

"My friends were in the café last night. They had dinner, wine, and dessert, but I don't see a ticket," she said in that squeaky, high-pitched voice of hers.

A cold chill ran through me. I didn't have an answer for her. "Carmen, it was busy at the end of the night, I'm not sure what went on at closing."

"Cuba doesn't know anything either, but he said it was your table."

I thought of that line by Mark Twain—"Get your facts straight first, then you can distort them." But the facts were not in my favor.

"Carmen, I don't really know what to say."

"I know what to say. You're fired," she said, her squeaky voice shaking. Then she hung up.

I'm sure she was angry at my disloyalty, but everyone who worked at the café was in the system. I chose not to rat on anyone else. We were all looking for ways to get out of there at that point.

Cuba Montez called me at home and said that everyone wanted to walk out because she fired me, but I told him not to be ridiculous.

"Don't quit. Decent jobs are hard to find," I said.

"Everyone's pissed off at her," Cuba said.

"She started that bullshit on opening night when she finally got the restaurant in her name, remember? We set up in the courtyard rolling out the tables and chairs. We filled all the coolers with ice. Then, at the end of the night, after she raked in the bucks, she told us to split our tips with the cook and busboys, because she couldn't afford to pay them."

"She'll lose everyone if she keeps this shit up," Cuba said.

"Anyway, I'll miss all of you, so please keep in touch," I said.

I hung up the phone wondering what my next move would be. The crazy twists and turns to my life in Florida never seemed to let up.

It wasn't long after that when Jules decided to go back to England. A friend from London informed him that they were looking for a chef at the restaurant where he had worked before. He felt that being a chef at the Circus in London, England, was way more prestigious than being a cook working on tips at Café L'Oiseau in Miami, Florida. I had to agree with him. I wasn't sad at all—well, I wasn't in love. Jules Buckingham got me through a difficult time in my life, and I was grateful for him.

Leon Roberts had been working behind the bar at Sportrooms, a members-only health club, for a long time. He'd laugh and say, "Yeah, they spend an hour working out in the gym, then they come to the bar to get trashed on liquor, and clog their arteries with burgers and fries." When he heard that Carmen Lopez fired me from the café, he said to give him a couple of weeks, and he'd have me working in the club. Sure enough, in no time I was slinging drinks and making lots of cash at Sportrooms with my best friend Leon Roberts.

Kamikaze night was every bartender's nightmare. Like the night a regular was sitting on a barstool when I noticed her eyeballs began to rotate. I glanced up from the speed rack again, and she had that faraway look. Soon she slipped off the barstool and onto the floor. Leon found an empty swivel chair, slumped her in it, and wheeled her past the table where the racquetballers were drinking pitchers of beer, and munching on onion rings. What a scene it was as he wheeled her, totally passed out, from one end of the room to the other, looking for a place to hide her before the boss arrived. I just kept slinging drinks behind the bar and delivering pitchers of beer to the tables as if nothing out of the ordinary was going on. It was quite the knack I had developed, balancing a sloshing pitcher of beer in one hand, and five glass beer mugs in the other.

I knew nothing about mixing drinks, so I suppose my good looks got me through the first few weeks at Sportrooms. Leon signed us up for a bartending course because he was winging it as well. We spent two months tossing colored water over plastic ice cubes. We learned the basics of bartending and the character of mixed drinks. That's how I became a bartender. I never gave up my hand-painted clothing business, but bartending provided me with a lot of cash. I knew I'd be able to pay off the Jeep Cherokee in no time. That New Year's had me looking forward to 1988 with a renewed sense of independence, and a dream of better things to come.

CHAPTER 6

AN UNLIKELY MESSENGER

The truth is rarely pure and is never simple.
—Oscar Wilde

I needed self-examination. I was stuck, yet another year, living in a place I wasn't happy in, while attempting to quell the memory of a place I missed. I seemed to have lost power over my destiny once again. Staying in the apartment after Derick Ellis left me was a mistake. I was confronted daily with flashbacks and dreams of what might have been. Derick's philosophy was, "Right is what you get away with, and wrong is what you get caught at." I was like a rat in a maze looking for the truth.

I was angry with myself for bringing us to this place, as if what had happened in Florida was all my fault. When anger and disappointment didn't force me to make a change, despondency set in. Without a conversation between us I felt no closure. Is there ever really closure with someone you love?

I became close with two of the neighbors in my apartment complex. Madeline Walsh lived in number 8. She loved animals and always made a fuss over Rebel. She often had me over for dinner. She'd sweat profusely, her eyeglasses fogging up as she talked, and she always had a glass of wine in her hand. I'd often sit at her table attempting to decipher her slurred dialogue. I found myself answering yes, nodding, or shaking my head, when I hadn't the faintest idea what she was talking about. I'd park the Cherokee, walk up the stairs, and notice her standing at the railing outside of her condo staring off into space, her front door wide open. She mentioned having a brother who lived in another state, but that she hadn't seen him in five years. I found myself feeling sorry for her.

I never had what I thought of as an addictive personality until Leon Roberts introduced me to horse racing. We made so much cash at the sports bar that we were at the track a few times a week spending it. I loved everything about the race track—the outdoors, the beautiful horses, and the excitement of it all. I would walk to the paddock before each race to watch the trainers dress the horses. I'd get a feel for the temperament of the horses and the attitudes of the jockeys. Then I'd watch the jockeys mount up and walk the horses onto the track. I'd always bet on the biggest, most beautiful horse. My choice was rarely the favorite (the horse projected to win) because I liked the bigger odds on a two-dollar bet.

I got acquainted with some old guys who were at the track every day, especially if I went without Leon or Flavio. These old guys read and followed the daily racing form like it was the Bible. They almost always bet on the favorite to win, and often just came to the track to bet on a particular race or a specific horse. They'd bet that horse fifty ways to Sunday, pairing it with other horses in perfectas and trifectas. It mystified them when I won a race by betting on a horse because I liked the way it looked, because its name meant something to me, or because I had a good feeling about it. After I'd had a few good wins, they nicknamed me Longshot Louie. Over the next year betting at the race track became an addiction.

With Flavio at Gulfstream Racetrack

Leon quit Sportrooms when he got a job as the banquet beverage manager of the Hotel InterContinental Miami. "I'm taking you with me; just give me some time," he said.

As soon as Leon was secure in his new position at the hotel, he had me apply for a bartending job in the private men's club on the first floor. It was an easy job. I never saw the patrons. The waiters came to my little window to order, and they delivered the drinks on trays to the men in the club room. Even though I worked in a tiny cubicle, and no one saw me, I had to wear black-and-whites with a formal hotel jacket and heels. My feet killed me at the end of each shift, but that job was a gateway into the hotel, which paid top money and offered excellent benefits.

I received a call out of the blue from Ross Grant. I'd heard through mutual friends from our commune days that he'd been in a horrific auto accident. He asked me to meet him at a bar in his neighborhood. I wondered why after all this time.

That evening I drove to the bar he'd mentioned and parked in the back. I walked toward the entrance wondering how I was going to feel when we were face-to-face. As soon as I scoped out the people sitting around the bar I saw Ross Grant talking to Derick Ellis. What the hell? I hadn't seen or heard from either of them for at least three years, and it felt like a setup. After everything that had happened, did Ross think we should all just make amends, join hands and sing "Kumbaya"? I had often wondered if they had remained in touch after everything went down. I sat next to Ross, not wanting to be next to Derick. Ross's face had been rearranged. He looked different yet the same.

"Hey, I'm glad you could make it," Ross said.

"You look different. What the hell happened?" I asked.

Ross said, "Well, I was on one of those crazy runs between New York and Florida. It was the middle of the night, I hadn't slept in two days, and I'd smoked a lot of weed. I knew I was in trouble when I saw a large fish pass my car." He gave a little giggle, telling the story.

Derick and I laughed in spite of ourselves.

Ross continued, "Then, all I saw was black. Some jerk's car had stalled in the middle of the I-95 thruway, and I smashed right into him. I went through the windshield. I needed plastic surgery to put my face back together."

"Jesus Christ," I said.

I couldn't help but wonder if he'd had elective plastic surgery to change his appearance, and questioned if he'd made up the story. Maybe someone was after him. Derick didn't say much after I sat down. He smiled at me a couple of times, but I averted my eyes not wanting to be drawn in by them. Funny how when faced with something you've wanted is right there in front of you, and all you can do is dwell on all the bad stuff that happened. Ross did enough talking for both of us.

It was sad sitting there with two men I'd loved so much at one time—my sweetheart, my lover, my everything; the other, my longtime friend, my commune brother. All I felt was disappointment and betrayal. As Ross blathered away, my mind drifted to that horrible last scene with Derick in our bedroom, when I turned into Medusa. I remembered a similar scene I had with my mother many years ago. The time I lunged at her, and we began fighting. My father had to break us up. When the people who are supposed to love you the most in the world, say and do things that destroy you to the core, you lose total control of yourself. That song "Somebody That I Used to Know" by Gotye began playing over the bar's sound system, which snapped me back to the present, and I felt the need to escape. I gulped the rest of my drink and abruptly announced that I had to meet someone. I stood up and walked out.

Leon Roberts was beginning to worry about my addiction to the race track. He'd chastise me when I came home having lost money. He'd say, "Adriana, you could have bought a pair of Johnny Versace shoes with the cash you dropped at the track today."

I'd ignore his words, and would find myself on the commuter bus with all the old codgers. On the bus I'd converse with the guys who'd read to me from the daily racing form, giving me advice and tips. I'd arrive with the optimism of the day ahead, then leave walking through the turnstiles after the last race tearing up my losing tickets, feeling shitty.

Leon's boyfriend, Flavio, was out of the picture, and another young Cuban guy named Roberto was Leon's new love interest. Robo, as we called him, never had much to say, but I assumed conversation wasn't why Leon kept him around.

It wasn't long before Leon got Janet Prescott into the hotel with us in banquets, and the old crew was back together again. We had fun from the beginning of each night to the end. The InterContinental Miami is a large hotel with a lot of banquet rooms. There could be eight different functions going on at the same time on a given night. Leon twirled through the hallways like a whirling dervish to keep up with each one.

The first crazy party I worked was a large Cuban wedding. The father of the bride walked into the banquet office with $40,000 cash in a brown-paper bag to pay for the event. He handed Leon a few hundred extra in cash and winked, insisting that a bottle of Black Label scotch be on every table. Leon happily obliged. By the end of the reception people were salsa dancing on top of the tables, and the party descended into total chaos. But we were all tipped out big time.

I was walking into Coconut Grove to cruise the boutiques and do some shopping when I saw two guys on bicycles coming toward me. I had the feeling they were looking to rob me. I held my purse tightly to my body and readied myself. One guy knocked me over, and the other one grabbed my purse. I stood up, a little dumbfounded at their success. *These thugs must take lessons*, I thought. I ran after them for a few blocks, and when they turned into the ghetto I followed them. They disappeared into a maze of rundown buildings. I walked up to a guy who was working under the hood of a car.

"Hey, some guys robbed my purse and ran in here. Did you see them?"

The guy stopped what he was doing to look up at me, but said nothing.

"Look, I don't care about the money in my wallet, but all my identification, my driver's license, my credit card, and my address book, were in that purse. Please help me. I'll pay you to just get my purse back," I pleaded.

Without smiling the guy said, "If you give me your number I'll see what I can do."

"Oh, bless you, thank you so much," I said.

He tore a page out of a notebook he had on the front seat and handed it to me with a pen. I wrote my name and phone number and gave it to him.

"I'll contact you later if I find out who took your purse," he said.

As if he doesn't know, I thought. I figured the same guys in their community committed these petty crimes, and I was convinced everyone knew who they were.

As I was walking away, I realized that my address and car keys were in my purse. I raced home thinking that while I was talking to him, these same thugs could be burglarizing my apartment and stealing my car. I rushed home fearing the worst. I ran up the stairs and banged on Madeline's door. She had a key to my apartment for emergencies. I called a locksmith and had the locks on my door changed.

That evening I received a phone call from the guy I'd talked to in the ghetto. He had good news. He had my purse and would bring it to me if I gave him sixty dollars for his trouble. I agreed to meet him in front of Zayre's not wanting him to come to my house. He handed me my purse, which I examined to make sure my wallet was still in it, along with the other important items. Everything was there, so I handed him the cash.

"You were very brave to do what you did," he said, as he turned and walked away.

I usually took the commuter bus to Calder Race Track, but once in a while I drove the Cherokee Chief. It was a beautiful day to be at the track. I had a hot dog with mustard and sauerkraut, and I checked in with the old codgers to get their recommendations on the horses running that day. Although I had my own methods and superstitions. I walked to the paddock to check out the horses. I noticed a horse that tickled my fancy. I had a good feeling about him. I could see he was a male. They usually didn't run male and female horses in the same race. I was told that the male horses instinctively would let the female win. I watched the trainer dress him for the race. He was a beautiful, big, black horse. His coat was shining, and he had a sparkle in his eye. The old guys told me I'd be throwing my money away on a losing horse, that there was nothing good about him in the daily racing form. He was a longshot.

Something about that horse reminded me of Devil's Bag, a famous racehorse I'd seen run at Gulfstream Park with Leon and Flavio. Devil's Bag not only won the race, but he won by fourteen lengths. When the race was over, the jockey rode Devil's Bag around the track alone for a victory lap. Everyone in the stands stood up and cheered as he pranced around the track. That horse knew he was a winner; I was sure of it.

I plunked two dollars to win on the big, black horse. I can't explain the feeling when the horse rounded that last turn and forged ahead of the other horses down the final stretch, and like Devil's Bag, he won by many lengths. I screamed with joy waving my winning ticket in the air. I won $300 just like that, on a two-dollar bet. I walked to the window to collect my winnings and passed the old codgers, who were ripping up their losing tickets and throwing their racing forms in the trash. They walked away from me in disgust, but I'm sure, with a little envy. I doubt they had admiration for me, and probably considered my win dumb luck. Still, after that win, I seemed to have gained some credibility, because the old guys began asking me who I liked in upcoming races.

My hand-painted clothing business was going strong. I experimented with so many different designs. I was painting on T-shirts, sweatshirts, dresses, tank tops, and skirt sets. People loved them, and my creative juices flowed, which kept me sane through those years in Florida. My mother only visited me once, but flights were so cheap that I flew to New York about every six months.

Janet Prescott and I worked a Bacardi promotional party at the InterContinental. We killed ourselves setting up the bars, shoveling ice, pushing the bars on the elevator, and rolling them into the banquet hall. As soon as the party was about to begin, Bacardi bartenders swooped in and took over our bars. We were pissed off because we knew these guys would be making all the tips, while we had done all the hard work. Leon said he couldn't do anything about it, that Bacardi brought their own people. To top it all off, we had to break down after the function, clean the bars, and push them back to the store room. I left the hotel about midnight. The guard who worked at the employee exit made a big deal out of searching my purse. I was annoyed that he always picked me out of a line of employees leaving the hotel. I couldn't stand that guy and didn't trust him.

It was a lazy Sunday morning. I was reclining on the couch drinking coffee. Rebel was chewing on a rawhide I'd given him. The phone rang. It was Leon.

"Are you reading the Sunday paper?" he asked.

"No, I just got up a little while ago."

"That bastard is in the paper—a big article."

"What bastard? Who are you talking about?"

"You know, the guy who always hassles you and rifles through your purse to see if you took anything from the hotel."

"What happened?"

"He and his son were arrested and carted off to jail in handcuffs. I guess they'd been under surveillance for quite a while. They were stealing from the hotel, big time," Leon said.

"Oh my God. No wonder that guy was always so meticulous about searching my bag. He must have had a guilty conscience."

"They found hotel furniture, cases of wine, wall art—all manner of stuff from the hotel—in their house."

"Well, there's one bastard who got what he deserved," I said.

It was about that same time that a new guy began as the food banquet manager for the InterContinental Miami. Harry Hackman was very efficient and personable. We all liked him. He had a girlfriend named Helga Hargrove. We teased them about their names and referred to them as the four Hs (HHHH). Leon Roberts and Harry Hackman worked well together. Leon dealing with the alcohol and bartenders, and Harry dealing with the food and waiters. They worked together with skill keeping the Banquet Department of the InterContinental Miami running like a well-oiled machine.

That summer, Leon and I went to see the Scorsese film *The Last Temptation of Christ* at the Grove Theater. As soon as I heard that the pope had warned Catholics not to see it because it was sacrilegious, I knew I had to check it out. Leon and I agreed that Willem Dafoe was great as Jesus of Nazareth. He portrayed the Christ as a real man, not God. I suppose that is what the church objected to. But didn't Jesus say that we are all the son of God? The character wrestled with all the weaknesses of the average man. Barbara Hershey was excellent as the prostitute Mary Magdalene. Some scholars claim that evidence shows Mary Magdalene was one of the disciples, as in Leonardo da Vinci's painting *The Last Supper*, where he has her seated at the table next to Jesus. They say she had a relationship with Jesus that was more than as a follower. Ancient scrolls state that Jesus kissed her often. I was fascinated by the film. It was the way I had always pictured Christ to be. We walked out of the theater in a philosophical mood, and went to a café on Commodore Plaza for a beverage and a deep religious discussion.

Also that summer a new drug called crack, a derivative of cocaine, appeared on the Miami scene. I never tried it because I'd heard bad things about it. It was said to be way more addictive than cocaine. I don't know anyone personally who used it; then again, would they even tell me? No one I knew ever offered it to me, and if they had, I would have turned it down. I had enough problems in my life, which continued emerging from a dark hole.

I took the metro to Gulfstream Race Track alone. Leon refused to go with me anymore. He was trying to convince me that it was a bad habit, one that I should cure myself of.

It was toward the end of the day, maybe the fifth or sixth race. I had placed my bet and was waiting at the rail for the race to begin. I watched the horses and jockeys walk out onto the track and load up in the gate. I was excited for the race to begin. The bell rang, the gates opened, and the horses raced out onto the track. As they rounded the final turn and were running to the end post I saw a commotion—horses falling and jockeys flying off. One of the horses didn't get up. It was right in front of us at the finish line. The jockey kept smacking the horse with his whip and pushing him down. The horse had broken both front legs and was trying desperately to get up. It was a horrible scene. An ambulance showed up immediately with two trainers who set up a large screen to block the flailing horse from the viewers in the stands. They killed the horse on the spot by lethal injection. Everyone in the stands got up in disgust and began to leave the park, like plebeians leaving the Roman Colosseum after watching Christians being torn apart and eaten by lions. All you could hear was the displeasure and shock from the crowd. I left with everyone else. I walked to the Metro train station and vowed never to go to a horse race again.

I spent that Christmas with my family on the East coast. Couldn't take the cold anymore. I was back in Miami for the New Year. I spent the Eve with my neighbor Madeline. She was already drunk when I arrived, and I was drunk when I left. I ushered in 1989 quietly, with Rebel lying at my feet.

I was setting up my bar for a party at the InterContinental when I saw a new guy in the ice room. He stopped scooping ice long enough to stare at me. I stared back.

"You wan' I push your bar into banquets?" he asked.

"I think I can manage," I answered, smiling.

"Which party you work?"

"The wedding," I said, mesmerized by his clear gray eyes.

"I work that one too," he said.

"I guess I'll see you there."

I watched him walk off, pushing his bar with such ease, like it was a baby stroller. He was a big guy with massive shoulders, nice-looking, with a fair complexion. I could tell he was Cuban by his accent and broken English. I scooped the ice into the small sink of my bar, and the rest into a bucket underneath. I saw Leon twirling down the hallway. "Lee!" I shouted.

Leon spun around. "Whatcha need?"

"I don't need anything. Just curious about the new guy."

"Manny Torres? The boxer?" he asked.

"The Cuban one. He's really buff, light-brown hair, light-gray eyes."

"Uh-huh, so you noticed his eyes?" Leon said, rolling his. "All the gay waiters are lusting after Emanuel Torres."

"Well, I can see why. I think he's cute."

"You're not telling me anything I don't already know. I'll bet he's a hunka-hunka burnin' love."

"He offered to help me with my bar," I said.

"And you didn't let him?" Leon asked, grabbing my bar. "Here, I'll help you."

Leon walked beside me pushing my bar onto the elevator. When we reached the banquet room where the wedding reception was taking place, he combed the room looking for something. Then he pushed my bar right next to Manny's. The bars were usually set up in pairs. I was a little embarrassed as Leon flipped his hair, laughed, and walked off.

"Hello again," Manny said, smirking.

"I hope we make some good tips tonight," I said, fanning my paper napkins with a water glass.

"Cuban wedding? You know we gawn make good tips," he said.

All evening we found ourselves stealing glances at each other during the lulls. When the music stopped a crowd of guests would swamp the bars. The women lined up at his bar, and the men lined up at mine. We smiled at each other in affirmation of just how human nature showed up, even in a situation like this. When the wedding was over and the hall emptied out we pushed our bars back to the store room together. There was definitely a mutual attraction. I knew nothing about him—he could have been a married man. Still, I went home in a good mood that night. It always left me feeling good when a hot guy found me attractive.

The next time there was a big function at the InterContinental, I showed up early to stop by the banquet office to see Leon. I hadn't spoken to him all day. I found him in the walk-in cooler boxing up bottles of wine.

"You're working the wedding on the third floor tonight," Leon said.

"How many people?"

"It's not a big reception, seventy people. Manny Torres was asking me about you."

"Really? Is he working tonight?"

"You two are working this wedding together," Leon said, with a devious smile.

"Lee! When did you become a matchmaker?"

"It was Manny who asked to be put with you tonight," he protested.

I walked out of the office and down the hallway. I saw Manny coming toward me.

"You wit me tonight," he said.

My sensibilities were stuck on his massive shoulders. I pretended I was just hearing it for the first time. We walked to the ice room together.

"I get the ice; you get the napkins, straws, and cut a few lemons and limes."

I did what he asked. I watched him shovel ice into both bars, his hotel jacket bursting at the seams. *God, he's really something*, I thought.

When the bars were ready, he pushed his along the hallway and dragged mine behind him with such ease, like they were two shirts on hangers. He was a powerhouse, and it turned me on. When we arrived in the banquet room, he set the bars next to each other in the corner. Two of the gay waiters we passed had their index fingers in their mouths and bit down hard as they looked him over. A smile broke out on my face as if to say, *"Sorry, boys, it's me he's after."* We had fun working together, and from that night on we were a team.

Not long after we worked a few more parties together, I took him home with me. He left his car in the hotel parking lot, saying he'd have a friend drive him to pick it up. We drove to my apartment on West Pelican Drive in my Cherokee. "Take Me Home Tonight" by Eddie Money was playing on the car radio. We glanced at each other and laughed. Manny told me he owned his own house, and that he was working toward being a professional prize fighter. I wondered why he'd want to mess up that beautiful face. He told me about his routine—he ran five miles every morning, and worked out at the gym every afternoon. I heard nothing about a wife or a girlfriend. I was nervous as we walked up the steps to my apartment. As soon as Manny followed me inside, Rebel circled him suspiciously.

"You din say you had a dog."

"He's just checking you out to make sure you won't hurt me. He's been that way since my boyfriend left a few years ago," I said.

Manny cautiously walked in patting Rebel on the head. Soon, the situation eased and we sat on the couch. Rebel didn't take his eyes off Manny for a second. Once in a while the dog's ear would twitch.

We started to make out on the couch, and he was all over me like ketchup on fries. Rebel was watching with his head on his paws, so I figured he'd made up his mind that this guy wasn't a danger to me.

"The bedroom upstairs?" Manny asked.

"Yes, let's go upstairs."

"Your dog gawn let me?"

"I think its fine. He seems to trust you."

I closed the bedroom door in case Rebel developed a concern hearing me grunt or breathe heavily. We undressed and flopped on top of the covers. I felt his shoulders which were as big and hard as two large slabs of beef hanging in a meat locker. I glided my hands along the front of his chest as he got on top of me. I closed my eyes and readied myself for impact. It was good, but I didn't have a climax. I was too nervous. I *guess I'll have to get myself off when he leaves*, I thought. But Manny ended up staying over that night.

In the morning Manny tugged at my robe while I was setting up the coffee pot on the kitchen counter, hinting he wanted to have sex again.

We walked back up to the bedroom for another round. It was over pretty quick.

"Why you don' take me to get my car?"

"Okay," I said, heading to the bathroom to take a shower.

Manny was reclining in bed when I reemerged.

"I'm going downstairs to have a cup of coffee," I said, getting dressed.

Manny tsked. "That's not coffee! We stop for a bullet on the way to the hotel."

"I have to walk Rebel. You can take a shower if you want."

When I came back, Manny was already dressed; his hair wet from the shower. "Today, I take you to Versailles for lunch," he said. His clear gray eyes disarming me.

"I love Cuban food, and I haven't been to Coral Gables in a while."

I drove him back to the hotel to get his car. We headed to Calle Ocho in Coral Gables and parked our cars in front of Versailles. That was the beginning of my affair with Manny Torres. He was a really nice guy, very attractive and funny, but I felt no emotion at all. I guess he just made me feel wanted, sought after, and beautiful at age forty-three.

> I knew you would do me some good, in some way, at some
> time—I saw it in your eyes when I first beheld you.
> —Charlotte Bronte, *Jane Eyre*

That spring was filled with news about the students demonstrating in Beijing's Tiananmen Square. There was daily TV footage of Chinese students defying military tanks.

Leon got me connected with the Castle Hotel on Miami Beach, which had a kosher kitchen. They were having some big parties and needed extra help. The first party I worked was a doctors' convention. After we set up the bars, a rabbi scrutinized them to make sure everything on the bar was kosher. We served bloody Marys out of IVs. The doctors were annoyed when they found out that the rabbi had banned dry vermouth from the bars because it wasn't kosher. They ranted and raved at the fact that they'd spent all that money for tickets, and couldn't even drink their martinis.

Another party we did there had a *Phantom of the Opera* theme. Guests were lifted up to the ballroom on the freight elevator amid a thick smokescreen that was very impressive. The music from the Broadway musical played in the background.

Then there were the senior citizen club dinners, which mostly consisted of women. They were seated with empty chairs between them. When we asked which entrée they preferred, they would say, "I'll have the chicken, and my husband"—they would point at the empty chair beside them—"will have the fish." Tin foil was given out with dessert. We shook our heads watching them wrap the untouched plates to take home. It was both funny and sad at the same time.

I was driving home very late from the Castle Hotel. I stopped at a red light in a sketchy neighborhood, and two guys approached my car from either side of the street. They had handguns drawn, pointed at me. They intended to either rob me or carjack me. Either way, I stepped on the gas and sped through the red light. There was no fucking way they were getting me, the cash I'd made that night, or the Cherokee Chief!

The next day I called Manny Torres to tell him about almost getting carjacked on my way home from the Castle Hotel. He invited me to his house for lunch. I hadn't been to his house before, though I had a general idea where it was. He gave me detailed directions. When I got to his neighborhood I reached in my purse for the piece of paper with his address on it. That's when I realized that I'd left it at home. I pulled over when I saw a public phone booth. I searched frantically for his name when I noticed pages and pages of Manny Torres' and Emanuel Torres'. I shook my head, got back in my car, and drove home. The next day I did go to his house, and we laughed over lunch about his name being all over the Miami phone book.

Leon called to tell me that the hotel banquet managers, from the two hotels where we worked, were sending each other checks without ever appearing at their respective hotel functions. They had the scam all set up, and had been doing it for a long time—until they got caught. He also reminded me that we were invited to Janet Prescott's anniversary party that weekend, and he was on his way to pick me up. We were going to a fancy shopping mall, Bal Harbour, to shop for presents. I had him run me to the bank in the Grove to get some cash out. Waiting in line I noticed a guy standing at one of the tellers who looked very familiar. He soon came into focus. It was my friend Bjorn, the ex-surfer from Maui, known by all the girls as Gorgeous George. I flashed on that one time we had sex, and giggled. He was a classically handsome guy who looked like Clint Eastwood, now that he was fifteen years older.

"Bjorn, is that you?" I called out.

"Oh my word, Adriana. What are the odds?"

"What are you doing in Florida?" I asked.

"I married a nurse, and her family lives here, so we moved to Florida."

"Wow, it's so good to see you again. God I miss Maui," I said.

"Who doesn't?" he replied.

"I have a friend outside double-parked waiting for me."

"Here's my phone number. We'll get together," he said, handing me a scrap of paper.

I took the note with his number scribbled on it, got my cash from the bank teller, and rushed out to the car. Running into Bjorn was an omen to me, and reignited my longing for Maui. That day started the ball rolling toward destiny.

When Leon dropped me off at home that night, I sat on the couch for a long time, pondering my life. I had been living in Miami for almost eight years. It was never planned that way; it just happened. I had been back to Maui four times over those eight years, but the last time I knew I wanted to move back. I'd watch *Magnum, P.I.* or the golf tournament from Kapalua, Maui, on TV, just to see the familiar places I missed. I thought of the six-month quarantine Rebel would have to go through. I didn't want to put the dog through something like that at his age. Another excuse to resign myself to the situation.

A few weeks later I worked a party at the InterContinental. Manny Torres worked it with me, but he was very standoffish. He helped me with my bar like he always did, but he didn't set his bar next to mine. It was a Cuban party, and most of the guests seemed to know him. In fact, one of the tables insisted Manny sit with them and have a drink. I was overwhelmed with curiosity. There was a very young, beautiful girl sitting next to him.

When the party was over we broke down our bars together in the ice room like we always did. He told me that this was a family he knew very well, and that he was putting that girl through college. I stared at him. I remembered seeing her photo among a number of other photos on a round end table in his living room. I felt like a fool when he admitted that he was planning to marry her. He wanted to still see me, but I told him it wasn't a good idea. I dropped by the beverage office to tell Leon.

"Adriana, you're not in love with Manny, are you?"

"No, hardly, but still I feel a bit used."

"I'd like to be used by him," Leon said, grinning. We both laughed.

That was the end of my affair with Manny Torres. I made sure that Leon got me more parties at the Castle Hotel on Miami Beach. When I had to work the same night as Manny at the InterContinental, I asked Leon to schedule us on different functions.

> Sex and a cocktail: they both lasted about as long, had the
> same effect, and amounted to the same thing.
> —D. H. Lawrence

The other neighbor in my apartment complex with whom I got friendly was a guy from Racine, Wisconsin. He lived in apartment 9, right next to mine. He owned a luxury boat that did charters and catered functions on the bay. Ian Brody was looking for someone to make reservations and answer phones. This worked out well for me, and I was able to bring Rebel to work with me. A redhead named Chloe Connolly lived with him. I couldn't tell if she was his girlfriend or just an employee, but he liked to boss her around. She trained me on the computer how to schedule parties and make reservations. Chloe and I also bartended the reggae cruise every Thursday night on Ian Brody's boat. It was a very popular cruise, and we made tons of cash. Ian had a strange payment system. He would quote us the price he'd pay us for a particular party. Then, at the end of the night he'd deduct our tips from the amount he quoted us. It didn't take long for us to get a scheme going. Chloe would take the downstairs inside bar, and I'd take the upstairs deck bar, and we'd keep tabs on each other throughout the cruise. She'd call me on the boat's phone, and ask if I had twenty dollars in tips yet. If I said yes, she'd tell me to put it in my pocket. We did that all night long. Ian never could figure out why we made so little in tips.

One of the nicest things we did on Ian Brody's boat was to be a shuttle for the U.S. Navy on an aircraft carrier that was docked offshore. Our boat came alongside the carrier, which was as large as a small city. It was awe-inspiring. Ian's boat actually fit in an opening of the aircraft carrier, which had an inside docking station. The servicemen were so appreciative to be shuttled to shore for a fun night in Miami, so Ian had a decent side to him. I did enjoy working for him, and I was happy for the friendship that developed between me and Chloe Connolly. She finally admitted to me that she'd had a relationship with Ian at one time; their affair was over, but they'd remained friends.

I called my Maui friend Bjorn, who I'd run into at the bank in Coconut Grove, and invited him to come visit and bring his wife. They came to my apartment. We sat around drinking wine and listening to music for a few hours. Bjorn and I reminisced about our time hanging out on Airport Beach on Maui in the late '70s. I got the impression his wife felt left out of the conversation, and perhaps imagined there was something more than friendship between Bjorn and me.

I confessed to them that I'd thought about moving back to Maui but hadn't worked out a definite plan. "That six-month quarantine is a long time for an older dog to be in confinement," I said.

"No, haven't you heard? They recently lowered it to four months," his wife said.

"Oh, that's good news, but still I wonder," I said.

"If Rebel was a really young dog, I think it would be more worrisome. An older dog mostly lies around anyway," Bjorn said.

"Well, it's something to consider," I said. I turned to his wife, "You know, all the girls used to call Bjorn 'Gorgeous George.'"

"Really?" she said, smiling at me, then turning to him with a different expression.

Bjorn and I laughed, but I guess she didn't see the humor in it.

After they left, I had another glass of wine and watched television. That November the Berlin Wall came down between East and West Germany after thirty years. I watched people from both sides of the wall chip away at it. That's how I felt about my life in Florida. I was chipping away at a wall between where I was, and where I wanted to be. I wanted to move back to Hawaii, but I felt tied up in red tape with my family, my friends, and the fear of another big change in my life. I wasn't that young anymore, and feared making another life-altering mistake. I needed someone or something to show me the way forward, because I was stuck in quicksand. I turned the TV off and switched on the stereo. Tom Petty's "Free Fallin'" was on the radio. As 1990 approached I was free falling somewhere between worlds.

Leon got me a gig working a small wedding at the Castle Hotel on Miami Beach. I was to deal directly with the bride and groom, tending to their every need and desire. I showed up at the hotel early and went to the office. The banquet manager sent me to a private room where the bride and groom were sitting on a couch. I entered carrying a bottle of champagne, an ice bucket, and two glasses. They basically ignored me at first, nuzzling and kissing each other. I was an intruder.

"How about a glass of champagne?" I said, when they came up for air.

"That would be wonderful," the bride said, finally acknowledging me.

"Make believe I'm not here," I said, handing them two flutes of champagne.

They never answered me, and I stood there feeling awkward.

After about twenty minutes the groom said, "Why don't you leave the bottle of champagne in the ice bucket? We can manage on our own."

I left the room and looked for the banquet hall where the wedding reception was to take place. Waiters were stacking cooked shrimp on a tower of ice, sneaking a few and eating them. Other waiters were setting the round tables with silverware and glasses. I went to the store room, got my bar, filled the ice bucket, and rolled it into the banquet hall. I fanned the napkins, and checked to make sure I had all the juices and mixes I needed. I looked up, and out of nowhere, a man was standing there. He had a large box camera slung over his shoulder that looked like a contraption from another century.

"Could I trouble you for a Coca-Cola with some ice?" he asked.

"No trouble at all," I said, reaching for a glass. I filled it with ice and pulled the tab up on the Coke can.

He stood there intently observing me as I continued setting up my bar.

He finished the Coke and placed the empty glass on top of the bar. I could feel his eyes on me, so I looked up and smiled, but he didn't smile back. His stare was intense. He reached his hand out for mine, so I figured he was going to give me a tip. Instead he grabbed my hand. I'll never forget the feeling when his hand touched mine. It was like an electric current traveling from his body to mine, and I couldn't pull my hand from his grip.

"Adriana, life is short. Do what you really want to do," he said, his eyes piercing mine. And with that, he let go of my hand, giving it a little tap.

I was frozen as he turned and walked away. I stood there, my mind going totally blank. When I came to my senses, I wondered how he knew my name. I certainly didn't tell him. I looked up again, and he had disappeared. I hurried to the food table and asked the waiters where the photographer went.

"What photographer? No one's been in here," they said in unison.

I thought, *That's odd.* I walked to the private room where I'd left the bride and groom. "Did the photographer come in here?" I asked, peeking my head in the slightly ajar door.

"No, we don't have a professional photographer. We have a family friend coming later to take photos," the groom said.

I walked back to my bar in a state of confusion, and poured myself a Perrier over ice. I gulped it down quickly. I got through the function that night, but my mind was preoccupied. I didn't comprehend any of it. What exactly had happened, and what did it mean?

On the drive home I felt chills every time I recollected the feeling of his hand on mine. I played the scene over and over in my head. I thought of the way he looked at me, as if he was looking into my third eye. It was then I knew that God had sent me an angel, a messenger. It took me a long time to fall asleep that night, but in the morning I woke up strangely refreshed and exuberant. I knew exactly what I was going to do. I got on the phone and purchased a one-way ticket back to Hawaii.

CHAPTER 7

MAUI NO KA OI

I am strangely glad to get back again to you: and wherever
you are is my home—my only home.
—Charlotte Bronte, *Jane Eyre*

The 1990s was known as the decade of peace and prosperity. That year
also saw the collapse of the Soviet Union, and the birth of the World Wide
Web. What that would mean to me, I had no idea, but I was hoping that
there were no more major collapses on my horizon.

I called Leon Roberts and told him I was moving back to Hawaii, and
that I'd be leaving in a few months. It was no surprise to him, and even
though we'd miss each other, there was no chance of his changing my
mind. I had a harder time telling my family, but promised I'd visit often.
I made arrangements for the four-month animal quarantine for Rebel in
Honolulu on the island of Oahu. I felt reborn, and although I had a lot to
do during those last few months in Florida, I got through the tasks with
joy and excitement for the future.

At the InterContinental Hotel I had become close friends with the four
Hs over the past year. They were at my house often, and always wanted
to hear about Hawaii. We were all standing around in the banquet office
waiting to hear which functions we were working, when I announced that
I was moving back to Maui. Harry Hackman admitted that he and Helga
Hargrove had been discussing a move there as well. I was in a cloud of
questions as he talked.

"We'll let you know what we decide," he shouted, walking out of the
banquet office.

Janet Prescott regarded me pensively. "Think of it this way kid. Life
is like a hotel. You check in, you enjoy your stay, because you WILL be
checking out! So do what makes you happy."

In February, I wanted to spend time with my family before leaving the mainland. Who knew what my life would be like when I landed back in the islands, and what sort of financial situation I'd be in? I bought a round-trip ticket to New York and left Rebel at the dog kennel for two weeks.

One of the first things I did was to take the subway into Manhattan to visit my old high school. I walked along Fifty-Seventh Street, then turned the corner onto Second Avenue. I walked through the glass doors at the entrance to the High School of Art and Design. The doors were unlocked, but the building looked deserted. I noticed a group of men sitting at a table playing cards. They looked like watchmen or maintenance staff.

I asked, "Where is everyone?"

"The school is closed until further notice," one of the men said.

"Is there anyone in the office?"

"No, the building is empty, going through renovations."

"Any idea when it will reopen?"

"Ma'am, I told you the school is shut down," he said, seemingly annoyed with me.

I left the building and backtracked along Fifty-Seventh Street, past so many of the shops I'd passed during the three years I'd attended the school. A surprising handful of them were still there all these years later. I walked down to Lexington Avenue and up to Bloomingdale's on Fifty-Ninth Street. I was in that department store every day because the subway stop was on the basement level of the store. I remember being sent to Bloomingdales with my sketch pad for a class project to copy the latest designs hanging on the racks.

As I walked through the various clothing departments on different floors, I thought of how far removed fashion was from my original concept of art. I was always into fine art—painting and drawing. I was so disappointed in the fashion world I found upon graduating, which consisted mainly of simple alterations to patterns and garment construction. I doubted there was much room at the top of the heap of designers, the ones who became famous and could be as creative as they wanted. It didn't have the essence or soul I was seeking. I'd found a compromise, painting on clothing, which was my link to Gauguin (art).

When I arrived back at my parents' apartment in the Bronx, my mother was on the couch watching television. It was an old movie with

Cesar Romero, her heartthrob. She had a thing for him, and would talk about him with a smile on her face and lust in her eyes.

"Where's Daddy?" I asked.

"Your father said he was going to the store, but I think he's seeing that crazy woman."

"What crazy woman?"

"He thinks I'm stupid, but I know what he's doing," she said.

"Ma, Daddy is in his eighties!"

"This is not new. I think he met her when he was still working in barber shops."

"Ma, what the hell?"

"Really, I don't care, although the woman is not all there. Even he calls her the nut."

I was taken aback, but then again nothing my parents did or said phased me anymore. They always had a dysfunctional relationship. I knew that was where a lot of my subconscious issues in my own relationship problems with men came from. I had to admit they did have stick-to-itiveness. They stayed together all those years through thick and thin. I supposed that counts for something. Just then, my mother mumbled, "Now that Cesar Romero—he can park his shoes under my bed any time."

My aunt Porciella, my mother's oldest sister, came by with her daughter, my cousin Gia. We sat at the dining room table drinking coffee and eating the cake they brought from a bakery in Manhattan. Our mothers talked about the old Victorian house in Harlem where they lived when the family first came to America from Bari, Italy.

"We lived with a ghost," Porciella said.

Gia and I laughed.

"No, there really was a ghost," my mother said. "He was small, like a leprechaun, and had beady eyes, red as coals. He would walk around the bed and tug at my arm. He'd say something to me, but I could never make out the words. It happened almost every night, but I was afraid to say anything." My mother trembled at the memory.

"We were so many kids that all of us sisters slept in one bed. I didn't think much of it when your mother asked me to sleep on the outside of the bed," Porciella said, with a giggle.

"Well, she soon found out!" my mother interrupted, laughing.

Porciella said, "I was the one sleeping on the outside, and your mother was sleeping next to the wall. I was woken up by this little man—he looked like an elf. He was sitting on the corner of the bed next to my feet. He was muttering something, but I couldn't understand him, and I was frightened. I pulled the covers over my head."

My mother said, "So the next day, Porciella told me what had happened during the night, and asked if that was why I wanted to change places with her."

"We told our mother, your grandmother, who quickly hung a crucifix over the bed, and that little man never came back again," Porciella said.

Gia and I gazed at each other. Were they telling us a tall tale? Then again, I'd lived with ghosts.

I went to Pelham Bay Park that Sunday with my father. We walked along the tree-lined path for a while, not saying anything. It was winter so the trees were bare, and everything looked lifeless and bleak. It was too cold to walk to the lagoon, so we sat on a bench and watched a group of old men play bocce ball.

My dad said, "When you were younger, there was a newscaster who would break into the regular TV programing to say, 'It's nine o'clock. Do you know where your children are?' I'd always answer the TV and say *no!*"

I laughed at my father's admission, remembering I was regarded as a handful.

"Dad, who's the nut?" I asked, changing the subject.

My father turned to me. "She's a woman I've been seeing for a while. It has nothing to do with your mother."

"But Dad, why?"

"She's a little crazy but very affectionate. She makes a fuss over me, which is something your mother never did."

"Dad," I said, taking his hand. I thought of the song by Nazareth "Love Hurts."

"I don't think your mother ever really loved me. I stayed with her because of you."

"Dad, please don't say that. I've been on my own for a long time now, yet you're still together."

"Who knows what keeps people together? Tradition, family, convenience, so many different things."

I felt sorry for my father, yet I knew there was something between my parents.

"Your mother never kisses me anymore. That woman kisses me and appreciates me."

"I'm a woman now Dad. I understand. Whatever makes you happy is okay with me."

"Don't be alone, Adriana. That's my advice. Derick was a nice guy, and he really loved you."

"I know that Dad, but things happened in Florida, and we couldn't seem to get back on the right track."

"Find someone to love darling. You'll always be my darling," my father said, rubbing my hand. He reached over and hugged me.

I wanted to cry for all of us. Perhaps love, marriage, and children, weren't in the cards for me.

My parents drove me to LaGuardia Airport. We hugged and kissed. I wasn't sure when I'd see them again. I took solace in the fact that it was a place I could always come back to, where there was endless love and affection for me. Even though they didn't understand me or my life, I was always welcomed with open arms.

As soon as I landed at Miami International Airport I numbly walked to baggage claim and stood there waiting for the carousel to start. I thought of how little love or affiliation I had for Florida. As the cab drove along the streets of Miami toward Coconut Grove I wondered why I stayed so long in a place where I wasn't happy. I didn't have an answer.

When we reached West Pelican Drive, I paid the fare and got out. I looked up at the building and a flood of emotions overwhelmed me. I gathered myself and walked up to number 10, remembering the first time Derick took me to see the apartment. I unlocked the door and set my suitcase on the floor. They say when someone lives in a place for a time, a part of them remains behind. I felt his presence heavily in that moment. I immediately drove the Cherokee to the dog kennel to pick up Rebel. He was very excited to see me, so I let him sit in the passenger seat next to me. He put his paw on my leg and looked at me with love. He was the only happy remnant left from my years with Derick Ellis.

Florida isn't so much a place where one goes to reinvent oneself, as it is a place where one goes if one no longer wished to be found.

—Douglas Copland, Australian economist

Harry Hackman and Helga Hargrove telephoned from Denver, Colorado. They had gotten married on Vail Mountain. They contemplated living in Lake Tahoe or Maui. They decided to give Maui a test run for a year. They told me that they were not coming back to Florida; they'd both quit the InterContinental Hotel. I gave them Annie Hughes's phone number on Maui, since that is where I would be staying while Rebel was in the animal quarantine on Oahu. I had a strong feeling that the universe was finally kicking in.

Ian Brody threw me a going-away party in his apartment. I invited all my friends, and even Bjorn came with his wife, the nurse. She was sort of a stiff, although a very nice one. Bjorn confessed that he wished he was going with me.

I was walking up the staircase in Ian's apartment to the upstairs living room, Bjorn following behind me. He rested his hand in the crack of my ass. *I hope his wife didn't see that,* I thought. When I turned around, he grinned and whispered, "For old time's sake."

I remembered the last reggae cruise I worked on Ian Brody's boat …

As I hurried along the dock toward the boat, "Many Rivers to Cross," the Jimmy Cliff song, was playing on the sound system. I thought I was late because the boat was packed with people when I walked up the plank. I rushed through the crowd to get to the downstairs bar and set it up as fast as I could. As the boat left the dock, I heard the theme song from the TV show *Hawaii 5-0* blasting through the sound system.

Ian shouted though a speaker, "Let's have a round of applause for our bartender, who's leaving us and going back to Hawaii."

After I had a bout of the gulps, as I was filled with emotion, I went to work and made plenty of cash tips that night.

It was the spring of 1990 when I left Florida and moved back to Maui. I arranged for the Jeep Cherokee to be trucked to California and shipped to Hawaii by barge. I loaded Rebel into his travel kennel and had no idea what was about to ensue. The flight took off late from Miami International Airport. When we landed at Chicago O'Hare I looked up at the screen, and luckily, I was still in time for my connecting flight. I hurried to the gate, which was at the very end of the terminal. When I reached it, my connecting flight had already left. I spoke to the agent at the counter and pointed to the clock on the wall, showing her that I was on time.

She said, "I'm sorry ma'am, the flight took off early."

When the hell, in all the years I've been flying, has a flight ever taken off early? I thought. "But my dog is on that flight," I said, panicking.

"No, don't worry. We took your dog off the flight."

"Oh God, what do I do now?" I asked.

"You'll have to pick the dog up at the animal holding station. We've arranged for you to spend the night at a Red Roof Inn, which accepts pets." She gave me directions to the holding area where the dog was being held.

When I arrived there, not only was Rebel waiting for me in his kennel, but so was the whole flight crew, who also missed their connecting flight. Before we all loaded into a van, I took Rebel for a short walk. Rebel was sort of a celebrity. The two pilots and stewardesses made a fuss over him on the ride to the Red Roof Inn. I went straight to the room to get settled in. There was a knock at the door; it was one of the pilots, who handed me two cheeseburgers from the restaurant—one for me, and one for Rebel. It turned out to be a wonderful experience. I called Annie Hughes on Maui to let her know that I wouldn't arrive until the following day.

Annie told me to take the small prop plane from Honolulu into Kapalua Airport so she didn't have to drive to the big airport on the other side of the island. Before taking my connecting flight to Maui, I dropped Rebel off at the animal holding station in the Honolulu airport, where he'd be picked up and brought to the state animal quarantine. I cried and hugged him before they took him away. The dog looked confused and perhaps thought I was abandoning him. That's when I wondered if what I was doing was the right thing.

Back in those days, Kapalua Airport was set in the middle of pineapple fields. I observed the mountains and the glistening Pacific Ocean as the prop plane landed. It was like returning to a lover I hadn't seen in a long time and missed. Annie was waiting for me with a plumeria lei, her gray hair whipping in the trade winds. She still had that old beat-up station wagon. "Riana!" she shouted. It was still her affectionate name for me. We hugged and kissed. She said, "So the Dalai Lama was right? Love *is* the absence of judgment!"

That's when I began to bawl.

We walked to the station wagon, and I tossed my suitcase in the back seat. As I was getting in the car I heard someone yell, "Adriana!" I turned my head to see Harry Hackman. He was driving a taxi and was letting someone out. *This is a good sign,* I thought. *Either that, or a very weird coincidence.* He yelled "I have your number. We'll talk soon. Aloha!"

"You know that guy?" Annie asked.

"Yeah, we worked together at the InterContinental Miami."

"I'm so glad you're back," she said, looking at me for a moment.

"I can't explain how I feel, except to say I feel like I'm finally home."

"Riana, this is where you belong, where you've always belonged."

"I know that now, but it's been a long road back."

"*Maui no ka oi,*" she said. "Never forget that again."

"Yes, there is no place better. It's the only one for me."

Entering Annie's apartment I noticed an extra single bed. I wondered if she'd done that for me. I was definitely happy about it, because the thought of sleeping on her floor at forty-four years of age was unappealing. I walked through the apartment and out to the porch, the familiar odor of Lahaina town and the ocean embracing me. I watched the people below walking along Front Street. Then I raised my eyes toward the ocean across the road. "Thank you God for putting me in this beautiful place again," I murmured.

That is when I regretted the years I'd wasted in a place I wasn't happy in. I thought of something my father always said, "The best years of our lives are from ages forty to sixty." I had some hope that maybe there was something beautiful ahead of me. Right then, I was just basking in the happiness of the moment.

"Let's go to Kimo's. We'll sit at the bar. We can even eat there if you're hungry. I thought the Yacht Club might be too much on your first day back," Annie said.

"Yes, the Yacht club would me a bit much."

We walked across the street to Kimo's and sat at the bar. I was thankful that no one looked familiar. I wasn't in the mood to be answering a million questions about why I hadn't been around in such a long time. Kimo's was the same as always. I gazed toward the water and thought of all the times I sat there with Dominick French. The bar was always Annie's domain, and on that day I was thankful we were sitting there. We ordered drinks and were chatting away when I felt someone's hand on my shoulder. Before I could turn around, two hands covered my eyes. They were rough hands, so I knew it was a man.

"Guess who this is?" the man said.

"I don't even recognize the voice," I said, feeling Annie pinch my leg.

He took his hands away and I turned around. A chill ran through me. It was Lucky Kamalani.

"Lucky! What the hell are you doing here?" Annie asked.

"I've been back on the island for a few months now."

"Too soon," Annie muttered under her breath.

"Well, I don't want to disturb your drinking ladies, so I'll catch up with you later," Lucky said, clearly not expecting such a chilly reception. He hurried away from us to a group of guys who were sitting at a table by the water. Annie's eyes followed him until he was at a safe distance before she spoke.

"That fucker showed up back on the island and he's in trouble already."

"What did he do this time?"

"Same shit as last time" she said, wrinkling her nose. "He was hanging around with an underage girl. He beat her up so bad he put her in the hospital, almost killed her."

"That bastard," I said. "Up to his old tricks."

It was the custom years ago in the islands to send delinquent young people away. Instead of putting them in jail, the family would make them disappear by sending them off the island. Back then, Lucky Kamalani had beaten his girlfriend so bad that she died. No one saw him for years after that.

"I'm sure the cops are keeping an eye on him, so he'd better watch his ass."

"Somehow, I don't think he'll get away with it this time," I said.

"My son is coming to live here on Maui. An apartment opened up in my building."

"Which son?"

"Sonny. Tony Jr. has a girlfriend in Vegas and won't leave.

"Annie, are you looking forward to Sonny living here?"

"Yes and no. I'll be happy to have my son here, but I really can't stand his wife."

"In-laws, it's the classic thorn in the side," I said.

"She thinks she's better than anyone else. I think she's a *puttana*."

"Annie, you will need to find a way to get along with her."

"Oh I know, but she's a real piece of work."

We had a wonderful afternoon at Kimo's, and when we'd had enough to drink we walked back to her apartment arm in arm. I collapsed on the bed and fell asleep to the familiar sound of Annie frying eggs in the kitchen.

Annie flew to Honolulu with me to check on Rebel in the quarantine. I rented a car and we drove to Aiea. I had directions, but I missed the exit on the H-1 freeway, which took us miles out of the way. When we finally found Aiea, we followed the signs to the state animal quarantine. Annie stayed in the car reading a book while I walked to the front desk. I wasn't sure what condition I would find Rebel in. When I saw him in the cage I cried. I opened the door and sat down on the concrete floor with him. I petted him, but the dog seemed confused. He even ignored me for a bit. He whined and whimpered when I left. I walked past so many servicemen whose dogs were quarantined there.

I checked on Rebel in the kennel each month, and got lost on the H-1 freeway every time. At one point, I had to bring a case of Kal Kan because Rebel had dropped weight, and wouldn't eat the food they supplied. I brought him a pool float to sleep on, but every time I visited, it would be as flat as a pancake, and I'd have to blow it up again. I'd see the same servicemen there visiting their dogs. They were stationed at Pearl Harbor and could drop by as often as they wanted. I lived on a different island. It was a long four months.

While the Cherokee was in transit across the Pacific, I looked for a job on the west side of the island. I had some crazy jobs those first few months. I briefly worked for a fabric shop on Front Street, which was only a few blocks from Annie's apartment. When the fabric store closed suddenly, I answered an ad in the local newspaper looking for a seamstress at one of the resort hotels north of Lahaina. Annie let me borrow her station wagon to drive to work each day. They set me up on a table in the cafeteria with a sewing machine, where I repaired towels and hotel uniforms. I stayed there not because I liked the job, but because I needed the money.

Annie and I were sitting at the bar in the Lahaina Yacht Club. I could tell she was ready for me to find my own place, and I was feeling the same. Two women in a studio apartment was not the best living arrangement. We heard a guy at the opposite end of the bar ranting and raving about Lucky Kamalani.

"What did he do now?" Annie asked.

"He din do nahting. He dead man now," Bully said, in pidgin slang.

"Dead?" Annie and I asked in unison.

Some other guy at the bar came over to us and told us that Lucky was found on the floor of the Laundromat. Someone had poured Clorox down his throat.

"Islan' [pronounced eye-lynn] justice," Bully yelled across the bar, raising his fist.

Annie and I exchanged glances but didn't say anything. I guess island justice got to him before the law did. He'd never hurt another girl. Lucky Kamalani's lucky days were over!

A bunch of guys sitting at the far end of the bar were going sailing and invited me to come along. I jumped at the chance; I hadn't been on a boat in the Pacific in so long. I knew most of the guys, and there were a few girls going as well. We motored away from the dock looking forward to a beautiful day in the channel between Maui and Molokai. When the wind kicked up they cut the motor and hoisted the sails. The boat cruised along at high speed, driven by the trade wind.

The guys had been drinking all day and were visibly inebriated. The boat began to heel from the wind, and I held on for dear life. It leaned so far over that my feet were actually in the water. I had a panic attack, thinking that these guys didn't know what the hell they were doing, and that we were all going to end up in the drink. I began to panic. *I don't want to die! I just got back to Maui,* I thought.

One of the guys zigzagged over to me, put his hand on my leg, smiled and said, "Don't be afraid, this is what we're out here for."

I calmed down and even felt a little foolish as the boat glided along the waves.

Rebel's incarceration in the state quarantine was almost up, so after I picked up the Cherokee Chief at the dock in Kahului, I began looking for a permanent place to live. No one on the west side of the island wanted to rent to someone with a dog. I began searching upcountry on the crater. I answered a few ads in the local paper, and checked out some creepy situations in my price range. Some were just a room in a house with kitchen privileges, and one only had a hot plate. Harry Hackman and Helga Hargrove told me that they lived in their car for a while when they first arrived on the island.

I finally found a cottage in Makawao. The *ohana* (family) extension was off a large main house. I shared it with a woman named Brittany. It was a prefab construction cottage on a large piece of land. I fantasized it being lifted off its foundation with strong trade winds. But when I walked outside to the deck, I could see all of Maui with the ocean in the distance. Occasionally, we'd wake up in a morning mist, and when the sun came out I'd notice that we were actually above some of the clouds. The air was brisk and fresh with a whiff of eucalyptus when the trade winds were blowing in our direction.

Cottage in Makawao

Brittany was very attractive but had a million insecurities. She was a tall, slim blonde with big lips coated in dark-red lipstick. She had the air of an old Hollywood actress. She drank wine out of a box—and a lot of it. Her morning beverage was Metamucil, not coffee. She had a very good-looking boyfriend, insisting she wasn't in love, just in lust. They worked in the same real estate office. He stayed over a lot, although she claimed they were just friends. Brittany and I were different in every way, so we had a chilly relationship. She was snooty and looked down her nose at me for some reason. I put up with her crabbiness because I didn't have options. I figured in time a better living situation would open up. When I flew to Oahu to bring Rebel home it all changed. My situation became more tolerable— I had Rebel for emotional support. Sometimes when I hugged him I felt a twinge of guilt and sadness for Derick. Rebel slept in bed with me. We helped each other through some rocky times.

There was a large German shepherd who often roamed the neighborhood. I wouldn't even know he was around until I'd hear Rebel growling at him through the large picture window in the kitchen. They'd pace back and forth snarling at each other through the glass. I had seen that dog on a runner chain in a yard at the very end of our street. They were two males that weren't neutered, so I made sure I kept Rebel locked inside when he was around. After the dog appeared at our window a few times, I walked down the road to speak to his owner. The guy who opened the door was an older Hawaiian man who said the dog's name was Kimo (which is Hawaiian for Jim), and he wasn't sure how the dog got loose from his chain. I told him that his dog was showing up at my house wanting to fight with my dog. He assured me he'd be keeping a close eye on Kimo.

I was in my bedroom reading when I heard the phone ring. I had an extension in my bedroom, but it was almost always for Brittany, so I didn't bother answering it.

I heard her call out, "Adriana, it's for you. It's a guy," she said, in a sarcastically surprised tone that I didn't like.

I picked up the receiver.

The voice on the other end of the line said, "It's Derick."

I was caught off guard for a moment and couldn't answer him. *Why is he calling me now?* I'd lived in that apartment on West Pelican Drive for at least five years after he left me, and I never heard a peep from him. What could he want? I figured some girl he'd been living with dumped him. All this was running through my brain as I waited for him to say something heartfelt or meaningful.

"How are you doing?" he asked after a long silence.

"I'm okay," I said. "How did you find me?"

"I called your mother. She gave me your phone number."

"Where have you been, and what have you been doing?" I asked.

"I'm a DEA agent. I'm gonna take down Ross Grant," he said.

From drug addict to drug enforcement agent, I thought, laughing to myself. "Really Derick? I don't think you should tangle with Ross. He might be living high, but he has friends in low places."

"How's Rebel?" he asked hesitantly, probably wondering if the dog was still alive.

"He's fine. He's lying right next to me."

There was a brief silence as if Derick was struck with emotion. "Are you ready to date again?" he asked.

At first, I couldn't imagine what he meant. Did he mean date *him*? Or date in general? Did he think I was saving myself for him? Waiting for him all those years? As if my life stopped because he walked out on me. Instead of being happy, I was getting angrier by the minute. He wasn't expressing emotions or feelings. He seemed to be blaming Ross Grant for everything that had happened in Florida. Sure, the guy left us flat, but Ross wasn't responsible for the things that went wrong between Derick and me.

"No, not really," I said.

"Really? Are you sure?" he asked.

"Derick, I just moved back to Hawaii, and I'm trying to put my life back together."

"All right," he said. "I just thought I'd try."

I hung up the phone a little shaken up. It was a voice from light-years ago, and I felt it was too late for us. It was like that old Joan Baez song "Diamonds and Rust." He let too many years go by without a word or a concern for me or his dog. Something must have happened in his life to turn it upside down, and he thought he'd see if maybe I still wanted him. He didn't even say that he was sorry about how everything ended. That day, I realized I was holding a lot of anger inside that I didn't know I still had, anger that I needed to deal with. Time hadn't healed that wound.

I immediately called my mother in the Bronx.

"Ma, why did you give Derick my phone number?" I said, as soon as I heard her voice.

"He sounded so nice on the phone," she said.

"Ma, after all I went through in Florida?"

"We had a nice conversation, and he really wanted to talk to you."

"It's okay Ma. I didn't mean to jump down your throat."

"Adriana, I thought you'd want to talk to him. You two were engaged at one time."

"I know that. But he just walked out on me. Didn't even leave me a way to reach him. Never called me or tried to contact me for years."

"Adriana, maybe he's changed."

"He doesn't ever talk about things. He's impulsive. I'd just be waiting for him to leave me again."

"Maybe. But Adriana, you're not a girl anymore. You're forty-five years old."

"You think I don't know that? But that doesn't mean I should take up with someone who did me wrong."

"Adriana, there's no such thing as a perfect man."

I got off the phone wondering if maybe I'd made a mistake. Perhaps I should have given him a chance. But he didn't say anything I needed to hear. He didn't even say he'd thought of me, of us, or that he missed me. He was tossing the ball in my court, and I wasn't having it!

> Forgiveness is the fragrance that the violet sheds on the heel that crushed it.
>
> —Mark Twain

I found a job waitressing at Polli's Mexican Restaurant right in town. Makawao is an old cowboy town, but most of the cowboys and gals had been replaced by artists and hippies. I started out doing Sunday brunches at the restaurant. Customers would ride up on their horses, tie them to the hitching posts, and walk in for breakfast. I made quite a bit of money over the four-hour shift. Polli's was a mainstay with upcountry residents, and the bar was the local watering hole just about every night. After a few weeks I was working more shifts and getting to know the customers. The waitresses were all in a clique and raked me over the coals during training, but eventually I got with the pace.

I worked a Friday night shift at Polli's, which was music night. I was standing at the waiter's station at the bar ordering two margaritas for my table, when I caught sight of a familiar form. A guy walked in with his guitar case like it was a machine gun. It was my old boyfriend from the seventies in San Francisco, Blake Middleton. I realized that he was that night's entertainment. His long black hair was in a ponytail, and he was wearing dark aviator sunglasses. He caught sight of me in the ruffled Mexican dress we were required to wear, with a large flower in my hair, and was about to burst out laughing.

"Don't you dare," I said, glaring at him.

"Can't I even laugh? I mean, this is quite a vision." He took off his sunglasses revealing his piercing baby blues.

"Go ahead and laugh if you have to," I said.

"Adriana, how'd you end up with this gig?"

"I live right up the road. Besides I get a burrito at the end of my shift."

We stood there laughing at each other for a while, then we hugged.

"This isn't the first time I've played here on a Friday night, but it's been a while."

"Where are you living?" I asked

"I rent a small house on the beach, not far from Willie Nelson's place."

"Do you know him?" I asked.

"I've played a few tunes with Willie."

"Well, I have to get back to work. We'll get together soon," I said.

"Yeah, I'll have you over to my place. I'll cook a brisket and play ya some tunes."

"I look forward to it," I said, walking back to the bar.

I hung around for a while after my shift to listen to his last set while I ate a beef burrito. I walked out before the end.

It was very early on a particularly cool Sunday morning. I put on my robe and fetched Rebel's leash. I figured I'd walk him while I checked the mailbox at the end of our driveway. I was still groggy from sleep. I heard a growl, looked up, and there was Kimo, right in front of us. He lunged at Rebel and began tearing at his leg. I dropped the leash and grabbed Rebel's collar. The dogs were going at it, and I couldn't stop them. Kimo bit me on my thigh, like it was a turkey drumstick. I began to scream. Our landlord, who was a big black guy—very sweet but a powerhouse—must have heard me screaming. He came running toward us with a two-by-four, which he used to beat Kimo over the head until the dog got off Rebel and ran down the street. He helped me up. I stood there staring at my leg, which had large bite marks in a circle that looked like I'd survived a shark attack.

"You'd better go to the emergency room and get a tetanus shot," he said. I was shaking like a leaf. He took off his white T-shirt and wrapped Rebel's mangled leg. I got dressed, carried Rebel to the Cherokee, and drove him to the vet. While he was getting cleaned and stitched up, I drove down the mountain to the emergency room for myself.

I went to work at Polli's that same day. I had the Sunday brunch shift and was able to make it to the restaurant by 11:00 a.m. I couldn't afford to miss out on the cash. I left Rebel at home resting.

The next day I marched myself to Kimo's owner's house, carefully walking past the dog on the runner chain. I knocked on the door, not taking my eyes off Kimo for a second. The old Hawaiian man came to the front door a little surprised to see me again. I showed him the horrific bite on my thigh, which was now black and blue. I handed him the vet bill. He paid for everything, even my emergency room visit. He was very apologetic, but it wasn't the first time his dog got off the chain. I told him I'd spoken to neighbors, who said his German shepherd was a menace. I reported Kimo and his owner to the Humane Society, and found out they'd had quite a few complaints about the dog. I wondered why nothing was ever done about the dog, or why the owner was never fined. I was just happy we both survived the attack. That large scar remained on my thigh for twenty years.

It was the end of the month, and I was having trouble coming up with my half of the rent for the cottage. I assured Brittany I'd get it somehow. It was October, and the Maui County Fair was happening down the mountain in Kahului. Harry Hackman had mentioned that he and Helga were planning on working the fair, so I asked if there was a chance I could work it too. Helga suggested we go down to the recruitment office together. It was easy to sign up, but I had to commit to working all four days of the fair. Working in those game booths was crazy. People threw stuff at me, and an arrow flew past my head one too many times. Each night we'd leave exhausted, as if we'd worked a long day in the pineapple fields. But at the end of the four days, I had enough money to pay my share of the rent. I mentioned to the four Hs that I was miserable living with Brittany. They talked about us getting a place together. I had a six-month lease, but we began making plans and combing upcountry Maui for a house to share.

Somehow, through all of the instability in my life, I managed to keep painting. I ordered cloth labels embroidered with my last name, Bardolino, as if I were a famous Italian designer. I carefully hand-sewed the labels into the necks of the clothing. I continued to feel artistically motivated, even though my life seemed to be dangling at the edge of a cliff. I figured that was the way my life was going to be, and I had better get used to it.

When Christmas rolled around, Brittany's boyfriend surprised us with a Christmas tree, which we put up in the living room. This seasonal formality was sort of ironic, since I was basically living out of boxes. Brittany went to a Christmas party with her beau. I stayed at the cottage. For New Year's I got together with Hackman and Hargrove, as I often called them, and we went to Polli's and got drunk. We rang in 1991 with bright hopes for our collective futures. My six-month rental agreement on the cottage with Brittany would be up soon, and I was so ready.

After the holidays, I received a call from Blake Middleton, who invited me to his house down the mountain for supper. He lived in a small house right on the beach in the town of Sprecklesville. I drove the Cherokee down the mountain and followed the directions he gave me. I turned onto his street, drove along a dirt road, and parked right next to his house. I walked through sand to get to his front door.

At first I noticed the place was in disarray, and I didn't smell a brisket cooking. There were a couple of guitars standing against a wall, some big-ass speakers, and a microphone on a stand, but Blake wasn't playing any tunes. He was sitting on his couch smoking a joint. The couch was the only piece of furniture in the living room, so I sat down next to him. He kissed me, but I felt nothing romantic, just familial affection. After we talked for a while we both were bored.

I left him on the couch as I headed for the front door saying, "See ya around." He was still toking on a joint and barely looked up at me as I walked out. "Maybe I'll see you at Polli's next time I have a gig up there," he said, as I shut the door behind me.

Funny how time changes the intensity we feel for a person, especially an old lover. There might be a hint of attraction in the familiar way they move, or the way they say something—maybe a laugh that brings us back to a time when we were so into them. But we can't stop time. It just keeps marching on.

I'd often spend a few days in Lahaina with Annie Hughes. She was still my Maui mom, and her place was like home to me. We were sitting at the bar having lunch at the Yacht Club, when my eyes drifted to a table where a tall, handsome guy was sitting with two girls. I stared at him, mesmerized. His looks and mannerisms were just like Derick's, and for a moment I thought it was him. I felt an attraction, a longing for him, even jealousy.

Then Annie tugged at my arm distracting me. "This is my friend Abigail Walton," she said, as a woman sat down on the barstool next to me. Abigail had a restaurant called Abigail's Place at the far end of Lahaina. She was looking for people to work in the restaurant, or bartend in her husband's bar, Bubba's Bar. There was no way I wanted to drive down the mountain every day from upcountry to work in Lahaina, but I was desperate for money. I figured I could maybe work two days a week and stay overnight at Annie's. I told Abigail I'd stop by the restaurant so we could talk about the possibilities.

After Abigail left, Annie told me she'd heard through the "coconut wireless" (local gossip) that the restaurant wasn't doing well, and that a lot of her staff was quitting because they were afraid the place was going under. During our conversation I found my eyes drifting back to the table by the ocean a few times. I didn't like what I was feeling. Why did I still want the man who had hurt me so much? *Love is weird*, I thought.

A week later I walked into Abigail's Place in Lahaina. I found her in the kitchen. It wasn't much of an interview, but she offered me a choice.

"I run a catering business out of this kitchen, so if you'd rather work parties with me, you could do that," Abigail said. "And by the way, call me Abby."

"Well Abby, that actually sounds more up my alley than working in the restaurant."

"You have to have good transportation to work onsite functions, because we work at different locations all over the island."

"I have a Cherokee Chief four-wheel drive. I can work anywhere."

"Can you bartend as well as do food service if need be?"

"I was a bartender at the InterContinental Miami, and I'm waitressing at Polli's."

"It's called Abigail's Distinct Affairs. You're hired," she said, handing me her business card.

I walked out of Abigail's feeling good. At that moment, I wasn't aware that Harry Hackman and Helga Hargrove had already worked for Abigail's Distinctive Affairs. I went right next door to Bubba's Bar, her husband's wing of the establishment, and ordered a top-shelf margarita. I noticed Bubba take a shot of something as he made my drink. I didn't think that was kosher, although I was well aware that bartenders often drank on the job. He seemed a lot older than Abigail. He resembled the handsome 1950s actor Glenn Ford. Abigail was such a beautiful, young, and charismatic woman. I wondered what her attraction to him was—well, besides the Glenn Ford thing. I finished my drink and walked out. I didn't feel like driving back up the mountain, so I slept at Annie's that night.

I had a day off and drove to Kihei to see my longtime friend Loretta Perino. Her baby was now an adorable little boy. She had found out that he was deaf and wondered if she might have to sell her house and move back to the mainland. She bemoaned the reality that there were no facilities to deal with deafness on the island, and that her son was just thrown in a class with children who had all degrees of disabilities.

I mentioned that I had volunteered at the Lexington School for the Deaf in Manhattan when I attended the High School of Art and Design. "They can do amazing things for deaf kids now. I worked the switchboard in the school's office. Kids would converse with me as if they had no hearing disability at all," I said.

"Believe me, Adriana, I don't want to leave the island. You know I love it here."

"When will you decide?" I asked.

"I don't like what I saw in preschool, so I should know pretty quicky."

"God, Loretta, I would miss you, and I know how much you would miss the island."

"I owe it to my son," she said, with a distraught expression.

We sat on her couch pondering our situations. I felt sad to know that such sacrifices were sometimes necessary.

"Remember what Hank Cooper used to say about life?"

"What's that?" Loretta asked.

"In life, there's a slap in the face around every corner!"

We both laughed.

"Speaking of Hank, I received a call from his brother, my ex, Sammy."

"You did?" I said, surprised.

"Well, with all I've been going through with my son and money problems, it slipped my mind. He mentioned nothing about Hank. Sammy went on and on about wanting to talk to me, that he fucked things up, and that he missed me. But I told him that he made his bed, and now he has to lie in it."

"Speaking of exes, Derick Ellis called my mother, and she gave him my phone number. He was very vague about his life over the past five years. He asked me if I was ready to date again. Didn't even say date *him,* or that he missed me. It was a weird conversation."

"Derick was never big on dialogue," Loretta said.

"Don't I know it!"

I left Loretta's house feeling glum, wondering what she would be forced to do. I knew the last thing she wanted was to leave Maui. I thought about my years with Derick, how it had deteriorated into a relationship I didn't even recognize. I wondered what my future life would have looked like if I'd given him another chance. Maybe he'd walk out on me again. Perhaps the way things turned out was for the best. Funny, that's what Derick would say every time we had an argument and he'd walk out the front door—"It's for the best!" As I slowed down at a stoplight, I thought, *The universe sure fucks with us sometimes..*

When I got back to the cottage in Makawao, I checked the mailbox at the end of the driveway. I had a flashback of the dog attack. There was a package in the mailbox from my mother addressed to Rebel c/o me. Rebel was right there to greet me. I opened the package while he nuzzled his nose through the postal paper—I'd told Rebel it was for him. It was a red-plaid doggie coat. I put it on him and walked him out to the deck. I took a photo of him to send to my mom. I had mentioned on a phone call how chilly it was up on the crater at night, and that Rebel liked to hang outside on the deck watching over the neighborhood. He was getting up there in dog years, and his hips bothered him when it was cold.

I took Rebel for a walk, keeping an eye out for Kimo at the end of the road. I could see that he was tethered on his runner chain, so I felt we were safe.

Harry and Helga came by the cottage to see how I was doing. They'd found a really great house farther up the mountain in Olinda on Red Road. They had been living in a condo in Kihei for the past year. We both wanted to get out of our current living situations. On the weekend they took me to see the house.

Off the main road, down a long private drive was a house set in the middle of a grassy field on five acres, which bordered a state forest. *Rebel would love this place*, I thought. As we walked up the driveway, I saw a row of gardenia bushes on one side of the house. I said to myself, *This is the place for me.* In the distance, across the field, we noticed a foundation for a second house. Walking through the front door, I saw a skylight over an island in the center of the kitchen. I thought, *A perfect place to paint.*

The house was all wood-beamed with high ceilings, a modern kitchen, and an open floor plan with a sunken living room. There were glass windows from ceiling to floor on one side of the house. From the suspended outside deck you could see the forest at the edge of the property. In the living room was an open-faced wood-burning stove, and I pictured nights around the fireplace. The house was fully furnished, and I spied a nice stereo system in a large piece of furniture along one wall of the living room. We heard that the owners were going through a divorce, so they just left everything behind. Two bedrooms and two baths were perfect for our situation. I picked the bedroom with the gardenias right outside the window. The garage was big enough for two cars, plus room to work on projects.

Harry Hackman and Helga Hargrove signed the lease, and I gave Brittany notice that I wouldn't be staying in the cottage past my six-month agreement.

CHAPTER 8

TEARS IN HEAVEN

> Man is the cruelest animal.
> —Friedrich Nietzsche

Random Thoughts:
I was definitely functioning in self-protection mode, not wanting to let anyone in emotionally. I found solace in painting, music, reading, and in the rustic beauty surrounding our house on Red Road. The state forest visible from our deck inspired me artistically, and offered me peace.

Harry waved as he pulled into the driveway. I continued watering the gardenias. Rebel was beside me investigating the bushes and everything around us. The dog loved it in Olinda. Rebel had plenty of land to roam around on, and there were other dogs—friendly dogs—along our road for him to play with. I took him to the local veterinarian for a checkup. When we arrived the vet was out in a field tending to a horse. The horse was lying down, obviously sedated. The vet said he was working on the horse's teeth. Rebel approached the horse very cautiously in slow motion. The vet said not to worry, that it would be quite a while before the horse would be able to stand up. Rebel got his checkup right there in the field, not taking his eyes off the reclining horse for a moment.

I loved spending my afternoons in the kitchen painting under the skylight. I had plenty of alone time, since Harry worked for UPS and Helga worked for FedEx during the day. I worked for the catering company at night.

Helga and I had a rare Saturday off together. I found her in the kitchen, turning something in a large bowl with a wooden spoon.

"It's such a cold day, I thought I'd bake cookies and make a fire."

"Yeah, cookies are always a good thing on a nippy afternoon. What kind?" I asked.

"Chocolate chip. It's Harry's favorite."

"Helga, isn't it everyone's favorite?"

She stuck her finger in the bowl to test the consistency of the cookie dough, then tasted it. "Here, see what you think. Is it too moist?" she asked, pointing a spoonful in my direction.

She took another spoonful, and so did I. As a child, I loved eating raw dough whenever my mother was baking something. She'd chastise me, warning that I was going to get a stomach ache. I loved raw dough of any kind, and it never made me sick.

"If we keep eating this cookie dough, there won't be anything left to bake," she said.

"I think it needs more flour," I said.

"I was just thinking the same thing."

Helga sifted more flour into the cookie dough. After she shook it all in she said, "There's something wriggling at the bottom of the strainer."

"They're worms. They must have been in the flour. Didn't you see them?"

"I didn't strain the first batch of flour, she said."

We were sick to our stomachs realizing that we'd eaten all that wormy cookie dough.

Harry roared with laughter when we told him about it.

Harry Hackman had gone through two years of culinary school on the mainland. His father was understandably upset when Harry decided he didn't want to be a chef afterall. Helga and I were the beneficiaries of his cooking skills. Harry was a nice-looking, even-tempered guy. I never saw him get angry or raise his voice. Helga was a pretty blonde with a freckly complexion. Her family was from Germany, and I often felt the temptation to call her Gretel, like from the German fairytale *Hansel and Gretel*. They made a great couple. That evening, Harry cooked a wonderful dinner worthy of five stars at a fancy upscale restaurant. The tale of the wormy cookie dough was a subject that lingered for weeks.

Nights up on Haleakala Crater were cold that winter. The wood-burning stove did a great job of heating the living room, but the rest of the house remained cold. We often sat on the couch watching television wrapped in blankets. I didn't have a man to sleep with, but Rebel was my constant, loving companion who always slept on the bed keeping me warm. On a phone call to my mother in the Bronx I mentioned how awful it was taking a shower when the temperature was forty-five degrees. Next thing I knew, a box with a small electric heater arrived with the daily post. I'd blast that heater to warm up the bathroom each morning before taking a shower.

I was enjoying my morning coffee when I heard a vacuum. *What the hell is going on?* I wondered. Walking into the living room, there was Helga on her hands and knees vacuuming the ashes out of the fireplace with my handheld Kirby. It was a gift from my mother when I bought the Cherokee Chief.

"Helga, what the hell are you doing?"

"Vacuuming the ashes. Easier than sweeping them out with that tiny whisk broom."

"You do know that you've ruined the Kirby."

"No, that's what it's for," she protested.

The vacuum never sucked up anything again. I reflected on my mother telling me never to lend anyone my sewing machine, car, or vacuum cleaner, and from experience, my mother was always right.

I received a call from Abigail Walton. She had a catering function in Wailea and wanted me to bartend with her husband, Bubba. I asked her if I should meet her at the location, as I didn't want to drive all the way to Lahaina, but she stressed that she needed my help at the restaurant. I had picked up a white shirt and black pants at a secondhand shop in preparation for catering. I already had the black bow tie from the InterContinental Miami. I hung my black-and-whites in the car and drove down the mountain. When I walked into Abigail's Place, the restaurant was pretty empty. I went directly to the kitchen in the back. Everything was in chaos, and I found her in tears.

"Abby, what's wrong? What's going on?"

"Bubba's drunk, and he always takes care of the booze. I don't know what to bring."

"Maybe I can help," I said, letting her know I knew my stuff.

"I don't even know how much wine to bring to this function," she said.

"Well, I know you can figure about five glasses per bottle," I said.

"Really? I rely on Bub, but he's useless right now."

She liked to call him Bub. Every time she did, I'd think of Uncle Victor, my mother's brother, who had the habit of calling everyone he met *Bub.*

"Tell me how many people are at the event, and I'll tell you how much wine to bring."

"Oh, thank you, Adriana. We will bring Bub along anyway. We need two bars."

"Calm down. We've got this. Just get the food ready, and I'll organize the bar," I said.

Abby concentrated on packing up the food, and I figured how many cases of wine, and how much beer and liquor to bring. I noticed two guys loading the truck. One of them was a good-looking Hawaiian guy with a mass of long, frizzy, dark hair. We smiled at each other briefly. Abby filled Bubba with black coffee to sober him up on the drive to Wailea, so he'd be ready to bartend by the time we got there. I followed the van because I wanted to drive straight home after the function was over. I was not leaving the Cherokee Chief in Lahaina.

Bubba set up my bar at the party so that I just had to walk behind the bar and start twirling drinks. He preferred that I help Abby with setting the tables. I figured he didn't believe I was really a bartender. Bubba was a very quiet man. He barely said a thing all night, unless it was to ask me if I needed anything. I had to ask him a question to get him to speak, and even then, I'd receive a very brief response.

The party went off without a hitch, except at the very end when everyone was leaving. One of the guests, a very drunk older lady, missed a step and tumbled down a walkway cracking her two front teeth. She was still smiling when she got up, blood dripping down her chin. I could smell the alcohol fumes coming from her direction, which probably insulated her from immediate pain. I imagined she'd wake up the next morning with a bad hangover and a huge dental bill.

Abigail whispered to the guys, "Just load up the van"—also referred to as the shit wagon on occasion—"and let's get out of here before something else happens."

I drove home that night laughing at it all.

Working for the catering company was like working for a traveling circus. I had to drive to different locations around the island. It sometimes required setting up tables on a lawn or in a tent, and regardless of how sweaty I got in the process, I had to be dressed in my black-and-whites with a bow tie before the guests arrived.

Sometimes we worked on rambling estates. These huge homes were historic, some dating back to the early missionary families who came to the islands in the eighteenth and nineteenth centuries. Houses were filled with antiques, artwork, Hawaiian memorabilia, and interesting family photos of old Hawaii passed down from one generation to another. One house we worked a birthday party in was like a museum. Not much about the house had changed in the past hundred years. The owner was an old man who sat at a piano and played while we set up. The house sat on a vast expanse of land with breathtaking views of Haleakala Crater, and the ocean visible in the distance. The large trees off the kitchen were filled with peacocks honking and flying.

The hosts were most often nice, but sometimes they were nasty or argumentative. Abigail Walton was always calm, sweet, and accommodating. Behind the scenes we often made jokes about everything and everyone to counteract our feeling abused.

My coworkers were a riotous bunch, all characters in their own right. We worked together for many years, and some became like family to me. The luggers and loaders were a motley crew. Paki Makani was the good-looking Hawaiian guy with long, wild hair, and Logan Baxter was a young, buff guy from California—I had a little crush on him. It was hard not to get attached when we worked together all the time. Then there was a guy we called Jumpin' Jimmie, who always had cocaine with him, which he hid for us in various places. It got us through some long, rough nights. The wait staff was a revolving crew according to who was available on a given night. Most had regular day jobs. There were two sisters from Milan, Italy—Italian Jews, Mara and Zenda Schwartz, very pretty and always stylish. They liked to yell orders at us in Italian, but we never knew what they were saying. Last but not least was Filippo Rizzoli who had a bad temper, was as tan as a California raisin, and liked to serenade us with Frank Sinatra songs. All these characters made going to work fun. I have a million crazy stories but will share some choice ones.

Things often went awry, like an important pan or a box of desserts was forgotten back at the kitchen on the other side of the island. Then there were unfortunate accidents, like the night Abigail painstakingly carved fifty giant onions to be used as bowls, and made a delicious onion soup from scratch at the kitchen. Someone in a rush at the venue bumped into the portable stove toppling the whole pot onto the floor. Logan Baxter was sent to the nearest supermarket to buy dozens of cans of onion soup. When he returned, we had to open up all the cans, heat the soup, ladle it into the onions, and cover them with crostini and melted cheese. Dinner went off without a hitch, and the night was saved. Everyone raved about the onion soup!

"How do you do it, Abigail?" the host said, heaping praise on her for another party well done.

One evening I was bartending a wedding on an estate in Kula. My bar was set up on a wooden terrace, which was uneven and rickety. Thousands of plumeria blossoms were dropped over the bride and groom by a helicopter above. I was serving champagne when my leg went through the floor, and I nearly disappeared. Luckily, Logan Baxter was right there filling my ice bucket when it happened. He lifted me out of the hole, and I went on working as if nothing had happened.

I arrived home on Red Road after a day in town. Rebel wasn't in the house or in the yard. I went looking for Helga.

"Helga, where's Rebel?"

"He's playing with the neighbor's dogs."

"Helga, he's not fixed. I don't want him roaming when I'm not here."

"None of the dogs up here are on leashes. They just run around."

"I don't care what the other dogs do. I don't want him running around loose. He could get into trouble, or fight with another dog," I said, annoyed.

This wasn't the first time I'd come home and had to go looking for Rebel along Red Road. Despite numerous warnings and concerns about it, they continued to let him out when I wasn't home, insisting I was being silly. On one occasion, I found Rebel walking into the woods. He refused to come to me, and I had to shout his name a few times before he finally turned around and walked toward me. I quickly latched his leash to his collar and walked him back to the house. I wondered why he was so determined to enter the woods.

A few days later, Harry told me that they were walking in the woods behind the house and came across a dog tied to a post. He said there were no houses around, and the dog looked half-starved but that he was friendly. I thought that maybe that dog was why Rebel was sneaking off into the woods. We went for a walk a few days later in the same area. We passed a field with horses and stopped to pet them, but I didn't see a dog around. Little did I know that Hackman and Hargrove were feeding that dog every day, until one day I came home and found the dog tied up in our garage, Rebel lying beside him. He was a spotted pointer, very young. They adopted the dog and named him Gizmo. I had a funny feeling about the situation early on, but after the dog lived with us for a while, he became part of the family.

I found a job at a clothing boutique in Makawao Town on Baldwin Avenue. It was only a fifteen-minute drive from Red Road, and I was able to bring Rebel to work with me. The store carried painted clothing and unique jewelry. Ethereal music played, and incense burned at all times. I convinced them to carry some of my hand-painted T-shirts, so I had yet another outlet. I also worked a couple of parties a week with the caterer. This afforded me the time and money to paint. I was waltzing into a nice stride. I quit my part-time job waitressing at Polli's Mexican Restaurant, but still stopped in for a margarita and a burrito now and then. Driving up that windy road to Olinda in the dark was scary, so I limited my drinking to the daylight hours. The only lights along that dark road were the headlights on the Cherokee Chief. I always made the sign of the cross when I pulled into our driveway.

I ran into my former roommate, Brittany, while shopping at the music store in Wailuku. We went to a café for coffee. Well, I drank coffee; she drank wine. We were discussing the death of Freddie Mercury, the lead singer of Queen. He'd died of AIDS, as so many of our friends did back then. She told me she'd lost her job in the real estate office, and her friend/boyfriend hadn't called her in a long time—he was the one she'd insisted she was just *in lust* with. She yapped away as I stared at her full lips covered in deep-red lipstick. Funny—she was such a pretty girl, yet I found nothing attractive or endearing about her. I was glad I got out of that prefab cottage we lived in together. She confessed that she either had to find another roommate or find another place to live. She no longer could afford it on her own. She also mentioned that the landlord's wife, Sheila, in the main house, hadn't been seen for months. There were rumors that she'd left her husband.

I was surprised because they had plans to move to the Big Island, Hawaii Island, and start a business together. One afternoon, by chance, I saw Sheila with Paki Makani, the Hawaiian guy who loaded the trucks for Abigail's Distinctive Affairs. They were smooching at a bar in Kahului. Abby confirmed that Sheila had indeed left her husband and had been boinking Paki Makani on a regular basis. I was certainly glad I was far away from that den of snakes. I wouldn't have wanted to be around the cottage when her husband found out.

That Christmas one of Harry's brothers came to stay with us on Red Road. Harry had nine brothers; he was the baby. We played games in the yard, went on hikes, and had some epic dinners. I was getting back into playing my guitar which gave me some joy. Work kept me busy.

I spent a few days with Annie Hughes in Lahaina every now and then. I finally met Sonny's wife Gloria, the puttana. She was younger than him, thin, attractive, and very New York Italian. She got a job as a waitress at Lahaina Broiler. There was constant bickering and door slamming going on between Annie and her daughter-in-law. From what I picked up, Annie loved Sonny's first wife and never accepted Gloria. "That puttana is just a user," she'd say. Personally, I never saw that her boy Sonny had much to offer any woman. I told her she had common ground with Gloria—that was Sonny—and I hoped she'd come to terms with it. Of course, Annie wasn't giving up breakfasts at the Broiler, so she always put on a phony smile when Gloria waited on us.

On New Year's Eve, Abigail's catering company worked a party at Puamana in Lahaina. That whole evening Filippo Rizzoli was acting crazy, throwing one hissy fit after another. Abby was losing her patience. Sparklers were inserted in Eskimo pies for dessert, and delivered to the seated guests to ring in 1992. Filippo blew up, yelling and cursing about a task Abby had given him, not just behind the scene, but in front of the guests. She tried to calm him down, but he kept up his tirade about some ridiculous, inconsequential thing. Bubba finally told him to leave and not to come back. That was the last time we saw Filippo Rizzoli at a function for a long time.

Occasionally the catering company had a huge function requiring a U-Haul truck to transport everything to the venue. That didn't happen very often, but when it did, we knew we were in for a long, hard night. We worked a real estate function on vacant land up on a hill in Kahana, West Maui. It was the proposed site for a future residential condo complex. Tables had to be unloaded from the U-Haul, rolled onto a very uneven field, and set up. The wind was so strong that day we used clips to keep the tablecloths from flying away. Everything regarding that event was difficult. I cut up lemons and limes for Bubba's and my bar, while Logan Baxter loaded us up with ice. When he was finished, he lingered around my bar.

"Logan, can I get you a soda or something?" I asked.

"Yeah, I'll have a Sprite?"

"Sure," I said, filling a plastic cup with ice. I was just about to pop the top of the Sprite can when he grabbed it.

"I'll do that," he said, his hand lingering over mine on the can.

I stared at him until he took his hand off mine. His dark curly hair wet with sweat, and his ruddy complexion were disarming. He was a handsome guy.

Bubba walked off, telling me that he was going to check on Abby, who was setting up a makeshift kitchen on the other side of the field in the food tent. I wondered if he'd noticed Logan's amorous gesture aimed at me. I told Bubba not to worry, that I'd have everything ready before the realtors arrived.

Logan was hanging around my bar for no apparent reason. He was giving me suggestive looks with his big, brown, puppy dog eyes. I was attracted to him, but he was so young. I thought, *When has that ever stopped me?*

"What are you doing after the party tonight?" Logan asked.

"I'll probably stay in Lahaina. I don't want to drive up the mountain."

"A few of us are going out for drinks. Why don't you come with us?"

"That would be fun," I said, excited at his interest in me.

He smiled and mouthed an affectionate kiss in my direction as he walked off.

Once the party started, Bubba and I were in the weeds with ice and drinks flying, and there was no looking up. We were using real glassware for the main luncheon, so I was very careful not to break a glass in the ice bin. I'd learned in bartending school that doing so would require me to empty out the entire bin and start over with fresh ice.

I saw very little of Logan for the rest of that evening and thought perhaps that was a good thing. When the function was over we began breaking everything down. Bubba said he'd take care of both bars. Abby needed me to help strip the tables, so they could be rolled onto the U-Haul. I looked up to see the most epic island sunset over the ocean with Molokai in the distance and thought, *God, I'd love to live up here!*

We were just about done when Logan passed me, and I felt a pinch on my ass. He didn't say anything but shot a playfully suggestive grin in my direction. *Oh God*, I thought.

Logan told me to meet him at the Mission Bar at the back of the Missionaries Hotel, which was having live music that night. I still liked that place, even though Dominick French didn't play there anymore—he'd moved off the island. Logan had to drive the U-Haul back to the restaurant and unload the perishables in the walk-in freezer. Everything else would be done the next day. While he was doing that, I stopped at the Yacht Club where I found Annie. I had a drink with her and made sure it was okay for me to stay at her place that night. I had told Logan I'd meet him in an hour, but when I got to the Mission Bar he wasn't there. I sat at a table near the band feeling a little awkward, and wondering what I was getting myself into. Just then, I saw him walk in with Jumpin' Jimmie. He smiled at me as he took the empty seat next to mine. Jimmie sat next to Logan. I swear that guy looked like he was moving even when he was sitting still.

"Whatcha drinkin'?" Logan asked.

"Tanqueray and tonic."

He ordered himself a rum and Coke and another Tanqueray and tonic for me. I looked around the place, which was filled with so many memories. I stared at everything on the walls and pictured the characters who used to hang out there on a nightly basis in the old days. I recognized one of the bartenders, and the same woman was behind the front desk when I walked through the lobby.

After a few drinks the liquor began to cloud my judgment, and I was feeling pretty reckless. Logan was a hottie, and even though I knew getting involved with someone I worked with could be a death sentence, I was tumbling into the I-don't-care phase of the evening. That night I was out for a little flirty fun, and wasn't thinking about tomorrow—or anything that made any sense. I just wanted someone to kiss me and hold me. Maybe my desires were sparked by the place I was in, and memories of being loved by someone, and being in love. I missed that feeling. I'd been without a partner for a long time—too long!

We talked and laughed about that day's realtor function and all the crazy things that went wrong and what went well. It was all work talk, which is what Logan and I had in common. I began to relax and enjoy myself.

After an hour or so, I stood up and told Logan I needed to leave. "I'm staying at my friend Annie's house, and don't want to get there after she's gone to bed."

He insisted on walking me to her door. When I turned to walk up the stairs to Annie's apartment, Logan reached for me, turned me around, and planted a soft, sweet kiss on my lips. Nothing passionate, no tongue, just a good-night kiss. "See you next time," he said, with a lingering smile as he walked away.

I had a warm glow about me walking through Annie's front door. I found her sitting on the porch.

"I saw you walking down the street with a hunk of a guy," she said.

"Yeah, Logan Baxter, a guy I work with."

"Uh-huh. What's the plan?"

"I don't have a plan. I don't want to get involved with him. He kissed me, but it was just sweet."

"Uh-huh. I've heard that before," Annie said.

"The longer I'm alone, the less I want to get involved with someone."

"You're still young and beautiful. Don't waste that! Anyway, I have a feeling that good things are coming your way."

I didn't share Annie's notion. There weren't many men my age with whom I clicked. I wasn't feeling anything special or deep with Logan. We were so different, not just because of our age gap, but he didn't evoke that special feeling, that je ne sais quoi.

"You hungry?" Annie asked, drinking milk out of the carton. "I'm making myself fried eggs."

"No, I just want to sleep. I'm exhausted. It's been a long day."

I threw myself on the bed and stared up at the ceiling. I thought of all the times I'd slept on Annie's floor after a night on the town drinking in all the bars. I remembered the Halloween Dominick French and I had slept on her floor. She came home and tripped over us on her way to the porch, cursing like a sailor. I thought of all the twists and turns in my life; random thoughts flew through my brain, and soon I fell off to sleep—a very deep sleep.

I was curious to know how I was going to feel when Logan and I worked another party together, because that was inevitable. Abigail's Distinctive Affairs had a small dinner party at someone's house not far from Red Road, so I had a short drive to work. I saw Logan unloading the truck. He and I were the only people working that night. Abby figured the three of us could handle a small dinner party. Logan and I teased each other and horsed around all evening, and there was no uneasiness.

Abby asked me what was going on between Logan and me.

"Nothing," I responded, "although I'll admit he's cute."

Abby laughed. I didn't mention his kissing me the other night. Logan and I had an attraction for each other, but as time went by, we became work buddies. It allowed for a fun, easygoing, work environment. I knew there would be no connecting with him in a sexual way, but it opened my mind to the realization that I wanted that in my life again. How or when that would happen, only God and the universe knew.

I had a day off and hung out at home on Red Road. After lunch I watered the gardenias and painted T-shirts. The dogs were outside in the garage, which is where they liked to hang out in the shade on a hot afternoon. I put music on the stereo while I did yoga. I heard them barking, as I often did, and figured some kids on bicycles were riding down our road. It was the most beautiful, calm day. I heard scratching at the front door, so I opened it and let Gizmo in. I walked out to the back deck and sat in a chair staring into the forest. Gizmo jumped in my lap and I began petting him. We stayed there like that for a long time.

Suddenly, I had a cold feeling in the pit of my stomach. I thought it might be guilt, knowing that Rebel would be jealous if he saw me petting Gizmo in such a way. Instinctively, I knew something was wrong. Rebel would have barked to come in by now. I pushed Gizmo off my lap and walked outside. Rebel wasn't in the garage where he always was. Maybe he'd walked down the road and was at a neighbor's house. I ran down Red Road knocking on doors. No one had seen him. I began to panic. *Why didn't I go outside to check on them when I heard barking?*

Some kids told me that a crazy guy came by in his truck. He'd run over dogs before on the main road, and he could have taken my dog. They said that he owned some land in the woods behind our house but never built anything. It registered in my head that maybe Gizmo was his dog, and he might have been looking for him. Maybe he saw his dog in our driveway and decided to take the other dog as some sort of revenge. Why would someone do something so devious and so cruel? Why not just knock on the door and talk to us?

When Hackman and Hargrove came home I told them that Rebel was missing.

"He'll come home," they said.

But I felt something terrible had happened, and it was all my fault. If they had been home, and I'd been at work, I would have blamed them for Rebel's disappearance. I just couldn't think straight. The next day I drove around like a maniac, putting MISSING posters on trees with Rebel's picture that stated $500 REWARD. Every time I heard a dog bark, I thought it was Rebel. I'd get in the Cherokee and drive toward the barking, only to hear it somewhere else. I'd yell out his name and could swear he answered me, but from where?

I called a local radio station to see if they would make an announcement.

"You sound distraught. I can hear it in your voice," the announcer said.

"He's lost, I'm lost, and I don't know what to do."

"I know a guy who's a ranger for the forest service up there on Haleakala. He's familiar with your area. If I send him to you, you can just give him lunch and pay him whatever you feel is right. He loves to do that sort of thing. Would you like me to ask him?"

I felt momentarily hopeful. "Yes, please, I'm more than happy to pay him."

The forest ranger arrived at the house. He was a weird guy who seemed as if he was more comfortable in the woods than he was around people. He was dressed in army green and had a red scarf around his neck. He looked like an overgrown Boy Scout. His hiking boots looked worn, and his hair was greasy peeking out from under his cap. I flashed on a childhood fantasy I had of marrying a forest ranger, but this wasn't quite the image I'd had back then. I would have laughed if I was in a humorous mood.

I explained that I'd hiked all around the area with my roommates to no avail. I told him I was sure he was out there somewhere, and that I had heard him bark. I handed him a photo of Rebel to take with him on his search, along with a ham-and-cheese sandwich, an apple, and bottled water. I watched him disappear into the woods and felt guardedly hopeful. He came back to the house a couple of times to report that he'd found nothing. On his final trip back he had no news.

"I combed every gulch, ravine, stream, everywhere, and I know this area like the back of my hand. I didn't find your dog, dead or alive. He's not here."

I handed him cash. "Thank you for trying," I said.

"I feel bad taking it. I know how you must feel. I have a dog," he said.

"No, please, I want you to take it. You searched for hours out there."

He reluctantly took the cash and left the house. I went into my bedroom and sat on the bed. I couldn't remember the last time I'd eaten, yet I had no appetite. Helga came in and sat down next to me. She took my hand, and I broke down crying.

"I think that crazy guy took him. The kids said they saw his truck on our road."

"I can't imagine someone would do something like that—be so cruel and vindictive."

"I can't function. I can't think of anything else but Rebel."

"Some people have no heart," Helga said.

"I don't know what to think."

"Sometimes when a dog is old, they walk off into the woods to die," she said.

I wondered if Rebel felt rejected after my roommates adopted the other dog. I did look in the woods where I'd seen him walk in and disappear that one time. I yelled for him, but he wasn't there. It crossed my mind that maybe he was angry about Gizmo and wanted to hurt me by running away. Then, when he decided to come home, he couldn't find his way back.

I called my parents to tell them what had happened.

"You've always been careless," my father said. He was angry and didn't even want to speak to me. My mother got on the phone to grill me about the details, and why I was letting Rebel outside by himself. I tried to explain that it was a rural area, and that all the dogs were outside. She was a little more compassionate, but still, my conversation with my parents certainly didn't make me feel any better.

I was devastated and heartbroken. I was in a cloud and didn't know if I would ever come out of it. I thought of Derick Ellis, and I felt shame and loss all over again. He entrusted Rebel, his dog, to me. It was March 1992, Rebel's twelfth birthday, and I didn't know where he was. I prayed that God would take care of him in my place. If he was hurt or had fallen into bad hands, I prayed that God would take him so he wouldn't suffer. But most of all, I prayed that somehow, by some miracle, he'd come back to me.

On the fourth day, I worked at the boutique in town, hoping I could occupy my mind. A guy walked into the store, a quirky guy who hung out in the cafés along Makawao Avenue. He'd been in before, and we'd usually have silly metaphysical conversations about nonsense. He was a very spiritual, ethereal, type.

"Where's your dog? He's always sitting on the floor next to you."

I teared up a bit. "He's missing, or someone took him, or he ran away."

"Oh, that's too bad. He was such a beautiful dog."

I didn't like his talking about Rebel in the past tense.

"I'll buy you a coffee? We can walk to Casanova's and sit outside."

"That sounds like just what I need."

I called the owner of the boutique and explained the situation. He said he understood and told me to take a lunch break and open back up in an hour. I walked to Casanova's with the guy, and we sat outside on the porch. I loved that place.

Back in the day Casanova's not only had an Italian restaurant with a firewood pizza oven, but they also had a deli, which stocked imported Italian grocery items on shelves, and cooked Italian delicacies that were displayed in a glass showcase. I always bought freshly made ricotta there, which could be purchased by the pound. The owners were from Italy and France, and prided themselves on serving authentic Italian food.

We sat on barstools, and he ordered us coffee and pastries. I was numbly observing passersby walking along Makawao Avenue. People wandered in and out of shops on Baldwin Avenue, and stopped in the general store, where Harry liked to buy his special cuts of meat.

"So are you feeling any better?" he asked.

"Not really, but thank you for inviting me. I appreciate the diversion from work."

"I didn't want to talk in the store. I want to inform you of something."

"Inform me of what? I don't understand."

"Yours is not the only dog missing."

"What are you saying?"

"There are cults I've heard about, cults that sacrifice animals."

I stood up. "Why are you telling me this? You're certainly not easing my conscience."

I left him sitting at the table and stormed off in a huff. I quickly walked down the street to the boutique, my heart racing. *What a horrible thing to say,* I thought. *What makes a person act like he wants to help you when what he really wants to do is to hurt you?* I didn't know, but I knew that guy better not ever walk into the boutique again.

My heart was aching. I called the owner again and asked him if he could relieve me for the rest of the day. He came by often anyway to check on sales, and to move merchandise between this store and another store they had down the street in a small marketplace. The owner told me he understood, and he'd be right there to relieve me. He walked in, eyes blazing, carrying an arm full of clothing from the other store. He always looked and acted like he was on something. He noticed my downhearted expression and took my hand.

"Adriana, go home. I can imagine what you're going through. We have two little Yorkies that we treasure. My wife and I would be devastated if anything happened to them."

"Thank you so much. I just can't get through this day," I said.

I walked out of the boutique, got in the Cherokee, and drove up to Red Road. The car smelled of Rebel. On the radio Eric Clapton was singing "Tears in Heaven." I looked out the window at all the houses along the main road and thought of how I'd driven up there with such joy, yet that day I felt overwhelming sadness. I couldn't hold back the deluge of tears that was bound to come sooner or later. I seriously thought I might have to move off the mountain. I would forever conflate it with my great loss. Every time I drove up the mountain to Red Road, I'd think of Rebel.

No one was home when I parked in the driveway. I went directly to my bedroom. I had some serious thinking to do. I sat alone on the bed staring out the window at the gardenias, with thoughts and memories running through my brain. *God, please, something or someone, take me out of this sorrowful, miserable place. There's nothing here for me anymore.*

He was born like a thought and died like a sigh and disappeared like a shadow.
—Khalil Gibran, *The Broken Wings*

CHAPTER 9

REPARATIONS FROM THE UNIVERSE

Life, death, people, the allies, and everything else that surrounds us. The world is incomprehensible. We won't ever understand it. We won't ever unravel its secrets. We must treat it as it is, a sheer mystery.

—Carlos Castaneda, *A Separate Reality*

That spring, Abigail Walton closed the restaurant. She bemoaned the fact that she was six-hundred dollars in the hole every day she kept Abigail's Place open. She rented a kitchen in Lahaina's industrial area. I hand-painted a tile with palm trees and tropical fruit that read, "God Bless Our Kitchen," which Abby displayed on the wall behind one of the stainless-steel counters.

Bubba Walton had a breakfast-basket contract and needed someone to assemble and deliver them to vacation rental properties along the lower road on the west side. I filled that need. Assembling the breakfast baskets was a breeze—one papaya, two pastries, and two pineapple juices. I'd use the small company van to deliver them, and I got through my daily routine like a mindless automaton.

I began spending a few nights a week at Annie's apartment in Lahaina, not being able to face the house upcountry. Driving up Red Road I'd pass telephone poles with Rebel's MISSING posters still displayed.

I was still working part-time at the boutique on Baldwin Avenue. Everyone asked about Rebel, not seeing him on the floor next to the counter, and I'd have to relive that horrible saga each time. I found being up on the mountain depressing.

The house on Red Road was for sale. The owner offered it to us, but who the hell had $265,000? Harry and Helga began searching for another house in that area. I was simply looking for salvation and peace, and was getting none of it up on the mountain.

I was putting breakfast baskets together in the kitchen, planning to meet Annie at the Mission Bar after work for a happy-hour drink. We were resurrecting our old habits. When I arrived at the Missionaries Hotel, she wasn't in the back-room bar. I waited for quite a while, nursing a drink, watching locals and tourists engaged in conversation. One group at a table next to mine raved that there were still whales out in the ocean, even though it was May and humpback whale season was over. I could have interrupted their conversation and told them that some whales stay in the Hawaiian Islands longer if they haven't mated yet, or if their new calves weren't ready to make that long journey to Alaska, but I wasn't in an informative mood. After half an hour I figured Annie wasn't coming, so I paid my tab and left. I walked along the seawall to her apartment.

I found Annie on her porch, upset and crying. Her son and daughter-in-law Gloria, the puttana, were standing next to her.

"What's the matter? What's going on?" I asked.

Sonny blurted out, "My brother Tony Jr. is dead."

"How?"

"He was found dead in the trunk of his car on the Las Vegas strip."

"Jesus Sonny, what the hell happened?"

"Just like his bastard father—couldn't keep his thing in his pants," Annie squawked.

I put my arms around her while she rocked back and forth crying.

Sonny said, "I knew he was sleeping with some Vegas mobster's wife, but I had no idea it would ever come to this."

"Really Sonny? Screwing a mobster's wife. You didn't figure it?" I said.

"I'm taking my mother to Las Vegas. We have to deal with funeral arrangements for my brother," he said, ignoring my comment.

"That's good Sonny," I said.

I left them to grieve in their own way. Tony Jr. had been sleeping with a mobster's wife; now he was sleeping in the trunk of his car. Gloria never uttered a word. I suppose she knew Annie didn't like her, and figured this wasn't the time to butt in. I walked across the street to Kimo's and ordered a shot of tequila. I had to settle my nerves before driving up the mountain. There was no way I was staying at Annie's that night.

Abigail Walton had a new chef working with her, a big German guy named Hans Berlin. He was very funny, talked fast in his German accent, and kept Abby laughing. I knew Abby's husband was a lot older than her, but it never dawned on me that something might be going on between Abby and Hans—until one afternoon when we were in the kitchen loading up for a function in Kapalua, and I happened to see Hans shove his hand down the front of Abby's apron and fondle her breast. I pretended I didn't notice. I imagined Bubba was at a bar somewhere getting drunk.

I picked out bottles of wine and liquor for Logan to load on the van. Woman's intuition told me there was trouble in paradise. At the time, I wasn't aware that Abby had given her husband an ultimatum regarding his drinking. I knew firsthand what drunkenness could do to a woman's sensibilities in a relationship, but I wasn't one to give ultimatums. Perhaps I should have.

It was an ordinary day, with not much going on. I had been at the kitchen in Lahaina, putting Bubba's breakfast baskets together. Hans (Abby affectionately referred to him as *Schweinhund*) was at the large butcher-block table chopping up vegetables for a soup he was making. He looked up and smiled at me. I told him I'd finished all the baskets and was on my way to deliver them to the properties. Bubba liked to have them in the condos so guests would see them as soon as they checked in. When I was finished, I returned the van to the kitchen and emptied the previous day's baskets. I tossed out any leftovers and recycled unused canned juices for the next day.

It was Friday, and I had planned on driving up to the house in Olinda for the weekend, but at the last minute something compelled me to stay in town. On what some might call a whim, I decided to go drinking by myself, which was something I never did. I walked along the seawall toward the Pioneer Inn as if a magnet was drawing me there. I figured I'd get a table near the window to watch the sunset, and observe the boats coming in and going out of the harbor, like I did in the old days. As I turned the corner and walked toward the dock, I could hear live music coming from the Inn. The place was crowded, not even one empty table. I caught sight of a bunch of guys motioning for me to sit with them. I eased my way through the crowd and sat down at their table. They asked me what I wanted to drink. I told them I liked Tanqueray and tonic, and they ordered one for me. We were all talking and joking around for a while. When the music stopped, the good-looking guy at the far end of the table leaned in past his friends and stared at me.

"What's your name?" he asked, drawing me in.

"Adriana Bardolino."

"I'm Cheyenne Bremmer," he said.

"Where are you visiting from?" I asked.

"Oh, I'm not a tourist. I live here."

"Really? I live here too. I'm glad to meet you Cheyenne."

"Me too," he said, with a smile that destroyed me.

We carried on a conversation; the other guys sitting between us seemed a bit annoyed. He had a fair complexion, blue-green eyes, and long, thick, straight, reddish-brown hair. Native American–looking hair. I figured if his name was Cheyenne, he had to have some tribal DNA. I noticed a couple of tattoos on his arms. Basically, he was a hottie, and definitely my type. I looked out the window noticing it was getting dark, and realized I'd missed the sunset.

"I have to get going," Cheyenne said, standing up. "I have an early day tomorrow."

"It was nice to meet you," I said, taking note of his solid form.

"Can I walk you home or to your car?" he asked.

"Actually, I'm staying right down the street."

"Well, I'd like to see you again," he said.

"This is my phone number," I said, handing him a piece of paper with my number scribbled on it.

"I'll be calling you for sure," he said.

As he was walking away with his friends my eyes drifted down to his butt, which was firmly packed into his jorts (blue jean shorts). Then I noticed another large tattoo down the back of his leg.

Annie had told me I could stay at her apartment that night. She was back from her son's funeral in Las Vegas and relished the company. I finished my drink and motioned the waitress for a check.

"The guys took care of the tab," she shouted.

I stood up and walked out into the balmy night air. I strolled along the seawall listening to the waves. I stopped to watch the ocean for a while. I gazed up at the stars, which were numerous and bright. I saw a shooting star and took it as a sign that something wonderful was about to happen.

I drove up the mountain on Saturday. The closer I got to Red Road, the sadder I became. I passed a missing-dog sign, though not Rebel's, and sighed. I thought of that guy telling me there was a cult of people who kidnapped and sacrificed animals. It enraged me. What the hell kind of evil people would hurt innocent animals? Dog nappers, who broke the hearts of loving families, children, and people like me.

Hargrove and Hackman were home eating lunch. I briefly went to my bedroom to put my dirty clothes in the laundry basket. I stared at the bed and pictured myself rolling around in the sheets with Cheyenne Bremmer. Just then I heard the phone ring.

She poked her head in my bedroom and said, "It's for you; it's a guy."

My stomach did a flip-flop as I walked toward the telephone.

"Hey, it's Cheyenne," the voice on the other end of the line said.

"I was wondering if I was going to hear from you," I said, picturing his eyes like oceans of blue.

"I can't talk long. I'm at the end of my lunch break. When are we getting together?"

"Actually, I live up in Olinda, way up on Haleakala Crater."

"Oh, I thought you lived in Lahaina."

"Well, I stay at a friend's house when I work on that side of the island."

"So when is the next time you're working on this side?"

"I'll be on the west side on Thursday."

"There's a restaurant called Luigi's at the main entrance to Kaanapali on the left side. Right under the restaurant there's a bar. Can you meet me there?"

"I know where Luigi's is, but I didn't know there was a bar downstairs."

"It's a really cool place, and they have great pizza."

"I'm Italian, so I'll be the judge of that," I said, laughing.

"I'll call you before Thursday."

"I look forward to it," I said. My stomach rolling over as I hung up the phone.

The very essence of romance is uncertainty.
—Oscar Wilde

Even though I'd felt an attraction, I had a hard time resurrecting his face. I only remembered his eyes and the tattoo on the back of his leg. That week, I worked at the boutique on Baldwin Avenue. The empty spot on the floor next to the counter haunted me, and I was glad when my three days were over. I wasn't sure how many more days or weeks I could stand to work there or to live on the mountain. Abigail's Distinct Affairs had a function in Lahaina that Thursday night, so I called Annie to make sure I could sleep at her place.

On Thursday, I drove to the kitchen in Lahaina and found everyone already there.

Strangely enough, we were working a party at the Whaler in Kaanapali, which was only a few minutes from Luigi's. The party was in a condo on the top floor owned by an art collector. It was a small affair, so it was just Bubba doing the bar, me helping Abby with food service, and Logan doing the loading and heavy lifting. Abby left Hans Berlin back at the kitchen cooking for a big function that was to take place on the weekend.

Toward the end of the party Abby fixed me and Logan a plate of food. The host of the party happened to come into the kitchen inquiring about dessert and coffee. He saw us sitting at the table eating, and threw a hissy fit, saying that he hadn't planned on feeding the help! Abby tried to calm the situation, telling him that it was customary to feed the staff.

The guy was a first-class jerk, complaining that he wasn't paying for us to eat his food. Somehow, Abby sweet-talked him off his pedestal, and basically made him feel like the asshole he was. He backed off, but I placed my dish, food and all, in the sink. Logan kept eating in defiance—he had done a lot of physical work, dragging coolers and cases of wine up to that pompous ass's apartment, and he wasn't about to put his fork down.

Once we were alone in the kitchen, Abby said, "The prime rib wasn't the only thing I wanted to carve up tonight."

When the party was over we cleaned and packed up. I left Logan loading the van in the parking lot. He smiled at me and said, "See you this weekend, and let's hope we won't be working for another jerk." I laughed nodding my head.

I drove to Luigi's, which was only a few minutes away, and parked in the lot alongside. I wondered if I'd feel the same magic when I saw Cheyenne that I'd felt the night we met at the Pioneer Inn. I found the entrance to the bar down a set of stairs. It was a small bar, very dark inside, with a jukebox in the corner. Most bars had jukeboxes back in those days. I didn't see any familiar faces right off, but then my eyes settled on a familiar form, and I remembered he had long hair in a ponytail. *That's him,* I thought, smiling and walking over. He turned only his head, following my approach with his eyes as I sat down beside him.

"You made it," he said. "I wasn't sure you'd come."

"Sorry I'm late. Actually, I worked a party right here at the Whaler, and it took us a while to clean up."

"What do you do?" he asked.

"So many things—bartender, waitress, store clerk, delivery person."

"Wow, a jack-of-all-trades," he said, laughing. It was a deep laugh in short bursts. He was sweet, charmingly handsome, and very sexy.

"And you? What do you do?" I asked.

"My dad is the chief engineer of the Royal Lahaina. He secured a five-year contract, so we left Arizona to come here. I'm his assistant, an all-around Mr. Fix-It." He hesitated, then said, "I have a band too. We have a studio in the Lahaina industrial area behind the Sly Mongoose."

"Really? The catering company I work for has their kitchen in that same area."

"No way! It's a small world," he said.

"So you're a musician? What kind of music?"

"I play bass guitar in a heavy metal band called Black Tar. Come by the studio. We practice just about every night."

"I don't know much about heavy metal, but I'd love to hear you play."

"Jesus, sorry, I didn't even get you a drink. I got sidetracked looking at you. You're so beautiful."

"If it wasn't so dark in here you'd be able to see me blush."

"Come on, I can't be the first guy to tell you how beautiful you are."

"My mother says, 'Your looks and a token gets you on the subway.'"

"You must be from New York," he said.

"Yeah, the Bronx."

"I was born in New York too, but my family moved to Arizona when I was a kid."

"You must be part Native American with a name like Cheyenne."

"My father is German with Sioux Indian, and my mother is Irish and Cherokee."

"But they named you Cheyenne."

"They couldn't name me Cherokee, and who'd want to be a boy named Sioux?"

We both laughed. We talked for a long time. He didn't look or act that young, so I wondered why he was living with his parents. *Maybe a bad marriage or a breakup*, I thought. Lots of people go back and live with their folks when things go awry. I did.

He walked me outside. When he saw I was driving a Jeep Cherokee Chief he grinned and said, "Must be a sign." He pushed me against the SUV and kissed me, opening my mouth and darting his tongue around.

Oh, this is going to be good, I thought. I pulled away. I wasn't jumping into anything that fast.

"Why don't you come back to my house? I'll play you some riffs."

"Another time. I promised my girlfriend I'd be there before she went to sleep."

I was about to get in the Cherokee when he turned me around again and kissed me.

"Think about that when you're with your friend. I know I'll be thinking about it."

I hesitated staring back at him, feeling butterflies and thrills like I'd just gotten off a roller coaster ride at an amusement park. I climbed in the Cherokee Chief and drove away.

Two weeks passed without seeing Cheyenne Bremmer. Most of the parties I worked with the catering company were upcountry, so I had no reason to drive to Lahaina. Cheyenne and I had some very long telephone conversations, almost every night, which gave us a chance to get acquainted without sex being a driving force.

The next time I worked a function on the west side, we got together at the same bar in Kaanapali. I felt a strong connection as soon as I caught sight of him. We'd spoken so much on the phone that I felt like I'd known him for years. Cheyenne followed me with his eyes as I walked into the bar and took the seat next to him. He had a funny way of turning his head without turning his whole body. It reminded me of the way a cowboy in the Old West would eye an approaching woman.

Once I was seated, he called out to the bartender, "A Tanqueray and tonic with a lime." Then turned to me. "So how was the party?"

"It was an easy one, and I got to eat a great meal at the end."

"I was going to order us pizza," he said.

"You go ahead. I'll watch."

"My parents owned a restaurant in Arizona. I loved cooking on the outside grill."

"My parents both owned their own businesses. My mom had a dress factory, and my dad had a barber shop. I spent a lot of time in both of those places when I was growing up."

"That's way cool," he said.

We talked for over an hour at the bar. Cheyenne ate pizza, and I drank. When it was time to go our separate ways, I knew he wanted me to go home with him, but I wasn't ready.

"You staying in Lahaina tonight? You can stay at my place," he said.

"I'm staying at my friend's house. She's really my Maui mom. She worries about me."

"I was hoping we could spend the night together."

"We will, but not tonight," I said.

"You don't like me that way?" he asked, innocently.

"It's not that. It's been a while since I've been intimate with a man. I want to go slow."

Cheyenne paid the tab, and we left the bar. As soon as we stepped into the night air he took my hand and rubbed it. My stomach turned to mush, and I felt throbs down below.

"Why don't you spend this weekend up at my place in Olinda?" I said.

"I'd like that," he said. He leaned in and kissed me.

We were tangled in a French kiss until I pulled away. "I've really got to get going."

"Aw, I don't want you to go," he said.

"I don't want to go either, but I have to. We have the weekend to look forward to."

"That's true. I'll plan on it," he said, hugging me and kissing me again.

I got in the Cherokee; neither one of us wanting to look away. I watched him get on a golf cart, which is how he navigated around the golf course. He waved at me, and I waved back. I drove away with mixed feelings of excitement and fear. Was I really going to take the plunge into another relationship? What was my reluctance? Perhaps the universe chose this person especially for me. I didn't want to be a woman, finding myself old and gray, regretting not having paid attention to the people the universe tossed in my path.

All that week I was preoccupied with bringing Cheyenne Bremmer to the house on Red Road. I knew I had a party in Lahaina that Friday night, so I had to say something to Harry and Helga. I walked in the house on Red Road and abruptly announced, "I'm bringing a guy home this weekend."

Harry and Helga stared at me, a little surprised.

"You are? How did this come about?" Helga asked.

"We met at the Pioneer Inn in Lahaina a few weeks ago."

"You never go to that place anymore," Harry said.

"I know. I guess it was meant to be.

After the Friday night function in Kapalua on the west side, I met Cheyenne Bremmer at Luigi's. We had drinks and pizza, then headed up the mountain in the Cherokee Chief. He had a small duffel bag that he tossed in the back seat as we drove off. It was pitch-dark as we turned onto Red Road, so there wasn't much to see. I parked in the driveway since the two other cars were in the garage. Gizmo was there to greet us.

"You have a dog?" Cheyenne asked.

"Not anymore. That's my roommate's dog Gizmo. I'll have to tell you about my dog Rebel some time."

The air was really brisk, and we could smell the wood from the fireplace. We walked in and went straight to the living room.

"There you are," Helga said.

"Guys, this is Cheyenne Bremmer," I said.

Helga said hello, and Harry stood up to shake Cheyenne's hand. I sensed trepidation in Harry's gaze. It was awkward at first, but when we sat down on the floor next to the wood-burning stove it all jelled. We hung out and talked for an hour or so, then Harry and Helga went to bed, leaving us alone.

I was nervous. I got up to get a glass of water and Cheyenne followed me into the kitchen. As the water was running, he stood behind me and circled his arms around me. I felt he was hard against my behind, and was rubbing it back and forth to make sure I could feel it.

"Let's go to bed," he whispered in my ear, tickling my neck. We walked to my bedroom and closed the door. I stared at the bed and thought of all the times over the past weeks I'd pictured us rolling around in those sheets. I shut the light and fell down on the bed, and he lay next to me.

"I guess I'm afraid it's going to hurt. It's been a while."

"I'll take my time. I'd never hurt you," he said.

"I didn't think you would."

I remembered getting my ears pierced when I was a kid, and my mother saying, "Adriana, if you leave that earring out too long, the hole will close up!"

The room was completely dark, and I tried to picture his face and his eyes. I concentrated on that while he undressed me. I wanted him, so I welcomed his hands all over me. He brushed his lips along mine. He stood up and took off his clothes. He lay back down and began moving his hands all over, examining my body. First my breasts, then his hand wandered down to my crotch. He slipped his tongue in my mouth, almost down the back of my throat. I liked the way he didn't hesitate. He put his finger inside me, and I let him play around down there for a while. My hand wandered and played with his member. He jumped on top of me, but for a while didn't do anything but kiss me. A feeling of calm came over me like ribbons of satin enveloping my body. In my head I was hearing that song I liked, "Black," by Pearl Jam, while he made love to me. I was a living sexual being again. I saw it as reparations from the universe. Afterward, he slid off and covered us with the quilt, the bedroom being so cold. He whispered, "I love you."

I didn't say anything. I'd heard that men always fall in love faster than women, and I wasn't sure of my feelings. We held each other and fell asleep. The act was repeated during the night.

In the morning Cheyenne slipped into his jeans, and I grabbed my robe. We walked into the kitchen together. He stood at the sink filling a glass with water. That's when I noticed two women tattooed on his back.

"What's that?" I asked.

"The tats on my back? That's my girls," he said, with a little chuckle.

"Cheyenne, how many tattoos do you have?"

"Seven," he said. "Well, so far. Why? You don't like tattoos?"

"Oh, I like tattoos. And I like that you have a smooth chest."

"Maybe the Cherokee and Sioux in me."

"It's what I think a man's chest should look like, because my father doesn't have hair on his chest. You know what I mean. That first image of a man from childhood."

"You hungry? I'll make us eggs," he said, peering in the refrigerator.

"Yeah! I'll get the toaster and bread out of the cupboard."

Just then, Harry walked into the kitchen. "Hey, I was planning on making us a big breakfast this morning. Why don't you let me do that?"

"No worries. I like when other people cook," Cheyenne said.

"You need any help?" I asked.

"Nah, I got it covered. Helga will be out in a minute. Relax, I got this under control."

I was standing at the island in the middle of the kitchen when Cheyenne came up behind me. I could feel how hard he was against the crack in my ass. I was hearing that line Mae West always said, "Is that a gun in your pocket, or are you just happy to see me?" I snickered to myself.

Cheyenne whispered in my ear. "Let's go to your bedroom for a while."

I smiled and followed him in. I jumped on the bed, tossing my robe on the floor. He took his jeans off and got on top of me. We communicated with our eyes, not wanting to make noise. It didn't take long for me to climax. I fell off to sleep soon afterward.

When I woke up, Cheyenne wasn't in bed. I lay there for a while under the covers rubbing my eyes, then I heard voices in the kitchen. I got dressed and found him sitting at the table in the dining room talking with Harry and Helga.

"You were sleeping so soundly I didn't want to wake you," Cheyenne said.

"There's plenty of scrambled eggs, and I made batter for pancakes." Harry said.

"I'll have pancakes," I said, putting my arms around Cheyenne's shoulders.

"This is some place you guys have here," Cheyenne said.

"It's for sale," Harry said. "Wish we had the money to buy it. There's already a foundation for a second house on the five acres. No one will build behind here because the property borders a state forest."

"Well, let's enjoy our last few months here till the lease runs out," Helga said.

After breakfast, I took Cheyenne for a walk around the property. I was well aware of how rustic and beautiful it was up on the mountain. I wasn't a fool. But its beauty became tainted after Rebel disappeared. As we walked along, I told him all about what happened to my dog. He rubbed my hand as I told him the painful story. He mentioned having a cat, and that he couldn't wait for me to meet him. He stressed that I could stay with him when I worked on the west side of the island.

"I look forward to that," I said, following him into the house.

"Hey, Adriana, did you go to that Santana concert in Tampa in '82 when you lived in Florida?" Harry yelled out, catching sight of us walking through the front door.

"No, but I did see them in Colombia, South America, in 1971."

Cheyenne stared at me as if something clicked in his brain. I ignored it, but my comment revealed that I was older than he thought I was. He didn't ask me about it that day, but in days to come, there were other hints that let him know I was quite a bit older. I still didn't know how old he was—and was I in for a surprise. In subsequent weeks reality hit. I was in my forties, and he was in his twenties. Funny thing was, he looked older than his age, and I looked younger than my age, so visually, none were the wiser. I had held out telling Cheyenne my age for a long time for fear of losing him. When I finally told him, he laughed and said he really didn't care, that he loved me. At the time I felt relieved. We clicked in a way that I hadn't with a man in a very long time, but I wasn't sure I was in love.

Cheyenne said, "You know what they say."

"What's that?"

"Twenty goes into forty a lot more times than forty goes into twenty!"

"Show me," I said, pulling him to me.

I was offered a part-time job at an Italian restaurant in the Kapalua shops. I started out as daytime bartender and manager three days a week. I made more money behind the bar than I was making at the boutique on

Baldwin Avenue, so I quit the boutique. On the weeknights when I worked at the restaurant in Kapalua I'd stay at Cheyenne Bremmer's house. On the weekends we'd drive up the mountain to the house on Red Road.

Meeting his folks for the first time was a bit daunting. Cheyenne's mom greeted me openly hospitable, but his dad regarded me warily. I imagined he wanted to know why his son was hanging out with an older woman, when he should be interviewing women his own age as marriage prospects. Cheyenne took after his mom, Pricilla. She had the same eyes, hair color, and complexion. His dad, Jim Bremmer, was a very tall man with dark hair and eyes. He walked and talked like Johnny Cash. He was a man of few words. Cheyenne told me that Pricilla and Jim tried to have a baby when they were first married, but she couldn't get pregnant, so they adopted a little girl. A year later Pricilla was pregnant with Cheyenne.

The very first night I slept at Cheyenne Bremmer's house was crazy. His cat was jealous of me, and wouldn't let me get close to him in bed, so we had to lock him out of the bedroom. I woke up around 3:00 a.m., slipped my panties on, and one of Cheyenne's T-shirts, and drifted across the hall to the bathroom. I was startled to find his parents sitting at the dining room table drinking coffee and smoking cigarettes. I halted, frozen in my tracks, like a deer in headlights. His mom smiled at me; his dad just stared. When I was finished, I quietly left the bathroom and ran back to Cheyenne's bedroom.

"Your mom and dad are awake watching TV and drinking coffee!"

"They get up at that time every morning to watch the lies."

"What lies?"

"You know, what some people call the news!" he said.

"Cheyenne, I was embarrassed," I said.

"Adriana, like they don't know what we're doing in here?"

"It just made me feel funny."

"Come here, hon." He liked to call me that. "I can make you feel another way, and I promise it won't be funny."

He pulled my panties down and put his head between my legs. When I finally came, he held his hand over my mouth so my moans were muffled.

I was certainly making up for lost time having been without regular sex in my life for a while, but somewhere deep inside me, I wondered how long this love affair could possibly last. It's difficult to overcome a big age difference, especially when it's the woman who's older. Society seems to accept it when the man is older in a relationship, but not when the man is younger.

When I woke up the next morning, Cheyenne was still asleep. I got dressed and opened the bedroom door. His cat was right there waiting to take my place. The gray tiger cat with green eyes leaped on the bed as I closed the door behind me. I walked into the kitchen and found Pricilla sitting at the table drinking coffee and still smoking cigarettes.

"Do you drink coffee?" she asked.

"Couldn't start my day without it," I answered.

She set her cigarette on the edge of the ashtray and walked to the counter, reached for a mug in the cabinet above and poured me a cup. We sat there together not saying much.

"Where's Jim?" I asked, pouring milk in my coffee.

"He's gone to work."

I felt awkward until Cheyenne walked into the kitchen carrying his cat, wearing only his jeans; his numerous tattoos visible. I felt a glow until he went to the sink to get a glass of water, and my eyes settled on the scratches down his back. Scratches that I'd obviously put there during sex. I was embarrassed and horrified.

Pricilla looked at his back, then looked at me, but she didn't comment. I wanted to crawl into a hole. Cheyenne popped a slice of white bread in the toaster and asked if I was hungry. I got up and stood next to him at the counter. I whispered in his ear that he had scratches on his back. His face broke into a self-satisfied grin, and he was about to laugh when I kicked him. He went back to his bedroom and put on a T-shirt.

His dad walked through the front door, and I could tell he wasn't in a good mood.

"Just getting up now? Does this mean you're not working with me today?" Jim asked, looking at his son. Then his eyes shifted to me, hinting that I was the cause of his truancy.

"I'm taking the day off. Adriana's here, and I want to show her around the property."

"I'll leave the golf cart for you," Jim said, reluctantly. He lit a cigarette and poured himself a mug of coffee. He didn't sit down at the table, just stood against the kitchen counter staring at me.

I felt very uneasy. I sensed a strained dynamic between Cheyenne and his dad. I understood that dynamic. You never quite live up to their expectations or standards. Jim finished his coffee and stomped his cigarette out in the ashtray. He kissed Pricilla on the cheek, gave a disapproving glance in my direction, and walked out the front door.

The Bremmers had a nice setup in staff housing on the golf course—a two bedroom, two bath, with an enclosed porch, which Cheyenne used as a music room. Cheyenne took me by the hand and led me to the porch. I saw a bass guitar against the wall and a large amplifier. He plugged his bass in and sat on the couch. I sat on the opposite end listening to him play riffs. His fingers were fast, and the sounds were random. Nothing I heard reminded me of a familiar song, but I could tell he was talented. He'd look up once in a while. His eyes were deep pools of turquoise blue, the color I once saw in the shallow areas of the ocean in Puerto Rico. *One could get lost in those eyes*, I thought.

That next weekend, we drove up the mountain to the house on Red Road. I let Cheyenne drive the Cherokee. As soon as we turned off Haleakala Highway and headed up that winding road to Olinda I was overcome with emotion.

My eyes teared. "I can't stand it! Every time I drive up this road my stomach falls out thinking of Rebel."

"He's in a better place now; you know that."

"I wish I did, but the truth is I have no idea what happened to him."

"Don't believe the crazy shit people tell you," he said.

"Honestly, I would have rather had him put to sleep then not know what happened to him. At least I'd know he's at peace, and not suffering or starving somewhere in the woods."

Cheyenne caressed my hand. "I understand, but there's nothing you can do about it."

"Life can be brutal sometimes," I said.

"Just have faith that if anything bad happened it's over by now."

I stared straight ahead as we forged our way up the mountain until we turned onto Red Road. When we arrived at the house Helga and Harry were in the kitchen.

"I figured you guys were driving up, so I made dinner," Harry said.

"I'll start a fire," Cheyenne said.

Cheyenne tossed wood in the wood-burning stove. I wanted to show him how good I was at making a fire, but I let him do it. My mind drifted to the past Christmas, sitting in front of the fire with Rebel. I have a beautiful photo of Rebel and me sitting on the floor next to the wood-burning stove. Rebel had a white beard by then. Perhaps Helga was right—that Rebel, being an old dog, went off somewhere to die. I felt no redemption, only guilt, in the way Rebel came to his end. Derick Ellis flashed across my mind. The one loving thing he did before walking out on me for the last time, was to leave Rebel behind to love me. A warm feeling swept over me, and I mouthed "thank you," as if maybe Derick could hear me.

"Whatcha thinkin' about?" Cheyenne asked.

"Crazy shit," I said.

I watched the flames flare up in the open stove and felt the warmth of the fire on my face. Cheyenne put his arm around me, and we hung out quietly until Harry called us into the dining room for dinner. There was a jovial atmosphere at the table. Helga mentioned that she had made an apple pie for dessert. There was no mention of the wormy cookie dough.

Harry took the bottle of tequila out of the pantry, and we did some shots. He whispered in my ear that there was a present for me in the bathroom. I excused myself from the table and went to the bathroom to investigate. I looked behind the Buddha—that was our hiding place—and found a halfie plastic bag of cocaine and a tiny spoon. Helga didn't like Harry doing that stuff, but we liked it once in a while. I snorted up a bit in each nostril and came back to the table.

Harry looked at the remenants of the apple pie and then at me. "The rest is for you guys," he said. I knew exactly what he meant. Before we went to bed that night I retrieved what was left of the coke from behind the Buddha, and walked to my bedroom. I couldn't wait to share it with Cheyenne, and looked forward to a night filled with chills and thrills.

In the morning, I left Cheyenne in bed sleeping. Harry and Helga took Gizmo for a hike farther up the mountain. I was in the mood to paint. I took out some white T-shirts and set myself up on the island in the kitchen under the skylight, covering the counter with newspaper. I hadn't painted in a while and was feeling motivated. Images flowed out onto the cloth easily. I was so lost in creativity that I didn't notice Cheyenne.

"You didn't mention you were an artist," he said, rousing me from my concentration.

"It's been a while since I painted. I lost my artistic mojo when Rebel disappeared."

"I love the way you put your hair up with a chopstick," he said, with a dreamy gaze.

"I left barrettes behind when I moved to Maui."

He hesitated and didn't put his arms around me keeping his distance. I suppose he didn't want to disrupt my creative energy stream. He walked past me into the living room and switched the radio on. His choice of a music station was unfamiliar to me.

"Who's that?" I shouted.

"Metallica! Their song, "'Nothing Else Matters.'" Cheyenne said. He walked out to the deck and slumped in one of the chairs, gazing toward the forest.

We were in our own worlds, yet very much together.

CHAPTER 10

BACK IN THE HOOD

Love is the flower of life, blossoms unexpectedly and without law, and must be plucked where it is found, and enjoyed for the brief hour of its duration.

—D. H. Lawrence

It was a busy summer. I was working all over the island with Abigail's Distinctive Affairs, and bartending part-time at the Italian restaurant in Kapalua. I tried to limit my days helping Bubba with breakfast baskets at the kitchen, unless he was really in a bind. When I did, I'd invariably end up at Black Tar's music studio. I was introduced to some heavy metal rock bands I'd never heard of like Slayer, Megadeth, Alice in Chains, and Cheyenne's favorite, Pantera. This music was foreign to me. It sounded angry, had a beat but no rhythm, and seemed so different than his sensibilities. Cheyenne was actually a very caring and sensuous guy. None of it added up in my head. Of course it was a generational difference I didn't want to admit at the time.

There were three other guys in Black Tar—a guitar player with a very biblical name, Ephraim, who had a wife and kid; a drummer, Tom, who was a close friend of Cheyenne's; and the singer, Dunk, who ran back and forth on stage yelling the song lyrics in a hoarse voice. Dunk was an attractive guy—most lead singers are. He had a shaved head, a patch of hair under his lip, and nice features. I never understood why a young guy would shave his head while he still had hair.

We frequented the Sly Mongoose bar, which was conveniently located between the catering kitchen and the band's studio. Back then it was a ratty, no-frills watering hole for locals, as it was off the tourist's beaten path. A real French bakery was in the same perimeter, but you had to get there before noon if you wanted your breads and pastries of choice.

It was a particularly hot summer that year. Cheyenne and I went to the movies in Lahaina to see the new Clint Eastwood flick, *The Unforgiven*. The movie theater was a place to spend a couple of hours to get out of the heat. I stayed at his house that night. He had a huge fight with his dad. It was an ugly scene. Jim had an idea of what Cheyenne should be doing with his life. Cheyenne had his own aspirations.

Cheyenne's mom, Pricilla, stood up and stepped between them breaking up the argument. Cheyenne and I retreated to his bedroom.

"What the hell do you think that accomplished?" I asked.

"He pisses me off."

"I get that, but you are living under his roof. His rules, no?"

"He doesn't understand me. He thinks I'm a dreamer."

I laughed. "Parents never understand their offspring."

"Maybe so, but I'm beginning to think it was a mistake coming here with them."

"What would you be doing back in Arizona?" I asked.

"I don't know. I was going through a breakup with this girl I'd been seeing. And the band I was with back there dissolved. I guess I needed a change of scenery."

"Oh, I know how that is, but we bring ourselves with us wherever we go."

Cheyenne was digesting my words. "Let's go to the studio so I can clear my head."

He borrowed Jim's van, and we drove to the studio.

"I need a shot of something to calm me down," Cheyenne said. Tom, Cheyenne's drummer, was sitting at a table with a woman when we walked into the sly Mongoose. We sat at the bar. Tom smiled at me, but Cheyenne didn't acknowledge him. We did a couple of shots of tequila gold, and Cheyenne had a beer chaser. We walked out of the bar and up the stairs to the studio.

Cheyenne leaned against the wooden railing and took out a pack of Marlboros from the pocket of his tight black jeans, lit a cigarette, and took a drag.

"Cheyenne, how come you didn't say hi to Tom?"

"He's with a different chick every time I see him. They're all whooahs (whores)."

"That's harsh," I said.

"He does too many drugs and sleeps with too many different women. He's gonna get something. There won't be a good end to him if he keeps this up."

"Who's being daddy now?" I asked, playfully.

"I've tried to talk to him, but he won't listen. He just laughs it off."

"You can't tell other people how to live their lives. Isn't that what you were just complaining about with your dad?"

"I guess you're right, but this could be a matter of life or death with AIDS spreading."

"I told you I was a hippie once and lived on a commune. My life is different now. Monogamy is a personal choice. I have friends who died of AIDS."

"So you understand my concern. I love the guy," he said.

"But you can't control someone else's behavior, only your own, and sometimes not even that!"

He unlocked the door and we went inside the studio. Tom's drum set sat in the corner, and there were a number of guitars scattered around. Large speakers and amplifiers were stacked one on top of another, and there were empty beer bottles, ashtrays full of cigarette butts, and a synthesizer. Cheyenne liked to work on that for special sound effects when the band was practicing. He plugged in his bass guitar and began playing riffs, and he seemed transported to a calm and happy place. I liked when he played by himself. I was able to follow the music better, and could actually hear harmonic tunes. When the whole band was playing, the music moshed together, got random and crazy, and it was hard deciphering anything.

He slipped a cassette in the stereo receiver, as he often did, because he wanted me to listen to something he was into. I flashed on Dominick French, and how he would put me through hours of records that he'd chosen specifically for me to listen to. Was it a musician thing, or a man thing? I wasn't sure.

"Cheyenne, I really like that. Whose music is it?"

"Nirvana. Kurt Cobain's song 'Come as You Are.'"

"It has a unique style and sound," I remarked.

"Finally found something you like hon?" Cheyenne said, smirking.

When the song was over Cheyenne played it on his bass. It was so beautifully done that I teared up a little.

"Chey [pronounced Shy], that's beautiful. You're beautiful," I said, touching his arm. "I love you."

He put the bass down standing it against the wall, and reached his arm out for me. He pulled me to him, hugging me tight, and kissing me on the lips. He held me away from him and said, "I needed that. I love you too Adriana."

> Music is the divine way to tell beautiful, poetic things to
> the heart.
>
> —Pablo Casals, cellist and composer

The next morning I woke up before Cheyenne. I got dressed and opened the door letting his cat in. I went to the kitchen where I knew Pricilla would be sitting with a cup of coffee. Sure enough, there she was. She smiled at me, watching me get a mug out of the cabinet and pouring myself a cup of coffee. I sat down at the table with her, ignoring the nasty ashtray filled with cigarette butts.

"You guys got home late last night," she said.

"We stopped at the studio. Cheyenne can spend hours there."

"Do you think my son is talented?" she asked.

"Very," I said.

"I do too, but Jim thinks he should be thinking of a career that pays."

"I hear ya, but discouraging someone's talent won't end well."

"I'm between the devil and the deep blue sea," she said.

"I can just imagine," I replied.

"Cheyenne thinks he's going to be a rock star."

"I'm sure he does. Why don't you let him find out for himself?"

"It's hard being between father and son."

"Pricilla, I feel weird about our age difference," I said, abruptly changing the subject.

Pricilla laughed. "When Cheyenne was seventeen he dated a forty-year-old woman."

I stared at her. "So are you saying he's always liked older women?"

"He's had young girlfriends! What I'm saying is my son's an old soul."

Cheyenne walked into the kitchen so I switched the topic of conversation.

"We were just talking about the Woody Allen scandal," I said.

"That guy is a creep," Cheyenne said, lighting a Marlboro. "He took up with his wife's daughter. Isn't that called incest?"

"She was adopted. There's no blood relation there," I said.

"But she's just a kid," Cheyenne said.

I got up from the table. I had to work my day shift at the Italian restaurant. I took a shower, got dressed, and drove to work. Cheyenne was working with Jim at the hotel that day. He did maintenance, handyman, and electrical work. On the drive to Kapalua I thought about Pricilla's comment about Cheyenne being an old soul. He did come across as old-fashioned for such a young guy, and a heavy metal musician to boot. He and I connected as if we'd been partners in another life. It was weird. But where was our relationship going? Could it be the right person but the wrong time?

When Cheyenne got out of work, he often hung out at the bar in the Italian restaurant. He knew I'd slip him beers while I was bartending. He would chat with the regulars who came in for happy hour each day. One of the regulars worked in a jewelry store in the same shopping center as the restaurant. She was having an intimate conversation with Cheyenne, and I wondered what it was all about. When the bar began to get busy, Cheyenne faded with a, "See you at home."

"What's going on?" I asked, after he'd gone.

"Your boyfriend is looking for a piece of jewelry for your birthday."

"I don't know now if I should have asked you," I said.

She laughed. "Why don't you come by the store and I'll show you what he's been looking at, and you let me know which rings you like. I'll steer him in the right direction."

A few days later, I walked to the jewelry store when I finished my day shift at the Italian restaurant. I browsed through the ring selections Cheyenne had set aside. My eye drifted to a mostly white opal set in gold, with three small diamonds on either side. I let her know that was the one I preferred.

On my birthday Cheyenne watched me open the jewelry box. It was the ring I'd most gravitated to. I threw my arms around him, "I love it Chey."

"Happy birthday hon," he said, beaming with pride.

On September 5, 1992, Hurricane Iniki struck the Hawaiian Islands, devastating the island of Kauai. I went to the Italian restaurant to help them board up, while Cheyenne helped Jim ready the Royal Lahaina for impact. It was a scary time. Luckily, the island of Maui escaped disaster, but the island of Kauai got the brunt of the storm. A few days later, I was at work when Cheyenne called to tell me that he and his father were being sent to Kauai to work on a hotel there that was owned by the same company as the Royal Lahaina. It was a beachfront hotel that had been hit hard and was without electricity.

"My mom knows more about the situation, so get with her after work. I don't have time to explain everything," he said, hanging up the phone.

After work, I drove to their house and found Pricilla sitting at the dining room table, smoking a cigarette.

"You do know that will take at least ten years off your life," I said.

"It's too late. I've already had cancer," she said.

I stared at her thinking she was being reckless as she took another drag. "What's going on?" I asked.

"Jim and Cheyenne flew to Honolulu. They will be flown by military jet to the island of Kauai, since no commercial flights are running. The runway there was damaged, and I guess all of Hawaii is under a state of emergency."

"Wow. For how long?" I asked.

"Who knows? We'll have to wait until we hear from them."

I stayed with Pricilla that night, feeling like a deserted World War II war bride. The next day I felt the need to drive up the mountain to the house on Red Road. I hadn't been up there for almost a week. I drove past boats washed up on the beach, downed trees and utility poles, with debris all over the roadways. I had that same awful feeling as I turned off Haleakala Highway and headed toward the road up to Olinda, praying I wouldn't see any missing dog posters. It was a beautiful sunny day—the calm after the storm. People had stripped the stores of canned goods, bottled water, and paper products, which was common during emergencies. Living on a remote island in the middle of the Pacific Ocean, you rely on most products to be flown in, or arrive on barges by sea. I wondered if we'd have to use leaves for toilet paper, but found an adequate supply of TP at the house. I sat on the outside deck for a while, staring into the forest. I knew Hackman and Hargrove were looking for another house in the area. I didn't want to live up on the mountain any longer, but this wasn't the time to discuss it.

The next week I drove to Lahaina to work my three days at the Italian restaurant, and Pricilla was happy I was staying with her. She felt alone with both of her men gone to Kauai. It was like sending them off to fight a war, only we knew they were coming back alive. Two weeks passed without a word. On the third week, I happened to be sitting with her in the living room watching television when the phone rang.

"It's Cheyenne," she yelled.

I stood in front of her. "What does he say? What's going on over there?"

She waved her hand shushing me while she talked to him. "He wants to talk to you," she said, handing me the phone.

"Cheyenne, how's it going over there on Kauai?"

"It's a total mess, like a war zone. The lines to use the telephones are fucking crazy. I had to wait over two hours for my turn," he said.

"I miss you," I said.

"Damn, I miss you too. I'm not sure how long we'll be over here. I rigged the electricity in our room so at least we have lights, but the rest of the hotel is still in the dark."

"What about the grocery stores?"

"things are being black-marketed. I had to pay twelve dollars for a six-pack of Coca-Cola. It's ridiculous."

"Jesus. That's just nuts."

"Well, I have to get off. There's a line of people waiting to make calls."

"Okay. I love you," I said, handing the phone back to Pricilla.

This situation went on until things were stabilized at the hotel on Kauai. It was a strange time in the islands, one that none of us will ever forget.

The Italian restaurant asked me to work full time. When Harry Hackman told me they'd found another house in Olinda, I told them I'd decided to move back to the west side of the island, and that I would be working in Kapalua full time. Driving up and down the mountain every day would be ridiculous, and I wasn't going to pay rent on a house to only spend weekends there. Living with Cheyenne at his parents' house was out of the question. I found a studio apartment in Napili Hui, the same complex I'd lived in back in the mid-seventies. I was back in the hood. The condo apartment was a corner unit on the ground level next to a gulch. I was familiar with the property, and it was not far from the Italian restaurant.

When Jim and Cheyenne finally returned to Maui from Kauai, Pricilla told Cheyenne that I'd gotten an apartment in Napili. I was home when the phone rang.

"My mom gave me your new phone number," Cheyenne said.

"I'm so glad you're back on Maui. You'll like this place. It's small, but it's mine."

"You mean you're not gonna live here with me?" Cheyenne asked.

"Chey, that won't work. It would be too uncomfortable for me."

"How do I get to your place?" he asked.

"This guy upcountry helped me move with his pickup truck. The owner of the house on Red Road said I could take the bed. He was selling the house anyway."

"What guy?" he asked.

"Just a friend of ours, a neighbor."

"Just tell me how to get to your place? I want to see you. It's been a while."

I gave him directions to Napili Hui, which was only about a fifteen-minute drive north of Kaanapali. I was putting away dishes in the kitchen cabinet when I heard a knock at the door. Cheyenne was standing in the doorway, his long reddish-brown hair loose. He stepped inside and closed the door. He stood there staring at me, then rotated his eyes around suspiciously, as if he thought someone was hiding behind the drapes or under the bed.

I stared back at him. "Chey, what are you looking for?"

He zoomed in on the bed like a hawk looking for prey. Realizing I was alone he turned toward me and smiled. We embraced and he kissed me long and hard. He led me to the bed and sat down. I stood in front of him staring down at the intense expression on his face. Then his eyes softened. I sat down next to him and took one of his hands. That's when I noticed his hands were filthy.

We started making out; his tongue ran across my lips and into my mouth. "Take your panties off," he whispered.

"Did you wash your hands?" I asked.

A strange look inhabited his face. He stood up and walked to the bathroom, and I soon heard the water running.

He walked toward the bed with his hands up in the air, like a surgeon wearing latex gloves ready to perform surgery. We both began to laugh. Then we became quiet. I pulled my dress up, took my panties off, and fell back onto the bed. His hands were all over me like cream cheese on a bagel. He unhooked my bra and played with my breasts under my dress, making the nipples hard. Then he moved one hand down to my snatch, using his fingers to see if I was wet. He got on top of me and fucked me hard, like he hadn't been with a woman in years. There was a lot of grunting and heavy breathing. It was quite invigorating.

After we came back to our senses, he told me he'd had an accident.

"You had an accident? Where? Is that why your hands were so dirty?"

"I borrowed my friend's car. I didn't see a median, and I flattened two of his tires."

"Oh shit. Where's the car?" I asked.

"It's here on the street, but I think I ruined the rims driving the rest of the way."

"What are you going to do?"

"I'll call Tom to help me out before band practice. I'm sure I'll have to buy two new tires. I'm hoping the rims won't need replacing. Still, I'm glad I'm here."

I thought that was a crazy thing he did, but it showed me his determination to be with me, like in that old acoustic Elvis song "Trying to Get to You."

The truth is that Cheyenne Bremmer never left.

Cheyenne purchased a used Camaro. I loved driving that car. If Black Tar had a gig somewhere on the island, he'd take my Jeep Cherokee, which had room for all the band equipment, and I'd take his Camaro. Driving the Camaro was like driving a hot rod. It had a lot of power. As soon as I stepped on the gas, that thing went from zero to sixty in a second.

We were both making descent money, so we took a weekend trip to Honolulu to do some shopping and have some fun. We flew out of the small Kapalua Airport, which was only a few minutes from the hood. I remember that day so well. I wore a black pencil skirt; a tight-fitting, sheer, paisley, stretch blouse; and tights with a bold pattern. Cheyenne paraded me around like I was a model. I was still hot at forty-seven years of age.

When we arrived at the outer island terminal at Honolulu International Airport, we hailed a taxi to the Ala Moana Hotel, a place I'd stayed many times with Annie Hughes. We checked into our hotel room. I was hanging up some stuff in the closet when I saw Cheyenne fanning a stack of hundred-dollar bills. I suggested we meet at the Steakhouse for lunch at noon, as I walked out the front door. I liked shopping alone. I hit all my favorite stores, dodging the men and women in the mall who accosted passersby with hand lotions and hair straighteners. Sears, Liberty House, and JC Penney, were the anchor stores back in the nineties. Those stores are all gone now.

I walked toward the Steakhouse and saw Cheyenne standing against the building in his tight black jeans, white T-shirt, and aviator sunglasses, like he was posing for a men's magazine. He had one leg bent against the wall and was smoking a Marlboro. I noticed a package on the ground next to him. He looked up and smiled at me. We went into the Steakhouse and found a table. He ordered a Steinlager, and I ordered a bloody Mary.

"You know, Annie and I had lunch here when I had my kidney stones blasted at Queens Medical Center a couple of years ago. I woke up in the hospital to a huge teddy bear just inches from my head on the pillow," I said, laughing.

"She's a riot. She treats you like a little girl."

"After the procedure, she wouldn't let me be alone in the hotel room. She went to the lobby for a drink and returned with a figurine of a Hawaiian man and woman on a canoe. "So you won't ever forget me,'" she said. How in the world could I ever forget Annie?"

"You're like a daughter to her."

"Chey, what's in the package?"

"I bought a camera and some lenses. Blew my whole wad of cash!"

"Are you telling me you didn't save any money for tomorrow?"

"Don't be mad at me," he said, reaching for my hand and rubbing it.

"I guess I'm paying for the next couple of days."

Cheyenne stared at me with a sullen expression, not answering. Suddenly my mood turned somber. I was pissed but wasn't going to let his thoughtlessness ruin the trip. He ordered a steak, and I ordered a Caesar salad with blackened Ahi. He jabbered away about the telephoto lens while we were eating. I sipped my bloody Mary in silence. When the bill came, I handed the waiter my credit card. Cheyenne turned his eyes away.

I got up from the table and announced, "I'm going back to the mall. I'll see you back at the hotel."

Later that evening he told me he'd found a great head shop with all sorts of bongs and related drug paraphernalia (he liked smoking pot), and he'd seen a cool T-shirt but didn't have the money to buy it.

Lesson learned, I thought. Then I realized that I did things like that when I was his age. I marked it up to youthful folly. Our weekend trip to Honolulu together was more of a lesson than a vacation for both of us.

I worked a function up on Haleakala with Abigail's Distinctive Affairs. It was on a big estate with a lot of land. I parked on a slope and walked to the house. The host of the party had two beautiful golden retrievers that just had twelve puppies. Despite its being a beautiful estate home with very expensive furniture and rugs, these puppies had the run of the house. I was setting up with Abby when the host walked into the kitchen carrying one of the puppies in his arms as if it was his new grandchild. This very wealthy man definitely had a big heart; in fact, the function was a philanthropic group meeting to discuss problems facing Hawaii.

After we cleaned up and the guys loaded the van, I walked to my car, got in, and turned the ignition. Every time I stepped on the gas pedal the car slid backwards, even though it was in drive. I tried again, and it slipped farther toward the edge of a deep gulch. Abby's son Ben, who was in charge of parking cars, motioned for me to roll the window down.

"I'm afraid the Jeep will tumble down into the gulch with me in it."

"Put it in park, set the emergency break, and get out," Ben said.

I did as Ben directed. I watched him get in the driver's seat and shift the Cherokee into four-wheel drive. He very slowly let the Jeep slide down the hill backwards until he reached a place where it leveled off, and he was able to turn it around. He drove the Cherokee straight down into the steep ravine. I saw the Cherokee smoking as he drove it up the opposite side, so much so, that I was afraid the engine would catch fire. He finally reached the road and drove back up to the house. I hugged and thanked Ben. I got in the Cherokee and drove toward Haleakala Highway, relieved and thankful, but checking for smoke the whole way home.

It was late when I reached the kitchen in Lahaina, but I figured the guys were still at band practice. I walked into a loud, smoky studio. Tom smiled at me, and the other guys stopped playing. Cheyenne put down his bass and walked outside with me.

"How was the party?" he asked, lighting up a marlborough.

"Party was great. Getting my car off the precipice of a gulch, not so easy." I told him the story of how Ben saved the Cherokee Chief, and me, from tumbling into a gulch. While we were standing there talking, Tom came out to join us. He leaned against the wooden railing of the staircase.

"You're a good drummer, Tom," I said.

"Thanks." He smiled, his blue eyes widening with appreciation. He rattled off the names of some drummers he admired.

"Are you familiar with Gene Krupa?" I asked.

"Who's that?" Tom asked.

"They say he was the best drummer who ever lived."

"Never heard of him," Tom said.

I wasn't surprised since it was a totally different generation—my parents' generation, in fact. "Well, you should look him up. They say he was the fastest drummer ever."

"I will," he said, still smiling.

Just then, a beautiful girl walked up the stairs and right over to Tom. He hugged her, and they walked down the stairs together and into the Sly Mongoose.

"Another one!" Cheyenne remarked.

"Stop it. Stop judging," I said.

When we were home that night, I asked Cheyenne what his bandmates thought of me. He began to chuckle, and I could tell he wasn't keen on telling me.

"Come on, tell me," I said.

"They used to tease me a lot when I first started dating you. They'd ask me if I was going to see my mother."

"Oh God," I said.

"Now that they know you, they like you."

"That's hard to take," I said. "But I did ask."

"What about you? What do your girlfriends think about you living with a young stud?"

"Some of them nervously laugh about it. One woman remarked that I was the only one in our group actually having sex."

"I don't care how old you are or how young I am. We're good together, he said"

"I feel the same way." *You can't help who you fall in love with*, I thought.

Cheyenne became tight friends with the surfer dude who lived in the condo apartment above ours. Brice Gordon was about thirty. He was always tan, had a sleek surfer's body, and dark, short-cropped hair. He had a habit of squinting his eyes to make a point when he spoke. He told us he'd grown up on the island of Oahu, and that his mother still owned a house there in Ewa Beach. She was Japanese, and his dad was German. Cheyenne spent hours upstairs in Brice's condo.

Driving to the other side of the island, the original dirt road is carved into the hillside, still visible from the highway that connects east to west Maui. Brice told us that his mother used that old dirt road in a horse and buggy when she was young, and that the trip took most of the day.

Napili Hui had a nice-sized pool, and we enjoyed swimming on hot afternoons. I was sitting on the edge in my bikini, enjoying the sun. Cheyenne dove in headfirst. I slid off the ledge and bobbed around in the cool water. He came up from under the water, stood up, and stared down at me.

"You know you have a better body than some of the younger girls I see."

"Everyone is beautiful when you're in love with them," I said, instead of taking the compliment.

"No, I mean it. I've looked around," he said.

"Chey, you're hot stuff yourself. I see the way women look at you."

He laughed in short bursts and splashed me.

I caught sight of Brice Gordon walking past the pool with his surfboard under his arm. He was dripping wet from the ocean.

"Brice!" I yelled.

He walked toward the pool and peered over the wall. "Come upstairs when you guys get out."

"We'll be up in an hour or so," Cheyenne shouted from the water.

We walked back to the condo and took a shower together. Cheyenne slipped into his rice bag pants, I put on a sundress, and we walked upstairs to Brice's apartment. He had some strong weed. He rolled a joint and passed it around. I wasn't that fond of marijuana anymore, so I didn't stay long. I left the two guys toking and talking story (Hawaiian phrase for sharing personal experiences and tales.)

Brice Gordon had an old beat-up car, what locals call a Maui Cruiser. Being an avid surfer, there were always surfboards on the roof of his car in case he ran into some killer waves while driving around the island. I was watching TV when the guys knocked on the door. Brice wanted to take a ride up north to Slaughterhouse Beach. He'd heard there were some big sets going off due to a sudden swell.

We were driving north on a winding road, the three of us in the front seat, when a pigeon flew into the windshield with a loud thud. Cheyenne yelled out, "Stop the car!"

Brice pulled over, Cheyenne jumped out, and we followed.

"What are you doing?" I shouted.

"It's probably just stunned," Cheyenne said.

I'd heard of clubs that raced pigeons from one island to another for money. Most pigeons were never seen again. But if a pigeon succeeded and was found on another island, the owner received prize money.

Brice and I watched Cheyenne pick up the lifeless bird and hold it between his hands very gently. I wasn't sure what Cheyenne expected to happen. The bird opened its eyes, Cheyenne opened his hands, and it flew away.

"Was that a fucking miracle we just witnessed?" Brice said, squinting his eyes.

"I've done this before," Cheyenne said.

"The bird whisperer," Brice said, laughing.

"Cheyenne, that was amazing," I said, touching his arm affectionately.

I could tell he was proud of himself, but I felt there was so much more to it. He seemed to not even believe for a moment that the pigeon was dead. Perhaps he had an uncanny cosmic connection. That was the day I fell totally, and hopelessly, in love with Cheyenne Bremmer.

> If you talk with the animals they will talk with you and you will know each other. If you do not talk to them you will not know them and what you do not know you will fear. What one fears, one destroys.
> —Chief Dan George, Tsleil-Waututh Nation

A heavy rainstorm flooded low-lying areas of Maui. Cheyenne and I were hanging out in the condo when there was banging on our front door. It had been raining hard for hours. I opened the door and water rushed past the entrance. The guy standing in the doorway was yelling for us to come help fill sandbags because some of the ground floor units in the hood were getting flooded. I walked to the edge of the gulch beside the condo, which was always dry, and saw it had become a raging river flowing swiftly toward the sea. I wondered what had happened to the goats that always grazed in the gulch. I'd hoped someone had rescued them, so they weren't washed out to sea with the flash flood.

We joined a line of neighbors filling plastic bags with sand as the rain beat down on us. It was a crazy day, and we were relieved when the storm subsided. It was still raining when we walked back to the condo.

"Shots are in order," Cheyenne said, taking the Jägermeister out of the freezer.

We spent the afternoon doing shots, listening to music, and talking story. Wasn't much else to do on a stormy day. I knew what was on his mind when Cheyenne locked the front door. He smiled at me coyly. I lay down on the bed and took my bra and panties off. I left my dress on, pulling it up to the top of my thighs. Perhaps I wanted to leave a little mystery in his mind, or maybe I felt uptight about my age.

He walked toward me and stood beside the bed. "Come on, stop teasing and take it off," he said. He unzipped his jeans and I watched them drop to the floor.

The lower half of my body was on fire. He took his T-shirt off and got on top of me, his weight heavy. I could hear the rain beating against the door which added to my sensibilities.

The next day, in total contrast, was bright and sunny as if there had never been a rainstorm. A neighbor who lived in the next building was giving away cockatiels. Cheyenne coaxed me into walking to her condo to see them. I was reluctant to get a pet of any kind. I was still wounded from the loss of Rebel, but he was keen on the idea. He knocked on her door, and she let us in. She introduced herself as April. She was a big girl, not fat, just tall and solid. She had long, wavy, blonde hair and a pleasant face. She seemed to like Cheyenne a little too much to my liking. I noticed that she let her birds fly loose around the apartment. Her cockatiels had just had babies, and they were awfully cute.

"I'd like you guys to take a pair, brother and sister," she said, explaining that they'd have each other for company. I watched Cheyenne play with one of the adult cockatiels. The bird took to him right away. *Sure, the bird whisperer*, I thought. I was astonished that one of the birds jumped right on his finger and let him massage the back of its head. We agreed to take two of them when they were older. I always found it interesting the way men felt the need to nest immediately upon falling in love, no pun intended.

As soon as we were back in our condo, I told Cheyenne that I thought April had a thing for him. He told me I was being silly. I wasn't really jealous. I suppose I knew there was no way I could possibly compete with women his age. But still, it bothered me. On the other hand, Cheyenne was jealous of Logan Baxter. One of the waitresses I worked with at the Italian restaurant, Mary, lived in the hood. She also worked for the catering company. Sometimes we'd all hang out together before or after work. If Cheyenne came home and found me in her apartment, and Logan Baxter was among the group, he'd throw a hissy fit. At the beginning I marked it up to youthful insecurity.

I was sitting on the couch in Mary's condo, Logan was sitting next to me. We were all talking and laughing about the party we worked that night. Out of the corner of my eye I noticed Cheyenne standing in Mary's doorway wagging his finger at me to come home, like I was a naughty little girl. When I got back to our condo he was so mad he took his hand and shoved me backwards onto the bed. This was getting out of control. That night when Cheyenne went to the studio for band practice, I marched myself upstairs to talk to his friend Brice Gordon.

"Brice, Cheyenne got a little rough with me today and I don't like it. I haven't given him any reason to be jealous of me. I don't know what to do."

"Really? That's not good. You leave him to me," Brice said, squinting his eyes.

I have no idea what Brice told him, but Cheyenne never got rough with me again.

That September, I knew I wanted to spend the holidays with Cheyenne, so I planned a short trip to New York to visit my family before Thanksgiving. My dad wasn't doing well, and my mother wanted to talk to me about looking for a nursing home. She said that he was becoming a handful, leaving the house at all hours of the day and night, and would often get lost. My dad was well into his eighties now, and even though my mother was younger than him, she had health issues. The situation was becoming too much for her to handle. She told me she'd explain it all when I got there.

Cheyenne handed me a list of heavy metal rock band cassettes that he wasn't able to find on Maui. I told him I'd try my best to look for them in a music store in New York City.

On the day I left, he drove me to Kahului Airport. We kissed goodbye at the gate. I hated leaving Maui, but most of all, I hated leaving Cheyenne Bremmer.

CHAPTER 11

YOU'RE A BIG GIRL NOW

To be a man of knowledge has no permanence. One
is never a man of knowledge, not really
When a man starts to learn, he is never clear about his objectives.
His purpose is faulty; He hopes for rewards that will never
materialize, for he knows nothing of the hardship of learning.
The *Teachings of Don Juan* by Carlos Castaneda

I arrived at LaGuardia Airport in the afternoon, but no one was there to meet me. It wasn't a surprise, as my parents weren't driving anymore. In fact, their gold Oldsmobile had been stolen right out of the hospital parking lot while they were at their doctor appointments. I sincerely hoped that whoever stole their car appreciated the statue of the Virgin Mary on the dashboard, and the St. Christopher medal clipped to the sun visor. My mother was actually happy about it, because my father fawned obsessively over the car. He'd peer through the blinds checking to make sure the car was still in the parking space downstairs in front of the apartment building. Still, it was sad.

I hailed a cab from the airport to the northeast Bronx.

I found my father Andre in bad shape. When he hugged me I could feel how frail he was. I had to hold back tears. He did have his lucid moments, but he would sink into bouts of confusion and anger. I imagined it was anger at life in general.

"Don't get old Adriana," he'd say. But how in the world could any of us evade time. We all get old eventually; that is, if we are lucky enough to reach old age. I thought of so many of my friends who were already dead and buried, some of them for a long time; they'd died in their twenties, robbed of their youth. My father basically lived in his pajamas and often slept during the day. My mother Vita remarked that he'd sleep so deeply that she'd hold a mirror under his nose to make sure he was still breathing. I knew it was going to be a difficult trip, but it was more than I'd bargained for. While my father was in the bedroom napping, my mother and I discussed the situation.

"Adriana, since I had the heart attack, only half of my heart works. Then I had a couple of attacks of angina. I just can't deal with your father anymore. I want a divorce."

I listened to her in disbelief. "Ma, Dad is eighty-seven years old. Why now?"

"I can't take him anymore. I don't have the strength I used to have. Your father was always a little crazy, but I had a lot more patience when I was younger."

"Ma, better that we scope out nursing homes than you talking about divorce. At this point that would be abandonment, and you would never forgive yourself."

My mother began to cry. I reached across the dining room table and held her hand. How difficult this was for her. She met my dad when she was eighteen. They'd spent a lifetime together, and went through everything life threw at them.

"Your father wakes up in the middle of the night and fries eggs. When I ask him what he's doing, he says he's making breakfast for Millie. Then I remind him that his sister Millie lives in Brooklyn. The other day I went grocery shopping. I told him to stay on the couch, and that I wouldn't be gone long. When I came home he was gone. I was frantic. Then the bakery called. "'Mrs. Bardolino your husband Andre is here looking for you.'" I had to go back out and get him."

"No Ma, you cannot go on like this. We'll do some research."

My dad walked into the dining room dressed in a suit and tie. We watched him put a tube of Ritz crackers and a banana in one pocket, and an Almond Joy candy bar in the other. Then he took a handful of Brioschi (Italian Alka-Seltzer) and tossed it in the pocket of his white shirt. This was nothing new; he never left the house without snacks and Brioschi.

"Where are you going?" Vita asked.

"I thought I'd open the shop," Andre said.

We stared at him. It had been years since my father retired and closed his barbershop. I wasn't sure how to react.

"No, today's not a day you work," my mother said. "If you want to go out I'll walk with you."

He looked at her a little confused, but then he said, "Yes, I could use a walk."

My mother put on her jacket and they left the apartment together. How quickly he had deteriorated from my last visit. He seemed a little off then, but not to such a degree.

I was so depressed that first day that I actually put my coat on and walked to the OTB (Off Track Betting) parlor that was a few blocks away under the train station. I hadn't even thought of a horse race since I'd left Florida. I realized what my betting addiction was all about—a kind of self-destructiveness in the face of unhappiness, punishing myself for all the things that had gone wrong in my life. I walked through the entrance and saw mostly men staring up at televisions broadcasting the races from Belmont Race Track. I looked at the roster of horses in the upcoming race, and their odds. I picked a couple by their names and placed two-dollar bets on them to win. I'd stare up at the TV screens along with everyone else. I'd either win or lose; it really didn't matter. After the race I watched people tear up losing tickets, some even walking out pissed off. Who knows how much money they bet? Maybe it was money they should have used to make a mortgage payment, or pay a utility bill, not to mention they'd have to face their spouses.

When I got back to my parents' apartment one of my cousins was there with her husband. Ariel was my mother's niece, Victor's stepdaughter from his wife's first marriage. She was quite a bit older than me, so we were never close. She and her husband Bruno had helped my parents a lot as they got older. They'd check up on them, and take them to doctor appointments if needed. They were great people. My not being there to help my parents wore on me, and was a source of guilt. Ariel knew of a state home we should consider for my father. Her own mother was there. Just the title "State home" made me cringe.

My mother's first cat, Alfie, the chocolate point Siamese, had recently died. He lived twenty-five years. He was my mother's first cat-baby, her love, her pride and joy. The other two cats, females, were also well into their twenties. One of my tasks when I visited was to take them to their vet appointments.

I was checking Cookie's claws with the intention of clipping them, when I noticed that they were so long that the tips were curling under and piercing her paws.

"Ma, when was the last time you checked Cookie's feet?"

"I don't know. I've had so much going on with your father."

"Ma, this cat has to go to the vet. She doesn't look so good to me. She's too thin, and her coat looks shabby."

My mother looked dismayed, and I could see that she felt bad. "She hasn't been eating so well lately."

Just then, my dad walked in from the kitchen saying, "Don't take her to the vet. She'll be fine here with us. Nothing good will come of it."

"No, Dad, she's suffering with her paws like this. How can she even walk right?"

"I'm telling you there's nothing but trouble with the vet," he reiterated.

My mother told me to make an appointment and take the cat in. My father shook his head annoyed and left the room.

The next morning, I coaxed Cookie into the cat carrier and took a cab to the vet. The veterinarian checked her over and gave me the diagnosis. Besides her claws, her teeth needed to be cleaned. He imagined she was thin because her gums hurt when she ate. I told him to do whatever was needed. My father was upset when I came home without Cookie, as if the cat was doomed.

The next day, Cookie looked like death warmed over when I picked her up, and the bill was exorbitant. I thought perhaps she was groggy from the anesthetic. When I got her home my parents were relieved.

I was awakened by the sound of my mother in the kitchen making the morning coffee. She disappeared into the bathroom while it was percolating. I got off the couch and immediately looked for Cookie to see how she was feeling. I searched all of her favorite haunts, but no Cookie. I looked under one of the recliners in the living room and found her dead, as stiff as if she'd been stuffed by a taxidermist. I was mortified. This was all my fault. My mother set the coffee pot and cups on the dining room table. I got up and sat across from her. I let her have a few gulps of coffee, waiting for the right time to tell her. Is there ever the right time for such news?

"Ma, I found Cookie dead under the recliner."

She stood up and rushed to the recliner, got on her hands and knees, dragged the stiff cat out, held her, kissed her, and wailed, "Cookie, oh my God, Cookie."

My dad rushed in yelling at me, "I told you not to take her to the vet." He was angry until grief overtook him and he began to cry with my mother. The guilt I felt that day stayed with me forever.

After we all cried we calmed down. My mother told me that she had gotten the cats a plot at Hartsdale Pet Cemetery in Upstate New York after Alfie died. It was quite a drive there, but my cousin Ariel and her husband Bruno offered to take us. Before we left my mom showed me a photo of Alfie in his coffin. At first it seemed weird, but these cats were part of the family so I understood. I took a copy of the photo of the cat in his tiny coffin to show Cheyenne when I got back to Maui.

The pet cemetery was a beautiful, serene place. Walking among the stone monuments that people had erected as memorials to their pets was impressive. I'd heard that Rin Tin Tin, from the famous TV show, was buried there, but we didn't come across his gravesite.

My mother and I went to a lawyer in Manhattan, who advised her to turn over one of her stock funds to me. There was a limit on how many assets, and how much income you could have to enter a state facility, which was really all they could afford. We spent a good portion of the day filling out and signing documents, but neither one of us was ready to bring my father to the nursing home. We hemmed and hawed over the decision. We told my father that he might have to go to the hospital for a few weeks. He had lucid moments when he knew what was going on. He'd comment, "Your mother is sick of me. She wants to put me in a home." I'd been through some painful things in my life, but had no idea just how wretched this was going to be.

My cousin Ariel mentioned that Filomena Genoa was in this particular state facility we had decided on. Filomena was the woman who had taken care of me when I was a child—the woman I thought was my real mother. I decided to visit her, and at the same time I would check out the nursing home. It was a short bus ride from my parents' apartment, which was a deciding factor that helped my mother make the choice. She could visit as often as she liked. I asked at the nurses' station which room Filomena Genoa was in. I got on the elevator and rode up to the second floor. I glanced in each room as I walked along the corridor. I saw old people in various states of health and sanity. I peeked in her room and saw her daughter, Anna Maria, sitting on a chair beside the bed. She stood up, surprised to see me, and we hugged.

"Mom's been here for a while. I spend time with her every day," Anna Maria said.

"She looks good," I remarked.

Then I noticed Filomena had no legs. I didn't want to cry or show her how upset I was.

"Mom, its Adriana. You remember Adriana, don't you?"

Filomena stared at me blankly, not even an inkling of recognition in her soft blue eyes.

"I'm sure Mom remembers you," Anna Maria said, but I knew better.

"It's all right. At least she still knows you," I said.

"Mom lost her legs from diabetes."

"Anna Maria, I'm so sorry. My dad will be coming to this home. Sadly, they probably won't remember each other. He's only lucid part of the time."

I was holding back tears like a fire hydrant that was turned off, not wanting to let loose. After I spent an hour talking to Anna Maria, I hugged her and squeezed Filomena's hand. She smiled at me through vacant eyes. I walked out of the room and down the long corridor. As soon as I got on the elevator the dam broke, and a flood of tears gushed out.

I would eventually go home to Hawaii leaving my mother to go through this on a daily basis. I was overwhelmed with guilt and sadness. For the first time in a long time, I felt the need to go to church. The next day I walked to Our Lady of the Assumption Church, sat in a pew, and prayed for my parents. I prayed for forgiveness for living so far away. I suppose I was aiming for redemption. I was relieved that my mother had three sisters and wonderful neighbors to help her. The woman next door in 3C had been a nun at one time. She offered my mother emotional and spiritual support. That would ease my mind a little when it was time to fly back to Hawaii, but it didn't relieve my guilt.

After Cookie's demise, a trip to Hartsdale Pet Cemetery, and that morose visit with Filomena Genoa in the nursing home, I was feeling depressed and wondered if I was helping my parents at all. I needed a break from doom and gloom. I took the subway to Manhattan. I got out on Forty-Second Street and walked to Fifth Avenue. I had arranged to meet my cousin Jenny for lunch. On my way to the building where she worked, I passed New York City's main public library. The stone lions at the front entrance sat regally, as if guarding the building. It's a fabulous architectural structure, inside and out, often the backdrop for wedding photos and ceremonies. My cousin Jenny had a high-powered job with an international bank. We went to a deli for lunch, and it was nice to catch up. After she went back to work I wandered around the city with my camera taking photos. I had purchased a few rolls of black-and-white film, which suited photographs of skyscrapers and monuments. I flashed on Erik Eschweiler, my German-American boyfriend from the late sixties. We enjoyed roaming around Manhattan taking photos. I had a sudden pang of missing my darkroom, and couldn't even remember what I'd done with the enlarger, chemical trays, and all the photo equipment, when I moved to Hawaii. But this bit of creativity put my head in a much better place.

> We are making photographs to understand what our lives
> mean to us.
> —Ralph M. Hattersley Jr., American photographer

I was putting on lipstick in front of a small gilded framed mirror in the living room. My father asked me where I was going.

"To the OTB," I said.

"Why do you need makeup? The men will think you're a whore."

"Dad, I'm just putting on lipstick. I won't be there long, and I'm not going there to meet someone. I have a boyfriend."

I could see his reflection in the mirror, staring at me with disapproval. Then I heard my mother scream. I ran to the bathroom where she was leaning against the doorway.

"Ma, what's the matter?"

"Your father put his shit in the cat box."

My heart began pounding, and I couldn't get out of there fast enough. I knew it was definitely time for the nursing home.

My father wasn't feeling well, so it seemed like the perfect excuse to make the move. We packed a suitcase and helped my father get dressed, telling him that his doctor wanted him to have a stay at the hospital for observation until he felt better. We took a cab to the nursing home and signed all the necessary forms at the front desk. A nurse walked us to a nice room where my father would be staying. There was another man in the room. At first we thought it was a good thing that my father had company. We got Andre settled in and stayed with him for a couple of hours. It was so hard leaving him there. I was glad that he didn't have all his faculties about him. My father never knew he was in a nursing home; he always thought he was in a hospital and would ask when he could go home.

My mother and I didn't say a word to each other on the bus ride home, or walking up the stairs to the apartment, but as soon as I unlocked the front door my mother broke down. The feeling of walking into the apartment knowing that my father was never coming home, was indescribable. There were no words, only hugs, as we held each other and cried.

After that day Vita settled into a daily routine of visiting him, sometimes twice a day. She'd find that the nice sweater my father had on the day before had been replaced with an old sweater that had holes. Nice clothes and blankets seemed to disappear. There were challenges, but she made sure that he never felt deserted. Occasionally one of her sisters would go with her, and while I was still in New York, I went with her or went by myself to give her a break.

I met my cousin Gia Ferrari in Manhattan on the last week I was in New York. We wanted to go to the Episcopal Cathedral of Saint John the Divine. Our uncle Victor had designed the marble in the main nave of the church. He was a young man at the time, one of many Italian immigrants who came to America in the early 1900s. As we entered the cathedral and walked to the altar, I admired the marble work. I giggled thinking of how my father would always refer to my mother's brothers as The Marble Heads because they were all in the marble business, but also inferring they were blockheads!

I pictured the tomato plants growing in my Uncle Victor's garden, pushing up along a marble pathway. It was the only fit of laughter I had while in New York. We wandered around the different chapels and buildings, which take up quite a few city blocks. We looked for the name plaques of the men who'd worked on the building of the cathedral, but didn't see Uncle Victor's name. The work began in 1892 and continues to this day. The cathedral is one of the largest church buildings in the world. My day in Manhattan was a short reprieve from what was happening back in the Bronx.

Walking to the train station I passed Tower Records. I wasn't planning another trip into Manhattan before going back to Hawaii, so this was my only opportunity to pick up the cassettes on Cheyenne Bremmer's music wish list. It had begun raining, so I put the hood up on my hoodie, but still I got drenched.

I entered Tower Records looking like a drowned rat, my dark hair flattened and stuck to the sides of my face. I approached one of the young guys behind the counter, asking him if he could help me find cassettes for the bands I had listed on a piece of paper. He came out from behind the counter and walked me to the heavy metal section. He fished through the scribbled list and found most of them. I thanked him profusely following him back to the desk. I watched him ring up the cassettes on the register and handed him my credit card. He took the card, and before completing the transaction, he asked, "Can you think of anything else your son might want?"

I stared at him for a moment, stunned, as if he'd slapped me across the face. "No, that should do it," I said. I thought about his comment on the train ride back to the Bronx, wondering how something society saw as so wrong could feel so right.

> She considered the demands of reality as something to be
> entirely crushed in favor of love, that obedience to reality
> meant a weakness in love.
>
> —Anais Nin, *Stella*

I visited my father in the nursing home one more time before going back to Hawaii. I walked in his room and found him sitting on a chair beside the bed.

"Dad, why don't we go to the recreation room?"

"Hi my darling," he said, with outstretched arms.

"How are you feeling today?" I asked, hugging him.

"Why is that guy over there again? What does he want?"

"What guy?" I asked.

My dad became agitated. "The guy sitting on the windowsill. He's right there."

"Dad, I don't see anyone on the windowsill."

"You can't see him?" he asked.

"Dad, let's go to the cafeteria and get something to eat?"

"I'll need the wheelchair," Andre said.

I walked to the nurses' station, fetched a wheelchair, and enlisted a nurse to help me get my father in it.

I was struggling to push him through the doorway, but he blocked it with his foot against the door frame like a stubborn child. The other man in his room was lying on his bed half nude, his private parts exposed. The nurse noticed it and went to his bedside to cover him. Eventually I got my father out of the doorway and pushed him to a table in the cafeteria. Nothing looked good in the showcase, but I came back with chocolate pudding. He ate the pudding but had no interest in talking to anyone. He just scanned the room regarding everyone with suspicion.

"Is your mother cooking for me? She always brings me something."

"She was tired, so I came today. Tomorrow she'll bring you something special."

I hung out with my father for a couple of hours, but there wasn't much dialogue. When I wheeled him back to his room, the nurse told me she had to change his clothes and get him ready for bed. She asked me to step outside, which was just as well. I'd never seen my father naked, and wasn't going to start now. Soon, she emerged from the room signaling me it was okay to go back in.

"Adriana, I was afraid you left," my father said, looking at me with relief and joy.

"No Dad, I'm still here."

"Did they tell you when I can go home?" he asked. "Please don't leave me here."

That's when my heart broke. My dad was never going home. I told him I'd come back the next day. I had to leave because I felt a wave of sobs coming on, and I didn't want him to see it. I kissed him gently on the forehead and then on his lips.

"I love you, Daddy. Sleep well," I said.

"I love you too, my darling," he said, not wanting to let go of my hand.

I walked out and cried all the way down the hallway, on the elevator, and into the night air. Looking back, I don't think I ever left that building without crying. I stood at the bus stop feeling numb. *Is this what our lives come to in the end?* I wondered and feared.

I had a 7:00 a.m. flight out of Kennedy Airport, and left the apartment in the middle of the night. I hated leaving my mother alone. On the taxi ride to the airport I thought of all the times I'd left my parents' apartment, torn between two worlds. I'd been forced, perhaps a bit late, into the harsh reality of adulthood, and my carefree youth seemed so far behind me. I was like the bird on the fence in the Bob Dylan song "You're a Big Girl Now." I knew my parents were elderly, and that it was only a matter of time before they would be gone from this world. I'd be on my own, without a family, hurtling like a tiny planet through the vast universe.

> Youth is a beautiful dream, but its sweetness is enslaved
> by the dullness of books, and its awakening is a harsh one.
> —Khalil Gibran, *Nymphs of the Valley*

I had purchased a cheap flight, so I had two connecting flights on the mainland, and then a flight from LAX to Honolulu. There's always a feeling of suspension in time while rushing through airports in different cities. There are usually interesting art displays, cafés, ice cream stands, and bookstores to wander through. There's that urgency you feel when your connecting flight has a gate change, or the flight you're on is delayed and you might miss your next flight. That is exactly what happened that day. I called Cheyenne from LAX to let him know that the flight leaving from California to Hawaii had been delayed. By the time the flight would land in Honolulu, there would be no more commuter flights to the island of Maui. We agreed that I'd spend the night in Honolulu, and I'd fly to Maui the following day.

I arrived in Honolulu after midnight. I was freaked out and exhausted. All I wanted was to sleep in my own bed, and for Cheyenne to hold me. I needed to feel some sense of normalcy. I begged the ticket agent behind the United Airlines counter at the gate to find me a way to Maui that night.

"Only thing I am able to find is the helicopter that delivers newspapers to Maui."

"I'll take it," I said.

I called Cheyenne and woke him from a dead sleep. I told him I was coming home on a helicopter flight with the Honolulu Advertisers.

"Are you crazy? I thought you decided to stay overnight in Honolulu."

"Please Chey, I just want to come home."

"Okay, I'm getting dressed now. I'll pick you up at cargo."

I was afraid he'd be annoyed with me and the change of plan, but when he saw the state I was in he just hugged me. We drove away from the airport, and I fell into a restful, secure sleep. As soon as we were inside the condo I flopped on the bed.

"You don't have to tell me anything tonight. It can wait until tomorrow," he said.

At some point during the night we made love. I didn't enjoy it; my mind was suspended in a weird space from that unsettling three weeks in New York. Cheyenne had a calming effect on me, and was always emotionally supportive. My time back east contributed to the death of my creative energy. "I never see you paint anymore," he'd say. I played my guitar once in a while, but the routine of everyday life overtook my sensibilities. I was missing Gauguin who seemed to have disappeared from my life.

Cheyenne began working as a prep cook in the kitchen of the Italian restaurant where I was working. He always made me a Caesar salad, just the way I liked it, with extra Parmesan cheese and extra lemon. He'd sit at the bar and drink a beer while I set up for the evening rush. We tried getting shifts together so we didn't have to use two cars, but it didn't always work out. We had a nice group of friends that we socialized with—the restaurant staff, the crew at Abigail's Distinctive Affairs, and his bandmates.

Abby rented Silver Cloud Ranch in Kula for the weekend of Thanksgiving. The house sat on top of a hill overlooking Maui below, with the Pacific Ocean visible in the distance. There were bunkhouses on the property, which is where Cheyenne and I slept. He tooled around on the piano in the living room of the main house, although his thing was bass guitar. It was an appreciation holiday weekend for all of the employees who worked for Abby. There were horses grazing on the side of the mountain behind the house. Driving along Thompson Road to the house, one might have to pull over for a cow or two. We all loved it up there. It was a place of peace, joy, and relaxation.

These days it's owned by Oprah Winfrey and is no longer available to the public.

The hill behind Silver Cloud Ranch

The holidays were joyous that year. We spent Christmas Eve home alone. Cheyenne surprised me with a Hawaiian heirloom solid-gold bracelet (which I still have and wear). My name in Hawaiian is etched in black on the outside, and on the inside the inscription reads, "Merry Xmas love Cheyenne." I encouraged him to buy his mom a similar bracelet. When Pricilla opened her gift on Christmas Day, she beamed with delight, smiling at Cheyenne. Jim Bremmer looked at his son with pride. I think it was the only time I saw a smile crack on the stoic face of that Johnny Cash character. I doubted he'd credit me in any way for his son's thoughtfulness.

In the New Year we adopted two baby cockatiels from our neighbor April. She had gotten so attached to them that she almost didn't want to part with them. We named the male Pua (flower) and his sister Honey Girl (a popular Hawaiian girl's name). 1993 found us in a good place.

"While you were in New York, April tried to get me to have sex with her."

"I told you she had a thing for you."

"Well, you know how hot I am," Cheyenne said, with a playful grin.

"Oh, I know, but nothing happened, right?"

"No. But when I wouldn't she offered to give me a blow job. More than once."

"Uh-huh. As if that isn't sex," I said, wondering what the truth was.

I figured I should give him what he wanted. I unzipped his jeans. He leaned back letting me fondle him. I stared up at his face moving my hands and fingers along his member, teasing him. Then I licked back and forth and did the lollipop thing. He tossed me on the bed, and in that little place there wasn't far to fall. He took his pants off, and we ended up in a tangled mess of arms, legs, and lips.

The catering company had a wedding in Wailea. We were all to meet at the kitchen since we were carpooling. Cheyenne dropped me off at the kitchen on his way to the music studio. Logan Baxter and Jumpin' Jimmie were loading up the van when I arrived. I rode with the Italian sisters, Mara and Zenda Schwartz. We had a good idea of the location of the wedding but followed the van anyway. Filippo Rizzoli and I sat in the back seat, and I sensed he was in a nasty mood.

When I was finished setting up my bar poolside at the venue, I walked to the ladies' room to get into my black-and-whites. I passed Filippo crafting floral arrangements as centerpieces on each table, and noticed his mood had lifted. The Italians were in the ladies' room smoking a joint when I walked in. I'd forgotten my bow tie, but Zenda had an extra one. She passed the joint to Mara, who took a long toke and passed it to me, but I shook my head. Getting stoned was not what I had in mind. Luckily Jumpin' Jimmie had some cocaine with him, which we did behind the men's bathroom.

The wedding reception was going normally until the bridal party got trashed. When dinner was over, and all the drunken slurred speeches had been made, the mother of the groom jumped into the swimming pool with her clothes on. You could see portions of her red sequin dress float to the surface. Before you knew it, everyone in the wedding party was jumping in and making fools of themselves. It was fun to watch them splash around while we cleaned off the tables and broke down the bars. We snagged two bottles of Chardonnay and poured ourselves a few glasses. Filippo Rizzoli got a bit twisted. His face was so tan that all you could see were the whites of his eyes, and his teeth flashing like neon Chiclets. When it came to worshiping the sun that guy never knew when to stop. On the ride home he lit into me about my relationship with Cheyenne.

"How do you justify robbing the cradle, Adriana?" Filippo asked.

"He's a man, not a boy, and it's none of your business," I answered.

"It's disgusting," he ranted. "You should be ashamed of yourself."

"You're just jealous," I said.

"A handsome young guy like that? You should be with a man your own age," he snarled.

"Someone like you?" I said.

I suppose if Cheyenne had been much older than me, there wouldn't be an issue. I found most men my age liked to tell me what to do. Cheyenne let me be myself, didn't criticize, and never used harsh or ugly tones with me. If we disagreed, we discussed it.

In the front seat, the Italian sisters were muttering Italian curses back and forth. I knew Filippo had anger issues. I'd heard that he'd been fired from his job at one of the hotels in Kaanapali where he worked in banquets, for holding an unwilling woman by the throat against a wall. I let him rant and rave at me with more insults as we drove along, not wanting to tangle with him while he was drunk.

We were following the van back to Lahaina when we saw them pull into a gas station. I jumped out of the car and told Abby I wanted to ride the rest of the way to Lahaina in the catering van with her, even if it meant sitting in the back with the leftover food and dirty dishes. When we reached the kitchen, I left the others and avoided Filippo Rizzoli.

I could hear music coming from Black Tar's studio behind the kitchen. I walked up the stairs and opened the door. Cheyenne broke out in a big smile when he saw me. He stopped playing, telling the other guys he needed a break. We talked for a while outside on the staircase. I wanted to go home, but he'd promised the guys another half hour of band practice. They had a gig coming up soon. I told him I'd wait for him in the Sly Mongoose.

Sitting in the Goose, my eyes narrowed in the dark and focused on Annie Hughes at the other end of the bar. She saw me, took her drink, waddled over and sat on the barstool next to mine.

"We haven't been out drinking together for a while."

"I know," I said.

"Where's lover boy?" she asked.

"He's at band practice upstairs in the back.

"I've been working at a jewelry store in the Hyatt. It's a change of scene."

"Is that the hotel with the penguins and the swans?" I asked.

"Yeah, that's the one. I love to watch the penguins walk around."

Just then, Cheyenne walked in. He stood behind me and ordered a beer. "We'll leave soon. I know you must be tired," he said.

"It's okay. Drink your beer. I know I'll sleep like a rock tonight," I said.

Annie smiled. She liked Cheyenne because he was a nice guy and was good to me.

We drove home in the Camaro, and I dozed off in the passenger seat. I didn't tell Cheyenne about Filippo Rizzoli going off on me. Not because I was afraid he'd want to thump the guy, but because I didn't want to cast light on our age difference. Cheyenne was a stabilizing force in my life at that time. *But for how long?* I wondered. I wasn't dumb. Eventually he'd want someone his own age. You can't fight father time. I just didn't know how or when that would happen.

Love is never planned; it just happens between the most unlikely people, under the most unexpected circumstances. I wanted to enjoy whatever time we had together.

CHAPTER 12

SNUFFED OUT

May the stars carry your sadness away
May the flowers fill your heart with beauty
May hope forever wipe away your tears
And above all, may silence make you strong
—Chief Dan George, Tsleil-Waututh Nation

Two new women showed up on the scene that year to work for Abigail's Distinctive Affairs. Lenora was one; she was called "Sweetie." She was very pretty, with short brown hair, fine features, and an air of class about her. I'd heard she was married, but I never saw her husband. The other was Veronica Dove, who became a close friend of mine. Vero—I liked calling her that—was a bit scattered but had an uncanny knack for describing people to a T. She could read a person's character like a clairvoyant. We spent a lot of time together outside of work. Cheyenne called her "Hoots" because of the way her large yellow-green eyes would rotate as she struggled to find just the right words. He said she reminded him of an owl. Of course, Cheyenne had a nickname for just about everyone we knew. He could do an excellent imitation of local jargon in pidgin, which kept me laughing.

The first time I went to Veronica's house, I had to move piles of clothing to create an empty space on her couch in order to sit down. Stacks of items were piled high in every available space in her living room. She was forever buying clothing at the Salvation Army, and picking up other treasures at garage sales. "It was such a good deal," she'd say, mentioning the label, or telling me about the designer. She just couldn't let anything slip through her fingers. She'd become visibly upset if she coveted an item, but someone else snagged it before she had a chance to. She rarely used or wore most of these things.

I was somewhat comfortably seated on the small section I'd carved out for myself on the couch while she went to the kitchen to make us tea. Her apartment was right next to the road, but close to the ocean, and I was soothed by the sound of the surf. She emerged from the kitchen with two cups of tea. She sat across from me on a chair that mysteriously appeared under a pile of folded blankets and a box of granola.

"Filippo Rizzoli invited me to breakfast in his condo at the Kuleana," she announced.

"Really Vero? How did that come about?"

"We both worked a banquet at the Marriott, and I happened to mention that my washing machine was on the blink. He told me to come by his place the next day for breakfast, and I could do my laundry in their Laundromat on the premises."

"Did you go?" I asked, staring at her sensual lips.

"Oh God, it's a story," she said, her yellow-green eyes darting around the room. "I showed up at his place in my sweatpants and an old T-shirt carrying my laundry basket. I was expecting coffee and cereal, or bagels with cream cheese. Instead, a table was set up on his lanai with a starched white-linen tablecloth, a crystal vase with fresh-cut roses, a bottle of champagne in an ice bucket, and poached salmon. Then Filippo waltzed out to the lanai all dressed up in a white shirt and black bow tie to greet me. I was taken aback."

"Vero, no!"

"When he poured the champagne he reeked of Karl Lagerfeld."

"Vero, I'm speechless."

"Oh, that's not all. After I checked on my load of laundry, I came back to find a dish of pasta with pesto sauce, which he made a point of telling me was his mother's recipe."

"Vero, it sounds like he has a thing for you."

"I was planning my escape when he put a Frank Sinatra record on the stereo and showed me his bedroom, which was partially converted to a workout gym."

I sat there, my mouth agape at Veronica's tale, but being familiar with Filippo Rizzoli I found it easy to picture the scene.

The catering company had a small, intimate wedding reception at a house in Wailea in a gated community. Abby was determined to cut down on any mishaps, so she made sure we all had the entry code written down.

When we arrived at the house there was no Filippo. He had forgotten the piece of paper with the code. Abby waited for over half an hour for him to show up. She relied on him to do the large floral arrangements and table centerpieces. Despite his explosive temperament he was definitely the master of that art. He finally got through the gate by piggybacking on the rear bumper of a resident's car that was going through. Abby refrained from chastising him because she wanted the party to go on without any glitches. Bubba stayed back at the kitchen and I bartended. Hans Berlin helped Abby with the food. We all noticed there was at least an hour when the two of them disappeared.

The wedding reception was a small family affair at their home after a religious ceremony in a quaint little church on the ocean in Makena. The bride was beautiful, and the groom was very handsome. Both were dripping with class, as was the entire wedding party. When the affair was winding down, we cleaned off the tables while Logan and Jumpin' Jimmie loaded up the van. Our bow ties were already in our pockets, when a piece of wedding cake flew past me. The bride's family and groom's family were engaged in a food fight with what was left of their beautiful wedding cake. When Abby saw chunks of white-frosted yellow cake land on, and stick to, the lavender leather sofa in the living room, she quietly signaled us to back away and get out of the house. She'd already received the check for the affair, and wanted nothing to do with cleaning that mess. We sneaked out in the middle of the sugary-frosting free-for-all.

I drove back to Lahaina in the van with Abby that night, avoiding another disciplinary rerun with Filippo Rizzoli. She and I were chatting about our escaping having to clean up the mess from the cake fight, when she noticed a warning light on the dashboard.

"I'm almost out of gas," Abby said. "There's a gas station before we get to the highway. I've used it before."

When we arrived at the gas station, it was closed.

"Now what are we going to do?" I asked.

"I'll call Bub at the kitchen, and ask him to get a container of gas and meet us here."

We sat on the curb outside the gas station for forty minutes. It was after midnight when we saw the small work van approach.

Bubba jumped out of the small van, and without a word, hopped in the big van to check the dashboard. "You said you were out of gas."

"That's what the needle says," Abby squawked.

"All you had to do was flip the switch over to the reserve tank."

"This van has another tank?"

"This van has two gas tanks."

"For Christ's sake Bub, couldn't you just have told me that when I called you at the kitchen?" Abby said, visibly annoyed.

Bubba flipped the switch and started the engine, then calmly and silently got out and hopped in the small van and drove off.

Abby and I got in the big van with all the dirty trays and leftover food from the wedding. "This shit wagon is full of surprises," Abby said, as we drove off.

In the spring of 1993 CNN had ongoing coverage of the Branch Davidians' religious compound in Waco, Texas, that had burned to the ground after a fifty-one–day standoff killing seventy-two people. It was sickening to watch. I sensed a disturbing, growing trend of censorship applied to citizens with opposing political views by the powers that be. Cheyenne knew I had been a hippie in the counterculture when I was in my twenties. He seemed to get a kick out of it. If I did or said something he considered odd, he'd laugh and remark, "Damn hippies." We definitely saw life through a similar political lens.

Also that spring, the first big-box stores opened on Maui. Abigail's catering company did the grand opening at Kmart. It was a huge event with balloons and giveaways to the first hundred customers. People were eating appetizers off the free Frisbees that were handed out, which worked well as plates. The soda was free, and we sloshed through the aisles to keep up with the demand for sheet cake.

At the Italian restaurant in Kapalua, I began working on Friday nights when the owner had Jazz Night. It was a popular event with crowds of local regulars, as well as tourists who loved jazz. We had drink specials and discounted food items. The place was packed, and I made lots of cash tips. I'd twirl around that bar like a pro, even receiving compliments on my martinis. Blackie, one of the regulars, always insisted that I stir his vodka on the rocks with my finger, or he wouldn't drink it.

The phone at the end of the bar rang. A guy asked to speak to Legs, the new waitress with the long legs. I yelled out, "Hey Legs, there's a phone call for you. It's Joey Buttafuoco!" The whole bar burst out laughing.

Joey Buttafuoco was involved in a huge scandal in 1992—a married man who got involved with an underage girl in his neighborhood in Long Island, New York. His paramour, Amy Fisher, became so jealous of Joey's wife that she knocked on their door one day with a gun. When Joey's wife opened the door, Amy shot her in the face.

Legs was about six months pregnant and still waitressing. She was a popular waitress, but I wondered how much longer she'd be able to work on her feet before that baby was ready to pop out.

My commune sister, Star Green, came for a visit. She insisted on referring to my boyfriend, Cheyenne Bremmer, as "The Youth." Yet to me, in so many ways, he seemed so much more mature than she was. I let her comments slip off me like a rain-soaked mudslide. She was on a kale-salad kick, which she coaxed me into trying. It was like grazing on a neighbor's lawn. She'd married a guy who was the inventor of a type of mountain bike. They had two kids together. Now he was divorcing her because of her runaway cocaine habit. While she was on the island we visited our favorite haunts, and in a few days she was gone.

Suki Rosmond, my other sister from the old commune days, also made an appearance that year. She stayed at her brother's house in Kula. He was an antiques dealer. She took me up there to roam through his warehouse filled with treasures. She was into body building, and had transformed her physical appearance. Suki and Cheyenne had something in common—smoking pot. They got along well, and there were no snide comments about his age. The days of the three musketeers were still alive, although over time distance diluted our connection. The remoteness of where I lived made it difficult to share important life events.

Time was sailing along at at a smooth pace until Pricilla called with bad news—Jim Bremmer, Cheyenne's dad, had been diagnosed with terminal lung cancer, and wasn't given much time to live. She told me it miffed her, and hurt Jim, that Cheyenne seemed to care more about our pet cockatiels than he did for his father. If I remember correctly, her exact words were, "Those damn birds."

"Please encourage him to come see Jim while he's still around," she said.

I promised her I'd talk to Cheyenne. Jim Bremmer never approved of me, but I understood he was looking out for the welfare of his son, and I didn't hold it against him. Pricilla set up a hospital bed in their living room in front of the large picture window overlooking Kaanapali Golf Course, so he could keep an eye on the property he'd taken such good care of. He was well liked by everyone at the hotel. Chemo did nothing for his advanced cancer, and just made his last months on earth a miserable, living hell. Pricilla took care of him until the end; she described how she had lightly stroked his arm as he took his last breath.

We were at home when we received the call from his mom. Cheyenne was sitting at the desk, and I saw him put his head down and cry. I rubbed his shoulder ever so lightly, not wanting to disturb the moment.

"My dad died. I didn't always get along with him, but he taught me everything I know," he said.

After Jim was cremated, Cheyenne took me on the golf cart to see the plaque the company had erected on the green in remembrance of Jim Bremmer for a job well done. Pricilla kept his ashes with her, and she eventually moved back to Arizona. Cheyenne told me they had five acres and a double-wide trailer there. Cheyenne stayed on Maui with me.

> When you were born, you cried and the world rejoiced.
> Live your life so that when you die, the world cries and
> you rejoice.
>
> —White Elk

I worked a morning function in Lahaina with the catering company. It was a celebration of life in the graveyard right across the street from Abigail Walton's new residence in the center of Lahaina Town. We all referred to the condo complex as the Pink Palace. It was an easy affair because it was just coffee, pastries, and fruit. The deceased man had planned his own funeral, requesting that little chocolate coffins be served, but Abby put the kibosh on that idea.

Filippo Rizzoli was one of the wait staff. We had made up since the time he went off on me. He and I were wheeling a large urn of coffee on a cart across the street—from Abby's condo to the cemetery. The ground was so uneven that the cart was jiggling around, and the hot coffee in the urn sloshing along with it. We began removing and tossing small stones in the cart's path to make it easier for us to wheel the coffee cart to the dessert table. We heard someone speaking on a microphone about the significance of the stones as grave markers for those who were buried there who couldn't afford a large gravestone or a monument. We realized that we were nonchalantly tossing what we thought were ordinary rocks, but were actually people's stone markers from their final resting places.

Filippo began to roar with laughter. There was no point attempting to undo any of the sacrilege we'd already innocently committed, as there were no names engraved on the stones.

Cheyenne quit the Italian restaurant, which I was happy about. His being there made it difficult for me to do my job, which was to schmooze the customers at the bar, and make big tips. I'd feel his eyes watching how I interacted with the male patrons, especially with the buff guys who worked out at the gym next door. He'd call me over and tell me he didn't like the way a certain guy was looking at me, or he'd ask why I was paying special attention to someone. I confessed my frustration to Abby one day, and she suggested he work in the catering kitchen for a while. She was down a prep cook and could use the help. It turned out to be a good thing. Cheyenne liked the fact that he could walk to his music studio when he finished his shift at the kitchen.

Abby told me that the first thing Cheyenne did when he walked into the kitchen was to take a loaf of French bread and slather it with a whole stick of butter. "I just marveled at his ability to eat that whole loaf," she said.

"Oh, he likes his bread," I said. "His mother told me when he was a kid he ate like a snake, going days without food, then eating a huge amount at one sitting."

Cheyenne was familiar with most of the characters who worked there, and enjoyed the easy vibe in the catering kitchen. He occasionally helped the guys load the truck, but I don't remember him coming to any of the functions. Cheyenne worked in the kitchen until he found a job in the maintenance department of one of the resort hotels closer to the hood.

We catered a wedding reception in Olualu at the old Plantation House on the ocean, about fifteen minutes south of Lahaina. The wedding was a beautiful event at the water's edge, with waves rolling onto the beach. Just as the music and dancing began we witnessed a glorious sunset.

We ate leftovers from the reception as we cleaned up. I sneaked a piece of wedding cake, and poured a glass of wine from a bottle we'd snagged and hid under the dessert table while everyone was dancing. I was almost back to Lahaina when I realized that I'd left my street clothes hanging in the bathroom at the Plantation House, but it was late, and I wasn't driving back.

I was at the kitchen the following day where we all met to go over the menu for a function that evening. The woman who lived in the Plantation House came by the kitchen to return the clothes I'd left in her bathroom. It was so very kind of her.

A few days later we heard that she'd been eaten by a shark. She had visitors in town for the wedding that week and they were snorkeling off shore. It was a place she had swam every day over the five years she lived in that house. A witnesses claimed she saw a shadow in the water and thought it was a turtle, so she swam toward it to get a better look. Once she realized it was a shark, she began flailing her arms and swimming toward shore, but it was too late—the shark had already taken her arm.

Her neighbor saw the fray, jumped on his surfboard and paddled out to help her. When he saw other sharks approaching, he realized there was nothing he could do. The woman's husband, who was the manager of the Pioneer Mill in Lahaina, was called to identify what was left of her body. It was a shocking and horrific end to such a wonderful person. I imagine the bride and groom had that awful memory regarding their wedding for the rest of their lives.

In an instant, when you least expect it, your life could be over. You might think, *No, not now. Everything is going so well. I'm not ready to die.* In contrast, I thought of my own life. I hadn't done anything creative in a very long time. I didn't even play my guitar anymore, which stood silently against the wall. Just then, the phone rang interrupting my thoughts. It was my mother informing me that my father had been put on a feeding tube and was living in diapers. I was mortified at this turn of events in the nursing home. To me, that was not living, only existing. She made sure she was there every day to check on him, but found him in someone else's clothes, and in a less-than-clean state. I flew to New York before the holidays.

I hadn't been back in Hawaii that long when a late-night phone call jarred me awake. I sat up in bed with the phone to my ear but heard no voice on the other end. Then I heard screaming and crying. I didn't have to ask my mother what had happened.

"Ma," I said, my voice cracking. Cheyenne didn't sit up but placed his hand on my thigh and his head in my lap when he heard me say, "Ma," again, and began to cry. When she regained the ability to talk, she told me what had happened.

"I was getting dressed to go see your father in the nursing home, when I received a call from the hospital. They said, 'Mrs. Bardolino, your husband Andre passed away this morning.' Just like that they said it," she lamented, crying again.

My aunt Porciella was there with her. It was a Sunday, and they had planned to bring my father Italian food, which he looked forward to.

"The home never even called to tell me he was ill and had been taken to the hospital. He was fine when I visited the day before. I never got to see him or talk to him before he died," she said, whimpering through tears.

Aunt Porciella got on the phone. "Adriana, your mother is distraught. Can you come back to New York?"

Despite having just been in New York, I had to go back immediately. I worked the day shift at the Italian restaurant that next morning. I had a hard time concentrating on anything. I went to the office and told the owner's wife that my father had passed away during the night. I said that I couldn't think straight, and that I was going back to New York. She immediately got on the phone and arranged an emergency plane ticket for me. I wasn't aware that airlines set aside seats for just such emergencies, especially on a holiday—it was New Year's Eve. My coworkers handled everything.

On the drive to Kahului Airport in the Camaro Cheyenne talked about how weird it was that we both lost our fathers so close in time. "They were snuffed out just like that," he said. When he dropped me off at the outside ticket agent, he hugged and kissed me. "I promise I'll call you every day."

On the overnight flight to New York the stewardesses served champagne when the clock struck midnight, and 1994 was ushered in as the plane flew above the clouds.

As soon as we landed I rushed through the exit doors with my carry-on, and immediately was hit with that familiar dense air. I took a taxi from LaGuardia Airport to my parents' apartment. I stared out the window at the familiar scenery along the freeway. I thought of all the times I'd done this. It was a fleeting thought that ran through my mind as the taxi sped toward the Bronx.

My mother buzzed me into the building, and I walked up the stairs to apartment 3B. My mother's neighbor, the ex-nun who lived in 3C, was standing there with her. She was helping my mother through this difficult time with prayers and spiritual support. Sanna, my mother's last surviving cat, ran into the hallway. I dropped my suitcase and ran after her. "Catch her before she runs down the stairs," my mother shouted.

All we need is another cat drama and more heartache, I thought. Vita hugged me and we both cried for a bit. Once inside the apartment the heaviness overwhelmed me—the loss of my father. Perhaps my parents weren't the same people they were when they first met fifty-five years ago, but they went through the changing tides of life together, and that stood for something. *She did love him after all*, I thought. I saw my own life as noncommittal and empty, well in the grand scheme of things.

The next day we walked to the funeral home, which was only a few blocks from the apartment house under the el (elevated train). She had already been there to discuss the funeral arrangements, and to bring my father's favorite suit. We looked through pages of coffins, and tufted fabrics for the interior lining, as if it really mattered once you're six feet under covered with dirt. The funeral home made the arrangements for the church, pallbearers, and limos. The funeral director and his associates gave off a crime-mob vibe.

We took a cab to a florist in the same neighborhood as her old dress factory. We ordered floral wreaths, one from her as wife, and one from me as daughter. To this day the aroma of carnations reminds me of funerals— and my first Holy Communion.

I was glad I was with my mother for the wake, which lasted three days. I sat right next to her and stood up to greet family and friends when they arrived. My father's sister, Millie, couldn't even enter the viewing room. She sat on a chair in the lobby and cried. "I can't see the dead," she wailed, through tears and sighs. My father's other sisters tried to comfort her. I thought back to when Millie's mother, my grandmother, passed away. Millie wanted to throw herself in the ground with the coffin. Her siblings held her back. They all cried, and screamed as my grandmother's coffin was lowered. It was very dramatic—a Sicilian thing.

All the family members I hadn't seen in years showed up, the ones who only come out of the woodwork for weddings and funerals.

I went up and knelt next to the coffin peering down at my father. I heard a woman remark to her husband, "I didn't realize he was such a tall man." He'd lost so much weight that his suit looked two sizes too large for him; his thin hands peeked out from the white shirt cuffs. I was wearing his garnet ring, which he'd given to me on one of my recent visits. I rubbed the stone and said, "Dad, I love you, and I will miss you so much."

On the last day, the day of the funeral, I let my mother be the last to say goodbye before they closed the lid. I took my mother's hand and we walked out together. The church service, with the sounds of crying, nose-blowing, organ music, and prayers was difficult. The ride to the cemetery in the limousine was a blur.

My father was buried in the same plot as my uncle Faustino, Gia Ferrari's father, who had been in the ground for many years. We all stood around the open plot on that cold day taking turns throwing flowers on top of the coffin as it was lowered into the ground.

My cousin Ariel leaned in to me and whispered in my ear, "We have an extra space in our plot at Saint Raymond's Cemetery if you have nowhere to go when you die." Being buried in the Bronx was the last place I wanted to spend eternity. I respectfully declined, saying, "I've decided to be cremated, but thank you for the generous offer." I don't remember what happened after that. The whole day was like one big dark hole we couldn't climb out of.

A few days after my father's funeral I walked to St. Helena's Church, where my friends and I had gone dancing as teenagers on Saturday nights. I suppose I always felt the need to take a walk down memory lane when

I visited the Bronx, the place of my birth. St. Helena's was about a mile from our old neighborhood, but excitement propelled us, so the walk didn't even faze us as teenagers. We'd congregate outside the church to see who would show up, what they were wearing, and how high the girls could tease their hair.

Downstairs in the basement of the church was an auditorium with a stage where plays were performed. A tiny record player with ginormous speakers sat on the stage, which funneled rock'n'roll 45s to eager dancers on an adequately sized dance floor. A priest mingled during slow dances to make sure bodies weren't touching. If a boy and girl were dancing too close—the priest would interrupt, tap the boy on the shoulder and say, "Now remember to leave room for the Holy Ghost." He was always present, monitoring the situation, and taking all the fun out of it.

I leaned against a car staring at the entrance door to the basement of the church remembering Ronny Donnelly, the boyfriend I had when I was fifteen. He was the neighborhood bad boy and heartthrob. He was barred from the church dances because of his hoodlum status. Women naturally gravitate toward the big fish and reject the guppies. I consider it proof of the power of natural selection to go for top dog in the pack.

Ronnie Donnelly would wait outside for me leaning on a car, just the way I was leaning now. I pictured his slicked-back, thick, dark hair; his tall frame; and his ruddy Irish complexion. I was hearing that old rock'n'roll song on a 45 by Rochell & the Candles, "Once Upon a Time." I saw him holding the door open to his friend's 1955 pink Cadillac convertible with a white interior, waiting for me to hop in. He'd grab me tightly around the waist and kiss me hard on the mouth. The thrill I felt, the electrically charged night air, the stars—how could I ever forget it? How long ago that was, and how strange life is.

I helped my mother go through my father's clothes, which we gave to Goodwill. I stayed for another week. We discussed the possibility of her coming to Hawaii. I flew home wondering if that would ever happen.

On the plane ride home to the islands I reminisced a lot. I saw my mother's face when she told me she'd be all right, but I knew she'd be struck with great loss. I thought of what a long life my father had. He was born in 1906. What changes in the world he'd witnessed. He was already forty years old the day I was born. I was barely seven years older than that now. He'd already lived a life before I appeared on the scene. He was eighty-eight when we buried him. It was sad, but then again, he did live a long life. I wondered how long my life would be.

As the plane approached the Hawaiian Islands, cityscapes were replaced with tropical scenes, and my spirit lifted. I had followed my dreams thus far. When the landing gear dropped I wondered what the cost of that would be. Like Star said, "Everything in life has a price!"

> What is life?
> It is a flash of a firefly in the night
> It is the breath of a buffalo in the wintertime
> It is the little shadow which runs across the grass and loses
> itself in the sunset
> —Crowfoot, Blackfoot warrior and orator (1830–1890)

In April of 1994 Kurt Cobain, lead singer of Nirvana, committed suicide. A young man with fame, talent, and everything to live for, chose to end his life with a gun. I'd heard he was into heroin. Kurt Cobain was only twenty-seven years old, the same age as Jimi Hendrix, Janis Joplin, and Jim Morrison when they died. I regarded that fact as slightly profound. It had to be more than a mere coincidence, although Cheyenne didn't share my assumption. I slipped a cassette in the stereo of Kurt Cobain's rendition of Lead Belly's song, "Where'd You Sleep Last Night," sat on the recliner, and stared off into space.

I liked the music of Nirvana, Guns N' Roses, The Red Hot Chili Peppers, and Metallica, whereas Cheyenne Bremmer went more for Iron Maiden, Judas Priest, Black Sabbath, and Slayer. I found myself tolerating his choices.

That June, Cheyenne joined a canoe club through his new job in maintenance at the Sands of Kahana, which he nicknamed the "Sands of Nirvana." I enjoyed going to canoe practice. I'd stand on the beach watching him paddle out, his tight butt visible through his wet white O'Neill shorts, and his thick hair tied in a ponytail. Spending a day at the ocean was always invigorating, filling me with a renewed sense of life.

At the end of the season we all stood on shore as the guys pushed the canoes from the beach into the ocean for the final competition. They jumped on board once the canoe was out far enough in the water, and frantically began to paddle. When the race began, everyone cheered their team on. Cheyenne's team did well but didn't win. The camaraderie was the take-away.

Canoe races, Lahaina

After the canoe races we hung out at home. Cheyenne took the bottle of Jägermeister out of the freezer, and we did some shots. We were not only lovers; we were friends. We lived in that tiny studio apartment for four years and never had a serious fight. That's hard to achieve in relationships, and I had a number of those to reflect on.

I watched Cheyenne search through the kitchen cabinets.

"What are you looking for?"

"Paddling out in the ocean today made me really hungry."

"What are you in the mood for?"

"I'm making us chicken and dumplings."

I took another shot of Jägermeister and watched him with a feeling of love and peace. It always gave me a serene feeling to observe someone I loved involved in a project they were really into.

"Can you get me a cigarette, hon?"

"You should cut that habit out," I said, grabbing the pack of Marlboros on the desk.

I put my arms around Cheyenne at the stove, hinting that I wanted to make love. He turned his face and kissed me.

"This will take a while anyway," he said, grinning at the thought of sex.

We moved to the bed, and soon he was all over me like an octopus. We made love to the sounds of the cockatiels chirping and the aroma from the chicken stew on the stove. When we were finished, he picked up my guitar and played for a bit. I curled up and closed my eyes.

"I have to stay awake to make the dumplings for the stew," he said.

I lay there listening to him play, and soon I drifted into a pleasant nap.

Black Tar had a gig to play in Kihei, so Cheyenne took the Cherokee and I drove the Camaro to work. At the Italian restaurant, everyone was talking about the murder of Nicole Brown Simpson and her friend Ron Goldman. Patrons stood around the bar, glued to the TV watching that slow-speed chase of the SUV with O. J. Simpson and his sidekick Al Cowlings along the freeways of Los Angeles. There was a gun in the vehicle, and everyone was convinced that the Juice was going to kill himself, rather than go to jail. The bizarre chase went on and on, but there was only so long that I could stand there gawking at the screen. Legs was the waitress in the bar section, and I finally got to meet her boyfriend, who was nothing like Joey Buttafuoco.

That weekend, Abigail's Distinct Affairs catered a wedding in Puamana. A Hawaiian holy man was to perform the ceremony, and the reception was to follow immediately after. It was a small affair. Abby and I were alone in the kitchen putting pu pu trays together. The plan was to walk around with bottles of champagne and trays of the appetizers after the ceremony.

The twenty-five-year-old bride slinked into the kitchen. She had a look on her face as if she was about to get a root canal. Abby asked her what was wrong.

"I can't go through with the wedding," the bride said.

Abby responded, "Everyone has last- minute wedding jitters."

"No," the bride said. "I don't want to marry this man."

I glanced at Abby to see what she would do. She grabbed the bride and shook her by the shoulders to wake her up to reality. She stared into her eyes.

"Just don't sign the certificate," Abby said.

"What do you mean?" the bride asked.

"Go through the motions of the ceremony, have the reception party, but don't actually sign any legal documents."

A big smile broke out on the bride's face, as if she'd looked in the mirror after having her teeth straightened. She turned herself around and walked out of the kitchen.

Abby swiped her hand across her forehead as if relieved.

"Abby, can you do that? Go through the motions but not actually seal the deal?"

"Yup. She's not the first bride I've seen have a come-to-Jesus moment."

The wedding and festivities went on as planned.

Two weeks later the bride called Abby from Las Vegas, thanking her profusely!

That Halloween, Cheyenne decided to dress as a Native American, which I thought was the antithesis of the premise of Halloween. Isn't it to dress up in costume to hide your true identity? He already had the long, thick Native American hair, which he wore with feathers. He war-painted his face so only his eyes were visible. The painted symbols continued down his arms. He looked like an Apache on the warpath. I dressed as a gypsy. I wore a lacy black top, a long patchwork skirt, and a large red-feathered mask. We cruised up and down Front Street with his work buddies, then walked up the steps to Annie Hughes's apartment, whose porch had a commanding view of the costume promenade along Front Street. One of his friends had cocaine, which we snorted up in Annie's bathroom.

Halloween in Lahaina, 1994

"So how's it going with lover boy?" Annie asked.

"Things are going great," I said.

"Enjoy it while you can."

I stared at Cheyenne, who was leaning over the balcony on the porch. "Oh, I'm enjoying it," I said.

Annie cackled and said, "A good man is hard to find, but a hard man is good to find."

I felt deeply about Cheyenne Bremmer, and wished we were closer in age. *Nature will win out in the end*, I thought. I knew that people came into our lives for a reason, even if they didn't stay. Like my mother always said, "Love isn't always a forever thing."

I was sound asleep when the pungent smell of steak being seared woke me up. Cheyenne's routine when he got home from band practice, often after midnight, was to cook himself a steak. I never ate steak, even as a child. The smell of seared flesh in the middle of the night made me queasy.

"I walked into the kitchen and put my arms around him at the stove. "My mother called. She coming to Hawaii for the holidays and staying for three months."

"Where are we going to sleep?" Cheyenne asked, innocently.

"I'll talk to my realtor friend and see if there's another studio in the hood I could rent."

"Do you think at eighty she'd want to move here now that your dad is gone?"

"I don't know, but I'm not ever moving back to the Bronx! If she wants to be near me, she'll have to move to Maui," I said, ending the conversation.

CHAPTER 13

A MOM FOR ALL SEASONS

You can lead a horse to water, but you can't make it drink.
—Twelfth-century English proverb

Thanks to my realtor friend I was able to rent an empty studio for three months in the hood. It was partly furnished with a bed and a couch. Cheyenne was lucky enough to find a round glass table and four tufted dining room chairs from someone who was moving out of the Sands of Nirvana, and was selling furniture.

I was not expecting the shape my mother was in when we picked her up at the airport.

We waited at the gate while the passengers disembarked. I impatiently searched for her face in the crowd. Then I saw Vita being wheeled off the plane in a wheelchair.

"Thank you. I'll take it from here," I said, to the attendant.

Cheyenne and I glanced at each other. My mother's face was pasty-white, and she was exhausted as I wheeled her to baggage claim. She talked about the flight and how terrible the food was. I was concerned about her health and well-being. I told Cheyenne to get the car and wait for us at curbside pickup.

"Are you sure you'll be OK?" he asked.

"Chey, I just want to get her in the car and home as quickly as possible."

I watched him walk away from us, and felt momentary desertion.

She was in such a weakened state, I wondered if this trip was a good idea. I had bought her a plane ticket as a Christmas gift to prompt her to come to Hawaii and check it out, to see if she might want to live in the islands. As I wheeled her toward the curb I wondered if I'd goaded her into making a wrong decision, and that my plan was one big pipe dream.

Cheyenne was sitting in the driver's seat of the Cherokee Chief as we walked toward the curb. I helped my mother into the front seat next to him. I figured she'd be more comfortable in the bucket seat. I sat in the back with her suitcase. Cheyenne shot me a strained smile as we set out for Lahaina.

The color began to return to Vita's face.

"Feeling better, Ma?"

"I feel so much better now," she said.

I reached my arm to the front seat and put my hand on her shoulder.

"How was the plane ride?" Cheyenne asked.

"I slept most of the way," she answered.

"We'll be home before you know it," I said.

When we arrived in the hood we parked the car and I helped my mother down the steps to the condo I'd rented for her. Cheyenne walked behind us carrying her suitcase. We settled her in and sat on the couch. Cheyenne got her a glass of water while I watched her eyes zoom around the apartment. I had purchased some groceries and put them in the refrigerator. She mentioned how much it looked like my first apartment, when she had visited me almost twenty years ago in the mid-seventies. We talked for a while. Vita seemed pleased with the condo and loved the fact that she could walk right out of the sliding glass door onto the grass.

"We're going home for a bit to let you get settled in. Take a nap if you want," I said.

"What do you mean? Isn't this your apartment?"

"Ma, I got this condo for you, so you could have your own space and privacy."

"You mean I'm not staying with you?" she asked, obviously disappointed.

Cheyenne walked out the front door. "I've got to get ready for band practice. The guys are waiting for me."

I had the feeling he was escaping an uncomfortable situation. I wondered how I would reply to my mother's surprise at not staying with us. "Ma, our place is so small. It's this size. You wouldn't be comfortable. Besides, where would we all sleep?"

I could tell she was digesting my words and sizing up the situation.

"I guess you're right," she said. "When will I see your place?"

"Take a nap, freshen up, and I'll come get you a little later." I set the key to her condo on the desk next to the phone, which I also obtained so she could call me, her sisters, and friends back in New York. I walked back to my condo a little upset.

"Abby called while you were at your mom's," Cheyenne said, as I walked in.

"I'll call her as soon as I calm down."

"It'll be fine," he said, hugging me.

"I suppose it's my own fault for not explaining the situation to her."

He kissed me on the lips and said he was taking the Camaro to the studio. I knew it was better if I dealt with my mom on my own.

After he left I called Abby. She mentioned that she had a small ladies' luncheon at the clubhouse in Puamana on Saturday. She asked if I wanted to work it with her. "It's a small affair, just the two of us. Bring your mom. She'll love it."

Later that day I walked back to my mom's condo. She seemed greatly rested and improved. I escorted her to my condo in the next building. She looked around and then sat on the only recliner we had room for. "It's nice but cluttered," she said.

"Well now you understand."

"Oh, those are your birds," she said, pointing at the cage.

"Yes, Pua and Honey Girl. They're brother and sister. We've had them for two years." I took Pua out of the cage and let him sit on her finger.

She was lost in the moment and smiled. "He's so friendly."

"He's my baby," I said. "He gives me kisses but snaps at Cheyenne."

"Remember when you were a little girl you had a parakeet?"

"Yes, I do remember. I think his name was Sparky. Then he flew out of an opening in the window and disappeared."

"Why is the other bird doing that funny thing with her neck?"

"Oh, she has that habit lately," I said.

"I don't think that's normal," Vita said.

"Honey Girl, the female cockatiel, loves Cheyenne. He can scratch the back of her head under her feathers. She won't let me do that."

"Cheyenne seems like a really nice guy Adriana."

"I think you will love him."

"Are we going to see Annie Hughes?" Vita asked.

"Tomorrow I'll take you to her place. We'll go for lunch and a drink."

Vita's eyes sparkled at the prospect.

That evening, I walked my mother back to her studio apartment. She probably was happier in her place because it was so sparse, while ours was crowded with electrical stereo equipment, large Jensen speakers, and ashtrays filled with cigarette butts. I stayed with her until it was time to go to sleep. The first day of my mother's visit went as well as could be expected, but I was relieved it was over.

I took my mom to see Annie Hughes. They were of the same generation and both native New Yorkers. Even though they had such different personalities they had things in common. Annie had visited my mom the last time she was in New York with her son Sonny.

Annie, my mother, and I went to the Yacht Club for lunch, then to the Pioneer Inn at the harbor for happy-hour drinks. We sat at the bar, me between the two moms. I looked at the bust of a mermaid hanging on a wall, which formerly had adorned the hull of a ship. I noticed the replica of an old iconic painting—I'd heard the original was in safe storage. I gazed at the harpoons and old photos of Maui and the Pioneer Inn on the walls. All of these treasures hit heavily. *What memories I have in this place*, I thought. I was lost in those memories when my mother blurted out, "Your cousin Jenny is estranged from her husband."

"What happened?" I asked.

"They're living separately. He moved down South for a new job. Jenny went down a few times and was supposed move down there. My sister Camille said that on one of Jenny's phone calls to her husband, a woman answered the phone. They're getting a divorce."

I was well aware of how a big move like that—leaving your family, friends, and your support system behind for a man, even a man you are in love with—could turn out. Being in love and having the best of intentions sometimes just isn't enough. Before you know it, it all turns to shit, spins in a downward spiral, and gets flushed down the toilet.

An orange tabby wandered into my mom's condo through the open lanai door. The cat befriended Vita and nuzzled up to her. She took to the cat right away, and wanted to buy cat food. I felt that whatever made her feel at home could only be a good thing. I wanted her to move to Maui permanently, but I could tell she needed convincing.

That Saturday I took my mom with me to the ladies' luncheon in Puamana. There were about twenty-five women, all around my mother's age. Abby set a place for her at one of the round tables, and she fit right in. She conversed easily with the other women and bragged to them that I was her daughter. I was working around her, opening up bottles of wine, filling glasses with ice and water, and serving the food. I thanked Abby in the kitchen when we had a quiet moment.

"I knew your mother would enjoy this," Abby said.

What's not to like? I thought—a beautiful clubhouse on the ocean, the sun shining, sailboats right offshore, guys surfing in the waves, and her daughter flitting around her, filling her every request and desire.

I needed to spend some time at Black Tar's music studio that following week. I promised the guys I'd take a black-and-white photo shoot of them, for a concert they had coming up. I dropped Vita in Lahaina at Annie's apartment. When I left them, my mother was trying on Annie's pants. I'd never seen Vita in anything but a skirt or dress. They were laughing up a storm, and I knew I was leaving her in good hands.

I walked up the steps to the music studio and through the door into Grunge Central. It was loud, smoke-filled, and loaded with testosterone. The guys smiled but continued playing as I stood against the wall listening. I did this often. In a few weeks, Black Tar was playing a gig at the Haiku Cannery, with another band opening for them. Excitement was in the air. Cheyenne created a flyer on the computer with his favorite photo from the shots I'd taken that day. I promised I'd get copies and distribute them around town.

We were up at Silver Cloud Ranch over the Thanksgiving weekend. I looked forward to a few days in the country on Haleakala Crater. My mother got a big kick out of seeing horses and cows wandering along the road to the house. Just about everyone we knew was there. It was wonderful catching up with Harry Hackman and Helga Hargrove. Vita was thrilled with the location and remarked that the main house reminded her of an old summer house in Upstate New York. Abby made sure we had one of the rooms in the main house. Vita stayed in the room with me and Cheyenne, which was weird.

Sweetie, one of the women we worked with, made a point of pulling me aside. "You are so attentive to your mother. It's nice to see."

"Well, she's my mom," I said, smiling.

"Yeah, but the way you hold her arm and walk with her, guiding her everywhere. You make sure she's taken care of. It's just so sweet," she said.

"Isn't that the way everyone is with their mother?"

"I'm not sure. I just wanted you to know how beautifully touching I think it is."

It was cold up there on the crater so we hung around the fireplace in sweaters and long pants. Cheyenne gravitated to the piano in the front room, where a little girl seemed mesmerized as she watched him play. The next day we walked around the property, petted the horses, and swooned over the potbellied pigs. When everyone was back at the main house, we ate most of the Thanksgiving leftovers. Abby insisted we all take doggie bags home.

Vita got settled in on Maui, and I felt hopeful that she'd want to stay. I felt it was time that I took care of her. Getting used to living on a tiny island in the middle of the Pacific Ocean would take some getting used to after living in New York, where anything you want is at your fingertips. *But she'd have me, her daughter*! I thought.

I dropped Vita off at Annie's house in Lahaina, while Veronica Dove and I rummaged around our favorite haunts on the other side of the island in Kahului. I'd promised Cheyenne I'd stop at Office Max to get copies of his band's flyer—BLACK TAR IN CONCERT AT THE HAIKU CANNERY. It was coming up in a week. I wasn't going to this one. It would be a long night with another band playing, and it was a ninety-minute drive from Napili. Besides, I wouldn't bring my mom to a heavy metal concert; I didn't want to freak her out. So far, she'd only heard Cheyenne play riffs on my acoustic guitar.

Vero was sitting in the passenger seat, looking out the window as we drove back to West Maui.

"I love it here. Can't imagine living anywhere else," she said.

"Believe me, I know the feeling."

"Do you think your mother will stay?"

"I hope so Vero, but I don't know."

"She'd be crazy to go back to New York."

"Cheyenne and I offered to go back with her and help her move."

"What did she say?"

"Nothing. She's eighty years old. It's not so easy to make a big move like that."

And that was the truth. I had absolutely no idea what was in my mother's mind. I was afraid to ask, afraid to know.

Abby had moved again. I swear that woman moved around more than a U-Haul truck. She was certainly keeping that franchise in the black. Her new apartment was in Kaanapali Royal on the golf course. I took mom there a few times. Abby made sure we were coming to her house for Christmas Day Dinner. That delighted Vita to no end. She admired Abby for being such a talented woman, and a successful entrepreneur.

I was sitting in my mom's condo when there was a knock at the door. I knew what was going on, so I let her answer it. Cheyenne had gone to look for a Christmas tree. She opened the door and there he was, the evergreen standing beside him. She watched him trim the trunk at the bottom. His friend Brice Gordon helped him set it up in her living room, and we had a fun evening decorating the tree. I had a box of Christmas decorations that I carried with me wherever I lived on the island. My mother made her famous eggnog, and we did shots of Jägermeister.

Vita made cannoli the day before. She kept the outer shells separate to keep them crunchy. She filled them with the cannolo cream that evening, and arranged them on a platter. My mom was an excellent baker.

There was a little wrapped box under the tree. Vita told me it was something special for the orange tabby. My mother understood that my gift was her plane ticket to Hawaii and the three months in the condo.

Abby had a small function in Kihei that week. She told me that a group of professors were meeting on Maui for a seminar, and would be arriving on different flights from various cities. It was their Christmas break and a sabbatical for these educators. She and I worked the party alone. It was just wine and a specific menu the host requested. Abby and I drove together in the small company van. We conversed the whole way and wondered how long the evening would be. When we arrived at the house we unloaded all the food, dishes, and glassware, carrying it up a long staircase.

The host, an older oriental woman, was standing in her doorway at the top of the stairs. She greeted me without a smile. She had a nasty disposition right off the bat, and was very picky about every little thing. She asked Abby if she had remembered to bring specific items she'd requested; luckily everything was on the van. It was Christmas week, so we brought Christmas-themed decorations. She eyed Abby walking up the stairs with a large plug-in Santa under one arm, and a coffee urn under the other. The woman shouted, "No Santa!" at Abby, who was a little stunned. Abby dropped off the coffee urn in the kitchen and carried the Santa back down the stairs and hid it in the van. I thought, *Maybe the woman is a Buddhist.*

This woman was critical of everything, from the size of the trays we used to the warming pans, which she claimed were too hotel-like. She insisted we use regular serving dishes—her dishes—but Abby explained that some of the food needed to be kept warm. The guests arrived late and not all at the same time, making serving difficult. They were all very educated and acted like they had sticks up their asses.

In the end, we got through a difficult night, and the host finally lightened up. We were cleaning the kitchen and packing up when a straggler arrived—everyone else had gone. Abby refused to drag out the warming pans again. She made the wayward guest a plate with a selection of food, with which he seemed very happy. In the end, the host was satisfied with our service and gave me a tip after handing Abby a check. On the way home we had a good laugh about the dancing Santa that never got plugged in.

That same week Veronica Dove told me she had worked a banquet at the Kapalua Bay Hotel. Filippo Rizzoli was working a different function at the same hotel, and he approached her about getting together after they finished work. "He insisted I come to his place when I was *pau* [finished with] work and have a drink," Vero said.

"You didn't go, did you?"

"Well, here's what happened," she said. "The banquet I worked ran about an hour later than I'd expected. I took a shower when I got home, and was getting dressed when there was a sturdy knock at my front door. It was Filippo in a drunken rage. He was all dressed up like he'd been asked to host the Oscars, holding a large wrapped present. I stood there, speechless, not knowing what to say. He was livid, as if I'd stood him up. Adriana, I thought we were just going to have a casual drink after we both finished work. When I told him that the banquet ran an hour over, and I had just gotten off work, he became unhinged. His face was flushed, and you know how difficult that is to see because he's always so tan. He yelled,

"'Merry fucking Christmas,'" and threw the present at me, adding, "'You fucking bitch!'" Then he slammed the door in my face. My own door!"

"Wow Vero, that guy is a snapper-head."

"I don't want anything to do with him anymore. I'm avoiding him at all costs."

"I'm dying to know what was in the box."

"I don't even want to go there," she said.

We spent Christmas Day at Abby's house in Kaanapali Royal. Her family was there along with all of her staff. She loved to entertain, especially on a holiday. I have some treasured photos from that day. My mom wore a silk dress I'd made during my days at the Crafty Mermaid. It wasn't tie-dyed, but had streaks of dye in lavender, purple, and gray. It fit her perfectly. I wore a tight black skirt, a tie-dyed silk blouse, and black booties. Like all holidays, we ate and drank as if we were participating in a Roman bacchanalian feast.

On the night of Black Tar's concert at the Haiku Cannery, Cheyenne took the Cherokee Chief, and I stayed home with my mother. She asked me why I didn't go to his concert. I was honest and told her that it was a very long drive to Haiku, and there would be another band playing as well, adding to the length of the evening. I didn't want to get into the mosh-pit thing. I wasn't sure how to explain it to her so she would understand. I could barely understand it myself.

Cheyenne got home really late from the gig in Haiku. He flopped on the bed waking me. He was so tired that he didn't even want to talk. But the next morning he had a lot to say. I had brewed coffee and was just about to walk to my mother's condo with two mugs when I heard him call out, "Hon." I turned around to see a grin on his face, and his arms stretched out for me to join him in bed. I giggled, noticing a peak in the sheet around his genital area. I set the two mugs of coffee on the counter and walked toward the bed. I took off my pants but left my T-shirt on. Cheyenne unhooked my bra, setting my breasts free. He nuzzled his face between my breasts looking up at me. "Miss me last night?" he asked, pulling my panties down. I didn't answer but gave him a warm, affectionate kiss. Soon, his hands were all over me, and I momentarily forgot about the coffee. I relished that feeling of urgency down below, anticipating waves of hot throbs. We always made time for sex. It was one of the plusses of being with a younger man. It was over pretty quick. I was just about to heat the mugs of coffee in the microwave when Cheyenne sat up in bed.

"I want to talk to you about something," he said.

"What is it?" I asked, wondering if it was something about us.

"Last night was weird. People didn't really dance. They stood around and listened to the music. I saw a few head-bangers and loonies in mosh pits, but that was it."

"Cheyenne, Black Tar's music isn't dance music. Sometimes it sounds a bit angry.

"Angry?"

"You know what I mean. Dunk screeches the words and stomps back and forth on stage. I mean, isn't that the whole point of it? Or am I missing something?"

"I don't know what I was expecting, but that wasn't it."

"It's the music young people like now. I thought that's what you were aiming for."

"I guess so. I was just curious to know what you thought."

Cheyenne lay back down. He seemed to be pondering my words, and I wondered if I'd said too much. *Will I ever learn to keep my mouth shut?*

It was a Tuesday, and I had the day off. I took my mom for a drive up north to Kapalua. I wanted to show her the Sacred Hearts Mission Church on Office Road, but the doors were locked. We walked down to a tiny church at the end of the road where many a visiting bride got married on a whim during a romantic vacation in Hawaii.

We cruised around the Kapalua shops, and I introduced her to the owner of the Italian restaurant where I was working. I promised to bring her to Friday Jazz Night, but reminded her that I'd be busy behind the bar, and she'd have to entertain herself. Everyone in the restaurant made a fuss over Vita. We had lunch in one of the booths. I didn't order the Caesar salad anymore, not since Cheyenne quit. The owner sat with us for a while. We discussed various Italian recipes he wanted to try in the restaurant, knowing my mom was Italian. Vita was having a wonderful time.

Cheyenne had a work buddy, Rudy Rodriguez, at the Sands of Nirvana. Rudy was married to a lovely girl; I think they were pretty close in age.

Cheyenne and Rudy were a great maintenance team, and kept that resort in tiptop shape. We'd been to their apartment a few times, usually after they worked a shift together. Rudy was an average-looking guy, nothing to write home about, and a bit of a tweaker. One evening after we'd settled my mom in her studio apartment at bedtime, we hung out watching TV in our condo. I could tell Cheyenne had something on his mind, but he was reluctant to say. Finally he came out with it.

"You know Rudy is really weird sometimes."

"Weird in what way?"

"I'm not even sure I should tell you," he said.

"Why? Is it something bad? Maybe it's something I don't need to know."

"It's just that his wife is so nice, so sweet, and so pretty. I just don't get it."

"What are you getting at Chey? Does he hit her? Spit it out already."

"There's an older woman who lives on the property where we work. He's been banging her regularly and bragging about it. Then he goes home to his wife."

"Oh God! How long has that been going on?"

"I don't know. I told him what he was doing was wrong."

"Maybe they have sexual problems. Not all couples are compatible that way."

"This woman's in her late sixties. What could he see in her. Besides, he has a wife."

"You don't know what goes on behind closed doors. Maybe his wife isn't into sex."

"I doubt that. She's a young girl. He says he loves his wife, and they have great sex."

"Chey I'll never look at Rudy the same way again, and I'll feel weird when we're at their place. Maybe he's just oversexed. I've heard some people are."

Cheyenne seemed to feel better after he got it off his chest. Rudy was a cad, and if he was cheating on his wife now when she was young and cute, what was he going to do when the bloom was off the rose? I was aware that some married people cheated. I'd been in enough relationships to know that people cheat for a reason. But having been the victim of it,

I knew that if his wife found out, she wouldn't get over it. When I was a hippie I cheated on two of my steady boyfriends. It was a retaliation for something they did or didn't do. It stemmed from an unhappiness in the relationship. But once you make that leap to infidelity there's destruction to the bond, and the relationship will never be the same.

On New Year's Eve, I took my mother to the Kapalua Bay Hotel, which was having an open house with a live band, champagne, and pu pus. We got all dressed up for the occasion. Susan Duffy, the deli manager at the Italian restaurant, came along. The three of us wandered in, looking to ring in 1995. I saw a young girl with a very tiny cinched-in waist. My mother commented about it. I reminded her that during the Victorian era, women of financial means had their lower ribs removed in order to wear those billowy dresses and maintain the tiniest of waistlines. Vita stared at me for a moment, processing what I'd said.

We headed to the bar for champagne when the band began to play. At about half an hour to midnight, I had so many things on my mind—my escape from the Everglades of Florida, the demise of Rebel, the death of my father, the future of my relationship with Cheyenne Bremmer, the disappearance of Gauguin (art) in my life, and my mother's thoughts about living in Hawaii. Everything good and bad was in a jumble rolling around in my brain. I knew what was behind me but not what was in front of me. It was one big unsolvable mystery in a swirling mosh pit. We rushed to the bar to fill our champagne flutes when we heard fireworks outside, just in time for midnight. I wondered what 1995 had in store for me.

> Until we accept the fact that life itself is founded in mystery, we shall learn nothing.
> —Henry Miller, American novelist

After the holidays life didn't slow down. I was working five shifts at the Italian restaurant in Kapalua, and one or two parties a week with the catering company. Very soon, the three months were up on the apartment I'd rented for my mother. She had to make a decision. Fearing her answer, I put off talking to her about it.

I had worked a back-to-back at the Italian restaurant, came home and took a shower. Cheyenne was still at work, so I walked straight to my mother's condo. I found her sitting on the bed with a glum look on her face. I wondered what had happened.

"I just spent the loneliest day of my life," Vita said.

I was a little confused. "What happened?"

"I haven't seen or heard from you since yesterday," she said, in an accusatory tone.

"Mom, I was racing from one shift to another at the restaurant."

"I think I'm ready to go home," she said.

Her words hit like a dagger to the center of my chest knocking the wind out of me. Disappointment sunk in. "You don't want to stay here in Hawaii?"

"I miss my friends and my sisters."

"Whatever makes you happy Ma? I just thought you'd love it here."

"Well, I really didn't see much of you. You're always busy. It's not a place where you can get around on your own, like in the Bronx."

I felt darkness sweep over me. "You know, I'm really tired. I think I'll go lie down and take a nap," I said, turning and walking out the door.

On the walk back to my condo I was filled with a feeling of helplessness, even some anger. I thought I'd bent over backwards to make my mom feel at home. I felt just like I did as a child—that she preferred her sisters over me, her daughter. I guess it was a selfish thought. I wanted to cry, but I was numb.

I walked into my condo with a heavy heart. I lay on the bed listening to the cockatiels chirp and whistle, but I was in a faraway place. I suppose I understood what she was trying to tell me, but I didn't have to like it. When Cheyenne came home, I told him that my mother had decided to go back to New York. As soon as he put his arms around me I began to cry.

"Hon, come on, it will be fine. You can visit her whenever you want."

"Chey, I haven't taken a real vacation for twenty freaking years. All my vacation time was visiting my family. I don't want to do that anymore. There's a whole world out there."

"It's going to be okay," he said, pushing me away and looking into my eyes.

"She chose her sisters over me, her daughter."

"She's just doing what's best for her. She's old. Let her enjoy what's left of her life."

"I guess you're right. It just hurts."

"Go over there. Let your mom know you're OK with it. Don't make her feel guilty."

Pricilla Bremmer was right—her son was an old soul, wise beyond his years. I made an effort to lighten my spirit as I walked to her condo. I found Vita in the kitchen cooking. We hugged immediately and professed our love for each other. She admitted how much she liked Cheyenne, and that she needn't worry about me anymore. I told her that I just wanted her to enjoy her life, and that I would visit her sometime in the near future.

The next day I confirmed her plane ticket back to New York. I made sure I set aside time to spend with her that last week before she left. I ordered her the use of a wheelchair and some assistance on her connecting flights. I was relieved to hear that one of her sisters was meeting her at LaGuardia Airport in New York.

It was brutal driving to the airport on the day Vita left. Things didn't turn out quite like I had wanted, but isn't that just the way life is? It hardly ever turns out the way you anticipate, and often not the way you wanted.

That night, I didn't want to have sex. I didn't want to hear any crazy stories about the guys in the band, or what was happening with Rudy Rodriguez at work. I just wanted the cocoon effect of a partner, and Cheyenne came through for me. Sometimes, all we need is for someone to hold us and tell us everything is going to be all right. I fell asleep after a few tears.

> Love as powerful as your mother's for you leaves its own mark.
>
> —J. K. Rowling

I went through weeks of moping around, but I kept myself crazy busy. I came home from my shift at the Italian restaurant and found Honey Girl on the floor in the corner. The bird looked stressed. I waited for Cheyenne to get home. He picked her up, as he often did, and put her on his chest. He petted her, but she didn't respond like she always did.

"Maybe my mother was right about something wrong with her throat."

Cheyenne didn't want to face the situation or talk about it. I searched through the phonebook until I came across a veterinarian in Kihei that specialized in birds.

"I found a bird vet. He even writes a column in a bird magazine."

"Really?" Cheyenne asked, brightening up with hope.

"I'll take her tomorrow," I said.

We had a small cage just for emergencies. The next morning, I coaxed Honey Girl on my finger, put her on the perch, and closed the cage door. Pua screeched as I took her away.

I was hopeful when I arrived at the Kihei Veterinary Clinic. I stood there while the vet examined her.

"I'm sorry to say she has a very bad crop infection. It's so advanced that there really is no treatment at this point." I stared at him waiting to hear what to do next.

"The humane thing to do is to euthanize her," he said.

I had a horrible flashback of taking my cat Boo to the vet because he wasn't eating, only to find out he'd been poisoned, and the vet telling me the same thing—"The humane thing to do …"

"You know what's best. I don't want her to suffer anymore," I said.

I was angry with myself for not listening to my mother's warning. She was right. Damn it, my mother was always right.

I walked out of his office with the empty cage and climbed in the Cherokee. I drove around looking for a public phone to call home. As soon as I heard Cheyenne's voice, my words began to break up.

"I had to have Honey Girl put to sleep. She had an advanced crop infection in her throat. It was beyond treatment." Then I began to cry.

There was no immediate response from Cheyenne. After a long silence he said, "I'll be here when you get home."

I drove home glancing at the small empty cage sitting on the passenger seat next to me. I parked on the street outside the hood and walked to our condo like a zombie. As soon as I walked through the front door Cheyenne stood up and hugged me. Pua, the male bird, seemed lost and confused. He paced back and forth on his perch. Cheyenne and I lay on the bed together, holding each other and crying, as if a family member had just died. Well, it was so. Cheyenne's mom, Pricilla, was right about her son. He cried more for that bird than he cried when his father died. I suppose we both felt loss and guilt at being neglectful. We remained that way until it was dark.

CHAPTER 14

DARK CLOUDS AND TUMBLING TIDES

Even as a small child, I understood that woman had secrets,
and that some of these were only to be told to daughters.
In this way we were bound together for eternity.
—Alice Hoffman, *The Dovekeepers*

My mother called me on Easter Sunday. I told her about Honey Girl, and she expressed her sadness in hearing of the bird's demise. I assured her that we planned on getting another female eventually, not wanting Pua, the male cockatiel, to be alone. We were talking like we always did on Sunday phone calls when she interrupted me.

"I made a big mistake," Vita said.

"What are you talking about Ma?"

"I should have never left Hawaii. I should have listened and stayed there with you."

"Ma, did something happen?"

"I'm spending the holiday alone. No one invited me for Easter."

"I'm sorry Ma. We're going to Abby's today." I immediately regretted the comment.

"And I could have been there with you. My sisters all went to their daughters' houses, and so did my neighbor. She'll be gone for three weeks. No one cared that I was alone."

"So what are you saying?" I asked, cautiously.

"I think I want to come back and live there with you."

"Ma, we will come to New York and help you pack."

"When can you come to New York?"

"I'll come for your birthday in September and we'll make a plan."

"Oh, I would love that," Vita said.

I hung up the phone feeling guardedly lifted in spirit. It crossed my mind that my mother was only temporarily let down, and that she'd get over it. Then again, being ignored by her sisters was a big thing. It was something I had no experience with. Being an only child forced me to have an independent nature.

That summer, a one-bedroom apartment on the second floor opened up in the hood. There was a tiled lanai with a fabulous view of the ocean. It was very spacious with an actual bedroom. It wasn't remodeled but had plenty of cabinets and storage. The owner was an Italian Jew from Milan, Italy, Lozano Manzoni. He was a good-looking man, a bit younger than me, with long, dark, curly hair and expressive brown eyes. I asked if he knew the Italian sisters, Mara and Zenda Schwartz, who were also Italian Jews from Milan, but he did not. He gave us a break on the rent, and we agreed to take the apartment. Annie Hughes gave us a sofa, which a friend had given her, but she claimed it was too big for her tiny apartment.

The new apartment upstairs in the J building was a big improvement over the tiny studio we'd lived in for four years. It didn't take long for the new place to get crowded with furniture and band equipment. Cheyenne set up the stacked sound system in a wooden étagère I found at a garage sale. The first night we watched the sunset from the lanai, I fell in love with the place.

I was settling in for the night after watching television. Cheyenne was at band practice. Our bedroom louvered windows faced the parking lot. I had already hung curtains, but they were open. I'd just jumped out of the shower nude, holding a towel as I fished though the drawers looking for a nightgown. I reached for my glasses and put them on. I heard strange noises outside. It didn't sound like an animal. I switched off the lamp on the dresser and peered through one of the louvers. There was a guy beyond the bushes in front of the parking lot, with his zipper down. He'd been watching me and jacking off.

I freaked out; I closed everything and ran out of the bedroom, shutting the door behind me. I did get a good look at the guy, because I had stared at the face that was staring back at me. I waited up for Cheyenne that night and told him what had happened.

"Adriana, that's what you get for prancing around nude."

"That never happened when we lived in the studio, and that was on the ground floor."

"This is not the commune you lived on in the woods. It's an apartment complex".

"I guess I wasn't paying attention."

"Damn hippies," he teased, hugging me and laughing.

A couple of weeks later I was in a salon getting my hair trimmed, when I gazed over at one of the hairdressers. It was the same face I'd seen outside the window that night. I was too stunned to even say anything. What makes a run-of-the-mill guy do something as crazy as that? I didn't have an answer. I certainly wasn't going to tell Cheyenne because he'd want to kick the guy's teeth out.

Our next-door neighbor was a divorced guy around my age. Our front doors were right next to each other, and his was always open. Unlike us, he had a screen on his front door. He'd often invite us in for a beer and conversation. Dash Kern was a Canadian transplant who owned his apartment—well, he had a mortgage. I liked playing with his black cat. We couldn't have cats because of the cockatiels.

We did get another female for Pua. We named her Cicci, after the famous Italian porn star Cicciolina, who founded a new political party in Rome called the Nature and Love Party. This erotic film actress was all the rage in Italy, fighting against government populism.

Watching TV one evening we heard moans and groans coming from across the way in the next building.

"Sounds like sex grunts," Cheyenne said, with an amused expression.

"I've heard women make noises like that during sex, but not men."

The sounds got louder until we could tell the sex act was over, and we both laughed.

"Chey, I promise I won't be that loud, I said."

"Wouldn't be the first time I've had to hold my hand over your mouth."

We heard that guy a lot in the weeks to come, no pun intended. Cheyenne nicknamed him "The Moaner."

That August of 1995 we heard that Jerry Garcia, lead singer of the Grateful Dead, had died. There was a rumor that he was still alive and secretly living in Paia, Maui. It is a thoroughly hippie town after all. Cheyenne and I drove to Paia and had drinks and lunch at Charley's Bar, affiliated with Willie Nelson. Walking through the streets that afternoon were plenty of hippies, but no sightings of Jerry Garcia.

The trend of big-box stores opening on Maui and the other islands continued; they popped up out of the red volcanic soil like pineapple pups. Abigail's Distinctive Affairs kept slinging Kool-Aid, buckets of Kentucky Fried Chicken, and endless boxes of sheet cake. The aisles were awash in sticky atomic-red liquid, and chunks of yellow cake with chocolate frosting.

Abby catered two small weddings in Lahaina on the same night. Somehow, the wedding cakes got switched. We didn't notice anything was wrong until the large white pastry box was opened in the kitchen at the venue, and the bride held her hands over her face in horror, saying, "That's not the carrot cake I ordered!" Luckily for Abby, both weddings were in West Maui, so the situation was easily remedied by sending Logan Baxter to the other wedding venue on the far end of town with the white cake, and exchanging it for the carrot cake—which luckily hadn't been eaten.

We became very friendly with our neighbor, Dash Kern, and often hung out in his apartment after work. Dash liked to drink vodka with Gatorade. Cheyenne preferred smoking pot, but never turned down a free beer. Dash was always watching a game of some sort on the TV. Neither Cheyenne nor I were into sports, so for us, it was just background noise. On one occasion, the three of us were standing at the counter in his apartment drinking beer. Dash was half watching a game when a bird flew into the glass sliding door of his lanai, dropping to the floor with a thud. We figured the bird broke its neck and was dead. Cheyenne scooped up the bird and cradled it in the palms of his hands.

"It's probably just stunned," Cheyenne said. He began to stroke the bird lightly and blew on it gently. After a few minutes passed, the bird twitched and opened its eyes. Cheyenne slowly opened the palms of his hands and the bird flew away.

Dash said, "What just happened? I thought the bird was a goner."

"He's the bird whisperer. I've seen him do this before," I said.

Cheyenne laughed and beamed, then reached for his can of Budweiser and took a swig. "Got any pot?"

"Can't stand the stuff," Dash said.

"I'm going next door and light up a bowl," Cheyenne said.

"I'm coming with you. I'm ready to eat something," I said.

I came home tired from my shift at the Italian restaurant, needing a drink after a very hectic day. When I got to the top of the stairs, I peered through my neighbor's screen door and saw Dash leaning against his kitchen counter.

"Hey, wanna beer?" he called out.

Instead of opening my front door, I opened his screen door. I set my purse on the floor and stood across from him at the counter. Dash walked to the refrigerator and got me a can of Budweiser. I never saw a foreign beer in his house. He claimed to be on a tight budget. He poured the beer in a glass mug, and we talked and drank the afternoon away. Through our laughter, I heard a voice and turned around to see Cheyenne peering through the screen door.

"Come on in," Dash shouted.

"Can I talk to you a minute?" Cheyenne said, staring at me—and not in a good way.

"I'll be there in a few," I said.

Cheyenne unlocked our front door and went inside. I got the vibe that he didn't like the idea of my talking to Dash alone in his apartment. At least, that was what I interpreted from his expression and tone of voice. I had experienced it before. I was a little miffed, to be honest, and was tempted to ignore him. After about fifteen minutes, I finished my beer and thanked Dash, saying we'd do it again. I grabbed my purse and walked next door.

Cheyenne was sitting on his favorite recliner staring up at the TV screen playing a video game, his thumbs darting along the game controller.

"Cheyenne, what the hell was that about? Why didn't you come in and join us?"

He continued playing the game for a moment, then looked up at me, a Marlboro dangling from his lips.

"Why were you hanging out with Dash? You like him or something?"

"Cheyenne, what are you even talking about? He's our neighbor. Lighten up."

"Have you done this before when I'm not home?"

"Are you out of your mind? I don't like being accused of something that isn't true."

He went back to playing his game and didn't say anything else. I knew he was jealous but couldn't figure out why. Was it because Dash and I were the same age? I'd seen an old photograph of Dash on the wall in his hallway. He resembled Don Johnson when he was younger. But there was only a trace of Don Johnson left in Dash Kern. Cheyenne felt threatened by him in some way. I knew how much he loved me; didn't he feel secure in the fact that I loved him? If I questioned him about a woman at one of his music gigs taking an interest in him, he'd say, "Don't be silly snapper-head." Men are masters of duplicity.

That fall, the Italian restaurant closed amid rumors of one of the owners disappearing and owing his partner a great deal of money. I wondered what I was going to do for work. I took the opportunity to carry through with my promise to go to New York and spend my mother's birthday with her. I was curious to find out if she was really serious about moving to Maui. I figured I'd look for a new day job when I returned.

I purchased a one-way ticket, hoping that I'd be helping her pack and move to Hawaii. Cheyenne dropped me off at Kahului Airport, expecting me back in a couple of weeks, three at the most. "I'll take good care of the kids [the cockatiels]," he said, as I got out of the Camaro. He smiled and blew a kiss at me watching me walk toward the outside ticket agent.

I landed at Kennedy Airport, which was farther from my destination than LaGuardia, but the ticket on that route had the best price. I took a taxi from the airport. It was a cool, rainy day on the fourth of September, gloomy compared to Maui. When the taxi pulled over in front of my parents' apartment building. I paid the driver who took my suitcase out of the trunk and set it on the curb. I looked up at the building and at the elevated train tracks that went past the bathroom window. A lifetime of memories passed before me. I felt nostalgic yet ominous.

I pressed the button in the vestibule, and my mother buzzed me in. I had called her from the airport to let her know I was on my way. When I reached the third floor, she was waiting in the doorway of 3B. We smiled, embraced each other, and went inside. The warm familiarity of it all was overwhelming. My mother had made supper, one of my favorites—cannellini beans with escarole. I took my coat off and sat at the table. All three of her cats were dead now, so we avoided talking about them.

"You must be hungry," Vita said.

"Yes, and tired, but this looks and smells wonderful."

"I made it especially for you because I know you don't have the time or patience to make it."

I reached for the grated Locatelli Romano cheese, sprinkling it generously over the bowl, taking delight in the toasted garlic garnish on top of the beans and greens.

"It's so good Ma," I said between bites. "It's having to wash the greens three times that annoys me."

She laughed and beamed with delight. "How's Cheyenne?"

"He's good. He's probably feeding the birds right now."

We ate in silence for a while with just the voices from the television.

After dinner she took out a folder of papers and statements from her investments. This was something I did in later years whenever I was visiting. She claimed she didn't have the head for stocks and bonds anymore. A few years back I'd convinced her to combine all the various investments under one company. That made it so much easier. There wasn't much of a portfolio left at that point, as she was using her savings to live on. The other thing she wanted to do was to fill out a health directive.

"I don't want to be resuscitated. If anything happens to me, and I'm in a bad state, just let me go. I don't want to be lying in a bed with a tube pumping food into my stomach, and someone having to wipe my ass, like your father in the nursing home."

"We can definitely do the health directive right away, Ma."

"You know, they can keep you alive for a long time, way past your expiration date. They collect money from procedures, medication, and hospital stays."

After supper, we watched television. We both liked *NYPD Blue*, and *Moonlighting*, with Cybill Shepherd and Bruce Willis . After we turned the TV off, I asked for sheets for the couch. Vita returned to the living room with sheets, a pillow, and a blanket. She set them on the couch and turned to look at me.

"I thought maybe you'd want to sleep with me," she said.

I was caught off guard and didn't know what to say. The couch had been my bed for so many years whenever I visited. I remembered sleeping with my mother as a child in the first house we lived in. It was when she had the affair with Dario. My father slept on my Castro chair-bed in the living room, and I slept with her in their bedroom.

"I think I'll sleep on the couch tonight, Ma."

"Oh, all right," she said. "I just thought you'd want to. I'll see you in the morning."

After that exchange, I had a hard time falling asleep. I wasn't expecting it and didn't know how to react, so I just went with my immediate gut feeling.

In the morning, I was awakened by all the sound effects coming from my mother, who was setting up the coffee pot in the kitchen. She huffed and puffed and groaned and gasped with each movement. She had arthritis and a bad back, not to mention a bad heart. A shoebox filled with various medications sat on the dining room table. I rolled over on the couch, waiting for the coffee to stop percolating. I glanced at the calendar that was sitting on the coffee table. I noticed a hair appointment that had been scheduled for the day before my arrival, and smiled.

"Don't look at the calendar," Vita said. "When you get to my age it's all doctor appointments."

I got up and put my robe on, walked to the table and sat down. I waited for her to bring the coffee pot and cups. I remembered that she always woke me up this way for school when I was a child, and for work when I was older. I never used an alarm clock.

There was a knock at the door. It was Nettie, her neighbor across the hall in 3A. "Did your number come out yesterday? Did you win anything?" she asked. Nettie lived with her brother. They were both retired, and neither of them had ever married. I liked her because she had been a seamstress in a prominent Manhattan dress design house. We often talked about it when I was there visiting. It was something we had in common.

Her brother was a weird guy; he was in the numbers racket. That was a big thing in the Bronx, betting the numbers. Every day they went to the corner store, got together with neighbors and played the numbers. It was a huge deal if they won money, especially if it was a thousand dollars or more. You never heard the end of the bragging. Mostly they lost or maybe won fifty bucks once in a great while, which hardly covered all the times they'd lost.

I got dressed and walked to the pasta factory to buy ravioli and a pound of fresh ricotta, which they made on the premises. On my way back to the apartment, I passed the restaurant where all the mob bosses ate. I saw two old waiters standing outside, leaning against the wall, with their long white aprons tied around their waists. The higher-end Italian restaurants in the Bronx only had male waiters. It was the custom. I'd eaten there only once. The food was very good, but you had the feeling that at any moment a table could get overturned and machine guns would come out.

When I walked into the apartment my mother was sitting at the dining room table. I was putting the groceries in the refrigerator when I heard her say, "I thought we'd take a trip to Connecticut and visit my sister Mari."

"Ma, I wasn't planning on renting a car and driving all the way to Connecticut. Maybe if it was the summer," I said. I was used to the small roads on Maui, and was not that keen on driving in New York City. Hell, I didn't even drive in the city of Honolulu anymore.

She looked disappointed, and perhaps I didn't pay enough attention.

"You know, I had an adverse reaction to the Coumadin I've been taking for years."

"What do you mean?" I asked.

"At first I didn't understand what was happening. About a month ago I had a period. I haven't bled like that for thirty years. I went to the hospital, and my doctor told me it was a reaction from the blood thinner. I was really scared, but they just said they'd cut the dosage. You know they play that game, adjusting your medications," she said.

"They're like witch doctors, but without that medication, who knows what would be?"

"I feel good now, but no one was around to help me. I went to the hospital by myself."

I took that as a personal dig at me. "Do you want to visit your sister Camille? We can take the bus," I said, ignoring her statement.

"Yeah, I'd like that."

When I called my aunt Camille she told me that her son, my cousin Rory who lived close by, would pick us up and take us home. I was relieved, not being that familiar with the bus route anymore. We had a wonderful day at Aunt Camille's house. We talked and laughed the afternoon away. We had cold cuts and crusty Italian bread with sesame seeds, then crumb cake and coffee. My cousin Rory drove us home. My mother was in good spirits. I felt unsure about bringing up the subject of her moving to Hawaii. Perhaps I realized the joy she experienced when she was with her sister Camille.

I was at the bathroom sink when I noticed my mother standing in the doorway.

"You still wash you face like a cat, with one hand," she said, smiling.

I grabbed a towel and dried my face.

"Come into the bedroom. I want to show you some things," she said. She was going through one of the closets when I walked in, tugging at dresses, searching at the bottom for shoes, and looking up at boxes. "See that box up there? I saved beautiful fabric for you from when I had the dress factory."

"Really Ma?"

"And if anything should happen to me, look through everything—all my coat pockets, behind picture frames, everywhere you can think of. I have jewelry and cash hidden."

"Ma, remember the time you sewed those diamond earrings into the hem of the living room drapes and forgot all about it when you sent them to the dry cleaners?"

"And you see this dress?" she said, ignoring me. "I want to wear this in the coffin. And for God's sake, don't let them see my feet. I want the casket to cover my legs."

"Ma, stop it. Why are you talking like this? It's not what I came here for. We're here to make plans for the future."

"I just want you to be prepared, you know, just in case something should happen."

I was troubled by the turn of conversation, but for now I felt I'd better keep my mouth shut about her coming to live with me in Hawaii.

The next day my mother's oldest sister Porciella came by. She took a cab from Manhattan, where she was living with her daughter, my cousin Gia. We sat at the dining room table reminiscing about all the holidays we'd spent together in the old days. The men would stay in one house playing cards and drinking, and the women and kids would be in another house, cooking and baking. Porciella told us about all the things that were going on with her daughter Gia, and with her granddaughter.

I could see my mother wasn't happy or smiling. I dwelled on the fact that I didn't afford any of that joy to my mother. No marriage and no grandchildren. My mother's demeanor changed, and she got a little nasty. She began questioning why I had to move so far away to Hawaii.

Aunt Porciella defended me, saying, "Vita, sometimes young people move away from their hometown to better themselves."

My mother wasn't satisfied with that comment. She began opening up old wounds—how I had turned away from her at my graduation from fashion school, refusing to go to a restaurant with her, and that she had gone home alone crying. "That's the kind of daughter you were!" Vita said, the pupils of her brown eyes sharpening into tiny beads.

My calm demeanor began to unravel. "Why don't you tell Aunt Porciella why I didn't go with you for graduation dinner that day?"

My mother stared at me. "What do you mean?"

"You came to my graduation with your boyfriend Dario, not with Daddy."

"What made you think of a thing like that?" she said, probably angry that I had exposed the truth.

"You wanted me to go to a restaurant with you and him," I said, angrily.

My aunt intervened suggesting we make coffee and have the Italian pastries she brought from Little Italy in Manhattan. That broke our angry exchange, but it was just a reprieve.

After Porciella left, my mother kept it up—all the things that bothered her about my not being like the other young people in the family, grievances I suppose she'd stored up over the years. According to her, I was the black sheep who had to do things differently.

"I don't understand why you didn't marry Troy Bloom. He was such a great guy with a good job at a TV station and a promising future," she said. "Why? I'm asking you why?"

"We weren't sexually compatible."

"I don't understand what that even means. What could have possibly been wrong?"

"He wouldn't eat me. Oh, he wanted me to do it to him, but he wouldn't do it to me. Who the hell wants to commit to a life together with someone like that?"

"Really Adriana? I never heard of such a thing to say—although I did do things with Dario that I never did with your father," she said, twisting her lower lip.

"Did you really have to tell me that, Ma?"

She struck blow after blow at me. I became unhinged and let her have it in kind.

"You made a fool of Daddy all those years. You dragged me on dates with your boyfriend, Dario, when I was just a child, using me as an excuse. But Daddy knew all along; the whole family knew!"

My mother became quiet. She sat there, stiff, as if I'd just stabbed her. "I think I'll go to bed," she said, standing up. Then she turned and said, "Adriana, let's not go to sleep angry with each other."

"No Ma, let's not. I'm sorry. I guess a cork just popped."

We didn't hug or kiss. My mother turned and went to her bedroom. I sat on the couch, angry with myself for blowing my top like a volcano going off after a hundred years of being dormant. It's amazing what anger and disappointments can be lurking deep in our subconscious, hidden for thirty years. Right there, I probably convinced her that moving to Hawaii to spend what was left of her life with me was not in the cards. It was just another thing I'd regret for the rest of my life.

I lay on the couch trying to fall asleep. I thought of my therapist, Joan, telling me that I was too hard on my mother. I was still punishing her for the affair she had with Dario. He always reminded me of that Italian actor from the 1950s and '60s, Marcello Mastroianni. I recalled my mother showing me a photograph of Dario in his army fatigues in Ethiopia, when he served during the Italo-Ethiopian War. I understood their attraction for each other. They were a good match with similar personalities. For Christ's sake, the man was dead and buried already. I'd loved different men in my life for different reasons, so why couldn't I afford my mother the same slack on the loves in her life? I thought of the day Dario gave me a beautiful gold medallion on a chain that he'd purchased while he was in Italy on a buying trip. He hugged me and said, "I love your mother so much," as if he was asking for my forgiveness.

I woke up to no coffee percolating. I was lying on the couch looking around. Soon I heard my mother walk to the dining room table and sit down.

"I'll make the coffee," I said, standing up and putting my robe on.

I set up the coffeemaker in the kitchen and sat down at the table across from her, listening to it percolate.

Vita said nothing, resting her head in her hands. Then she said, "I don't feel right."

"Did you take your medication?"

"No, I take my medication after breakfast."

I helped her up and walked her to the couch. She lay down and closed her eyes. I sat at the table drinking my coffee, wondering if she was still angry with me over the ugly words we'd exchanged the previous night. I was upset and couldn't eat breakfast. I took a dress out of my suitcase to show her. I walked to the couch blabbing about where I'd found it, holding the dress for her to see. There was no response. I thought, *Oh God, she's ignoring me. Maybe she's still mad at me.* "Ma, look at this dress I brought to wear for your birthday."

She didn't stir. I touched her shoulder to gently wake her, yet there was no response. I began to shake her. "Ma, Ma, answer me!"

I ran out into the hallway and banged on our neighbor's door. Nettie opened the door, and I began yelling that I couldn't wake my mother up. She ran back in the apartment with me. "Call 911," she shouted. I could hear Nettie yelling my mother's name over and over again. "Vita, Vita, wake up, Vita."

The ambulance was there in less than five minutes. The paramedics were working on her, and asking me questions about her medications, but I was in a panic, my mind a total blank. I handed them the shoebox filled with her medications. I don't know what they injected her with, but Vita revived. They sat her up and began asking her questions.

"Where are you? Who's that?" They pointed at me.

"I'm home. That's my daughter," she answered.

I was so relieved. They told me they were taking her to the hospital anyway to make sure she was all right. I rode in the ambulance with her.

At the hospital, she was kept on a gurney in the hallway for a long time. I didn't understand what was happening. I wondered if they had given her all of her medications. I stood next to her and rubbed her hand.

"I'm so hungry," Vita said.

I felt the urgency of her situation was not being addressed, yet it was a hospital, and I had blind faith that they knew what they were doing.

"I'll get you a sandwich from the cafeteria," I said, walking away. When I returned, I handed her a tuna fish sandwich on white bread, which she munched on cautiously. She seemed a little foggy. I asked her if it was good. She answered me, but her words were gibberish—they made no sense at all, although she seemed to think they did. I calmly stood up and walked to the nurses' station so as not to alarm her that something was wrong. I told a nurse that my mother was talking, but none of the words made any sense.

They immediately wheeled her into a room, and that was the last I saw of my mother for two hours. Eventually a nurse came out to tell me that Vita was having mini strokes, and that she'd have to stay overnight. I flashed on her story about bleeding like she'd had a period about a month back, and I hoped there wasn't bleeding in her brain. Suddenly I was terrified, but I had to remain strong and alert for her. I was aware that you need an advocate when you are hospitalized.

"Your mother is in a room on the second floor, if you want to see her," one of the nurses said. She suggested that I not stay too long because she needed rest.

I took the elevator up to the second floor and looked for her room. Vita's face lit up with relief when she saw me. I sat by her bedside.

"What do they say?" she asked.

"They want to keep you overnight for observation." I mentioned nothing about the mini strokes.

"You will come tomorrow, won't you?" she asked.

"How can you even ask me such a thing? I will be here first thing in the morning."

"This is turning out to be some vacation for you."

"Don't worry. You'll be fine, and we will make plans for Hawaii."

My mother smiled.

I stayed for a while; I kissed her and squeezed her hand. I told her that I loved her before I walked out of the room in a semi-trance. It had been a disturbing twenty-four hours. I was totally drained. I got my bearings and knew where I was, and by some miracle I remembered which bus to take from the hospital. My ride back to the apartment was filled with a sense of doom and lots of guilt.

The apartment was warm. I sat down at the dining room table in a numb state.

Mom's neighbor Nettie knocked at the door, and I let her in. "You know, your mother hasn't been doing so well the past few months. I think she was just waiting for you to come."

That wasn't what I wanted to hear, but it was the new reality I faced.

That night, I called Cheyenne back on Maui.

"Do you want me to come to New York?" he asked.

"I don't know exactly what's happening yet. Besides, who will take care of the birds? And it's not like you can just quit your job. We still have to pay the rent. I don't think it's a good idea, as much as I wish you were here."

"I guess you're right. Let's wait and see what happens," he said.

I got off the phone thinking that the closing of the Italian restaurant on Maui was the work of God or the universe, freeing me up to help my mother through a difficult time—as if it was all meant to happen this way.

I sat at the desk in the bedroom staring at the telephone. My eyes drifted up to the relief hanging on the wall. It was an art piece my old boyfriend Jamie Fitzpatrick had given my parents as a gift one Christmas. It was a scene of a deer in the woods with a stream and a cabin. The background was painted, but the deer and trees were actual figurines glued onto the surface. Why they would save that silly painting all these years escaped me. I imagine it had something to do with Jamie and I having been engaged, and my mother picturing the four of us living in a mother-daughter duplex somewhere in the Bronx, after I married him. But I was only seventeen and obviously didn't have that same vision. It probably reminded her of happier times in her life. I thought of the time I asked Jamie, "If I were pregnant, and there was a problem with the pregnancy and I might die, would you save me or the baby?"

When he said, "The baby," I made up my mind I wasn't marrying Jamie Fitzpatrick! Obviously I wasn't his priority. After the memory subsided, I stared at that silly relief on the wall and dialed my mother's sisters.

I watched television for a while but couldn't really follow any storylines. When it was time to go to sleep, I stood up like a robot and walked into my parents' bedroom. I laughed at my mother having told me once that she hated the bedroom set, but that my father loved Danish Modern.

Above the headboard hung a pair of scrolls in very ornate frames. I'd given them to my parents as an anniversary gift one year. They were black-and-white etchings of a Renaissance king and queen. I felt the need to sleep in their bed. As tired as I was, I had a difficult time falling asleep. I thought of a crazy routine my father had whenever I brought a new friend home. He'd lead them into the bedroom, switch off all the lights and close the door. He'd shine a flashlight toward the ceiling and ask, "See that? All that soot flying around in the air? That's what's killing me!" I sat up, shook my head and laughed. I figured that somewhere in that bedroom closet was a gas mask. After a fit of unexpected laughter I finally fell asleep.

The dark details of events and tumbling tides of emotions over the next weeks were like a Shakespearean tragedy. I watched my mother deteriorate, slowly and brutally. It was horrifying to witness. Her sisters took turns going to the hospital with me. The progression was first the loss of the use of the right side of her body; soon, she lost speech.

My aunt Camille walked with me to the bus stop after visiting hours.

"You do know about the ward Vita is in, don't you Adriana?

I stared at her blankly.

"It's the ward where people are sent who are not going home," she said.

I began to cry, realizing the gravity of her situation. In one of the beds in that same ward was a very young girl in her twenties who had just had a baby. She'd pushed so hard during the birth that she had a stroke. I realized that she was never going home, that her husband and family would go from the joy of the newborn, to the impending death of the object of their affection.

"You were always so difficult," Camille said.

"I know I was a disappointment to my mother, but we can't help who we are."

"I understand," she said. "I don't hold it against you, but she is my sister."

On week three, my mother spent her eighty-first birthday in a hospital bed. Two of her sisters came that day. I sat my mother up in bed, fluffing the pillows behind her and combing her hair. She'd lost a lot of weight. I could tell by the expression on her face that she was very self-conscious in front of them, and couldn't wait for them to leave. I never cried in front of my mother because I wanted her to remain hopeful. She wanted me to go back to Hawaii. I told her I wasn't going anywhere without her. She seemed relieved.

Each time I spoke to Cheyenne back on Maui, I'd let loose with sobs as soon as I heard his voice. It was a release from all the emotion and sadness I'd been holding in all day. Life would get even more difficult.

By week four Vita couldn't swallow any longer. I asked to speak to her doctor, who was a very young Russian immigrant. She updated me on a few things. She suggested that we put a food tube in Vita's stomach. I told her no; my mother specifically told me she didn't want that. I regretted that we hadn't had the time to fill out the health directive and give it to her primary care doctor.

"Well, then, you're killing your mother by withholding food," she said.

"Why don't you ask my mother what she wants?" I said.

The Russian doctor walked to the ward with me, and we stood beside my mother's bed. Vita lay flat on her back staring up at us.

"Ma, do you want a feeding tube in your stomach?"

My mother shook her head, unable to say the word no.

The young Russian doctor looked at me, exasperated, and left the room for a while. I waited. My mother's sisters, who also knew my mother's wishes, backed me up. The Russian doctor returned with a team of doctors. They stood outside in the hallway conversing. I walked out to join them.

One of the doctors—he looked Japanese—turned to me and said, "Your mother's brain is scrambled, so it really doesn't make a difference."

I wondered why in the world he would say something like that to his patient's daughter. I was confused and angry and didn't know how to react. I walked away from them and sat on the chair next to my mother's bed. I had to seriously think about what I needed to do. I was given the brochure of the same nursing home my father had been in. I was forced to go to an interview there—it had something to do with a requirement for the continuation of my mother's health insurance. We were five weeks in now, and I was feeling desperate.

That night I called Cheyenne. As soon as I heard his voice I broke down in sobs—that feeling of total helplessness and despair. "I had a bad day!" I blubbered. He repeatedly asked me if I wanted him to come to New York. For so many reasons, I thought it wasn't a good idea. Why I insisted on going through this on my own escapes me now. Looking back, part of it, I am sure, was not wanting to deal with the judgment of my family regarding our age difference. I was in a vulnerable state and didn't need more drama.

My cousin Angie and her husband, Ash, drove to New York from Cape Cod. They picked me up at the apartment, and we drove to the hospital together that evening for visiting hours. I had been there earlier in the day and found my mother slightly improved. When we arrived at the hospital, Angie and I took the elevator up to the room, while Ash looked for a parking space. We walked past the other beds in the ward and found that my mother was not in bed. The nurses had propped her up in a chair next to the window. She looked up at us with a vacant stare.

Angie and I hugged each other tightly. I whimpered a little.

I went to the nurses' station and asked them to please put Vita back in bed. "Your mother seemed much improved earlier," one of the nurses said.

Angie and Ash drove me home at the end of visiting hours. I sat in the living room looking at my artwork that hung in various places. I guess my mother admired my artwork after all. She'd had the art pieces framed a long time ago. I realized that she did admire me in some way, even if she was disappointed in the path I chose in life.

For the first time in a very long time I prayed. Vita's friend in apartment 3C, the former nun, came by to sit with me. We talked for a long time. She mentioned how she'd often overhear my mother and her sister Camille telling stories and laughing so loudly that she could hear them through the wall. I knew my mother's life was there in New York, and realized that she'd never be happy in Hawaii, even if it was with me.

Early on the morning of October 29, 1995, I was having something to eat before going to the hospital when the phone rang. I nonchalantly picked up the receiver, thinking it was my Aunt Porciella, who was meeting me there. But it was the hospital calling.

"We just wanted you to know that your mother Vita has passed away. If you want to see her you can come any time. You don't have to wait until visiting hours."

I hung up the phone and sat at the desk. I couldn't even cry. I calmly called her two closest sisters, who wanted to come to the hospital with me, but I wanted to say goodbye on my own.

I quickly got dressed and took the bus to the hospital. I gazed out the window along Moshulu Parkway—the parkway being the same place where the Moshulu Indians held powwows seventy years past. The same route I used to take to Noah Bernstein's house in the West Bronx. He was my first live-in boyfriend, whose relationship took me to San Francisco for the summer of love in 1967. The bus passed the Bronx Riding Academy, but there were no horses and riders on that bleak day. My mind was replaying an avalanche of scenes from my past.

When I arrived at the hospital, I took the elevator up to the fourth floor. I walked past the nurses' station and into the ward where my mother was. I passed the bed where the young mother in her twenties had been before she died. There were curtains around my mother's hospital bed. I walked through and sat down on a chair next to her. I touched her face and neck, which were still warm with life, even though she was gone from this world. In a way, I was happy her suffering was over. I wondered what was on her mind in those last few hours. Did she want me there holding her hand? I wondered if there was still a spark of life left in there, some part of her able to understand.

I stroked her hand which was still soft and pliable. I said, "Ma, Daddy will take care of you now." I broke down and cried. We often didn't see eye to eye, but she was my mom. I grieved my last grief at us parting after an argument in such a dramatic way, and I'd hoped I didn't cause this. I told her how much I loved her, and promised we'd meet again. I kissed her forehead and said goodbye. I stood up and walked through the curtains. I stopped at the nurses' station to thank them for the attention they showed my mother.

They advised me to make arrangements with a funeral home as soon as possible. I walked out into the hallway, through tumbling tides, past rooms filled with sick and dying people, in a state of numbness. I went through the hospital doors under a dark cloud, in a daze, for the last time.

A Pueblo Indian Prayer

Hold on to what is good,
Even if it's a handful of earth.
Hold on to what you believe,
Even if it's a tree that stands by itself.
Hold on to what you must do,
Even if it's a long way from here.
Hold on to your life,
Even if it's easier to let go.
Hold on to my hand,
Even if someday I'll be gone away from you.

CHAPTER 15

SEEKING SALVATION

I have seen that in every great undertaking it is not enough
for a man to depend simply upon himself.
       —Lone Man (Isna-la-wica), Teton Sioux

I called Cheyenne Bremmer in Hawaii and told him the news. There was
crying and remorseful tales of woe on my part, but he propped me up with
love and light. That lasted for the length of the phone call. As soon as I
hung up darkness returned.

I began going through all the closets like a sleuth on a mission of
discovery. I found large, gaudy rings with gems the size of quail eggs
wrapped in tissues in the pockets of house dresses and coats. I found the
2.5-karat diamond solitaire engagement ring Vita offered me and Jamie
when we got engaged. I heard Vita's words in my ear: *"Someday this ring
will be a condo."* She'd already given me most of her sentimental jewelry
years ago.

I found mementos from when Vita belonged to the Daughters of
Italy. She wore a wig with a fake diamond tiara, and a blue cape. I came
across a program and tickets to a dinner at the Loyal Order of the Moose,
which my father belonged to. I found hundreds of dollars in cash in the
backs of picture frames, and more cash at the bottom of the napkin box
that sat in plain sight on the dining room table. I was very thorough so
as not to miss anything. I thought of the time my parents and I were
eating dinner, when we heard a clanking sound coming from the kitchen.
My mother was defrosting the freezer, and silver dollars were dropping
which had been frozen to the roof of the freezer. I shook my head and
had a good laugh.

There were three fur coats in one of the bedroom closets—an autumn
mink cape; a jacket with the body of an actual mink, head and all, as
a collar; and a full-length luscious, dark ranch mink with a hood, that
she'd purchased from the fur coat designer I worked for in Manhattan. I

pictured my mother in that coat twirling around with a beautiful smile on her face, filled with life, and flashing her rings.

My style was native funk and flash; Vita's was mostly flash. The coat was too big for me, and where the hell would I wear it in Hawaii? I planned to take them to Ritz Furs in Manhattan, a fur thrift resale store, to see if I could unload them for a decent price.

I made a call to the funeral home to make sure they had picked up my mother from the hospital, and to set a time for me to come by and bring her clothes and shoes, the ones she instructed me she wanted to wear in the coffin. I also took the rosary beads I'd found in a drawer next to a missal I saw her read. Her friend, the ex-nun, told me she had the beads blessed at the Vatican in Rome.

I swung by the funeral home to give them her clothing. The funeral director had me look through a book with coffins in different price ranges. I picked out the one I thought she'd want. I'd gone through that same book less than two years ago with my mother when my father passed away, so I knew her preferences. He gave me some advice about the church service and the pallbearers, stressing they would all have to be paid in cash. Everyone in the funeral home seemed respectful, but I sensed an undercurrent which I couldn't quite put my finger on. I didn't notice any women, and all the men looked like they'd just completed a scene in a mob flick. Of course a funeral home is not a happy place to begin with, but still it was a bit odd.

I left the funeral home and went directly to the bank to close her accounts and empty the safe-deposit box. Luckily on one of my visits a few years back, she had added me on her accounts and on the signature card for the safe-deposit box. I brought her death certificate just in case. There was only about six thousand dollars left in her savings account, which I hoped would cover the funeral expenses. I called my cousin Gia and told her I needed the deed for the grave, since our parents had purchased a plot together at Woodlawn Cemetery when her father Faustino died a fairly young man. I had no clue as to how expensive it would be to have the grave opened. I left the bank with the cash in large bills stuffed in my bra, and a sack filled with jewelry, which I held very close to my body under my winter jacket.

Before I went back to the apartment I stopped in my favorite pizza joint, and ordered two slices of thin crust with extra cheese. I sprinkled oregano and hot red-pepper flakes on it and sat at a table. I picked up a slice, folded it the correct way, and watched the grease drip off onto the paper plate before taking a bite. I hadn't eaten since the previous day, and found the pizza comforting and filling. I watched people come and go as if it was just an ordinary day on Crosby Avenue.

At the apartment I went through all the jewelry from the safe-deposit box. The majority of the pieces were ornate and expensive, most of which I knew I'd never wear. I noticed that my mother had saved the simple wedding band that my father had given her when they got married. That was proof of love to me. Through all of life's trials and tribulations, cheating and arguments, they managed to stay together for fifty-five years.

Gia and her husband Stu came to the apartment. I made coffee, and we ate the cannoli they'd brought from a bakery in Little Italy.

She handed me the deed to the cemetery plot. "You'll need this to have the grave opened."

Our fathers were already in that grave six feet under; now my mother was joining them. Gia's mother, my aunt Porciella, was still alive, even though she was the oldest of all the siblings. She was living with Gia and Stu in their penthouse apartment, which was on top of an old hotel in Tribeca. It was quite a place, with a rooftop garden filled with trees, shrubs, and barrels of water lilies in summer. Walking out on their terrace was like a sunny day in Tuscany. I thought of all the Christmases we'd spent there. Their dining room is mostly glass. Snow would come down outside all around us, while we ate warm and cozy inside. My cousin Gia was like a sister to me, and I was happy to give her my mother's sapphire ring, a rather large stone encircled with diamonds. It was Gia's birthstone. I gazed at it on her finger as she poured more coffee in my cup.

When they left I felt empty but industrious, so I decided to go through the large junk drawer at the bottom of my parent's dresser. I opened the drawer and fished through papers, stocks and bonds, and insurance contracts. I found a large black cardboard folder with sketches and renderings I had done in art and fashion school. They were in good condition despite all the years that had passed. I came across a manila envelope filled with sheets of poetry and rambles I'd written. Then I came across my journals and letters, on which my memoir is based. I remembered hiding the journals at the bottom of that drawer on one of my visits to New York.

It was a bit of a shock to see that my mother had saved all the correspondence I'd sent her after I left home to live on a commune in Berkeley, California in 1967. I packed the letters and journals away in a box to read when I got back to Hawaii, but I found myself fishing through them while packing up the apartment. I got in the habit of reading a few journal entries each night while sipping a gin and tonic.

Journal entry 1971:

> It's been windy and cloudy for days and won't let up.
> Why won't the rain come down and cool everything off,
> cleanse our souls?
> Been thinking of having a baby.
> Never thought I'd say it, but there it is.
> I'm scared, don't want to do it alone, though that'll
> probably be the outcome.
> I fear the physical thing, and another life depending
> on me.
> At the lake I saw a girl nursing her baby.
> I'd just had an abortion. I couldn't watch.
> I am empty, a life is gone, taken away, no given away.
> She said, you'll have a baby someday.
> I cried and held hers.

It wasn't easy to remember how I felt that day. I set the journal down and stared at the large framed charcoal drawing I'd done of a mother and child that hung on the wall in the living room.

Charcoal of mother and child

The next day I called Woodlawn Cemetery. I was informed that it would cost approximately three thousand dollars to open the grave. I took the bus to a florist in Parkchester, near our old neighborhood. I ordered a beautiful floral arrangement for my mother to be delivered to the funeral parlor. My next stop was the funeral home. I handed the director cash, with which he would take care of the pallbearers. Then I walked to our neighborhood church and spoke with the priest about the mass. He said he'd coordinate everything with the funeral home. I did all these things alone. I realized that if I'd had a husband he'd be doing all this with me, helping me with this burden. *I should have asked Cheyenne to come to New York to be with me*, I thought. Then again, he wasn't my husband.

I came home and sat on a chair in the small room off the kitchen which was used as my bedroom when I was younger. It had no doors. Originally, there was a carved wooden lattice covering the archway to the living room, which I covered with an Indian bedspread that I'd purchased at the World's Fair, when Jamie Fitzpatrick and I went with my parents.

The three of them were troubled by my fascination with the Moroccan Pavilion, where I spent a lot of time roaming among the hanging rugs and Bedouin couches. The Moroccan teapot I took home that day was still sitting on a bookshelf. My parents never threw anything away.

A folding screen separated the tiny room from the kitchen when I wanted privacy. I thought of all the times I'd jacked off Jamie Fitzpatrick in that room. I saw myself sitting on the Castro chair-bed with my legs wide open, Jamie's head between them, eating me to the sound of clanking coffee cups and family chatter in the dining room. We never had intercourse; we were saving that for after we were married. I was only seventeen, and that never happened.

When I left the commune in Berkeley in 1969 and came to live with my parents again, I got rid of the Castro chair-bed and went through a phase of sleeping right on the floor atop my sleeping bag and a few quilts. It was actually very comfortable. I suppose that's how I developed a liking to sleeping on a mattress on the floor. I gazed up at an abstract drawing in colored chalk pastels that I'd done in high school. It was framed and hung on a wall facing the window.

Tomorrow was the beginning of the wake, which would run for three days. I had to be prepared to greet family members and friends. I made myself a stiff drink. I picked out another journal and settled on an entry from one of the hiking trips I'd gone on with Troy Bloom to the Grand Canyon in July 1972.

From my journal:

> Descending down into the canyon the sun scrambles your brain and sucks your energy. It's sweaty, nasty, and hot as hell. We walked for hours and still didn't reach the bottom. Thought we were on the wrong path in some remote part of the canyon. Slept right on the trail under the stars, scared, hot, and thirsty. Walked farther at dawn and saw a sign to the base camp. Relieved, happy, drank the rest of our water. Reached the bottom, dumped our packs, clothes, and dove nude in a rocky pool.

I wondered where Troy Bloom was now. Was he even still alive? I'd heard rumors that he committed suicide, but I thought they were unfounded. He was such a great guy, except in bed.

On the first day of the wake I wore all black, as is the custom when one is in mourning. It's an Italian tradition from Rome dating back to 700 BC. The funeral director told me my mother looked beautiful. He escorted me to the room were her body lay in view. I went in by myself, cautiously walking up to the open coffin. The bottom was closed, covering her legs as she wished. I knelt down and stared at Vita, who looked so peaceful with her hands clasped and her own rosary beads entwined in them. She looked beautiful but dead.

I felt nothing there; she was an empty shell of her former self. It was unsettling. After I stared at her for a while, I made the sign of the cross, stood up, and sat in a chair in front of a gallery of chairs, waiting for people to show up. At that moment, I think I felt more alone than I'd ever felt in my life. My immediate family was gone, and I was floating around in the cosmos by myself, not even wearing a spacesuit to protect me.

Soon people began to arrive. Greeting everyone was daunting and made me dizzy. People showed up that I hadn't seen since I was a child. They'd introduce me to their significant others, who I didn't know, and really didn't give a shit about. Others showed me photos of their kids and grandkids. It annoyed me as much as the trend of sending a Christmas card during the holidays with a studio photo of their kids who you don't even know, rather than a short sentimental note. It was ceremonial, impersonal, unfeeling, and sometimes fake. Of course, there were people I loved, but even some of them had morphed into their parents with age. At least I knew they all loved my mother. That was the first day, with two viewings, morning and evening. It was draining.

I was happy to get back to the apartment. I made myself a cup of tea and sat at the dining room table munching on a rugelach I'd picked up at the German bakery down the street. I stared at a painting I'd done that hung on the dining room wall. The still life was my first attempt at acrylics. The subject matter was a bottle of Chianti in a basket beside a wheel of Gouda cheese set on a wooden table.

I walked to the box with my journals and picked out a blue notebook from 1971.

From my journal:

> Never satisfied with myself
> My physical appearance
> Wanted to be taller, slimmer
> Not so serious, not so hairy
> Not so loud, not so angry
> Is this why I get frustrated?
> I am what I am
> People do love me for it
> So why can't I?

By the second day of the wake I was numb to it all. People came and went, but most of my close family members stayed. We all began sharing amusing family tales, and there was much laughter. At one point, I noticed that one of my mother's eyes had opened.

I told her sister Camille, who laughed and said, "That's Vita, she's listening to us and wants to be part of the conversation."

I alerted the funeral director, who told me that he couldn't imagine how that happened, as they sew the eyelids shut. That gave me a queasy feeling. He asked everyone to vacate the viewing room while he remedied the situation. We all filed into the lobby and patiently waited while he sewed Vita's eye shut.

My cousins Angela and Ash showed up at the evening viewing on the second day of the wake. They were staying in town for the funeral, and it was nice to catch up. I wanted to find out if the funeral director knew of a good restaurant where I could take the family after the funeral; it's an Italian tradition. When I stood up, Ash insisted on coming with me. Walking into the office I guess we surprised the funeral director. There were piles of cash—singles, fives, tens, and twenties—in neat stacks on the desk in front of him. Four big guys, who could have been in the cast of *The Sopranos*, were standing around looking very stoic.

"Excuse me," I said. "I didn't mean to disturb."

"No trouble at all. How can I be of help?" the director asked, in a Tony Soprano voice.

"I want to take my family to an Italian restaurant after the funeral tomorrow. I was wondering if you have any recommendations."

The Sopranos all looked at each other. Tony said, "Leave it to me. I know a guy who owes me a favor. How much do you want to spend?"

Ash shrugged his shoulders when I searched his face for an opinion.

"I'm not sure, but I know my mother would want a number of courses," I said, as if she was in the room on the planning committee.

"For fifteen dollars per person, you could have spaghetti marinara, chicken marsala, and cheese cake for dessert. But for twenty-three dollars you could have antipasto, Penne a la vodka, a choice of chicken or fish for the entrée, red and white wines, espresso, and spumoni or tiramisu for dessert."

"I'll go for the twenty-three dollars," I said.

"Tell me how many people, and I will take care of the rest," Tony said.

"Let's say fifteen people, just the close family. You're a lifesaver," I said.

Tony nodded in affirmation, and I smiled in appreciation.

"The limos will drop your family off right in front of the restaurant after the funeral."

Ash and I walked back to the viewing room a little bewildered but laughing about the scene in the director's office. I figured when Tony Soprano gave me the total price, I'd bring him the cash to add to his collection.

That night I was a bit on edge. It was the eve of my mother's funeral. I wasn't sure I could get through it alone, although I had done it so far. I needed to get my mind off it all. I knew it would be hell on the morrow. I reached in my box of journals and picked out a more recent book. I smiled at the thought of my cross-country trip with the bubble-headed O'Brien sisters, and the night we spent in New Orleans.

From my journal, 1976:

> Satin ladies, black and white gentlemen
> Flappers with red crystal beads and swinging fringe
> Patent-leather hair, spit curls, and marcel waves
> Hot waves and hot numbers in the Metropole Café
> Horns blowing, tubas buzzing, and banging drums
> All with an ace in the hole
> Dave Von Ronk, stoned to my soul
> Happy music making me dance and sing

It was a cold November day, day three, the day of the funeral. I walked alone to the funeral home. My family was already there. We had a final viewing of the body, and it was rough. Lots of tears and hugs. I asked Ash if he wouldn't mind staying in the room after everyone left, because I couldn't bear to watch them close the coffin.

"Of course! I'll stay with Vita and make sure she's all right," he said. I knelt to say goodbye to my mom. I slipped the original wedding band my father had given her next to her folded hands. I got up, and Ash hugged me. I walked out leaving him there to watch them close the lid and follow the pallbearers carrying the coffin out to the hearse.

We all got out of the limos at the church and looked for seats among the pews. My mother's youngest sister, Camille, and oldest sister, Porciella, walked me down the center nave. All I could think of was how I'd robbed my father of the joy of walking me down the aisle as a bride. Funny how the mind works at such times. The pallbearers set the coffin down near the altar to the sound of organ music while a woman sang Ave Maria. That's when the nose-blowing and tears began.

The priest's sermon started out beautifully, reminding everyone that my mother's name, Vita, means life. That was true; she was always full of life. Then the priest went off on a crazy tangent about Russia that made absolutely no sense. There were confused looks, heads shaking, and some snickering. I even pictured my mother rolling her eyes in the coffin until I remembered they were sewn shut. But I knew that for my mother, that day was deliverance. She was free from the bounds of life on earth.

It was snowing as the two limousines followed the hearse to Woodlawn Cemetery. It was about a forty-minute drive, but there wasn't much to see outside the window, just snow coming down. The weather cleared a bit as we arrived at the cemetery gates. The limo passed the monument to the *Titanic*, and once we saw Miles Davis's gravesite we knew we were close. My parents were in good company. Woodlawn Cemetery was built in 1863 during the Civil War. Many famous people are buried there. I thought of the day my mother purchased the plot, so many years ago. She had said to me, "At least I know where I'm going! We're on a hill under a willow tree."

We stood around the recently opened grave. The words spoken were a jumble. I stood there in black high heels, with the cold wind blowing up my dress. I stared at the willow tree which was bare. We all threw a flower on top of the coffin as it was lowered, and shovels of dirt were thrown in. The pallbearers placed all the wreaths and floral arrangements on top, the ones I didn't donated to the church for Sunday mass.

We all silently got back into the limos, and were eventually dropped off in front of an Italian restaurant right in my mother's neighborhood. *Wow, Tony Soprano came through for me,* I thought. A large family-style table was set with stemmed wine glasses and carafes of red and white wine, as much as we wanted to drink. Baskets of crusty Italian bread were spread along the table within everyone's reach. There were dishes with olive oil and balsamic vinegar for dipping the bread.

We took our coats off and sat down. A waiter appeared with small platters of antipasto, and we began picking. The talk was festive, and there was a collective laughing fit when someone brought up my mother's eye opening during a lively talk at the wake. We all agreed that she was sitting at the table with us, not wanting to miss out on a family reunion. She would have been the life of the party. The rigatoni al la vodka was good, but the sauce was not as good as Vita's. Lots of grated cheese on top remedied that. We ate and drank like Roman gladiators and told old family stories. It was all so wonderful. I hoped my mother was looking down pleased with it all, and pleased with me at how I had handled everything. I suppose I was seeking forgiveness, a bit of salvation, and yes, redemption.

After espresso and dessert everyone began getting their coats and leaving the restaurant. We stood outside in the cold talking and hugging. We kissed goodbye and went our separate ways. My family had come through for me. I was so thankful for my cousins and my mother's sisters, who never left my side that day. They wanted me to go home with them, but I told them that I just wanted to go back to the apartment and lie down. I was exhausted from the past weeks and needed to rest and gather my thoughts. The apartment felt strange as I entered. It was empty, yet I felt my parents still there, as if they would walk into the living room at any moment. I saw their three dead cats alive, creeping around corners and playing with toys.

Just then, the phone rang. It was Cheyenne.

"How'd it go today?"

"I think I'm fine. I surprised myself with the organization of the funeral and the dinner. I miss you."

"I miss you too," he said.

"I'll probably be here a while longer. I have to clean out this apartment."

"Whatever time you need. Do what you have to do. I'll be here when you get home."

We talked for a long time. Cheyenne told me about everything going on back on Maui. He suggested that we go to Tucson, Arizona, for Christmas to spend the holidays with his mom and sister. I told him it sounded like a good thing for both of us, and that we'd make a plan when I got back to Maui. When I hung up the phone I was slightly depressed. I walked to the cabinet, got the gin, and made myself a tall drink. I flipped through my journals, settling on one in which I seemed to reveal my disdain for New York City after living in Berkeley, California, for two years.

From my journal 1969:

> Sidewalks, freeways, statues
> Concrete! Concrete! Concrete!
> How lifeless can everything get?
> Or are we already there?
> Can't look at much, can ya man?
> Mr. Dylan, send us a dream
> Build its façade like peaches and cream
> Give us more trees of mint leaves and clover
> Then tell us that our concrete nightmare is over

And so began the dismantling of the apartment in which my parents lived for thirty-two years. Giovanna Ferrari came with me to a few auction houses in Manhattan, Christie's being one of them. I wanted a good price for my mother's jewelry—the pieces that had no sentimental value to me, or that I knew I'd never wear. The auction houses all had a similar rap—there was no guarantee of the price for which the items would sell, and the auction house received a third of the proceeds. Gia suggested that I keep the jewelry for now, and decide what I wanted to do with it later on. I went to Ritz Furs, but when they examined the large box with my mother's expensive furs, they told me that they were too old-fashioned, and wouldn't be able to sell them. I walked out disappointed.

My cousin Ariel came to the apartment with her husband Bruno to see how I was doing. I handed her my mother's full-length ranch mink with the hood. She'd always loved and admired it, and after all, she'd taken my mom to doctor appointments. I felt it should belong to her. She put it on and twirled around the living room, running her hands along the fur, smiling just like Vita would do.

"It's yours," I said.

"I'll always think of Vita when I wear it," Ariel said, her eyes tearing. "And I want you to know that regardless of what you think, your mother loved your father very much."

Inwardly I knew it all along.

I emptied the contents of the closets into large plastic garbage bags. There was so much junk, but I did find a few gems. Ariel had given me the card of an antiques dealer to call if I came up with any treasures. I found two vintage purses and three hats in very good condition, which I was sure were worth something. I also came across a crocheted Italian bedspread—a gift from a friend of my mother. Vita had given her a job in her dress factory when the woman first arrived from Italy. I called the antiques dealer, who gladly took those items, as well as two cherry-wood end tables that were hand carved and imported from Italy, along with the white fake marble coffee table, and two large Italian figurine lamps. My mother loved extravagantly beautiful things. I got a decent price for everything.

I took a break and sat in the living room. I searched through the box of journals and pulled out one from 1973.

From my journal:

> The two of us women hiked to the top of Mount Monadnock. I realized I was still in pretty good shape. We sat for a long time on top of the mountain and talked about ourselves, about men, and relationships. We saw berry bushes and ate from them. We hiked back down and went skinny-dipping in a quarry. We hitched a ride to the Cape and scaled the sand dunes filled with wild rose bushes, gnarled trees, and windblown shrubs. We

were overcome with joy at our first glimpse of the Atlantic Ocean. I watched her slide down a sand dune and run into the cold sea. That night she fucked the Italian Indian but had a hard time accepting it for what it was. I told her I fucked the young guy with the twelve-string guitar and didn't bat an eyelash. Summers in the northeast are the best, and you're sure to fall in love with Old Cape Cod.

After reading that entry, I laughed at how uninhibited I was back then. We just stuck our thumbs out and hitchhiked to the Cape on a whim, seeking adventure.

I told my cousins to come to the apartment and choose an item they wanted before everything was given to the Goodwill. My cousin Jenny took a hand-crafted soup tureen from Italy that she'd always admired. My cousin Cody drove all the way from Connecticut to take the nine-foot couch, the espresso machine, the table-sized wooden bread-and-pastry board, and a few other kitchen items. The ex-nun next door in 3C took my mother's raincoat. She handed me a beautiful mass card, along with two partially burned candles that were used in a memorial mass for my mother and other deceased parishioners of Our Lady of Assumption Church who died in 1995. I still have them in a drawer. I also kept the missal my mother used for daily prayer in later years.

I was emptying a few precious items from the china cabinet when a train passed by the bathroom window shaking the dishes and glasses. I gave a little chuckle. Everything else I would have professionally packed and shipped to Hawaii.

I took the train to Manhattan to visit my cousin Gia and her husband Stu. I loved going to their rooftop apartment. It was like a green oasis in the middle of a concrete jungle. We had lunch in the dining room because it was a little nippy outside. I stared at the plumeria tree that was standing in a pot next to the piano. The tree had taken over a large portion of the room. I remembered when it was just a tiny stalk I'd sent to them from Hawaii. I walked outside to the terrace and looked down twenty-four floors to the traffic in the street below. I turned my face south to see the arch in Washington Square Park. I thought of the pottery class I'd taken with Adam Hirschfeld so many years ago. I pictured us walking down

Fourth Street, arm in arm, in the late sixties, like the cover of a Bob Dylan album.

I handed Gia the deed from the cemetery so she'd have it in the event her mother, Porciella, passed away in the coming years. We vowed to have the gravestone carved for our parents, with all the names and dates after she was gone. At the time, just our two last names, Ferrari and Bardolino, were etched on the stone. I heard a roar above me and looked up. A plane was passing overhead, probably having just taken off from Kennedy Airport. It was so close I could smell the jet fuel.

On the train ride back to the Bronx I dozed off hearing the screeching of the train wheels over the tracks, as I had done since I was in high school. Riding those trains and subways was a big part of my early life. The noise was like a lullaby to my senses. Funny that I never missed my stop. I would miraculously wake up just in the nick of time. Walking to the apartment from the train station, I flashed on a day I was walking on that very street with my mother. I was about sixteen years old. A guy walked past us, and Vita squeezed my arm and said, "Adriana, that guy melted and fell apart just looking at you." I must have had my head up my ass, because I didn't notice it, but she did. It was the day I learned I was beautiful, and how that could have an effect on men. I realized beauty wielded a lot of power.

My mother's neighbors down the hall were renting the apartment when I left. They were an interracial couple who had the most beautiful little girl. They'd often gone grocery shopping for my mother when she didn't feel well. I asked the husband if he would like the Danish Modern china cabinet and bedroom set when I left. He was overjoyed at the prospect. I assured him the furniture was his. When he left, I made myself a drink and sat on the couch. I came across one of my LSD rambles in a red journal from 1970:

From my journal:

> Anything? Anymore? Alcoholic, junky, pimp, fag
> Can't you see we're all the same?
> Is it still light outside?
> How much is left?
> Did they give me too much? Did they give me enough?
> No more chemicals!

We take them to make the pain go away
We take them to make the pleasure more intense.
When is the end?
God, I'm god, we're all god.
Sometimes I think I'd be better off dead
Where's my baby? Are we all pregnant?
Where are the children?
Where are you at?
Don't bring those trips in here!
None of us know what we need
The birthday party gets bigger every year.
I don't know what's going on
Let's not mention any names.

I called a shipping company listed in the Yellow Pages of the phonebook. I needed them for items like a vintage Singer sewing machine from my mother's dress factory, and some of my larger framed artwork. They promised to pack my artwork very carefully. "It's our profession ma'am," the guy claimed. I took slides of my artwork before they were wrapped and packed. I took the smaller watercolors out of the frames and rolled them in tubes to take on the plane with me. I went to the post office and mailed three boxes to myself with personal items, like family photo albums, the box of letters and journals, all my sketches from art school, and a set of pots and pans that my mother had purchased as a wedding gift for me when I was engaged to Derick Ellis and living in Miami in the 1980s.

The apartment was pretty bare at that point, save for a Christmas wreath I had sent my parents for the holidays a few years back. I bought it when Abigail's Distinct Affairs worked opening night at the Hui No'eau's Christmas craft show in Makawao. The wreath was made of king and queen protea and eucalyptus, with a smattering of berries. It lasted a long time. Now, it was a dried-up dead thing hanging on the wall that needed to be tossed in the trash.

It was a week before Thanksgiving when I left the Bronx at 4:00 a.m. I'd arranged for a private cab to take me to Kennedy Airport for an early flight to Honolulu. I left the apartment house carrying my suitcase and my father's accordion—a beautiful instrument with mother-of-pearl–plated keys. I just couldn't leave it behind. (The accordion sat on a shelf in my parent's closet for years, and now it sits on a shelf in mine.)

It was a very cold night after a heavy rain. Icicles hung from the entrance of the building. It was like leaving the Kremlin in the midst of a dark, frigid, Russian winter. I felt great relief as the cab drove away. It marked the end of something I couldn't quite put my finger on. One thing I knew for sure was that after the loss of my mother I would never be the same.

CHAPTER 16

REDEMPTION

Dull Knife and the homeward bound Cheyenne, whom
the army tried to starve into submission, but who resisted
until the last warrior charged the troops with nothing but
his war cry and an empty revolver.

—Frederick W. Turner, *Geronimo*

I slept most of the way on the plane ride back to Hawaii, just staying awake
enough to exit one plane and drifting like a sleepwalker to the next gate
to catch the next flight. When I reached Honolulu though, I seemed to
resuscitate.

Cheyenne Bremmer picked me up at Kahului Airport, and we hugged
for a long time. I was too tired to cry or talk, so I waited at baggage claim
in a numb state while he went back to the parking lot to get the Cherokee.
Cheyenne flipped a Metallica cassette in the dash, and I began to feel
drowsy.

"I'll make us chicken and dumplings for dinner tonight," he said.

"Sounds wonderful, but I'm not that hungry."

"You look good. I was expecting you to be all haggard and *hammajang*."

"I guess I slept that off during the long trip home."

No sooner than I said that, I fell asleep listening to Metallica's "Enter
Sandman" on the car stereo.

Bob Marley said, "One good thing about music—when it hits you,
you feel no pain."

Pua and Cicci chirped and whistled when they heard my voice. I'd
missed the birds, and I could tell they'd missed me. Of course they had
no idea what I'd been through.

Everything was familiar, yet I felt detached. I'd been gone for almost
three months. I feared I had changed in some way—that I had experienced
a dose of hard-core reality. I wondered about my future with Cheyenne,

who was so much younger than me. I figured, as I always did, that the universe would sort it out.

I spent the next few days getting back in the swing of island life and getting reacquainted with Cheyenne—in the biblical sense. I didn't ask him what he did while I was gone. I never got the feeling he cheated on me, but the thought always dangles in a woman's mind. Cheyenne was an attractive guy with a great personality. He was a guy who loved his music, his bandmates, and close friends took up most of his time. One thing was for sure—I knew Cheyenne Bremmer loved me.

Everything seemed to get back to normal until one night I was awakened by someone's voice moaning and shouting. It was my voice. "Ma, Ma, Ma," I heard myself say because she was fading away. I sat up in bed.

Cheyenne shook me. "What? What's wrong?"

"It was my mother standing on the sidewalk in front of the first house we lived in."

"You were dreaming."

"No. It was real; it was her. She was holding her arms out wanting to embrace me."

"What did she say?"

"She didn't say anything. She was smiling at me. Then she put her hands together like she was going to pray. She always did that when she was happy about something. For the first time in my life I felt that she was finally pleased with me."

He put his arms around me, and I began to cry.

"It's only natural. You've been through so much over the past few months, but you're home now."

I stopped crying. We lay back down, and I nuzzled my head in the crook of his shoulder while he rubbed my arm with tenderness. Soon we both fell back to sleep.

That week I felt the urge to go to church and say a prayer for my mother. I hoped it would bring me peace. I parked across the street from Maria Lanakila Church, the church my mother loved when she visited Maui. The church was deserted except for two old Filipino women who were dusting the pews. I walked down the center nave breaking down in uncontrollable sobs before I even reached the altar.

The women rushed over. "What's the matter?" one woman asked.

"I lost my mother," I blithered through tears.

One woman gently placed her hand on my shoulder, and the other leaned in and held my hand. I recognized one of the women. She was the owner of the house I lived in on Nanu Street behind the sugar mill in the late seventies. She didn't recognize me. It was my friend Loretta Perino who had rented the house and usually dealt with her.

"Say a prayer to God for your mother," she said.

"She's looking down on you with love," the other woman said.

I gained my composure and thanked them for listening to me. I sat in a pew by the tall windows and gazed at the mango tree outside, the same tree my mother marveled at when she sat there. A calm came over me. After a while I noticed I was alone. The two old women who were cleaning the church had gone. I stood up and lit a candle for my mother in front of the statue of the Virgin Mary. I knelt there and said a prayer. I thought of Vita coming to me in that dream and felt a kind of redemption. I made my peace with the death of my mother. I got up and walked to the altar, crossed myself, placed my hand over the mosaic hand of Father Damien, and left the church.

We spent another Thanksgiving up at Silver Cloud Ranch, but Abby insisted it was a Christmas-themed event. We were all instructed to wear gaudy Christmas sweaters. It was so good to be up on the crater in the country. The horses and cows were still around, but I only saw one potbellied pig. The air was crisp and fresh at night with a million stars. Evenings were filled with stories while sitting around the fireplace. Cheyenne and I wore matching colorful flannel jackets that I'd picked up in New York City. Abby had someone dress as Santa, and the women took photos sitting on his lap. Everyone was there—Hans Berlin, the chef from Germany; Filippo Rizzoli; Hackman and Hargrove; Jumpin' Jimmie; Veronica Dove; the Italian sisters; and Logan Baxter. Paki Makani was there with his girlfriend Sheila, whose former husband had saved my life during that awful dog attack, as was all of Abby's family—her husband Bubba, and son Ben. Bub's son Bob from a former marriage was married to a Hawaiian woman. They were there with their whole clan. Bubba's thirteen-year-old granddaughter did a hula for him in honor of his upcoming birthday at the end of December. There wasn't a dry eye among us watching her dance.

With Thanksgiving behind us, Cheyenne convinced me that Christmas would probably be an emotional roller coaster, and that we needed to get off the island. We bought round-trip tickets to Tucson, Arizona, to spend two weeks over the holidays with his family. This was also an opportunity to take a vacation before I began a job search.

Pricilla Bremmer picked us up at the Tucson airport. She was filled with excitement to see her son. His grandma Willa sat next to his mom in the front passenger seat. I stared out the window as we drove along a very arid landscape filled with cacti of all types and sizes. It was a far cry from the tropical climate we'd just left on Maui. We pulled into the driveway of a double-wide trailer surrounded by a fenced-in-yard.

Once inside, it was like any other house. It was roomy with a number of bedrooms and bathrooms. Grandma Willa had a similar setup right next door. There was a Christmas tree already decorated in the living room, but Pricilla told Cheyenne that he was charged with the task of erecting the train set. I noticed a complete ceramic village on top of a large platform next to the tree.

A girl walked into the living room. I assumed it was Cheyenne's sister. "This is my sister Barbara," Cheyenne said.

She and I nodded and smiled at each other. Barbara lived there with her little boy, who was overjoyed to see Cheyenne. I didn't catch his name until his mother Barbara yelled at him: "Kevin, did you finish cleaning your room?"

I felt comfortable right away being with his family. Pricilla and I sat at the kitchen table together like we had done so many times when she lived on Maui. She asked me all about my mom and about New York. I told her an abbreviated version. I really wasn't in the mood to rehash it all just yet.

When it was time for bed Barbara told us we were to sleep in her room. She was bunking in with her son Kevin. We were happy to have the privacy of our own room, but I hated the idea of displacing her. Cheyenne had told me she had some problems, and that Pricilla and his grandmother Willa were helping to raise Kevin.

We sat on the bed, which was very bouncy and soft. We rolled toward the middle as if the mattress was on top of a ditch. We began to laugh until something else was on our minds.

"What's so funny?" Barbara called out from the hallway.

We didn't answer. "It's only for two weeks," Cheyenne whispered.

I woke up with a tweak in my back from the bed. I didn't wake Cheyenne; I let him sleep in. With the morning sun, I noticed a funny-looking jar on a shelf over the headboard, along with some photographs. I put my robe on and looked for Pricilla, who I found sitting at the kitchen table with coffee and a cigarette. *That's a familiar scene,* I thought.

Cheyenne's mother was less than ten years older than me, but we were worlds apart in so many ways. We did have something in common that was of great interest to both of us—Cheyenne. I was sure she wanted him to move back to Arizona, and she probably resented me for keeping him on Maui. She never said as much, but I felt it. We were having a nice chat when I heard Cheyenne call me from the bedroom.

"Hey hon, come in here."

I excused myself from the table and went back to the bedroom. Cheyenne was lying there with a smile on his face and a bump in the blanket. I laughed a little and got back in bed.

After we made love we talked about our plans for the day. He wanted to show me around Tucson. It was Christmas week, and we wanted to pick up gifts to put under the tree.

"What's in that weird ceramic jar?" I asked.

"That's my mother's first husband Slim."

"Wow, that's a little creepy!"

"I can bet ya she's got my dad in another urn in her bedroom."

We got dressed but didn't take showers. It was pretty cold in Tucson, and we were used to the tropics. Pricilla was making breakfast when we walked into the kitchen—corned beef hash and eggs with biscuits and gravy. I was looking forward to a day of sightseeing.

Cheyenne took me to an old mission church built in the 1700s. He knew I loved that stuff. San Xavier del Bac Mission Church was something unique and beautiful in the Moorish, Byzantine, and Mexican Renaissance style. It was filled with old religious icons. I knelt at the altar in front of a Madonna that was dressed in real clothing. I'd never seen anything that elaborate. On the way out we stopped at a market filled with religious trinkets and silver jewelry. I snagged a silver ring in the shape of a tarantula holding a moonstone. We drove around on mountain roads and then onto a main road. We stopped at a supermarket to get a six-pack of beer and a few items Pricilla requested. There was a sign at the entrance: LEAVE YOUR GUNS OUTSIDE. We certainly weren't in Kansas anymore, or Maui for that matter.

The next day, Cheyenne was in the process of putting the train set together with his nephew Kevin. I sat at the kitchen table with Pricilla and his sister Barbara.

Pricilla said, "It's been a couple of years since Jim died. I'm thinking of getting out there again."

"You mean date? You're still a young woman," I said. "Why not?"

Barbara glanced at me rolling her eyes.

"I get lonely sometimes," Pricilla said. "I did have a number of men over, but after a few dates nothing developed."

"I think the first thing you should do is get rid of those urns holding the dust of your late husbands in the bedrooms," I said, and the three of us laughed.

Barbara asked me if I'd like to take a ride with her while model train city was being erected. I figured it would be a chance to get to know Cheyenne's sister. As we were walking out the door Cheyenne gave me the craziest look.

We hopped in her old beat-up black car—I didn't pay attention to what kind of car it was. She took me on a wild-goose chase from one trailer to another, frantically searching for something. Each time we pulled into someone's driveway she'd ask me to wait in the car, assuring me that she would be right out. This was repeated at least four times. This rampage along trailer row took up the whole afternoon, until she got what she was looking for. After the second stop I figured out she was on a search for drugs. I was annoyed, but she was so erratic that I just let her do her thing without commenting. She drove along the dusty back roads until we finally ended up back at the house before dark.

There was conversation while driving, but she didn't have much good to say about her relationship with her mother or brother. I understood that she'd been adopted, but she was in no way appreciative. I made sure not to get roped into that situation again.

Cheyenne took me to see one of his cousins. It was a strange place in the middle of nowhere, but at least the girl was someone I could relate to.

She had a parakeet in a cage on the kitchen table. We spent an hour or so visiting with her. Cheyenne and his cousin passed a joint back and forth while I played with the parakeet. That night we hung around the house watching television. I wore the most luscious, tight, formfitting pants of a tie-dyed crushed pan-velvet, along with a sweater over a T-shirt. Cheyenne couldn't keep his hands off me. Even though it was all so Christmassy and homey, he soon marched me to the bedroom past the Christmas tree all lit up. He fucked my brains out to the sound of the toy trains rushing around the track through a miniature village.

The five acres the Bremmers owned wasn't far from mountainous terrain, so when Cheyenne's aunt and uncle came by we all went on a hike. I'd been in arid landscapes before when I backpacked in the Grand Canyon with Troy Bloom, and I had investigated various parts of Colorado, New Mexico, and Arizona. The endless varieties of cacti and thorny bushes was very interesting. There were no blossoms of any sort because it was winter.

This landscape was beautiful in a different way than I was used to; it just wasn't my way. I hoped Cheyenne didn't want to move back to Arizona. We saw mountain goats and got close enough to take photographs. That evening after dinner we all sat around the kitchen table. Pricilla told us about the first time she'd encountered javelinas (also called musk hogs because of their odor).

"You can smell them coming," she said. "I was sitting outside on the porch when I smelled something pungent, something I'd never smelled before. Then, there they were, a pack of pig like creatures as ugly as large rodents. They ran all over the place and right under the house. It's not uncommon to see them brazenly walk through the neighborhood in a pack."

We all ooo'd and ahh'd at her story. Then the conversation turned to tribal politics, and things got really heated. Being of Native American heritage they were all bitching and moaning about having to pay taxes to the government. They said this was really their land, and that it had been stolen from them. Instinctively I knew this wasn't my fight, so I kept my mouth shut.

The following day, Cheyenne wanted to get together with his old friends; I guessed they were his old bandmates. I stayed back with Pricilla. She and I were going shopping in town, and she wanted to show me the supermarket where she worked as the manager of the bakery department. I mentioned that I'd love it if she baked a chocolate cake with lots of chocolate icing—chocolate being my favorite. When we got back to the house Cheyenne wasn't home. Pricilla made coffee, and we sat and talked for hours. Still no Cheyenne. She became edgy and seemed troubled.

It was getting dark when Cheyenne staggered up the front porch steps and in the front door. He was totally drunk. Pricilla was visibly upset. I was just confused, never having seen him like that. Pricilla sat on a chair at the kitchen table and cried. I couldn't figure out her emotional reaction to his coming home drunk. Cheyenne slumped on the couch next to me. I had a momentary reaction of disappointment and disgust. I couldn't help thinking back to all the times Derick Ellis had come home drunk. I hated it, and had a hard time keeping my wits about me. But I chose to react differently than I had with Derick. I put my arms around Cheyenne, motioning for him to lay his head in my lap.

He did as I asked, like a little boy wanting to be cuddled. He stared up at me, his eyes like deep pools of seawater. Then he nuzzled his face against my pan-velvet pants, the ones he liked so much. I turned his head and lightly ran my hand back and forth across his forehead, which seemed to calm him. I remembered Pricilla telling me he loved that when he was a baby, and it worked like a charm. I think it stopped him from getting belligerent, and maybe saying things to me or his mother that he'd later regret.

I walked him to the bedroom and tucked him in. When I knew he was asleep I closed the door and walked to the kitchen. I sat at the table with Pricilla, held her hand, and asked her why she'd reacted the way she did.

Pricilla said, "Cheyenne's father, Jim, was a bad drunk for a while. It was a horrible time in our marriage. I was wondering if my son was following in his father's footsteps. Jim would get drunk in bars and pick up women. Sometimes he wouldn't come home for days. It was a difficult time."

"Men can be thoughtless idiots at times," I said. "I had a boyfriend who got drunk all the time and then started shooting up hard drugs. It ruined our relationship. We were engaged to be married. When I rebuffed him physically in retaliation, instead of working things out with me, he found another woman to screw and put up with his bullshit. Love can turn to hate when you feel let down and betrayed."

Later that evening, after Cheyenne sobered up, he explained that he and his friends had gone to a bar and got nostalgic about a tavern they all went to in the old days, the Stumble Inn. Once they were of legal age they frequented that place all the time. He claimed he just got lost in the moment.

"I understand," I said. "As long as this drunkenness doesn't become a habit. I wasn't really angry with you, just troubled. You should talk to your mother though, because she was really upset."

He stood up, walked into the kitchen, and sat at the table with his mom.

When Christmas was over we went with his aunt and uncle on a jaunt to Tombstone, Arizona—a total throwback to the Old West. There were cowboys and cowgirls riding horses, and a staged gunfight on a corner at high noon. We wandered in and out of shops with western-themed clothing, and Native American trinkets. Cheyenne fell in love with a long cowboy duster in one of the western shops. When he slipped it on, he looked very authentic, as if he'd just walked off the set of the movie *Tombstone*. We passed a storefront that took period photographs, and we had a professional photo taken of the two of us in early western garb. They dressed Cheyenne as an outlaw cowboy, and me as his Indian tracking squaw.

Tombstone, Arizona, 1995

We passed an old saloon and walked in. It was a big tourist attraction. I swore I could hear the ghost of an upright piano playing. I imagined painted ladies in seductive frilly dresses with lots of cleavage popping out of their bustiers, and long curls surrounding their highly made-up faces. Those who engaged in prostitution were sometimes called *soiled doves.* Upstairs there were small rooms, not like the colonial rooms I'd pictured in my mind. These were tiny closet-like rooms with just a single bed, a dresser, and a hanging mirror. On the bed posts hung a contraption that my eyes zoomed in on. It was a jar-like thing with a narrow hose. I asked Cheyenne if he knew what the heck it was.

"That's for the whooahs {whores}," he said laughing. "its how they douched between the men they entertained."

His explanation made sense. There wasn't much in the way of birth control back then.

We passed card tables on our way out. I pictured grubby cowboys who hadn't bathed in weeks, and slick-dressed dandies playing poker. Bottles of whiskey, shot glasses, and firearms laid impotent on the surface of the wooden tables. None of it matched the romantic image I had of saloon life, and dashed the thought that I could have been a saloon girl back in the 1800s.

Before leaving the iconic town of Tombstone we wandered through a graveyard taking note of the young ages of the people buried there, most in their teens and early twenties. Life expectancy a hundred years past was much shorter. If you reached thirty-five you were doing well or just lucky. Many died from diseases for which there was no cure back then. And, of course, it was the lawless Wild West. I got a kick out of some of the inscriptions on the tombstones and wooden crosses:

Here lies Lester Moore, four slugs from A-44, no Les, no more
John Heath, taken from county jail, LYNCHED
in Tombstone Feb. 27, 1884
Seymore Dye, 82, killed by Indians
Billy Clayton, Tom McLaury, Frank McLaury,
murdered on the streets of Tombstone, 1881

New Year's Eve was windy and chilly. I walked past the Christmas tree and the train set, and peered out the window. I could see tumbleweeds rolling along the street beyond the white picket fence, propelled by gusts of wind. I stared at the American flag in the yard lit by the rays of a spotlight. The flag was waving wildly, to the eerie sound of the rigging flapping against the flagpole.

I wanted to go home. I certainly didn't want to live among these flimsy trailers. I believed they could be lifted into the air and tossed around in a tornado, like in those newsreels where you see a cow flying. Cheyenne walked over and circled his arms around me. I had a forlorn feeling, a feeling that even love couldn't cure. I wondered what 1996 had in store for me.

"We're going back to Maui in a few days," he whispered.

I took note that he did not use the word *home*. "I'm looking forward to it," I said.

In the kitchen Pricilla had just taken a ham out of the oven. I watched her use the fatty grease at the bottom of the pan to make gravy, and my stomach turned. Cheyenne smirked at my expression. Dinner was really good, but in the middle of the night I was throwing my guts up in the bathroom toilet across the hall. Cheyenne knocked on the door a few times. I told him to go back to bed, that I'd be fine. I convinced him that it was just the rich food, but looking back, I knew it was much more than that.

Pricilla and Grandma Willa drove us to the airport on the day we left Tucson. Pricilla wouldn't take her hands off Cheyenne. She held onto him and wouldn't let go, as if a piece of her was being torn away. Never having been a mother, I had no idea what that felt like. Grandma Willa cried just to see her daughter so upset. Cheyenne seemed oblivious to all the love being thrown in his direction. *Just like a man to not have a clue*, I thought. We walked away from them to the gate and onto the plane. I looked back to see Grandma Willa holding her daughter who was in tears. Sophocles said, "Sons are the anchors of a mother's life."

Being back on Maui in the hood was a relief. I loved our apartment in the J building, and I couldn't wait to see an awesome sunset from the lanai. I drove to Kihei the very next day to retrieve Pua and Cicci, who'd spent the two weeks boarded at the bird vet. Two days later, the cockatiels flew out the front door while I was on the phone. We didn't have a screen door, but this had never happened before. I always made sure the door was shut when the birds were outside their cage. I ran outside and down the stairs. Pua, the male, was sitting on the ground waiting to be rescued, but Cicci flew right over the building and out of sight. I called Cheyenne at work. He drove home, picked me up, and we scoured the neighborhood. I brought along the small cage, and the fish net on a long pole, which I used to catch the birds when they refused to go back in the cage. We heard Cicci in a large mango tree quite a distance from our apartment complex. We parked under the tree. I spotted her, but every time I got near her with the net she'd fly to another branch. Soon she disappeared.

How will she eat? I wondered. Perhaps other birds would attack her. We couldn't sleep at all that night. We tried leaving Pua in the cage outside on the lanai. We hoped she'd hear him and fly to the cage, but that didn't happen. I made a flyer with a photo of Cicci and drove to Napili Market, which had a bulletin board back in those days. As I was fastening the notice to the board, I saw a large note: "I have your cockatiel. Call me." I copied the phone number, sped home, and called immediately. When I described Cicci, the guy said it was definitely her. Cheyenne and I drove to the guy's house. He told us that he'd heard a bird in the Norfolk pine tree outside his front door that wasn't familiar. He saw it was a cockatiel and trapped her by wetting her down with a hose so she couldn't fly. We were so thankful to get her home, and Pua was overjoyed to have his mate back.

Having no day job, my search began. I found work with a local landscape company called Ground Control in Kaanapali. It wasn't far from the main highway, with all the hotels visible from the outside porch. I was the sole employee, sort of a gal Friday. The first thing I'd do when I opened the place in the morning was head to the orchid room. I'd get the hose and water all the plants crowded on long wooden tables under a black gauzy tent. Then I'd check the computer for any orders or requests for specific plants or trees. Occasionally, one of the hotels would rent large plants or areca palms as decor for a meeting in a conference room. They always sent someone to pick them up and would return them after the function, so I never had to lift any large pots.

Once a week I ordered cut tropical flowers from Hana. When the truck delivered the flowers, I'd put them in containers filled with water and store them in the refrigerators at the back of the workroom. I'd spend the morning making large, tropical floral arrangements, which I'd deliver to various hotels with which we had weekly contracts. This usually took a few trips and most of the afternoon. I enjoyed the bit of creativity it afforded me; it was one of my favorite parts of the job.

The owner was a very tall, classically handsome man, who resembled a young Gary Cooper. He was the quiet type. He'd give me short, pointed instructions about what tasks he wanted me to perform on specific days. He lived in a really nice house on Kaanapali Hillside. Cheyenne had done some handyman repairs to his house. When it was payday, he'd walk into the office and turn his back to me, as if he were doing something top secret. He'd push some buttons on a hand-held device, probably one of those early huge cell phones. A few minutes later the printer would spit out my paycheck.

Around that same time Veronica Dove mentioned that they were looking for a ceramics instructor in a small studio on Office Road in Kapalua. Since I had a limited background in pottery, the director hired me as an instructor for two evenings a week. I did not work on the potter's wheel or load the kiln. The class was basically painting vases, plates, and figurines. The director would fire our pieces in the kiln when we were finished with our projects. I made some beautiful pieces in that class that I still use to display fresh cut flowers.

Painted and glazed pottery vase

Our apartment in the J building of the hood was already crowded with Cheyenne's furniture freebies from the Sands of Nirvana, electrical equipment, and speakers, so in preparation for the thirteen boxes that were being shipped to me from New York, Cheyenne rented a small unit in a self-storage building. We kept all sorts of things there—Christmas decorations, items his mother left when she moved back to Arizona, my portfolio of black-and-white photographs, and my guitar, which I didn't play anymore. Except for the creativeness of the pottery class and making floral arrangements for Ground Control, I was definitely missing Gauguin who was floating somewhere in the universe waiting to reconnect with me.

The shipment of boxes from New York never arrived. I called the Bronx district attorney. It took me quite a few calls to actually get him on the phone. He told me the owner of the shipping company was in jail for fraud, and that I wasn't the only person he'd ripped off. No one knew where my thirteen boxes were. I was devastated and angry but helpless in the situation. The Bronx DA told me to send him a copy of the shipping receipt, and he'd cut me a check for the full amount. That was the end of ever seeing all those treasures from my parents' apartment, along with two of my larger art pieces.

Black Tar began to get more gigs. I went to a few concerts, but the age range of people attending left me feeling out of place. I did love watching the guys play on stage, especially Cheyenne's solo bass licks. A new club opened in Kahana called Ludwig's—the same family dynasty as the famous drum set brand. It was a large warehouse with a stage and a second-floor balcony with cocktail tables and couches. It was close to home, and I enjoyed the openness of the venue. The place didn't last long. Residents in the area complained to the county about the noise, and the unruly crowds of people that hung around outside the club. In the end, the complainers won, and the club closed. Perhaps they weren't aware of what Beethoven had to say about music:

> Music is a higher revelation than all wisdom and philosophy. Music is the electric soil in which the spirit lives, thinks and invents.
>
> —Ludwig van Beethoven

Cheyenne on bass guitar

The year 1996 was whizzing by like a rocket ship hurtling through space. I was busy with two jobs, and Cheyenne was running from his day job to his music studio.

Hans Berlin went back to Germany for a while, and Abigail Walton hired a new chef in the catering kitchen—a woman, very talented and personable. She was a master pastry chef. Myrna Nichols was an all-American type from the Midwest. She was an attractive blonde who wasted no time in getting involved with one of the part-time chefs at the kitchen.

The three of us ladies took a short trip to Honolulu. I had to make up for two aborted trips I'd taken with Cheyenne. One where he blew his wad of cash on the first day in a camera store, and another when he took some weird drug that made him paranoid and he refused to leave the hotel room. Abby loved to drive in Honolulu; I hated it. She knew the city like the back of her hand, since her parents had lived there and were managers of a residential property. Abby and Myrna left the day before me. They had a list of catering warehouses and chef stores to visit. When I arrived at the inter-island terminal in the Honolulu Airport the next day, they were waiting for me. I threw my carry-on in the trunk of the rental car and got in the back seat. There was a cooler of ice with champagne. Myrna filled my plastic flute as the car lurched forward, the radio blasting. We were aiming to have a bang-up time.

Abby took us to a British pub in Pearlridge that her father frequented called Elephant and Castle. The place was filled with British memorabilia in a castle theme. They served little canapes for happy hour. I remember sipping a gin and tonic while staring at a seventeenth-century suit of armor, helmet and all. We went to Hy's Steakhouse for an extravagant dinner. The place was reminiscent of a library or a private men's club, and I felt momentarily removed from the tropics. We danced the night away in the disco of the Ala Moana Hotel. We shopped and shopped, and drank and drank. We laughed like hell when Myrna told us she'd spent the whole afternoon in the fragrance department of Liberty House. It was a wonderful few days. I thought, *Now, this is the way a Honolulu shopping trip should be.*

When we returned to Maui on the weekend, the catering company had a birthday luau at a house in Lahaina. This party caused Abby lots of frustration, but had the rest of us in fits of laughter. She sent Paki Makani, very early in the morning, to the venue to bury the pig in the *imu* (pit) with fire and hot rocks, so it would be cooked in time for the evening luau. It's not a luau without Kalua pork. When we arrived at the house that afternoon to set up for the party, Logan Baxter unloaded the van, but Paki Makani was nowhere to be found.

"I smell the pig," Abby said.

"I smell it too, but I don't see an imu," Logan said.

We searched all over the backyard, but there was no pig buried anywhere. Come to find out, the pig was buried at the house next door by mistake. Abby was livid. She made Paki dig it up, dig another pit in the yard of the correct house, start another fire, and bury it again. We laughed for days about the pig that got buried twice, but Abby didn't see the humor in it.

I received an unexpected phone call from the Bronx District Attorney in New York. My shipment of boxes were found in a warehouse in New Jersey.

"Are you kidding me? It's been over a year!" I said.

"We can resend them to you if you want, but we cannot guarantee the contents."

"What exactly are you saying? I'm a little confused."

"The boxes look like they've been repackaged. The guy might have sold all the good stuff at flea markets and auctions, so we don't really know what's in the packages. The boxes might be filled with rocks."

I told the district attorney I had to think about it. I mulled over it for a week or so. My feeling at the time was that after a whole year of living without all that stuff, I was just fine. I remembered what Leon Roberts had said when a thief stole his shirts out of the back seat of his car: "I guess God doesn't think I need that stuff."

In the end I called the Bronx DA and told him that not even knowing what was in those boxes, I had decided to let the stuff go. I thought it was uncanny though, that I'd packed the most precious things - my journals, letters, family photos, etc - and mailed them to myself in Hawaii. Perhaps that was the universe at work or someone guiding me from above.

The only things I really missed out of the whole thirteen boxes were my two treasured pieces of art. I had slides of them and planned on having them printed on canvas. After all, I wasn't Vincent Gogh, Pablo Picasso, or Paul Gauguin. They weren't worth any real money. Artists have to get used to parting with their work. I was reminded that I hadn't painted anything in ages. Maybe I was just going through a dormant phase. It was a different time in my life, a time of upheaval, and I let myself flow with the turbulent tides.

Speaking of Leon Roberts, I was home alone when I received another unexpected phone call with bad news. It was Janet Prescott, my friend from Miami. She told me that our good friend Leon was very ill. He had a really bad heart and was fading fast. "I think you should give him a call before it's too late," Jan said.

As soon as I hung up with her, I dialed Leon's number. "Lee, what the hell?" I said as soon as I heard his voice.

"Yeah, I'm not doing so well. I'm in bed right now. Don't have any strength at all."

"I held back tears not wanting him to feel my sense of doom.

"Flavio's back on the scene. He's been taking care of me, along with my mother," he said, in a very faint voice. "And my ex-wife is here too."

As Leon talked I pictured him the way I remembered him, like a whirlwind, flying along the corridors of the InterContinental Hotel in Miami. I wondered how long he had left. I thought of the dangerous lifestyle he'd lived. It was the wild drug days of Miami—dancing the night away in discos, doing poppers right out on the dance floor. That shit could stop your heart in a nanosecond.

Another friend was fading from my life too soon. I went around in a gloomy state for days. I imagined my dear friend Leon was headed for his own redemption. A few weeks later I got the call from Jan. Leon Roberts was no more. I could only dwell on that famous Shakespearean passage from *Macbeth*:

> To-morrow, and to-morrow, and to-morrow,
> Creeps in this petty pace from day to day.
> To the last syllable of recorded time;
> And all our yesterdays have lighted fools
> The way to dusty death. Out, out, brief candle!
> Life's but a walking shadow, a poor player
> That struts and frets his hour upon the stage,
> And then is heard no more. It is a tale
> Told by an idiot, full of sound and fury
> Signifying nothing.

That December of 1996, the first Starbucks opened on Maui in Kahului. I stood on line with Veronica Dove, waiting for a mocha Frappuccino thinking, *Maui is definitely marching toward the twenty-first century!*

CHAPTER 17

NOTHING ELSE MATTERS

> If you do it that way—that is, if you truly join your heart
> and mind as one—whatever you ask for, that's the way
> it's going to be.
>
> —White Buffalo Calf Woman

The year 1997 came in like a lamb but would exit like a nasty two-headed monster from an old black-and-white Godzilla movie.

I looked forward to my new gig as the instructor of an evening ceramics class in Kapalua two nights a week. It gave me a much-needed outlet for creativity.

My friend Veronica Dove found a job driving the beverage cart on one of the Kapalua golf courses. She drove around on a converted golf cart, which held a cooler with drinks, sandwiches, and sweet treats. She was sitting under a tree reading a book waiting for someone to request a cold drink. Two tourists on a golf cart rammed into her beverage cart, flinging her about twenty feet in the air and tossing her down a hill onto the green. It knocked her out cold. She woke up to a crowd of people standing around gawking down at her to see if she was still alive and coherent.

I went to her house to check on her, since they sent her home. She seemed OK, but I worried that there would be lasting effects. I moved some clothing and a couple of books to make room on her couch so I could sit down; she went to the kitchen to get us iced teas.

"Vero, what the hell happened?" I asked.

She walked slowly and carefully into the living room carrying the two glasses of iced tea. "I don't know. All I remember was soaring through the air and tumbling down a hill."

"Vero, you should sue those bastards."

"My boss said they were foreigners and didn't know how to stop the golf cart."

"They could have killed you."

"I don't want to lose my job," she said, her eyes darting around the room.

"I get that, but still."

We talked for an hour or so until it began to get dark. I told her to call me if she needed anything. Her roadside apartment had been the victim of a couple of incidents with cars coming around that turn and crashing into the side of her building. It was a precarious location, but the upside was that it was right on the ocean.

When I got home Cheyenne was sitting on the recliner watching *Beavis and Butt-Head*. What the hell is it with men that makes them like those dumb TV shows?

He motioned for me to come over to him. "I picked up a halfie for us," he said, putting the remote down. He spread the white powder onto a mirror and sectioned it off into neat little lines. I watched with anticipation, as it was a very expensive and rare treat. He rolled up a ten-dollar bill and snorted up two lines. He held the mirror out and passed me the ten-dollar bill. I quickly vacuumed up two lines. We went straight to the bedroom, got undressed, and made love. Afterward, we stayed in bed talking for a while.

"Let's save the rest for tomorrow," he said, getting up and putting his jeans on.

Yeah right, I thought. *That'll never happen.*

On Sunday, I cruised home after having a drink with Annie Hughes in Lahaina. I looked through the refrigerator for something to eat and found Monterey Jack cheese. I made myself a sandwich for supper. As long as there was alfalfa sprouts, mayonnaise, and avocado involved I considered it healthy. Cheyenne was watching television. I gave him a peck on the cheek, ate my sandwich, and went to the bathroom to take a shower. When I came out, I was feeling free and easy, loving my life. I got dressed in something casual, sat on the bed, and turned on *Mystery* on PBS. I was engrossed in the show until I noticed Cheyenne standing in the doorway.

"Don't you want to watch television with me?" he asked.

"Chey, you were already watching a program."

"Come on, we can watch something together."

"You don't like *Mystery!* You think it's silly, too British. You know I wait for Sunday night to watch it, and tonight it's Hercule Poirot."

"I guess," he said, in a disappointed tone.

As I watched him walk back into the living room, I couldn't imagine what this was about. It had to be more than a television show. I enjoyed watching the shows I liked, and if it meant watching them by myself on the TV in the bedroom, so be it.

A short time later he popped his head in the bedroom to tell me he was going to the studio to practice with the guys.

During the week I went shopping with Abby in Kahului. We had lunch at a popular restaurant called Marco's. In those days Marco's had the best blue-cheese salad with bacon, chunks of blue cheese, and a chopped hard-boiled egg. Out of the corner of my eye I glimpsed Mango Mike, an old boyfriend of mine from the seventies.

"Don't turn your head, but one of my old paramours is sitting at another table."

"Who is it?" Abby asked, ignoring me and turning to look at him.

"We had a brief summer romance years ago. His name is Mike."

"I went out with that guy," Abby said.

"You're kidding. When did you go out with him?"

"I think it was in the mid-seventies. My son Ben was just a child. I was the manager of a small complex across the street from Napili Hui."

Are you telling me you lived right across the road from the hood?"

"Looks like we went out with this guy at the same time."

"Abby, this is just too much. I'm going to freak him out."

"Adriana, what are you going to do?" she asked, watching me get up from the table.

I walked right over to Mango Mike and stood in front of him. It had been about twenty years since I'd seen him. Though older, he still had a little Omar Sharif left in him. Mike looked up at me and smiled. He was surprised to see me, but stood up and hugged me warmly.

"I'm here with a girlfriend," I said. "I think you'll remember her."

Mike leaned over and poked his head past me to have a look. When he caught sight of Abby waving at him, his demeanor changed. I wasn't quite sure what was going through his mind, but it couldn't be good. He slumped back in his seat and stared at me.

"Well, I'd better get back to my table. We haven't finished our lunch yet. It was good to see you, Mike," I said, walking away.

I could tell he was very uncomfortable at being found out as a cad. Abby and I laughed and exchanged stories. He never came to our table. When I got home that evening I searched through my jewelry box looking for the etched silver band Mike had given me all those years ago. I found it and tossed it over in my fingers. A million memories came back to me of my first few years in the islands. I carefully set the ring back in the box and closed the drawer.

I poured myself a glass of red wine from a bottle I'd rifled at the last party I'd worked for the catering company. I sat on the couch and turned on the TV to watch the nightly news. China was retaking Hong Kong, and there were huge protests in the streets of Bejing. The sun was setting creating a golden glow on the lanai. I put fresh seed in the bird's cup and opened the cage door. I placed a shallow dish on top of the cage and filled it with lettuce leaves and water. I watched the birds take a bath. I coaxed Pua onto my finger. He gave me little kisses with his beak. It was the end of another beautiful day in paradise.

Cheyenne walked through the front door. "Watching the lies?" he asked, laughing.

"Yeah, China is taking Hong Kong back," I said. My eyes followed him as he cruised around the apartment doing his thing. He sat on the couch next to me. I didn't tell him about running into my old paramour Mango Mike. I didn't think anything good or meaningful would come out of such a conversation. It was something I would laugh about with my girlfriends but not something I thought was a good idea to share with my partner. We became engrossed in a television program about unruly kids. We were laughing at the crazy things the kids were doing, and the lackadaisical reactions their parents had to their bad behavior.

"That will never happen when I have my kids," Cheyenne said.

"Your kids?" I asked. "When are you planning on having these kids?"

"Oh, I don't know," he said, probably realizing he opened a can of worms with his remark, but there was no taking it back.

"I'd like to know when you plan on having these kids."

"Sometime in the future, I guess."

Suddenly, I felt my whole world crash around me, and I became silent. I thought of that phrase my mother often said, "You can start the day laughing and end the day crying."

Cheyenne looked straight at me. "Don't you want to have a little us?" he said, reaching for my hand and rubbing it.

"Cheyenne, I still get my period, but I'm fifty-one years old."

"So, we can still have a baby, can't we?"

"It could be dangerous for me and the baby." *That ship's already sailed,* I thought.

"It just popped out of my mouth. I wasn't thinking," he said.

"It's okay. It was an innocent comment."

I stood up and went into the bedroom, threw myself on the bed, and quietly cried. I didn't want Cheyenne to know how upset I was. He stayed in the living room for a while, then came into the bedroom and lay next to me. He spooned me, resting his arm on my waist.

"I do love you very much," he said.

"I know," I answered, squeezing his hand.

But all I saw was the end of our relationship on the horizon. With talk of a baby I knew which way the wind was blowing.

That August Princess Diana died, her life snuffed out in a car crash, hounded by paparazzi. I had watched her wedding in the middle of the night, broadcast live from England in the summer of 1981. My life was whizzing by.

Abby introduced me to a couple from the East Coast. She figured we'd have a lot in common. They were from Massachusetts. He was a red-headed Sicilian, Joey Tarentino. His wife, Athena, was Greek and Irish. Joey had a quick sense of humor and kept us all laughing. He'd been a confirmed bachelor until he met Athena McElroy. She was a fiery Greek, smart-ass type, who had an answer and a detailed explanation for everything. It was understandable, as she was a schoolteacher. Abigail's Distinctive Affairs did their wedding ceremony at Joey's house in Lahaina, and I bartended.

Athena McElroy and I became friends over the next year. Joey Tarentino was a fabulous cook, and had a large plot in the community garden up north. They'd occasionally invite me for dinner if Joey was cooking Italian food. I marveled at how he made ravioli with wontons instead of dough—a Chinese-Italian fusion influenced by living in Hawaii. Athena often took vacations without Joey. I wasn't sure why, but after two disastrous trips to Honolulu with Cheyenne, I could definitely relate.

Athena and Joey owned a vacation rental condo on the island of Molokai. Athena often went to that island to check on its status, and one time she asked me if I'd like to tag along. Molokai always intrigued me. I knew from stories I'd heard that it was nothing like Maui, sparsely populated, and much less constructed. Athena said, "It's more like the Hawaii of olden days." I knew it was where Father Damien had lived with, and was the priest for the lepers. I knew all about his history, and I was excited about the journey.

Joey dropped Athena and me at Lahaina Harbor in the early morning hours to pick up the Molokai ferry. When we arrived at the dock there was a line of people waiting to board, but the ferry hadn't arrived yet. People had large coolers of food and all sorts of supplies they'd purchased on Maui. Finally, in the distance we saw the ferry approaching. I knew it would be about a three-hour trip, but I had no idea what we were in for.

We purchased our tickets and went aboard. There were rows of seats on the small ferry, and there weren't more than about twenty-five people in total. There was a television on board, but the picture jumped around with a loud buzz which gave you a headache if you watched the screen too long.

When we left the dock I stood up watching Lahaina Harbor slip away behind us, as the ferry headed toward the Molokai Channel. It was a very rough ride, akin to riding a bucking bronco at a rodeo. When the boat got going at a pretty good clip, I could see foamy ocean water coming right over the top of the boat as the small ferry slapped the waves, so I buckled myself in with the seat belt provided.

I'd had a dream of doing the religious pilgrimage into Kalaupapa on the back of a donkey, but that never happened. I thought of how people with Hansen's disease (leprosy) were tossed off ships close to the cliffs and had to swim to shore. If they survived, they were able to live out their lives as outcasts with other lepers on this remote island. Father Damien chose to be their priest and refused to abandon his flock. He eventually succumbed to the disease himself. He was buried on Molokai but later was dug up, and his body was sent back to his native Belgium. I think a piece of his foot is still buried in the soil on Molokai.

The ferry slowed down as we neared the towering cliffs of the rugged Molokai coastline. I pictured the poor souls swallowed up by the sea as they struggled to reach the shore. We disembarked the ferry and waited for a van to take us into the town of Kanakakai where Athena had rented a car. It was a very small town with a general store, a supermarket, a bookstore, and a bakery. We went straight to the Kanakakai bakery for breakfast and planned our first day.

We loaded our suitcases in the trunk of the rental car and headed out on an exploratory drive. Athena was like a tour guide, showing me where everything was. Once we got out of the main town there were tons of wild turkeys and other wildlife all over the roadways, which we had to dodge as we drove along.

Back then Molokai Ranch was the top dog in town. It employed most of the island's residents. I found it to be a kind of serfdom, in the same way serfs lived right outside of the castle walls in medieval times. Everything revolved around castle life, and this wasn't much different. We finally reached the complex where their vacation rental condo was located. It was on a golf course, but beyond the greens the landscape was scrub. The condo was a large studio with two queen beds. We brought our suitcases in and got settled.

Athena immediately climbed on a ladder and began taking inventory. I watched her measure the bathroom window for a new curtain. I walked out on the lanai, sat in a beach chair, and gazed out over the landscape. Even the palm trees looked scrubby. I loved the wildness of Molokai Island. After Athena finished her tasks, she took me on a walk around the property. We hiked all the way down to the beach which was deserted. The desolation was a little spooky at first. There wasn't a soul to be seen along the path to the ocean, or on the stretch of beach which went for miles. It was eerie staring at the tall cliffs, with us seemingly the only two people left on planet earth, but I loved it.

I tried to push Cheyenne out of my mind. I didn't want to dwell on the end of our relationship, which I imagined was coming at some point. I figured at my age there wouldn't be many men on my horizon. It was just the way of Mother Nature, and I wanted to milk my present life for all it was worth. I wasn't sure if anyone would ever love me in that intense, passionate way ever again. I'd heard that older women become invisible. I was happy for the time we had. I loved Cheyenne enough to want to see him happy. I knew he wanted a child, and I was well past that stage in my life.

I slipped into bed staring at the ceiling. Athena was sound asleep. I swear that woman could sleep on a dime. I heard strange noises coming from the lanai. A cat would yowl, and shortly after that I'd hear the gobble-gobble of a turkey. I woke Athena. "It's just the feral cats fighting with the wild turkeys," she said. We listened to the standoff for a while, giggling. I laughed myself to sleep thinking that this was total Molokai madness.

I opened my eyes very early to find Athena awake and sitting up in bed writing lists. I got up and walked out to the lanai without saying anything. I stood there in my nightie enjoying the sparseness of civilization on the island. I knew there were other people in the resort complex, but it was a very slow time of the year, and we rarely saw anyone.

"Let's go to the bakery for breakfast," Athena said.

"Yeah, that sounds like a plan. I'll jump in the shower."

We hopped in that dumpy rental car. It jingled and jangled down the roadways dodging wildlife. After riding for a while, I wondered if we'd pass anything that resembled civilization, but we didn't see a person until we arrived in town and parked in front of Kanakakai bakery. We walked in and found the place filled with local residents. It appeared to be the place in town where everyone congregated. I went straight to the showcase with all the homemade pastries and bought an old-fashioned jelly doughnut.

"Aren't you going to eat breakfast?" Athena asked.

"Yeah, but I couldn't resist; they look so good."

"We make them fresh every day," the woman behind the showcase said.

We scanned the chalkboard that listed the specials for the day, ordered our food, and found a table. There was nothing special about bacon and eggs, but it was what I was in the mood for. People sat at tables talking or reading newspapers. After breakfast we walked to the general store, which carried everything from onions to plumbing supplies. Athena found a curtain for the bathroom in a clear plastic package. I thought it was ordinary, but she thought it was stupendous. I imagined she was getting by with spending as little as possible on the condo, which couldn't be making much money without tourists around.

She held a four-pack of lightbulbs in one hand and a box of silverware in the other. "Honestly, I don't know where all the silverware disappears to," she remarked.

I followed Athena around the store looking at strange items in barrels. I was glad when I saw her at the checkout. We talked about taking an exploratory drive around the island that afternoon on our way back to the condo.

Athena replace light bulbs and hung a new curtain in the bathroom. I held onto the ladder to steady it while she balanced on the top rung. She washed and dried the silverware she'd purchased and set it in the silverware drawer while I packed snacks for our road trip.

As we got in the rental car Athena admitted that she'd never driven around the island in all the times she'd visited Molokai. It wasn't long before we came across a tiny church. It was no bigger than a large walk-in closet. We parked the car and walked inside the church, which was unlocked. There weren't many statues or religious relics. I saw mostly paintings and photographs under glass, the images of Father Damien and various other saints. We were both filled with reverence for Father Damien, who built a number of churches around the island with the help of his flock of lepers. I felt his presence heavily in that little building.

We hadn't gone much farther along the road when we passed another small church. It was larger than the last one, perhaps the size of a large room, but still very austere inside. We smiled at each other as we opened the front door and walked inside. A feeling of total peace swept my being. I saw a row of lit candles with a red hue. *Someone must maintain this little church if there are candles burning*, I thought. I walked toward them and knelt to say a prayer. I dropped a dollar bill through the coin slot and lit a candle for my mother. Athena and I had bonded over religion. Catholicism was something we had in common, although Athena McElroy had gone to a parochial school as a child, while I went to public schools. My mother told me I had to learn to live in this world with everyone. Athena was an avid churchgoer, whereas I hadn't been to mass in years.

We continued along the one main road that circled the island. One church had a life-sized statue of Father Damien at the entrance. He was dressed in all black, with his iconic black wide-brimmed hat and glasses. Someone had placed strands of white shell beads around the statue's neck. We stopped and said prayers in each church we passed.

Around a turn we found ourselves in a valley. The scenery was bewitching, with a rather large church in the middle of a field of green grass, and a tropical mountain range as the backdrop. A life-sized wooden cross stood in front with a white cloth draped over the top post. Christ was absent from the cross symbolizing a perpetual Easter Miracle. *He is risen.*

When we left that church we drove along silently until we came across a line of people who were standing on the road outside of a small shack with a tiny window. There were no restaurants to speak of on Molokai. There was the occasional picnic table outside of someone's home, where they served food cooked in their own kitchens. This particular place seemed to be a popular take-out spot. We watched jeeps and trucks come and go. We ordered burgers and fries to go and ate them in the rental car.

On our way back to the condo we passed the Molokai Hotel. I'd heard from Annie Hughes that it was a hot spot back in the day. We sat at the bar filled with locals sipping tropical drinks. I had the feeling that these days didn't match those days. Perhaps it just wasn't my cup of tea, but it did offer us a pleasant break from desolation row!

The day exhausted us, so that evening we stayed in the condo and watched television. I tried to fall asleep when Athena hit the bed but couldn't. She assured me that the sound of the television wouldn't bother her. I lay in bed thinking of how peaceful I felt on Molokai, and I realized it was because there was a body of water, the Molokai Channel, between me and my problem. I knew what was in store for me, and I really didn't want to face it—the inevitable end to my relationship with Cheyenne Bremmer.

I couldn't stop my brain from rehashing the mistakes I'd made in my choices of men. *Look before you leap* was never my practice. Not that they weren't all wonderful men, but I often chose situations with a built-in ending. I knew it had something to do with my *alone script*. I supposed somewhere deep inside me, I didn't feel deserving of a true and lasting love. Perhaps that was the reality of a lot of people's lives. I wondered if some people just settled on partners, and lived with the mediocrity and precariousness of it all. I guess I wasn't willing to do that. Finally, I fell asleep.

On Sunday, our last day on Molokai, Athena told me she was taking me someplace special. I didn't ask questions because I trusted her judgement. We drove to a coffee plantation that had a small gift shop, and a counter with snacks and drinks. I saw a stage set up so knew we were in for a concert. I'd guessed it was a recurring Sunday affair. Senior citizens showed up with guitars and ukuleles, and the music began. An older Hawaiian gentleman, a transvestite, was dressed in a colorful muumuu—this was common among the Hawaiian people. I was told that in the old days if there were no female children in a family, one of the boys was raised as a girl. It was an accepted practice, and unabashed on the island of Molokai.

We were treated to a great concert of Hawaiian music as we sipped on iced coffees and ate pastries. At the end of the concert everyone was prompted to stand at attention while the old Hawaiian Kingdom's national anthem was played. Athena and I didn't sing along or hold our hands over our hearts; we just stood out of respect for the old Hawaiian Monarchy.

Back in the town of Kanakakai Athena took me to the bookstore, which was another meeting place for Molokai residents. Athena knew the owner, who asked us if we'd attend a meeting about future plans in the works for a wind farm on the island. What I got out of the meeting was that the residents would not benefit from the wind farm, and that the electricity generated would be transferred to the city of Honolulu on the island of Oahu. It certainly didn't sound fair. It was a political football on the island, and some residents were up in arms.

We went on a last-minute hike through a pine forest. The majority of trees were ironwoods. Athena told me there was a large sculpture in the shape of a penis at the end of the trail called Kauie O Nanahoa (Phallic Rock). It was a relaxing walk through the woods. When we reached the top of the trail, there indeed was a huge stone penis staring at us. I imagined it was a fertility rock. We walked out on a plateau that had a great view of the town below, and the vast ocean encircling us. We walked along the ironwoods back to the car in silence.

In the morning we returned the rental car and took a shuttle to the dock to catch the ferry back to Maui. Three hours on that bucking bronco of a floating tub was a fitting end to a weekend of Molokai madness.

I found Cheyenne in the same recliner when I got home. Despite our chronological age difference, sexually we were the same age. They say men reach their sexual peak in their twenties and women in their forties. Emotionally, I knew we loved each other and enjoyed spending time together. Sex was one of things that kept our relationship afloat. All of this was well and good, but I had been preoccupied since our discussion about having a baby. The reality of the situation depressed me. I also felt guilt, as if I was holding him back from living his life to the fullest.

In months to come, Cheyenne began slacking off on paying his share of the rent, and at one point, he asked to borrow money to buy a pickup truck he had his eye on. I found myself paying for the storage unit a few times, and other things that had been his responsibility. I was digging myself into a financial hole, living on credit cards, and I wasn't liking it. I began to keep tabs. I knew it was wrong because love doesn't keep score. I fronted Cheyenne six thousand dollars to buy the truck he wanted, knowing his mother was going to reimburse me right away from his father's life insurance policy. He and I had been together for almost five years, but there didn't seem to be anywhere left to go. We were drifting in the ocean toward the future without a rudder or a paddle. I'd learned from my past that sometimes love just isn't enough.

Abby wanted to get all of us girls together for dinner at the Makawao Steakhouse . She said we didn't do enough fun things like that. She had a friend who owned a limousine company. We all met at Abby's house, and she had the limo pick us up for the drive upcountry. We were all good friends, so the ride in the luxury limo drinking champagne and talking story, made it all special. Driving up Haleakala Highway, the limo driver told us the story of how she found out her longtime boyfriend was cheating on her, and how she had ended the relationship. Somehow I knew my relationship was next on the chopping block.

We had a wonderful dinner at the Steakhouse. Anywhere we went with Abigail Walton we received special treatment. She knew so many people in the restaurant and food industry. Things came out of the kitchen that weren't even on the restaurant menu. Every course was a specialty of the chef.

When I got home that night Cheyenne wasn't home. I figured he was at band practice, but as the hours passed I couldn't sleep. I knew instinctively that something was up. About 2:00 a.m., I got up, put my robe on, and sat on a chair in the living room in the dark. I heard his key in the front door. When he flipped on the light over the desk he saw me sitting there, like a gargoyle in a horror movie. He was surprised and took a step back.

I stood up. "Where the hell have you been?"

"I fell asleep on my friend's couch," he said, not making eye contact with me.

I didn't believe that story for a second. I walked past him without saying another word and went to bed. I heard the water running in the shower; then I heard him throw his guts up in the bathroom toilet. I knew he was lying, but I didn't want to confront him. I didn't want to let him go, even though I knew it was the right thing to do.

Over the next few days we didn't discuss that night. I made believe I swallowed his story, and he made believe he wasn't lying. We went on with our lives as if nothing out of the ordinary had happened—until one evening when we were in the mood for pizza; We usually went to Pizza Hut in Lahaina, which Cheyenne nicknamed Pizza Slut, but he wanted to go to Dollie's, which was right across the street from the Sands of Kahana where he worked. We walked in past the bar and sat at a table. Cheyenne ordered a draft beer and I ordered a Coke. We were laughing and talking as we waited for the pizza. The overhead TVs were reporting the mass suicide of the Heaven's Gate cult in California. We agreed that crazy shit happened in that state. A girl walked right up to our table and stood in front of me. She stared at Cheyenne and smiled, then turned her gaze at me.

"Do you know how lucky you are?" she asked.

I stared at her, then I looked questioningly at Cheyenne for clarity.

She was a bleached-blond bubblehead type. I figured Cheyenne met her at the resort where he worked. *So this must be the bimbo he fucked around with*, I thought.

"Oh, I know exactly how lucky I am," I answered, staring back at her.

Cheyenne laughed nervously, acting flattered, as if he didn't know her. But my gut told me different. I had the urge to wipe that stupid grin off his face with the back of my hand, but my mind went blank. I couldn't help but flash back to the day I'd found the photo of Derick Ellis with a woman sitting on his lap, a big smile on her face. That horrible feeling in the pit of my stomach—I was feeling it again. It crossed my mind that, like Derick, Cheyenne wanted me to see this woman.

I figured she was a tourist screwing around with a local guy on vacation, and that she'd be flying back to the mainland soon, and our lives would go back to normal. That's what I tried to tell myself. Funny, the things you are willing to put up with not to lose the object of your affection.

My mind drifted off like a safety mechanism. I thought back to a vacation I'd taken to Puerto Rico with my girlfriends when I was nineteen. We hooked up with some local Puerto Rican guys. We took them back to our room and screwed them. In turn, they paraded us around the Condado Strip in San Juan like we were conquests to be proud of. It was part of the experience of being in a foreign land. When our vacation was over we went home and forgot about them.

Cheyenne grabbed my arm dragging me back to the present. "Let's get the check and take the rest of the pizza home." I stared at Cheyenne sitting across from me. The bubblehead had disappeared. I figured I'd let him find out for himself just how vacation romances worked.

I had a hard time falling asleep that night. When I finally did, we were jarred awake at 3:00 a.m. by a car radio in the parking lot blasting AC/DC's old rock song "Live Wire." I lay there listening, and even though Cheyenne was lying next to me, we were miles apart.

My periods had been sporadic of late, but one month it was really late. I thought, *Wouldn't it be ironic if I was pregnant?* I went to the clinic to see my doctor. She ran some tests, and no, I was not pregnant.

"Am I in menopause?" I asked.

"I got your test results back. Let's put it this way: your estrogen counts are much lower and show that you're definitely not going back."

I left the clinic relieved but a little disappointed. Despite how young I looked, I had just turned fifty-two years old, and that was a fact I had to face.

I was sitting on a chair in the living room mending a hole in a sock by hand. Cheyenne walked in and stood in front of me.

"We have to talk," he said.

I stared up at him over the rim of my glasses. He looked serious and definitely uncomfortable. "What is it Chey? You can tell me anything."

"I need to go my own way. I've been feeling this way for a while."

I put the mending down and took my glasses off. "Tell me more."

"I found an apartment. It's not far from here," he said, reluctantly.

"Next thing you're going to tell me is that you've met someone else."

"Well, yeah, but she's on the mainland."

"Uh-huh," I said, figuring that was the whole point of his getting an apartment, in preparation for the bubblehead coming back to Maui. *Funny how men suddenly step up financially for a woman they want!* I thought.

I was tabulating his words in my brain when Cheyenne said, "You seem relieved. I thought you'd be really upset."

"I knew this day was coming. I just didn't know when. You want a baby. That's something I can't give you. I love you enough to let you go."

Cheyenne looked surprised at my reaction to his announcement. I wasn't sure what he was expecting. Truth be told, I was relieved not to be waiting for something I knew would happen eventually anyway.

"I've got to get to work," he said, heading for the front door. "We can talk more later. Oh, and I guess you can keep the kids [our cockatiels]!"

I said nothing.

After he left the apartment I thought of how we had lived in that tiny studio for four years, never had a serious fight, and were happy together. I knew that was total bullshit. This was always the expected end. I'd be replaced by a young chippie. A self-fulfilling prophecy was coming to fruition. I had no one to blame but myself. He was leaving the birds behind! *Just like a man*, I thought. He was stepping into freedom while leaving the obligations behind, the pets that *he* wanted. I sat on that chair for a long time slinging all this back-and-forth in my head.

Ground Control, the landscape company I'd been working for, went out of business. Abigail Walton had a friend in the vacation-rental business. I'd seen her at a few parties I'd attended at Abby's house, but I didn't know much about her. Lana DeMarco was a tall Southern Italian bombshell with a big mouth and a lot of hair. She mentioned she could use someone part-time to answer phones and make reservations. I had that experience from Miami, when I worked for Ian Brody's boat excursions.

We met at a small café for breakfast in Lahaina behind the public library that I didn't even know existed. I went to the counter to get coffee and a pastry.

Lana said, "No, put your money away. It's my treat." I got us a table and sat down. She soon returned with two cups of coffee and one muffin. "I'm on a diet," she said, cutting the muffin and giving me half. At that point I stopped worrying about what sort of impression I was making on her.

The rentals Lana DeMarco managed were upscale properties, one of which was Willie Nelson's house, The Western Star. But there was a volatile dynamic between Lana and her business partner, which made for a tense working environment. I lasted there about six months.

I found a full-time job as a sales clerk in a boutique at the Hyatt Hotel. One of my tasks was to dress the mannequins in the sprawling display windows with new design arrivals that came into the store. That was something I enjoyed doing. My life was going through some major changes, and work helped to keep me sane.

Cheyenne moved into a little studio about ten minutes away from our apartment. Every time I drove past his place his door was always wide open. The bubblehead from the mainland dropped him like a hot potato when she left the island. He and I were still together in the biblical sense, but I never stayed overnight after we had sex. I felt at home wherever he was. My mind might have given up on us, but my body refused to.

I do remember the first time Cheyenne came back to our apartment in the J building of the hood. I watched him walk up the stairs. He was carrying a handful of palms for the birds. They loved to chew on the fronds. He had tears in his eyes. We stood there at the top of the stairs holding each other. We walked into the bedroom, got undressed and made love. It was hot, and seemed very loving. Afterward, he hugged me so hard I thought he would go right through me, like a ghost that had the ability to transcend solid form. I knew he still had love for me. We went on this way, together yet not together, for months.

I purchased an old-fashioned composition notebook and began journaling again. Sort of a daily bitch fest I called the Morning Pages.

From the Morning Pages:

> I don't want to hold you back from what you want. The
> last time we were together I saw love in your eyes, or was
> it the love in me I saw reflected in your eyes?

Black Tar played a concert at a club in Lahaina. Cheyenne's bandmates basically ignored me, except for Tom, the drummer, who stood at the bar with me when the band took a break. Tom had a floozy hanging on to him. She had jet-black hair, numerous tattoos, and a silver nose ring. Tom and the floozy walked off when Cheyenne stood next to me. We engaged in a dialogue that felt distant. When the guys went back to the stage, my attention flipped to an older woman paying a lot of attention to Cheyenne, like she was his best fan. She clapped, hooted, and hollered at his solo riffs on the bass. Cheyenne had aspirations of being a rock star, and fantasized going on tour with his band. I figured they were pipe dreams. During our conversation at the bar, he spoke of the future; I spoke of the past. I was remembering; he was dreaming. Our age difference was blatant. I snuck out of the building during their next set. I walked through dead streets, like the lyrics of Bob Dylan's song "Love Sick," with Cheyenne in my head.

I hadn't seen or heard from Cheyenne Bremmer in a while when he called me out of the blue. He told me he'd moved a couple of times. His new place was on the northern end of Front Street, right outside of town. After he lived there a while, he started a vegetable garden on the side of the condo, and wanted me to see it. I figured he was lonely. I started hanging out there and having sex with him again. I enjoyed swimming in the pool on the premises. Cheyenne would stare at me in my bikini, telling me what a great body I still had. He'd lost the storage unit for nonpayment. My guitar was in that unit, along with all my precious black-and-white photos from the days when I had my own dark room. I was pissed. I was rolling around in a den of snakes looking for a way out. We were sitting on the couch in his condo. I asked him for the key to my apartment, which he still had.

He handed me the key. "Look, I don't want to hurt you," he said.

"It a bit late for that!" I said.

I stood up and left, but I wasn't crying anymore. I didn't want to see him again. I was ready to move on.

I worked a function with the catering company up in Kula at Ulupalakua Ranch, way up on Haleakala Crater. A group of people were on an around-the-world trip, and a luau on Maui was on their itinerary. They arrived on the ranch via helicopter and were rushed to the bunkhouse, where we had prepared a light lunch for them. After lunch they were carted off for a horseback ride in the mountains while we prepared for the evening luau. There wasn't just a pig buried in the imu, but also a wild turkey and a Key deer for maximum effect. I could tell these people had beaucoup bucks.

Logan Baxter, along with some of the ranch hands, made a huge bonfire. I took delight in watching the expressions on the women's faces when two of the *paniolos* (cowboys) jumped up on a picnic table and danced the hula. Their reaction to the men's hand gestures and suggestive hip gyrations was priceless.

We loaded all the dirty dishes and glassware in the van, to be cleaned the next day at the kitchen in Lahaina. I rode back down the mountain in the van with Abby and took the opportunity to talk to her about what had happened between me and Cheyenne. I hoped she'd give me some honest advice, or at least have a sympathetic ear. She was married to a man who was almost twenty years older than her. She'd had her share of affairs. I imagined it was expected with such an age difference. But I also knew she loved her husband. She didn't say much, but at least I got everything off my chest.

A few months later I went to a movie in town with Abby and Bubba. I combed through the patrons while we waited for the doors to open. My eyes zoomed in on Cheyenne with a very young blonde girl, maybe twenty or so. She was very much pregnant. My heart sank. Was God punishing me for something? He walked over to us and introduced her. I smiled but didn't even hear her name. *How much could a woman take?* I thought. I remembered nothing about the movie. I hurried to the Cherokee and drove home after the movie, not wanting to cross paths with them again. The car radio was playing Metallica's "Nothing Else Matters." "Life is cruel," I blithered, through useless tears.

I wondered how couples dealt with each other after a breakup when they had children together. *Life must be a constant emotional hell ride*, I thought. That was one situation I managed to avoid in my life. But wasn't I on my own hell ride?

I walked into my kitchen and Pua attacked my feet. The birds had been spending a lot of time under the stove. It had been a cool fall in Napili, so perhaps it was warm under there. I decided to have a look. I got on my hands and knees with a flashlight to investigate. I saw something moving. It was a baby bird. "Oh my God, there's two!" I said, out loud.

Those clever, sneaky, little monkeys! I made a basket filled with soft grass for them to go into when the babies were ready to come out. Pua and Cicci developed voracious appetites feeding them. I cooked them rice and gave them scrambled eggs, anything to keep them nourished. After six months, I was paying more attention to their two babies than they were, so I gave the babies away. The cockatiels were a source of love and joy.

It was Thanksgiving 1997. I had a coupon for a free turkey at Foodland, and planned on making a big dinner with all the trimmings, and invite a few friends who had nowhere to go for the holiday. Cheyenne Bremmer called wanting to know what I was doing for Thanksgiving. Against my better judgement I told him to come over, not even asking any pertinent questions. A number of our friends showed up, including Filippo Rizzoli, who had just moved into an apartment in the hood. Brice Gordon walked over from his apartment. My next-door neighbor Dash Kern carved the turkey. It was a really nice afternoon.

Cheyenne had bicycled all the way from Lahaina to Napili. He told me he didn't have the truck anymore. *That was six thousand dollars down the drain*, I thought. I didn't ask about the pregnant girl I'd seen him with at the movie theater. I didn't want to know. After dinner, Filippo Rizzoli took a large pot from my kitchen cabinet, insisting that he start a turkey soup with the leftover carcass. There was much laughter when the sac with the giblets (which I had no idea existed) floated to the top. Cheyenne stayed over after everyone left. We had sex that night. I just took it for some unexplainable mutual attachment we still had.

I met Annie Hughes at the Yacht Club for happy-hour drinks. She was still my Maui mom, and we kept in very close touch. Her son Sonny was dying of lung cancer. It was a horrible thing. Annie had so many family headaches and heartaches.. I told her about my periods being sporadic and that my doctor told me that my estrogen count was dropping and it wasn't going back.

"Honey, it's not over till it's over," she squawked.

A friend of hers walked in and sat next to her.

"Adriana, this is my good friend Dourine Wicket—Dori, we call her."

"I'm about the give up my vacation-rental business," Dori said.

"What the hell's going on, Dori?" Annie asked.

"I discovered that two of the women working at various rental offices on the west side have been stealing from me," she said, with disgust.

Annie said. "My friend Adriana is looking for a job. She's competent and honest."

Dourine set her cigarette down on the edge of the ashtray and stared at me. She was a good-looking woman, very petite, with sharp features, impeccably dressed, with short blonde hair teased up like a Shiatsu.

"Come to my office next week and we'll talk," Dourine said.

That conversation was the beginning of a new career for me.

CHAPTER 18

THE OLD COUNTRY

Develop interest in life as you see it; in people, things,
literature, music—the world is so rich, simply throbbing
with rich treasures, beautiful souls and interesting people.
Forget yourself.

—Henry Miller

The year 1998 brought the Monica Lewinsky scandal in the Clinton
White House, with talk of a cigar and a stained blue dress. It was also
a very eventful year in my life. I began working for Dourine Wicket's
vacation-rental management company. Dori was moving me around to
different properties as a fill-in for front desk managers who were out
sick or on vacation. All of these properties were oceanfront. There was
a natural dichotomy between the condo owners who lived on property,
and the owners who rented their condos out to tourists. An ongoing
tension between these two groups existed on every property. The job was
a juggling act between the visitors, the owners of the condos, and the
management company, and required a great deal of patience. I had no idea
at the beginning that it would turn into a career. I'd just show up at any
office Dori sent me to, do the best job I could, and hope people liked me.
I finally had a job with a real salary and benefits. I was able to save money
and pay off my credit cards.

One of the properties I was sent to was very small. There were only
seven vacation rentals in the whole building. It had a tiny office with a
window that opened to the lobby. I shared it with another woman who
handled Dori's long-term rentals. Each morning I'd open the window
like a priest in a confession box, waiting to hear confessions (complaints).
There was always something crazy going on in the building—an unhappy
tourist expecting a better room or view; the report of a leak, and I'd have
to call a plumber; something broken in a unit, and I'd have to contact our
handyman, Garry Walker.

The owners had no mailboxes, so they'd pop their heads through that little window all day long like clowns springing out of a jack-in-the-box asking, "Has the mail come yet?"

At the end of January a group of us flew to Honolulu for the Rolling Stones concert tour at Aloha Stadium. Harry Hackman and Helga Hargrove rented a suite at a hotel in Waikiki with a hot tub. When we checked into the room, it wasn't much of a suite, and the hot tub was just an oversized jetted tub.

I was single and ready to mingle. We had drinks in the hotel lobby, then took a taxi to the concert. There was a huge tailgate party going on in the parking lot of Aloha Stadium, with bottles of booze, and people sharing drugs between cars. Rolling Stones music played over a loud speaker, so we didn't notice the end of the piped-in music, and the beginning of the actual concert. We were having so much fun that we missed the first fifteen minutes of the Stones' onstage performance. We raced in and found our seats. Mick Jagger pranced around on a moving stage that went way out into the audience. We were high on coke, liquor, and feeling good. Little did Helga Hargrove know that she was pregnant with her first baby.

That spring I became friendly with our handyman, Gary Walker. He was older than me but not by much. He'd had a heart attack, and his mother came to Maui from California to take care of him. I winced when he unbuttoned his shirt to show me his post-surgery scar, which was like a long zipper running up the center of his chest. Gary was our go-to guy because he was capable of fixing anything, quickly and efficiently.

I was just starting my day when Gary Walker appeared at the office window with the craziest look on his face.

"Gary, I don't remember calling you for anything. What are you doing here?" I asked.

He stood there stoically, not uttering a word. Then he took a large black binder and laid it on the counter inside the window. "This look familiar?" he asked.

I began flipping through the eight-by ten images in the loose-leaf binder. I saw an old black-and-white photo of my mother that I'd taken of her at the Cloisters Museum in Fort Tryon Park, New York, on the cliffs of the Hudson River. I'd developed it myself when I had a darkroom. I was silent.

Mom at the Cloisters

"There are nude photographs here I thought you'd want. Some are of you," he said.

I stared at the photographs and then at him. "Shit, these are photos from my darkroom. Where the hell did you get this?"

"They were in a pile of stuff I bought in an abandoned storage locker auction down the road. I recognized you right away. Well, it was your face. I haven't seen the rest of you yet," he said, with a smirk. "I just thought you'd want them."

"Gary, I don't know what to say. My ex lost our storage unit a while back for nonpayment. I figured all this stuff was lost. You didn't happen to see a Yamaha F180 guitar, did you?"

He ignored my question saying, "I just thought I should bring this to you."

"I'm so grateful you did."

He left the black binder on the counter and began walking away, but stopped in his tracks and looked back. "Did you hear? The FDA approved a little pill called Viagra as a treatment for erectile dysfunction." He was grinning as if hinting that he wanted to get to know me in the biblical sense.

I laughed and thought, *Just what the world needs—more stiff dicks!*

He turned and left the building, leaving me flipping through the photographs.

> What I like about photographs is that they capture a moment that's gone forever. Impossible to reproduce.
> —Karl Lagerfeld, American designer

That job lasted about six months. Then I worked at another property in Kahana with two towers of apartments. I was being trained by the woman who was retiring. The condos had been neglected and needed upgrades badly. I spent my days off shopping for toasters, curtains, bedspreads, and fake orchid plants. I did a lot of work whipping those condos into shape. Right before the holidays, they hired a different management company and gave us the shaft.

But Dori kept me busy. She liked and trusted me. She eventually sent me to a property in Honokowai called Kohola Look-Out, to fill in at the front desk while the regular manager was on vacation. *Kohola* is the Hawaiian word for whale. Walking into the office was like walking into a cold meat locker. The woman who managed the front desk was wearing a long-sleeved blouse with shoulder pads, even though she was big and tall. She told me she'd made friends with one of the owners, who was taking her on a $50,000 month-long safari in Africa. "Who could turn down something like that?" she remarked.

I sat in a chair next to her while she familiarized me with the ins and outs of the property. The phone rang and her expression changed. I imagined it was a guest who was missing Maui and wanting to know what the weather was like.

"Oh, it's miserable today, and it's raining," she said, rolling her eyes.

I gazed at the sliding glass door to the sunny walkway but said nothing. She hung up the phone and laughed. I wondered how she kept that job with her flippant attitude. An older man and his wife, who I later found out were owners, brought her a blueberry muffin with butter and jam, along with a cup of tea. She had a good racket going in that place.

When she finally went on vacation I worked the whole month and grew to like the property. I'd never been a morning person and didn't understand why what was done at 7:00 a.m. couldn't be done at 9:00 a.m. The hours took some getting used to. The owners really liked me and approached Dourine Wicket about my being the permanent manager of Kohola Look-Out. I was tickled pink at the prospect. Dori found money unaccounted for when she did the previous month's financial closing, and she asked me to look for it in the deposits on reservations. There was no internet back then. Reservation sources were from return guests, referrals, travel agents, and the odd walk-in off the street. I found the discrepancy in the reservation system. Five hundred dollars was missing from a future reservation deposit. The reservation was noted as confirmed and deposited, but the money was missing. I later found out that the manager, for whom I was filling in, had taken the five hundred dollars to Africa for spending money, planning to replace it when she received her vacation pay. At least that is how she later explained it to me. I didn't see it as a big deal, but Dourine Wicket regarded it as stealing.

When the manager returned from vacation, she called the office to see how everything was. I knew Dori had sent her a termination letter, but I could tell by our conversation that this woman hadn't gone through her mail yet. I didn't say too much, just that she needed to read her mail. And so, I became the front-desk manager at Kohola Look-Out by default.

I signed the papers in Dourine Wicket's office accepting the position. I told her that I'd had a horrible few years. My dog had been abducted, my father died and my mother soon after, my artwork and family treasures had been stolen, one of my birds had to be euthanized, and my boyfriend walked out on me. Dori stared at me wide-eyed. "Dori, before I start this job at Kohola Look-Out, I need a vacation."

"As long as you're back before the holidays, when the busy season hits."

I agreed to that condition. That was it; I was on my way to the old country, Italy.

I'd made friends with a woman who had her own condo-cleaning business. Donna Lamonzzoni was a Jew who'd married an Italian guy, but since had divorced. She told me she was so miserable that she walked out on him and their two kids. I didn't comment; I was not one to judge. She was a few years older than me but kept herself in top shape. We attended a weekly yoga class together. We saw life through a similar lens, and shared a compatible sense of humor. She owned her own house which was filled with a collection of interesting art pieces. She mentioned that she would be in Italy with two girlfriends the same time I was there, and that we should hook up.

A week before my trip to Italy, I was walking into Foodland to get a few groceries, and found myself face-to-face with Cheyenne Bremmer. He'd been totally off my radar for a long time. We froze in our tracks like two wolves caught in snares.

"How the hell are ya?" he asked.

"I'm good. I was just going in for a few groceries."

"I got something for lunch from the deli counter."

"I'm on my way to Italy soon."

"Whatcha doing tonight?" Cheyenne asked.

"Nothing really."

"Can I come over later?"

"I'd like that," I said, forgetting the pain of my foot in the trap.

"I'll be over about eight o'clock. We'll catch up," he said, with that smile I loved.

We stood there, our eyes connecting like magnets. Staring into his eyes was like staring into the deep blue sea, and I had a hard time pulling mine away. I managed to turn first and walked into Foodland with a sudden spring in my step. There were no inquiring questions on my mind, only the prospect of being with him later on.

When I got home I fed the birds and made myself something to eat. I could barely swallow my food, anticipating what might happen that night. About two hours later there was a knock at the door. It was Cheyenne. He walked in and looked around.

"Sorry the place is such a mess. I've been packing for my trip."

"Are you kidding me? This place is a palace," he said, his eyes sweeping the room.

Cheyenne didn't waste any time. He pushed me on the chair in the corner, lifted my skirt, and slipped my panties down. He was all over me like a rash, which I definitely needed scratched. He opened my legs, got on top of me, and fucked me hard. It was over pretty quick, but we moved to the bedroom and made love again on the bed. All the necessary questions I should have asked, I didn't. I was in the moment. Afterward, we got dressed and went back into the living room. Cheyenne played with the birds for a while. He seemed lost in transition, as if he missed it all. I figured he just missed aspects of his life with me. Then he whipped a cassette out of his jeans pocket and slipped it in the stereo.

"We've been working on this for a while," he said, wanting me to hear his band's latest creation.

I listened, somewhat interested. He jabbered away about the tape and some other stuff Black Tar had been working on. All I wanted right then was for him to leave. I was dwelling on everything that had gone down between us, and didn't want to repeat it.

I got up and took the cassette out of the stereo and handed it to him. "I think it's time for you to go home," I said.

He was a little stunned, but he slipped the cassette in his pocket and reluctantly walked toward the front door. He turned and said, "Are you sure you want me to leave?"

"It was really nice Chey, but I want you to go."

I walked to the door and opened it. He left looking slightly lost. As soon as he was completely outside, I shut the door behind him. That's when I became emotional, but refused to let myself cry.

I was getting ready for work the next morning, looking all over for my mother's comb, which I had saved along with her nail file. Having those items made me feel her presence around me. I kept her comb on the dresser, but it was gone. It crossed my mind that Cheyenne had taken it. But why in hell would he take the comb unless he needed one. I was momentarily angry, but I let it go.

Three days later Cheyenne called me with the news that Tom, his drummer, had died of AIDS. He was very emotional on the phone, and I choked up just listening to him whimper. He always said that Tom would come to a bad end, and he did.

I'd already purchased a plane ticket to Venice, Italy, when I received a timely phone call from Dominick French, the piano player who was my paramour for the first two years I lived on the island in the mid-seventies. He was visiting Maui and wanted to take me to lunch. "I'll be in Europe while you're there," he said, in between bites of his blue cheese salad. "I can meet you in Venice. I've been thinking about spending a couple of weeks there after my piano gig on the riverboat on the Scandinavian waterways is finished."

My thoughts were that I'd be spending a week on my own before joining a two-week Italy tour, and it would be nice to hang out with someone who knew his way around Europe. I wasn't expecting anything romantic with him; those days were long gone. But I knew he had friends in Venice, and I pictured myself in old apartments with high ceilings, cracked walls, peeling paint, and that Old World vibe.

On the day I left for Italy I took a shuttle to Kahului Airport, wanting to slip out of town unnoticed. I went directly to the United Airline's counter to check in. I felt like I was walking on air as I cruised to the gate. I remained in a state of anxious excitement, so much so that I couldn't nap on any of the flights. I did fade for an hour or so once we were flying over the open ocean—probably a safety mechanism to avoid my fear of the sea.

When the plane landed in Frankfurt, Germany, I followed the crowds of people from different countries wandering through that busy airport. There were numerous checkpoints, and police patrolling with assault rifles and German shepherds. They were stopping people at random asking to see their papers. It was totally weird and unsettling. I saw lines forming in front of three desks. The signs were all in German, and I had no idea if I'd picked the correct line. When I reached the desk I was told I was on the wrong line. I rushed to the back of the correct line, hoping I wouldn't miss my commuter flight to Venice. That's when Murphy's Law struck.

We were being detained in a holding area of the airport, and were told that there was a delay on the commuter flight. All of my connecting flights had been on time until that very last leg of my journey. I was only an hour away from my final destination, Venice. We were stuck there for four hours, screwing up the plans for my whole first day in Venice. When the commuter flight was finally ready to depart, we were bussed to the gate which was quite a distance from the airport holding area. There was very tight security. We were all screened, examined, and scrutinized again by more police as if we were potential terrorists. Going through the final turnstile, an airport attendant stopped me and took my camera.

"What is this?" she asked.

"What do you mean? It's my camera," I answered, annoyed.

"Then take a picture," she said, in English with a heavy German accent.

She handed me the camera and I pointed it at her and was about to click the shutter when she grabbed the camera and ripped the film out. *What the fuck is going on here?* I wondered. Then again, she seemed exasperated with me, and I didn't want to ruffle her feathers in such a way that she'd keep me from my flight. I let her throw the film in the trashcan, and she let me go through the turnstile. We were escorted onto the runway to the plane by more police. I'd hoped I wouldn't be connecting through the Frankfurt airport on my return trip to the US.

The plane landed at the Marco Polo Airport in Venice, but there was no Dominick French to meet me. I wasn't surprised since my plane was more than four hours late. He knew the name of the hotel where I'd be staying. I followed the crowd looking for a water taxi to Piazza San Marco, where I had arranged for a three-day rental in a bed-and-breakfast. Enough people spoke English for me to make sure I would get on the correct *vaporetto*. The operator of the water taxi let me know when it was my stop.

My first impression of Venice was that it could use a dunk in hot soapy water. Gliding along the canal through the still lagoon I saw black sludge at the bottom of the buildings at the water's edge. Black soot coated the buildings as well. Despite all of this, it was as beautiful as a fairytale.

I struggled with my suitcase over cobblestones, until I reached Piazza San Marco which was so vast that I couldn't see the opposite end clearly. The sun was setting, and it was imperative that I find my hotel before dark. I asked a few people who replied, "Which one?" Apparently, there were two hotels with the same name. Finally someone took pity on me and read my computer reservation printout and pointed me in the right direction, insisting that it was only a short walk.

His instructions led me through an alley which opened to a bridge over a canal. I lugged my suitcase up the steps and over the bridge. I came across a store window filled with costumes and ornate masks stocked up for Carnevale di Venezia, and for Halloween which was only a month away. He told me to look for that, so I knew I was on the right path. I came upon a very unimpressive facade with the name of the hotel stenciled in gold on a glass door.

A very young man with short brown hair and glasses stood behind the desk. He took my computer printout and mentioned that I was more than four hours overdue, but that they'd held my room. He explained all the amenities, like a daily cleaning service and a continental breakfast each morning. He handed me the key to my room and pointed to the elevator. Everything in the building was compact. Entering the room I saw a very old bed next to a window that opened to a canal. I unpacked a few things and immediately wanted to walk around Venice. I freshened up and took the elevator back downstairs to the lobby. I asked the same clerk if anyone had left a message for me.

"No one has called or come by looking for you Ms. Bardolino," he said.

"Where is a good place to eat for a reasonable price?"

He gave me the name of a local cafeteria, and spouted confusing directions, which I followed but never found the place. As soon as I left the confines of the bed-and-breakfast I was lost. I didn't notice many actual street names in Venice, only signs with arrows pointing in the direction of famous landmarks. Each day I left the hotel but never found my way back the same way. That first night I walked around Piazza San Marco lined with stores and outside cafés. I could vaguely see a spotlight on a trio performing in a sidewalk café at the far end, but couldn't hear the music. I went through an alleyway and walked over numerous bridges and canals until I came across a store with wheels of cheese and different kinds of salami hanging in the window. I bought a loaf of crusty Italian bread, Fontina cheese, and Genoa salami. I sat outside on the steps of a bridge eating. I found my way back to the hotel, but it took a while.

I checked in with the same clerk to see if there were any messages. With a negative response, I went up to my room. I fell back on the bed, which was lumpy and felt like the mattress was filled with straw. There was an odd pillow the size of a body bag that looked like it was stuffed with someone's overcoat. I put a sweater over the pillow and rested my head. That bed was in such a state that I wondered if Mozart himself might have slept in it two hundred years past.

I tried falling asleep but couldn't. I looked out the window and saw the moon glistening on the narrow waterway between buildings. Pigeons had flocked to the windowsills to sleep for the night. They cried and coo creating an eerie atmosphere.

In the morning I was roused from sleep by the loud bell ringing in the Campanile. I cruised down to the lobby to take advantage of the continental breakfast. The desk clerk pointed me to a small room off the lobby. I saw a few tiny tables and chairs, like one would see in an elementary school. A counter was stocked with trays of croissants, pastries, and wrapped butter and jam. I asked for a coffee.

The attendant asked, "Café Americano?"

I nodded, watching him pour a small cup of espresso into a large cup and fill it to the brim with boiling water. Even the tiny containers of creamer didn't mask the awful taste. The breakfast filled me up though. On the way out the front door I passed the desk clerk without asking if there were any calls for me. I didn't want to embarrass or make a pest of myself. I set out on a walk around Venice. The Basilica di San Marco is a medieval church of a thousand years filled with Byzantine mosaics and stained-glass windows, carved wooden pews, and an altar screen filled with pearls, rubies, emeralds, and other precious stones. Wandering through this building was an explosion to the artistic senses.

Walking away from the church I gazed up at the bronze horses on the roof which looked to still be in motion. This was just around the corner from my hotel. *How lucky am I with this location*, I thought, and had a momentary desire to kiss my travel agent.

I appreciated that there were no cars in Venice, which is a walking city. The number of pigeons throughout the city was crazy. People stood in the Piazza as pigeons lined up along their arms, waiting for the seeds and popcorn sold by local vendors. When the bells in the Campanile began again, the pigeons took off, en masse, creating a dreamy scene, like an old black-and-white Alfred Hitchcock film. I walked toward the canal and saw a line of gondolas bobbing at the water's edge. I took a photo with my wide-angle lens.

Gondolas

Strolling along a sidewalk next to a canal I stumbled across a sign that read, THE HOUSE OF CASANOVA. I'd been under the impression that Giacomo Casanova was a fictitious character, but he actually lived in Venice in the 1700s. He'd been imprisoned in the Palazzo Ducale for a year and a half for sorcery. When released, he'd become a spy for the Inquisition. I wandered up the stairs at the edge of the water and entered the House of Casanova. The ceilings were very high with long maroon-velvet curtains sectioning off very austere rooms. It was a strange place filled with glass cases of erotica and pornography from the fifteenth and sixteenth centuries. I could hear giggling among the visitors as they walked between rooms watching dirty films in flipbook form and kineographs from the eighteenth century.

Nothing looked familiar on my way back to the hotel, and none of the signs pointed to anything that I'd heard about. I walked along picturing Beethoven and Casanova slinking around corners in black capes. I walked over a bridge onto a street which opened into a residential neighborhood. Children were playing ball in a piazza, and there were trees—the first trees I'd seen in Venice. A woman was telling her dog in Italian to drink water from a fountain, and he did. I was lost, but in a good way. I sat on a bench for a while watching the children play.

San Zaccaria Church had a huge painting by Bellini hanging behind the altar, and a saint's relic on display. It was common to see a Michelangelo painting hanging on the altar of a church. Could they have been real, exposed to the public like that? I wondered, on my way out. I came upon a group of gondoliers wearing straw hats with red ribbons, and white-and-black–striped shirts. They smiled and pointed to their gondolas as I passed. I thought it would be silly for me to ride in a gondola all by myself, so I got that out of my head immediately.

I passed a restaurant with outside tables, and thought it would be the perfect place to sit with a glass of red wine and eat a caprese salad. A very young waiter standing outside leaning against the building smiled and motioned for me to come toward him. As I approached he stuck his tongue out and began moving it rapidly from side to side, as if advertising he was good at licking pussy. I quickly turned around and walked in the opposite direction.

I finally saw a sign with an arrow pointing to the Ponte Rialto (Rialto Bridge). I knew where that was, I had been there the previous day. When I reached the bridge I wandered among the tables of trinkets and fruit stands. I bought a bag of fruit and headed back to the hotel. I chuckled to myself at the memory of my father stuffing a banana and a tube of Ritz crackers in his jacket pocket every time he left the house. I passed a grocery store and purchased an Orangina, a lovely light orange soda in an oddly shaped bottle. When I reached the hotel I stopped at the front desk to hear there were no messages.

I wanted to watch the sunset from a boat on the Grand Canal, so I hopped on a vaporetto. On either side of the waterway were colorful palaces, some still inhabited. Small rowboats were tied up at the entrances. The water was a bit above the base of the doorways, so I doubted anyone was able to live on the first floors of the buildings. It was something you could only get the real image of from the water. A glorious sunset lit up the windows of the palaces in a golden hue as we glided by. I saw a large, stark-white domed cathedral in the distance and vowed to visit it the next day.

My last full day in Venice started out with an awful watered-down espresso. *What I wouldn't give for a cup of Folger's coffee*, I thought.

I inquired at the desk about the large white cathedral with the dome. The clerk said it was the church called Santa Maria Della Salute. He told me which vaporetto to take to get there. Walking across Piazza San Marco I gazed at the hitching posts, still there from ancient times. I pictured live animals tied up, and people being flogged in front of huge crowds.

The dome of the cathedral was like a white mirage shining in the sun. The steps up to the entrance were right at the water's edge; the waves lapping at the bottom step as I got off the vaporetto. The three chapels had paintings by the masters Titian and Tintoretto. At this point I was convinced that all of these paintings were copies, the originals locked up in storage somewhere, or hanging in museums. My eyes darted here and there taking it all in. I was the only soul inside the church at that moment. I knelt in a pew and said a prayer. On my way out I marveled at the marble floors and thought of my mother's brothers who were born in Italy and practiced their marble trade when they arrived in America.

On my way back to the hotel, I stopped in the famous Café Florian for an afternoon cappuccino and a very rich pastry. I had a flashback to all the Sundays after church my dad took me to our local soda fountain in the Bronx for a salted pretzel and a chocolate malted. I smiled at the memory, and the fact that the malted and pretzel tasted as good then as the Italian pastry did now. The Republic of Venice was way ahead on Europe's social and political stage when it was the mercantile center of Europe. I looked around the Florian and pictured well-dressed Bohemian men and women sitting at the tables discussing the political fate of Venice, and critiquing art in the eighteenth century. I wondered what it would have been like to be an artist at that time.

I found a public phone booth and called my friend Donna Lamonzzoni who was already in Italy. She invited me to come stay with her and her girlfriends. They were renting a villa in Umbria in central Italy. She told me to take the train south to Perugia which borders Tuscany. She assured me I would love it there.

The next morning I rolled out of Mozart's bed for the last time and packed my suitcase. I took the elevator downstairs and checked out.

"Don't forget to take your continental breakfast before you leave," the clerk behind the desk said, with a mechanical smile.

I had a terrible cup of coffee and ate a roll with butter and jam.

I crossed the Piazza San Marco which was empty. It was so early even the pigeons were still asleep. I hopped a water taxi to the train station on the outskirts of Venice. I never made it to the island of Murano to see the glass blowers, but Venetian glass was displayed in stores throughout Venice.

I purchased a ticket at the train station and stood in line at a counter with other people, waiting for an espresso. A man with sweat-drenched dark hair flattened to his forehead, wearing a long white apron tied around his large midsection, was pumping out espressos as fast as he could from a steam-hissing machine. I watched him slide the tiny cups along the counter with such skill. The coffee was hot and strong. I added sugar remembering how my father always heaped three demitasse spoonfuls of sugar into his espresso cup, along with a sliver of lemon rind.

I walked to the platform and waited for the train. Standing alongside me were two prostitutes—a tall white girl and a tall black girl, both in high heels, very short tight skirts, long earrings, and lots of makeup. When the train arrived, I rushed in alongside them looking for a seat; it was a three-hour trip to Perugia. They were on the move and immediately walked to the next rail car, probably attempting to drum up business. I sat down and looked out the window as the train raced away from Venice.

Donna Lamonzzoni and her two friends, who she secretly referred to as the wicked sisters, were there at the train station to meet me. Both sisters were very tall, and neither was pretty. One took my suitcase, and the other entwined her arm in mine whisking me off the platform, down the stairs, and directly to a gelato shop. It was a strange little town without any character. We walked along the streets, me licking my chocolate gelato, and the wicked sisters jabbering away about all the things they wanted to show me. Donna was silent, with occasional glances in my direction. They had the tiniest car—the four of us plus my suitcase, barely fit in it.

As we drove away from town the scenery improved dramatically displaying a marvelous landscape. *Ah, this is how I pictured Tuscany*, I thought. We drove through a vineyard. In the distance at the top of a hill stood a medieval villa. We had to beep the horn a few times to warn the alpacas hanging out on the road to the house. We dropped our bags inside and sat on the patio with a bottle of local red wine to watch the sunset. I was in a state of euphoria.

I was given my own room on the second floor. The electricity in the villa was sporadic, and when it got dark we relied on candles to find our way around. The windows had no glass, so when the shutters were closed we were in complete darkness. I remember that first night, walking up the staircase to bed, the four of us following each other carrying candles to light our way along the narrow corridor. We were like four nuns in a fourteenth-century monastery.

The bright sun blinded me when I opened the shutters in the morning, but I was able to look around and get my bearings. I knew I'd only be there a few days, so I didn't unpack, just hung a few dresses up. I walked down the staircase to the kitchen where I found the women making breakfast with the eggs from local chickens. I loved every minute in the villa.

That afternoon, we drove through the vineyard, past the alpacas, to the nearby hill town of Orvieto. It was a very old town at the top of a winding road. We parked at the bottom and walked up along the cobblestone streets. We passed a group of women who were sitting outside together snapping string beans into a large pot. We stopped to talk with them. They spoke in Italian with a few English words thrown in. I amazed the girls, as well as myself, by being able to carry on a simple Italian conversation. My mother and her sisters often spoke in Italian, so I guess I absorbed more of the language than I thought. All of these hilltop towns were remnants of medieval times—an old world in modern times.

Donna Lamonzzoni mentioned that the villa came with a chef who would prepare us an Italian meal on our last night—for an exorbitant amount of money. I suggested that I, being Italian, would cook us a meal. The wicked sisters were thrilled, but Donna seemed apprehensive, and an argument ensued. I was like Cinderella sweeping the kitchen between the two ugly sisters and their wicked mother. It was decided I would cook dinner.

I was at the stove, happily stirring the marinara sauce with a wooden spoon, while the wicked sisters were sitting at the table drinking wine. The three of us were talking and laughing exuberantly. Donna flew into the kitchen like a witch on a broom, chastising us for talking so loudly. "Can't you ladies understand that I have a migraine?" she blurted out.

We ate in silence after she left the room. Donna's plate sat empty while the three of us enjoyed the Italian dinner I'd prepared. Donna didn't make an appearance until the next day. I was miffed, but let the episode slide not wanting it to affect our friendship, which I knew would continue when we were back on Maui.

On the day we left the villa, we locked it up like a medieval monastery under siege from Norman invaders. The girls were on their way north to Venice, and I was on my way south to Sicily to join a tour. The women dropped me off at the airport in Florence and drove off. I was alone again on my journey in the old country. I'd heard from Donna Lamonzzoni that when they arrived in Venice, the streets were under water. They sloshed around in knee-deep murky water, looking for a hotel. I was glad I'd experienced Venice before the high tide.

My flight arrived in Palermo, Sicily after dark. I was in the birthplace of my father, a connection I felt immediately. I was instructed by the tour company to ignore any men approaching me asking if I needed a ride to a hotel, and to wait at the official taxi stand. Sure enough I was barraged by fast-talking Italian men, pointing to their cars for a ride. I waved them off and waited at the official taxi stand. I remembered my father telling me that his cousin was robbed by a taxi driver and left in the middle of nowhere when he visited his hometown, Castel Vetrano, in Sicily. I didn't want to repeat that.

"The Grand Central Palace Hotel," I said, to the taxi driver as I got in.

We drove for thirty-five minutes, past rundown buildings and scenes that reminded me of the Bronx. I wondered where the hell he was taking me.

The taxi pulled alongside the curb in front of a very stately building, which I later found out was once the mayor's residence. I paid him the amount on the meter with American money and gave him a little extra.

"*Grazie*," he said. He took my suitcase out of the trunk and handed it to me with a smile revealing a few gold teeth. In total contrast of the view out of the window of the taxi, walking into the lobby was like entering Nero's Palace. It had marble floors and ornate statues in nooks along the walls. I walked up to the desk and handed the clerk my reservation printout.

"Good evening, Ms. Bardolino," he said in English with an Italian accent. "We have your room ready. There will be a buffet breakfast served on the rooftop in the morning. I think you will like it very much."

The front-desk clerk had me fill out a registration form, handed me the key to my room, and pointed me toward a wide marble staircase. When I made the reservation, I'd indicated that I wanted a hotel in a central location so I could get around Palermo without the use of a car. I never expected to be staying in a palace. I walked down the corridor on the second floor, past tropical floral arrangements, looking for my room. I unlocked the door and entered a palatial room with beautiful furniture, and a large bathroom that was marble from ceiling to floor. I took a long, hot shower, pretending I was in an ancient Roman bathhouse. It was invigorating. I heard thunder and saw lightning as I was putting on my nightgown. I peered out the tall windows to see heavy rain coming down, and felt a chill as it beat against the windows. I felt my father's presence all around me.

The heavy rainstorm prompted a flashback of my first memory as a child. I was sitting in a highchair in the kitchen. My father was getting milk for my bottle out of the icebox. There was a terrible rainstorm beating against the window. The milk bottle slipped from his hand splattering the glass and milk all over the floor.

"My mook, my mook," I wailed.

My father put his coat on and went out in the storm to get another bottle of milk for me. I teared up at the memory. For sure he was with me on this night.

When I woke up the next morning, I went straight to the rooftop for the breakfast buffet. It was still drizzling outside so I took a seat inside under the glass canopy. I could see all of Palermo from the terrace, with Monte Pellegrino in the distance. Pellegrino is a very common surname name in Sicily, like Smith is in America. Pellegrino was my paternal grandmother's maiden name. I cruised the buffet table which had an array of cold cuts, fruit, sliced Italian bread, and a tray of freshly made ricotta. I filled a plate with a little of everything, but heaped on a mound of ricotta, which I went back for more a few times. I stopped at the desk to ask for a late checkout, as I was to meet my tour group at another hotel at 2:00 p.m.

I spent the day wandering around Palermo looking at the sights. So many of the street names were in Arabic, as Sicily was part of the Byzantine Empire for two hundred years. Sicily was the Islamic kingdom, a major cultural center of the Muslim world between the years 891 and 1091. I saw many Moorish influences, both in the buildings and in the food.

I stared up at the Church of San Giuseppe with statues at each level going up the façade of the building. The interior was over-the-top ornate. I said a prayer for my father in front of the statue of Saint Joseph.

There were palm trees everywhere in Palermo, and I realized why I was so comfortable in the tropics—it was in my blood, my DNA. It had stopped raining so I walked a little farther passing a courthouse, where I happened upon a plaza with a fountain surrounded by nude statues—Piazza Pretoria (Plaza of Shame). I thought it was thoroughly beautiful, even though some of the statues were missing limbs, and one was missing his dick.

I checked out of the Grand Central Palace, thanking the desk clerk profusely for such a wonderful stay. He gave me directions to the hotel where I was to meet my tour group. I took a taxi through yet another rainstorm. I walked into the lobby and found my fellow travelers sitting on couches. We greeted each other, and shared stories of our Italy experiences so far. There was a single woman from Staten Island, New York, Cathy Rubia, who I clicked with right away. She and I became buddies on the tour. One of the men had gone out earlier that day in the storm to get fresh-made cannoli from a popular bakery in Palermo. I regretted having arrived too late, missing the pastries. Sicily is the home of the cannolo. Our group spent that first night at the hotel, and were treated to a wonderful dinner with local wines.

After being on my own for over a week, I was happy to join a tour, where I wouldn't have to drag my own suitcase around, miss museums for lack of reservations, or worry about a meal at the end of each day. All that was taken care of by the tour company. Each morning we were directed to leave our suitcases outside of our rooms and go to breakfast while all the luggage was loaded on the tour bus. I sat with my new friend and companion, Cathy Rubia. Our tour director had a thing for Cathy, who had a pretty face and big blue eyes.

Southern Italian food was right up my alley with all the red sauces and hot spices. The farther north we traveled the less I liked the food. Every town we stopped in had locally crafted wines, of which we drank plenty. The town of Agrigento was filled with Roman and Greek ruins, temples, aqueducts, and an amphitheater which is still used for concerts two thousand years later. The landscape among the ruins was very arid. I spied a cactus with prickly pears which reminded me of Hawaii, and saw a bush of capers growing right out of a rock wall.

A few days into the tour Cathy noticed that every time the bus stopped in a new town, the tour director would buy a bouquet of flowers and disappear for a few hours. We were convinced he had a girl in every town along the route. Looking at him, I couldn't understand the appeal.

On the way to our hotel the bus stopped for gas. This was nothing like a gas station in the USA. There was a full restaurant, with choices like prime rib, lasagna and tiramisu for dessert. I saw the same two prostitutes hanging around the gas pumps that I'd seen on the train ride to Perugia. One of the clueless women on the bus asked me why those women were dressed like that. "Because they're hookers," I answered.

We stayed in the beach resort town of Taormina. Cathy and I had lunch at an outside café; the menu consisted of all seafood. A large platter of clams was being served to the people seated at the table next to ours. I had a flashback of going to Arthur Avenue in the Bronx with my father as a child. The first thing he'd do was order a dozen cherrystone clams on the half shell from a sidewalk restaurant. I'd watch him squeeze a lemon over them, trickle hot sauce, and eat the whole plate with gusto, slurping one clam after another.

Cathy and I were told to sit with our backs to the wall, as the Mafia was still a force to be reckoned with in Sicily, and a gunfight could break out at any time. I wasn't sure if our tour director was joking, but I wasn't taking any chances.

I ordered the fresh catch of the day in a lemon and caper sauce. Cathy had shrimp scampi. A secret admirer sent two shots of Limoncello to our table.

I used a public restroom down a long flight of stairs at the other end of town. An old man stood inside the doorway of the bathroom. I had to pay him to get toilet paper. He grinned and slapped my ass on the way out. Cathy and I laughed about that for days. When we grilled the tour director about the incident, he dismissed it by saying that there was no Social Security in Italy, and old retired Italians did odd jobs for money, which didn't really address our concerns.

We left the island of Sicily and boarded a ferry to the mainland of Italy. Andrea Bocelli's new hit song "Con te Partiro (Time to Say Goodbye)" was playing as the boat left the dock. I felt sad, as if leaving Sicily I was leaving my father behind. I heard that song everywhere we went, and it became synonymous with my trip to the old country.

I really wanted to spend time in Naples, the home of pizza and the opera, but we were told it wasn't a safe place to stay. I wondered if there was some truth to that famous line, "See Naples and die!" We made a short stop at the Port of Naples where Italians boarded ships for America in the early 1900s. As the bus drove out of town, I saw those same two prostitutes standing on the side of the road in the middle of nowhere. I suppose they were looking to be picked up by truckers on their daily delivery routes. These ladies of the night and day certainly got around.

Mount Vesuvius was on the horizon, and Pompeii was our next destination. We were dropped off and given the afternoon to wander through the streets and villas uncovered from the ash of Vesuvius's eruption in 79 A.D. There was a gallery with mummified Pompeiian residents in glass cases frozen in time with the most horrific expressions. They couldn't escape the volcanic eruption, except for those who had boats. Families were entombed in volcanic ash hugging each other, holding hands, or covering their pets. We were told that at the time we visited, the buried city of Pompeii had only been one-quarter excavated. What a strange and marvelous place.

Most villas were built around a central courtyard with greenery, fruit trees, birdbaths, and stone benches. They were so completely intact that I expected someone to walk into the courtyard at any moment to get a jug of water from the fountain. We walked through a very ornate dining room in a red hue. Frescos lined the walls depicting graphic sexual scenes. One man had a huge dick that would terrify any woman. We wondered why such a fresco would adorn a dining room.

Iridescent flecks were imbedded in the sidewalks to reflect the moonlight, which lit up the paths in darkness. Raised stones were placed strategically so you could hop across the street avoiding the water during heavy rain. The ingenuity and craftsmanship of these ancient Roman builders was incredible. I couldn't get over how one drastic event, the eruption of Mount Vesuvius, buried an entire city and killed all its inhabitants.

Courtyard in Pompeii

We stayed in Florence for a few days. I was disappointed when I found out the statue of David in the plaza was a fake. The real seventeen foot statue of *David* by Michelangelo had been moved indoors to the Academia Gallery in 1910. We were taken to a leather factory and prompted to buy very expensive coats, jackets, and purses. Cathy Rubia and I saved our money for the eighteen-karat–gold jewelry, for which Florence is also known. I bought a beautiful gold chain-link bracelet with dangling light-blue aquamarine hearts.

When we pulled into Rome, the Eternal City, everything we passed outside the bus's windows looked larger than life. Women zipped past the bus on Vespas, all dressed up for work in high heels. Red traffic lights are just a suggestion in Rome.

The tour of the Vatican was swift, as if on a conveyer belt. Michelangelo's sculpture, the *Pieta,* was enclosed in glass; we were whisked past it on an escalator. We were hurried through the Sistine Chapel, being told that our breath could destroy the frescos. At first I was annoyed; then I remembered seeing a documentary on the building of the subways under Rome. When the tunnels were dug revealing ruins, ancient frescos began to fade as soon as they were exposed to the air.

Saint Peter's Cathedral was huge and very crowded. We had to dodge gypsies and pickpockets. I guess the Swiss Guards, who patrolled Vatican City, weren't paying attention.

I was captivated by the Pantheon, which was an ancient pagan temple converted to Christianity over the centuries. Gods and goddesses had been replaced with saints and martyrs. The marble floors were pristine, despite the dome opening to the sky, which allowed rain to fall on that marble floor for two thousand years. I visited the ancient Colosseum on my own. I walked through the archways and alcoves. I gazed at the center stage hearing the ghosts of the Roman populace cheering for their favorite gladiators, or recoiling in disgust at the carnage of Christians being fed to the lions, or a plethora of exotic animals sacrificed.

On a free day in Rome, Cathy Rubia and I went on a shopping spree. I spied an eighteen-karat–gold ring with a light-blue aquamarine heart in the center. I had to buy it; it matched the bracelet I'd found in Florence. We walked to Trevi Fountain, and I made sure I threw three coins over my shoulder into the rushing water, which guaranteed my return to Rome. I pictured Anita Ekberg in that tight dress, wading in the fountain in the old black-and-white Fellini film, *La Dolce Vita*. We stopped in a café for an afternoon gelato and espresso. I looked up at the television, which was playing a popular Italian sitcom whose star was a German shepherd that solved crimes.

On our last night in Rome we were treated to a dinner and live band at the Brancaccio Palace. We drank, ate, and danced the night away, like anything but common plebeians.

Cathy Rubia and I exchanged addresses and phone numbers and vowed to keep in touch. I promised I'd visit her the next time I was in New York. I took a taxi to the airport and was happy to find that my return connecting flight from Rome would stop in Munich, Germany, not Frankfurt. This wasn't an over-the-ocean route. I was able to see land most of the way back to the US. We flew over Iceland, Greenland, and the Northwest Passage into North America. On my first airport connection in the United States I passed a McDonald's. I was more than happy to wait on line for an Egg McMuffin and a cup of real American coffee. Funny—the simple things you miss when you are away from the States.

I still had to fly to LA, then over the Pacific Ocean to Honolulu, Hawaii, and then on to Maui. I was able to slip back into town unnoticed. I spent a restful night alone in my apartment in the hood. I watched an episode of one of my favorite series, *Mike Hammer, Private Eye*, with Stacy Keach. I picked up the birds at the vet the following day.

My trip to Italy was unforgettable. I thought so much about my father while I was in Sicily. My big takeaways from the old country was that our family origins, and our DNA, impact the choices we make in the places we feel most at home, and our taste in food. Also, art was much more at the center of everyone's daily life during earlier centuries.

CHAPTER 19

BLOOD IN MY EYES

The conditions of a solitary bird are five:
It flies to the highest point
It does not suffer for company, not even of its own kind.
It aims its beak to the skies
It does not have a definite color
It sings very softly
—San Juan de la Cruz, *Dichos de Luz y Amor*

I was jotting random thoughts in my Morning Pages and contemplating my life going forward as a single woman, one who does not sing softly. I noticed that the fichus tree on my lanai was overgrown to the point of obstructing my view. I spoke to the resident manager of the hood, who told me he would plant it in the ground at the top of the gulch in a place where I'd be able to see it from my lanai. I hated letting it go, but it was time.

The management company I was working for hosted a Christmas party at a new restaurant in Lahaina. I got all dolled up and drove into town. I walked in and got settled at a table with one of the managers from a sister property, Susan Duffy. We had worked together at the Italian restaurant in Kapalua, and now we worked for the same Vacation Rental Company. We remained friends over the years.

Susan Duffy leaned in and whispered in my ear, "Isn't that Cheyenne Bremmer?"

My eyes cruised the room for him. "What the fuck?" I mumbled.

Cheyenne was the sound engineer for the band that was supplying the music for our Christmas party. He did that on a regular basis for a number of local bands. The death of his drummer, Tom, put the kibosh on Black Tar. Cheyenne walked to my table when he saw me. He always looked hot in black. He knelt down beside my chair and hugged me. My heart did a flip-flop and my eyes filled with blood.

After we chatted for a bit he took something out of his pocket. It was a photo of a little boy. "This is my son, Donny," he said.

My heart dropped, and for a moment I was speechless. "He looks just like you, except for the blond hair."

"Yeah. His mother took him to the mainland with her. She's hooked on drugs, and we don't get along. Her parents sent her to rehab, and now I'm taking care of Donny."

"That sounds like a plan," I said. The photo of his son imprinted behind my eyes.

"You look like a million bucks," he said, gazing at me.

I smiled and took a sip of chardonnay.

Cheyenne wanted to talk more, but the band was walking back to the stage, and our food was being set out on the buffet table. He kissed me on the lips, stood up, and said, "You're still beautiful hon."

Everything in front of my eyes went wobbly as I watched him walk away, and I thought I might pass out. I walked to the food table and made myself a plate. When I sat back down I just stared at the food and couldn't eat.

"Adriana, what's wrong?" Susan asked. "What did Cheyenne say?"

I stood up without a word and left through the back exit of the building. My head was exploding with memories and regrets. I don't remember the drive home. I walked in the front door of my apartment taking off my clothes, and making my way to the bathroom. I turned on the shower and hopped in letting the water rush over me, and cried it all out.

The next day I went to work at Kohola Look-Out as if nothing had happened. The crazy cast of characters on that property kept me busy and somewhat amused. Besides, all I had to do was leave the office and walk out front to the ocean and watch the waves roll in for a dose of peace and tranquility. I'd gaze out to the island of Molokai across the channel, and sometimes watch surfers in the waves, and my mind would go to a happy place. After work, I drove to Donna Lamonzzoni's house. We wanted to look through the photographs we'd taken in Umbria. She gave me a colored pencil drawing she had done of the medieval villa we stayed in. We drank wine, had a good laugh about the wicked sisters, and I went home.

About a week after the Christmas party Cheyenne called to confide in me about his tale of woe. I have no good explanation for why I was listening. I had no other love interest, and perhaps I still had love for him. Hell, I was still sleeping on my side of the bed! He told me that his very young twenty-two-year-old girlfriend, Ricki, was coming back to Maui after rehab and wanted them to live together again. He just wanted them to share custody of Donny. It sounded like a difficult situation.

I began seeing Cheyenne Bremmer again—in the biblical sense. I guess it filled a need in both of us. Subconsciously, I knew it was only temporary. Like the line in the Bob Dylan song "I Got Blood in My Eyes for You," we still had a mutual attraction.

Annie Hughes's friend Chip Newton was in town from Las Vegas. I met them for a drink at the Sly Mongoose. They were sitting at the end of the bar when I walked in. Chip moved one barstool over so I could sit between them. I was about to bring them up to speed on my situation when Annie told us a crazy story.

Annie said, "My daughter, the one who was in a mental institution, showed up on my doorstep unexpectedly. She'd shaved her head, had a nose ring, and a snake tattoo on her neck. She blamed me for everything that happened in her childhood."

"Well, she's nuts!" Chip said.

"My other daughter must have given her my address."

"Is she still here?" I asked.

"No fucking way! I had her sent off the island," Annie said.

"How the hell did you manage that?" I asked.

"I woke up with a knife at my throat. She threatened to kill me. I called Tim Kork, and he bought her a plane ticket off the island. He drove her to the airport and didn't leave until he saw her get on the plane. I told him to wait until the plane took off to make sure."

"Annie, that's horrible. Thank God you're OK."

"I told her if she ever came back to the island I'd call the cops and have her arrested."

"What about your other daughter?" Chip asked.

"She's fine. She's married and has four kids to keep her busy."

I nursed one drink while Annie and Chip were knocking them back pretty good. Chip brought up that crazy trip the three of us were on in

Honolulu so many years back, and we had a good laugh about the Monkey Bar in Pearl City.

"You going to the studio to see lover boy?" Annie asked, looking at me.

"No, the band broke up after their drummer died. I'll see him later on."

"Getting banged? Can't knock that. Get it while you can honey!" she said, laughing.

I kissed Annie on the cheek, hugged Chip Newton, and walked out of the Goose.

The year 1999 arrived with world paranoia about the Y2K bug. Everyone was waiting to see what was going to happen as the year 2000 approached. They assumed the world's financial markets were going to go through a major reset, and it was all going down the tubes. For me, it was a new year, and I was hoping for a new direction in my life.

I was into Guns N' Roses. I guess I was still a rocker at heart. I was driving to Kmart in Kahului in the Cherokee Chief listening to their old hit, "Sweet Child of Mine." I had the windows rolled down and was in a good mood. I needed to buy toasters and coffee pots for the condos at work. The condos were involved in deep cleanings and inventories. I drove along the lower road, past all the cars parked at the shore. The waves were up, and surfers were out in the water waiting for sets to roll in. I thanked God for putting me in this beautiful place. Despite all the crazy things that had happened in my life on Maui, I was grateful for my tropical surroundings.

When I arrived back at Kohola Look-Out all hell was breaking loose. A water heater in a condo on the third floor had blown, and the water leaked down two floors. The ceiling of the condo underneath it on the second floor had caved in and was laying in chunks on the bed. The condo on the first floor received the least damage, just bubbling and a water stain on the ceiling. The resident manager had already called a plumber to replace the water heater, and I called our handyman, Gary Walker. I liked him to size up the situation and get an estimate on how much it was going to cost to put the three condos back together as if nothing had happened. I had to move guests who were affected by the flood, and cancel other reservations for people who were due to arrive in those condos on the weekend. It was a jumbled mess, but something about the way everything came together in the end was very rewarding. I learned how to multitask, and I knew I was good at my job.

That summer John F. Kennedy Jr. was lost at sea. The plane he piloted disappeared in the Atlantic Ocean off Martha's Vineyard. The young, good-looking Kennedy prodigy was never seen again, along with his wife, Lauren Bessette, and her sister. There were rumors that they were actually alive somewhere in hiding. A few weeks later the plane wreckage was found and the bodies recovered. The Kennedy clan sure had their share of tragedies.

My aunt Porciella had died recently, and my cousin Giovanna Ferrari wanted to get our parents' gravestone etched with all the names and dates, now that all four were in the ground. I told her that when the stone was complete I would come to New York, and we would go to the cemetery to see it.

A month or so later I received a call from my cousin Gia. Our parents' gravestone was ready and would be reinstalled that month. I hadn't been to New York since my mother passed away in the fall of 1995, so I'd be seeing everyone for the first time in four years. Now that my parents were gone, I had little motivation to go to New York. I wanted to spend my future vacations going to places I'd never been before, but this trip was already charted. I purchased a round-trip ticket to the East Coast.

I arrived at Kennedy Airport in the first week of September. Gia and and her husband Stu were waiting for me at the end of an escalator in the main area of the airport. As soon as Gia and I made eye contact we walked toward each other and hugged. We drove straight to their roof top apartment in Tribeca; I never suffered from jetlag. When I get to where I'm going I always hit the ground running.

With the job I had, I was tethered to my cell phone. The woman who was covering the office for me while I was away was free to call me at any time for advice or to clarify an issue. I preferred that than arriving back in the office at Kohola Look-Out and finding a mess that had to be straightened out.

"We were thinking of meeting a friend in Greenwich Village for a drink. Are you sure you're not too tired?" Stu asked.

"No, I'm wide awake," I assured him.

After I freshened up and changed, we walked to an outside café in the Village. From there we went straight to their neighborhood restaurant, Knickerbockers, for drinks and dinner. I found myself easily falling back into city life.

When I woke up the next morning I walked out of the French doors onto the terrace. It was brisk but pleasant. Some of the shrubs and trees in their rooftop garden were turning fall colors. Birds of all varieties hung around the trees singing their unique songs. I spied a hawk sitting on the roof of the adjacent building. I sat on a bench under the trellis watching it until my need for coffee overtook me. I walked through the garden to the kitchen at the other end of the apartment and saw just the coffee pot. I could hear it percolating with the strong aroma of half Maxwell House and half Medaglia d'Oro Italian espresso. Gia was still asleep so I figured Stu set up the coffee, and had gone downstairs to get the morning paper. I got a mug out of the cabinet and poured myself a cup. I sat at the kitchen table and stared at the stained-glass sailboat dangling from the window with the morning sun shining through, the sailboat I had made for them years ago. It depressed me that I hadn't done anything creative in such a long time. The thought nagged me, and I wondered how I lost Gauguin.

Stu walked in the front door with the *New York Times* and a bag filled with fresh bagels. "I thought we'd go to the Statue of Liberty. Would you be interested in that?"

"I'd love to take a boat ride," I said.

"We'll wait for Gia to wake up. She can make breakfast."

"Stu, I think I can find something to eat in the fridge. You don't have to wait on me."

"No, she likes to do it," he said. I imagined he assumed she did.

"I'll go wash up," I said, walking out of the kitchen with my cup of coffee.

Stu had the latest gadgets and techie stuff. I was sleeping in the media room, which doubled as a guest bedroom. There was a desk with a computer monitor that was also a TV. I picked up my cell phone and checked in with the office at Kohola Look-Out to make sure everything was going smoothly back on Maui. When I got off the phone, I realized that I didn't miss work at all.

Stu knew everything that was happening in New York City. He'd often take us on walking tours, pointing out new buildings being constructed or older buildings being refurbished. He knew who owned them and who the builders were. He'd pointed out a huge apartment complex that Donald Trump had under construction. He told me that a visitor center was in the works on Ellis Island slated to open in the next couple of years. We'd be able to trace our ancestors back to when they arrived in America, and would actually see their names on the manifest of the ship they sailed from Europe on. Stu, a Russian Jew, knew his family came to America around the same time that Gia's mom arrived from Italy. Ellis Island was definitely a draw for me to visit again in the next few years.

We went to my favorite falafel place in Greenwich Village for lunch. Stu wanted to show me the Meatpacking District which was in the process of being gentrified. The streets that once ran with the blood of slaughtered cattle, were now filled with upscale restaurants and designer clothing shops. We walked into a warehouse-style store, where only a few items of clothing hung on the racks, but were very high end! Gia saw a white blouse hanging alone, picked it up, tried it on, and purchased it on the spot. It was very expensive. I shopped in department stores and tried on dozens of garments before making a choice, sometimes walking out of a store with nothing. Gia and I certainly had different shopping habits.

When we got back to their apartment twenty-four floors up on top of the building we discussed going to Woodlawn Cemetery the next day to view the gravestone. Gia and I weren't looking forward to it. We were afraid we'd be overcome with emotion. With a nervous smile Stu assured us we'd be fine.

The following day the weather had changed exponentially. I walked out of the French doors to the terrace from the media room to a chilly wind. We bundled up with sweaters and jackets while Stu went to retrieve the car.. The three of us got in the car. Gia and I didn't say much. Stu did most of the talking. He had something to say about almost every building and skyscraper we passed until we were out of the city. We drove along back roads until we reached Woodlawn Cemetery.

Gia spied a flower stand inside the gates at the entrance and bought a bouquet of flowers while Stu parked the car. The three of us wandered around for a long time but couldn't find the gravesite, so we went to the office which we'd avoided on our way in. The man on duty gave us a map and directions to the correct area of the cemetery. After walking about fifteen minutes I spotted Miles Davis' gravesite. "We're close," I said.

Gia entwined her arm in mine as we approached our parent's grave. We were ambivalent as to how we were going to feel. Stu stood a distance back, not knowing how we would react. Perhaps he'd have to deal with two women crying and tearing their hair out.

Gia and I scrutinized the engraved names on the stone. Everything looked right. Their individual names were listed, and they even spelled my father's first name the Italian way, as it appears on his birth certificate. It was an impressive thing to see. I skipped over the dates.

Faustino Ferrari
Porciella Ferrari
Andrea Bardolino
Vita Bardolino

"How do you feel?" Gia asked.

"I don't feel anything," I said.

"That's because they're not there," Stu said.

"The four of them are probably playing cards in heaven," I said, laughing.

Gia and I hugged each other tightly. Stu commented that Faustino's brother, who married Porciella when her husband Faustino died, had trimmed the fire bushes that were on either side of the stone. The story was that Faustino's brother always had a thing for Porciella, even when they were young brothers back in Brooklyn, but Porciella chose Faustino. It's a common thing in the old country for a brother to marry his brother's wife if her husband dies. He always reminded me of the Hungarian actor Bela Lugosi in an old silent horror film. He did have the most striking pale-gray eyes. I imagined he'd been a very attractive man when he was young.

We set the bouquet of flowers at the base of the stone and the three of us walked away, past Miles Davis, past the weeping willow tree my mother always bragged about, and out of the gates of the cemetery. I've never been back.

The second week I was in New York we set out on an excursion to the Hamptons, a trendy area of Long Island, New York, inhabited by movie stars and celebrity elites. Stu had rented a house right on the beach, even though it was fall and too cold to swim in the Atlantic. We went to a bar and ordered Irish whiskeys to warm us up. We visited a historic lighthouse that was filled with old photographs of the way things once were. On the drive back into New York City we stopped at a Native American trading post where they picked up cartons of cigarettes cheap, in preparation for an upcoming trip to Italy my cousins had planned. "We can't find our brand in Europe," Stu said.

When I stayed with my cousin in Manhattan, my routine was a morning walk through Greenwich Village via Washington Square Park. Musicians still played under the arch or next to the fountain. It was still a meet-and-greet place for local Village residents. Old retirees played chess on stone tables; people sat on blankets and had picnics on the grass where squirrels scampered up and down trees. There was the odd preacher preaching. *Some things never change*, I thought.

I left my cousins for a few days to visit my friend Adam Hirschfeld in Ithaca, in the Finger Lakes region of New York State. I'd never been to the house he built after our commune broke up. I took a commuter bus from Port Authority, and Adam picked me up at the bus depot in Ithaca. We spent a few fun days together. He took me to a botanical garden. Funny that we always ended up at a botanical garden whenever and wherever we reunited. We visited Aiden Wazansky (a former boyfriend of Adam's). Aiden had a get-together at his summer house on a lake. So many people from the old commune were there, mainly the gay contingent. It was nice catching up with everyone. Even Evelyn Moskowitz, aka Ivy, was there. She mentioned to me that she was rarely invited to these gatherings, and thought she was only asked to attend because it was a special occasion, my being there.

Through the bay window in Adam's living room was a commanding view of the Adirondack Mountains. His yard resembled a traditional English garden, with groups of wildflowers growing haphazardly. He'd built a fence around the vegetable garden, saying that the deer were eating everything, and that it was a constant battle to salvage his produce.

I spent some time tidying up because the place was a mess and needed a woman's touch. I cleaned off the large wooden dining room table in front of the picture window. I cut some wildflowers from his yard, arranging them in a vase with water and set them on the table. Adam, having been a chef for a long time, cooked us a memorable dinner. Sebastian Warren, also from the old commune, came to dinner. He drank quite a bit of wine and rambled on and on about nonsense. He'd grown into a crotchety old man, but we still loved him. I only saw him that one time. Adam avoided inviting him to do things with us after that, claiming he'd become ill-tempered and difficult with age.

Adam showed me the site where one of the twins from the old commune, who'd died of AIDS, was buried right on the property. It was in a beautiful spot, with the mountains as a backdrop. Adam's orange tabby cat, Albert, followed us around everywhere, unless he was napping in a ray of sunlight. He loved sitting on Adam's lap getting pets. Watching them, I couldn't help remembering all the times I watched Lonny Marcum's cat in Adam's lap on a chair by the window in their apartment in Manhattan where I lived with them in the late sixties. Adam and I were lovers back then.

Adam took me to Moosewood for lunch, the ethnic collective Restaurant where he worked. Lonny Marcum, who was now legally blind, walked in led by a companion who lived with him. We ordered drinks and had a wonderful afternoon reminiscing about the early days of the commune, and our magical summer in the Yellow House back in 1971. Lonny reached for my hand across the table.

"The only good thing about being blind is that I still see you at twenty-five years old."

"Lonny," I said, my voice cracking.

He stroked my hand and smiled.

I teared up. "We certainly have some wonderful memories, don't we?" I said.

"Yes, amazing and unforgettable."

After a few days in the Finger Lakes, Adam dropped me off at the bus depot. We hugged, and he promised to visit me again soon in Hawaii. I told him I looked forward to it.

Back in New York City, Gia and Stu took me to high tea at the Carlyle Hotel. The surroundings were opulent. It was a treat eating those tiny cucumber and cream cheese sandwiches, not to mention the pastry sampler. Another day, it was pastrami sandwiches at Katz's Deli, and ice cream sundaes at Serendipity's for dessert.

Sammy's was an out-of-the-way ethnic kosher food restaurant. Stu said, "You'll love this place!" It was down a staircase in the basement of a building. Stu ordered for the whole table—chopped liver, gefilte fish, and my least favorite, chicken soup with unborn eggs. They ate with gusto. I shifted the food around my plate while listening to Klezmer music.

New York is definitely a city of indulgence. Walking back to their apartment I saw rather large rats scurrying along the bases of buildings dragging food they'd scavenged.

When it got dark, we went back to the Carlyle Hotel to hear Woody Allen's Dixieland jazz band, which was a large fourteen-piece orchestra. The bar was so crowded that we had to split up to get a good view of the stage. I saw some famous people standing around. On another afternoon, we went to hear a jazz singer in a small club in Greenwich Village. The singer was marvelous. I thought of my introduction to the jazz world when I dated Zackery Darcy, the jazz drummer, who took me to see every popular jazz musician and singer back in the sixties. Everywhere I went I had memories haunting me, but in a good way.

I couldn't leave New York without visiting my friend Cathy Rubia, who lived on the furthest tip of Staten Island. It was a two-hour trek by bus over the Verrazano Bridge. We met at a restaurant in her neighborhood. Over lunch we discussed the Italy tour we'd taken that past year. We laughed about the tour director who had a woman in every town the tour bus passed through. We walked to Cathy's house from the restaurant. As we approached the tiny house I noticed it was leaning, and sand had heaped up at the bottom of the entry steps.

The interior of the house hadn't been remodeled since she lived there with her mother, who'd been dead a long time. She asked me if I liked oldies. When I said I loved old rock'n'roll, she put 45 after 45 on an old record player. I assumed it was the same one from her childhood. I was getting creeped out, and wondered if it was a mistake to agree to an overnight stay.

She walked me to the guest bedroom I'd be sleeping in, and set my overnight bag on the floor. The house had settled over the years, and every room was on a tilted angle. Walking through the hallway was like an amusement park ride, where the funhouse is tilted and you struggle to stay upright. I had to adjust my stance so as not to tip over. The whole house was sinking into the sandy soil. I wondered why she stayed in the house. Perhaps she couldn't sell it in that condition. She showed me photographs of her mother and brother, and talked about their wonderful early life together. I was glad I visited her, but knew I'd never go back to that slanted funhouse again. She left me off at the bus stop on her corner, and promised to visit me on Maui in the coming months.

Stu got us prime tickets to see Giuseppe Verdi's opera *Aida* at the Metropolitan Opera House at Lincoln Center. I'd heard that in Italy outside productions of *Aida* actually had live elephants on stage. This was not just a night at the opera. After a fabulous meal in their dining room, we were escorted to a private box over the stage, which an attendant opened with a key. The opera was beautiful—the music, the costumes, live horses prancing on stage. During intermission we were escorted back to the dining room for dessert and coffee. The finale was incredible, followed by a number of curtain calls. I was enjoying all the things I missed about living in a city.

Our last excursion was a trip to Connecticut to visit our cousin Cody. Gia and I spent many summers at his parents', Aunt Mari and Uncle Giuseppe's, mini farm. I was nervous about seeing my mother's nine-foot couch, which Cody and his son had taken after my mother passed away—the very couch that was my bed for so many years while visiting my parents in the Bronx. His house was beautiful, very spacious, on a good-sized property, and well landscaped with a garden. Cody was always into landscaping, even as a young man. He had constructed a pool in the back of the house, which was covered because it was fall.

He made hummus from scratch and served it with sesame breadsticks. My eyes zoomed around the kitchen searching for other familiar items from my mother's kitchen, which Cody also took after her death. We stayed overnight and I slept on my mother's couch enveloped in a cocoon of love and safety. I was happy that Vita's couch had a loving home.

My last few days in New York were filled with walks around the city, and a shopping spree in Macy's flagship store. I found navigating the eleven floors daunting.

On the flight back to Hawaii, I thought of how my cousins always wined and dined me when I visited, and how appreciative I was. As the plane took off from Kennedy Airport, I thought of the time they invited me to a rocket launch at Cape Canaveral in Florida. After the launch we spent a large portion of the day at the Kennedy Space Center. Then they flew me to a villa they'd rented on the island of Anguilla in the Caribbean. I spent two glorious weeks there. Goats roamed the streets. Pristine beaches with fine white sand surrounded the island. A private indoor/outdoor bathroom and shower was attached to my bedroom, which overlooked the ocean. On that trip, I flew straight back to Hawaii from Anguilla. The ferry took me to Saint Martin where the airport was. That island required numerous passport checkpoints because the island was split into territories controlled by four different countries. That was a fabulous trip I'd never forget.

I found life much the same upon my return to Maui, a life I'd grown used to. True, it was another place filled with memories. Every time I walked past the Missionaries Hotel, I heard the ghost of Dominick French banging on the piano keys, and thought of my first two magical years on the island. When I drove past the strip mall in Kaanapali where they rent mopeds, I pictured Derick Ellis emerging from the doorway with that marvelous mop of wavy blond hair, and remembering how in love I was.

Now, I was living in the apartment I'd lived in with Cheyenne Bremmer. All of our mementos around me. The day after I returned, I drove to Kihei to pick up the cockatiels from the bird vet. I settled in, the birds in their cage, and a heavy rain coming down on the lanai. I had my front door open and could hear music streaming in from Dash Kern's stereo. I was content and at peace.

I didn't work for Abigail's Distinctive Affairs any longer, but Abby and I remained friends. We met on the weekend for lunch in Lahaina, and she told me the crazy story of the marriage of Filippo Rizzoli. He had gone to Chicago indefinitely because his father was deathly ill. Filippo fell in love with his father's nurse. Dawn was her name, like the dish liquid. Perhaps there was an oath regarding the death of his father, but Filippo decided to make this nurse his wife. Abby put together a small wedding ceremony on the beach. When they left for Chicago as a married couple, Filippo left his wallet with all his credit cards and cash in Abby's van. I could just imagine how that honeymoon must have gone.

A group of us flew to Honolulu for Octoberfest. One of the hotels in Waikiki was having a big bash with green beer and German food. I didn't ask Cheyenne to go. Besides he had his little boy to take care of. We all got drunk and crazy. I distinctly remember the chicken dance. Hans Berlin was there, but Abby drank Hans, and everyone else, under the table with a beer mug hanging on a cord around her neck. We walked back to the hotel during the wee hours of the morning, my feet screaming in high heels.

Abby's son Ben was sweet on Sweetie, with whom I was sharing a room. She brought Ben back to the hotel room with us. I was too drunk to care—that is until I was awakened in the middle of the night by heavy breathing and grunts coming from Sweetie's bed. When I heard them start a second round I shouted, "I'd better not hear that again!" They got dressed and left the room to find somewhere else to screw.

Whenever I mentioned Sweetie in the months to come Abby would remark, "You mean the Sweetie who boinked my son?"

Filippo Rizzoli and his wife Dawn were passing through Honolulu on their way back to Maui from Chicago, so Abby arranged for them to join us for a Sunday brunch at a restaurant in Waikiki. We waited for over an hour at a reserved table in a private room. Abby kept checking her watch and gazing at the entrance, hoping to see the newlyweds. Finally, Filippo and Dawn waltzed in to cheers and congratulations. We were all famished and ordered food immediately. We knew something was very wrong when Dawn announced to everyone, in a very somber tone, that she needed to take a Valium just to look at Filippo's face every morning. I guess the marriage and honeymoon were a bust, and the rotten mess quickly got thrust down the mouth of a garbage disposal. I had an image of bullets instead of rice being tossed at their second wedding ceremony in Chicago. We made it through the brunch, but it was tricky.

Not long after that day, Dawn divorced Filippo and went back to Chicago. Filippo Rizzoli instructed us never to mention the word dawn around him ever again. Once, without thinking, I nonchalantly said, "I was up at the crack of dawn this morning." Filippo snapped his head in my direction, and if looks could have killed, I'd be dead.

Cicci was very lethargic and wouldn't eat. I wondered if she had an egg stuck inside her. She'd suffered from egg binding once before. I coaxed her in the small cage and took her to the bird vet.

"Are you going to give her an injection to induce her to drop the egg, like you did the last time this happened?" I asked.

The vet had a very concerned look on his face. "I will attempt it, but this might be a different scenario." He encouraged me to leave Cicci with him, and told me he'd see what he could do. I left his office with mixed feelings.

The next day the vet called me with an update. "The shell of the egg had broken in the canal. I cleaned her out as best I could, but this situation usually causes a type of peritonitis. She is awake and alert this morning, which is a good sign. I've been keeping an eye on her for any changes. She seems to be looking around for someone."

I immediately realized Cicci was searching for Pua, her mate. I thought, *Oh God, I should have left both birds there together.*

"I will call and let you know how she's progressing," the vet said. "She seems to be doing well, so I'm hopeful."

The following day the vet found Cicci dead at the bottom of the cage. He said that he tried everything he could to remedy her condition, but she didn't survive. I hung up the phone feeling sadness and loss. I took Pua out of his cage and held him on my finger. I gave him kisses on his beak and told him that Cicci wasn't coming home. The bird seemed confused. He refused to sleep in the cage after Cicci's demise. Cheyenne had made an elaborate perch for the birds, which I set on the nightstand next to my bed. That is where Pua slept from that day forward. He never went into the cage again unless it was to eat seeds or drink water.

Cheyenne and I drove upcountry to spend Thanksgiving with Harry Hackman and Helga Hargrove. I suppose we found comfort in each other even though the romance was gone from our relationship. Harry and Helga had bought a house on a corner in a residential neighborhood of Makawao. Helga had just given birth to a daughter. It was a beautiful cool day up on the crater. My landlord, Lozano Manzoni, who owned my apartment in the J building of the hood, lived right across the street. What kind of a coincidence is that? Or is it?

We had a wonderful turkey dinner with all the trimmings. After dinner, Helga showed us the outside yard. They had planted tropical bushes and fruit trees. This was something I never would have imagined they'd do when we worked in banquets together at the InterContinental Miami. Isn't life full of surprises? They showed us where they buried their dog, Gizmo, who had been poisoned by a neighbor. His resting place was under a large tree inside the white picket fence. All those awful memories about Rebel being abducted came back to me. I knew they were going through the same sorrowful feelings I had back then.

Helga made coffee, and we had apple pie for dessert. I was glad, not being a fan of pumpkin pie, unless it was smothered in whipped cream or vanilla Haagen-Dazs. We whiled away the afternoon reminiscing about our year in the house on Red Road in Olinda. I picked up the new baby and held her in my arms, twirling around and making a fuss over her. I stood in front of Cheyenne and said teasingly, "Maybe we should have a baby." The look on Cheyenne's face was a mixture of annoyance, disappointment, and a tinge of anger. It was as if he was saying, *You put us through all that bullshit, and* now *you want to have a baby?* When I sat on the couch with the baby on my lap he slinked over to the refrigerator to get another beer. He'd been drinking heavily all day, and God only knew what thoughts were running through his head.

When it began to get dark I handed the baby back to Helga and stood up. "It's getting late. We should be heading down the mountain," I said.

"I'm so glad you guys spent Thanksgiving with us. Let's not be strangers. Come up whenever you want," Helga said.

"Yes, whenever you want," Harry chimed in. "We'll always have a room ready"

Cheyenne was very quiet as we walked out the front door. He reached for the car keys in my hand when we got to the curb.

"I'll drive hon."

"You've been downing cans of beer all day long."

"I'm fine," he said stubbornly. "Come on! Don't be a snapper-head."

"You're not driving," I said.

Cheyenne gave up on getting the car keys out of my hand, and reluctantly sat in the passenger seat. I slipped a cassette of Guns N' Roses in the car stereo, and we drove toward Haleakala Highway to their song "Yesterdays." Cheyenne stared out the window for most of the trip. He smoked a couple of Marlboros while I waved the smoke away from my face.

I dropped Cheyenne off at his house. He'd moved yet again. It was a stand-alone house on a corner in Lahaina. The house reminded me of so many of the houses I'd stayed in when I attended the San Francisco Art Institute in the early seventies. The house was reminiscent of the stoned-out hippie era, with a fireplace in the living room, and a large tie-dyed sheet hanging on the opposite wall. Single mattresses on the floor against the walls with colorful Indian bedspreads were used as couches. It appeared as though *hippie* was making a comeback! We'd usually have sex in his room, but on this night I wasn't in the mood for hippie love, make up sex, or anything that reminded me of the past.

"Coming in?" Cheyenne asked with blood in his eyes for me.

"No, I just wanna go home."

He leaned in to give me a kiss with a drunken grin on his face and exuding beer fumes, but I didn't respond. He slammed the car door and walked up the driveway to the house. I guess the blood in our eyes had curdled.

I drove home wondering why the hell I was hanging on to this man who should be part of my past by now. Maybe love remains after a relationship ends.

> When I look back at all my relationships, beginning to understand that there are a few of them that never seem to diminish, neither in my mind nor in my heart. You just manage them. You can get over a person romantically and never fall out of love with them. I think when you really fall in love, there seems to be something permanent that happens to you.
>
> —Junot Diaz, Dominican-American writer

CHAPTER 20

THE VOYAGE

> Here he came then, day after day, week after week, month
> after month, year after year. He saw the beach trees turn
> golden and the young ferns unfurl; He saw how every tree
> and plant in the neighborhood is described first green,
> then golden; how moons rise and suns set; how spring
> follows winter and autumn summer; how night succeeds
> day and day night; how there is first a storm and then fine
> weather; how things remain much as they are for two or
> three hundred years or so, except for a little dust and a few
> cob webs which one old woman can sweep up in half an
> hour; a conclusion which one cannot help feeling might
> have been reached more quickly by the simple statement
> that 'time passed' and nothing whatever happened.
> —Virginia Woolf, *Orlando*

I was in my mid-fifties as the year 2000 crept closer. My desire turned
toward making my life easier and more secure. I had a job that gave me
some of those things, but something was missing—Gauguin. Art was
missing from my life, and as a creative person I needed that for fulfillment.
I could search for Gauguin, but I knew like love, it was something that
the universe would eventually present to me in the most unexpected way.

The revolving cast of characters at Kohola Look-Out was an endless
stream of fun and a great source of knowledge. I met people from all over
the world, some of whom had squirreled away their money over a lifetime
just to take a trip to Hawaii. These visitors had a hard time believing I
actually lived in such a place, which they'd always thought of as paradise.
Then there were those who expected to find a little grass shack, and were
disappointed to find most of the modern conveniences, big-box stores, and
a Starbucks on just about every corner. But by the time their vacations

were waning, they'd fallen in love with the island and didn't want to leave. Magic still exists if you look in the right places.

Kohola Look-Out is a property on the lower coastal road, built in the mid-seventies. One of the original owners showed me photographs of the huge sandy beach with palm trees when it was first constructed. By the time I worked in the office the beach was a moving target. Sometimes the ocean would dump tons of sand, providing a good-sized beach to sunbathe on. At other times Mother Nature took the sand away, leaving just a steep drop into the ocean.

One morning I opened the office noticing an awful odor. I walked to the front of the property and saw seaweed totally covering the sand. It hung around for days, stinking, until one day the ocean wiped it clean.

All the condos opened to the ocean, and each ground floor lanai had a blue acrylic whale imbedded in the cement.

There were a few residents on the property with whom I became enamored over the years I worked there. An elderly couple lived in a two-bedroom on the ground floor corner. The husband was retired from a car dealership he owned in California. He referred to his tiny wife as "The Mouse" and bragged about her having had a limitless credit account at a very expensive shoe store in California, back in the day. They were two wealthy but sweet curmudgeons, who were very generous with me. I received cash and gifts on special occasions, daily plates of goodies, antique collector plates, and a set of two iconic ceramic Disney mice, which I still have in my china cabinet.

Their son, who inherited the car dealership, couldn't have been more different than his parents. He was a total ass. He was referred to by the owners as "The Cowboy" because he always showed up on the island in a cowboy hat and boots. He'd stand in front of my desk with his shirt unbuttoned, tufts of wiry gray chest hair popping out, and blue eyes ready to toss fire at me like a dragon. He managed their one-bedroom rental unit in the building. It was basically a dump which he expected to rent out as a palace, bragging that it was right on the beach with a million-dollar view. He managed it via telephone and fax from the mainland. Whenever something was broken, or there was a plumbing issue, he'd yell over the phone, "When are these renters going to take responsibility?"

There were endless arguments with him, which usually resulted in his cursing at me and my hanging up the phone. This cowboy was a thorn in everyone's side.

Another notable owner was a woman, an ex-combat Vietnam veteran, who owned a center unit on the ground floor. She was a real piece of work. She'd come in the office with a list of complaints along with a list of demands, while her husband stood beside her grinning like a ninny. But I gained a lot of respect for her when she put the Cowboy in his place at a board meeting. He was pacing back and forth across the room like a rabid tiger, ranting and raving in a loud voice, when she stood up, leaned on her cane, and told him, "You've made your point, so sit down and shut the hell up!" The Cowboy stormed out of the meeting room but soon returned, sat down, and was as quiet as a church mouse for the rest of the board meeting. (A side note: the Cowboy was shot dead on his ranch on the mainland. I suspect he mouthed off at the wrong person.)

The corner penthouse was the largest condo in the building on the top floor of Kohola Look-Out. It was purchased by an older Indian couple. It was the designer's unit when the building was built and had a panoramic view of the ocean and neighboring islands. The couple were both born in India but met in South Africa. They remodeled the penthouse when they purchased it from a retired runway model. The management company wasn't sure we could even rent such a high-priced unit, but it became the most sought-after condo. They always took me to a restaurant for lunch when they were in town, and they were familiar with the names of every chef, manager, and waiter on the island. The husband was a googly-eyed internet genius, and the wife had a body like the Hindu goddess Shiva, with a tiny frame and jet-black hair. Fabulous people!

An older Japanese man, Gus Matzumura, lived with his wife in a townhouse on the two top floors in the center of the building. He was in the ocean every day with a spear, fishing for *taco* (octopus). He'd emerge from the waves holding the slithery thing, saying that he had to feed his wife. If no one was watching he'd ride up in the elevator, dripping wet, with the live taco's tentacles climbing over the side of the bucket, trying to escape, and leaving a slimy puddle. He owned the Texaco station in Lahaina near the sugar mill, and had been my mechanic when I first moved to the island in the seventies. That is until I met Derick Ellis.

A man who reminded me of my father, owned a two-bedroom condo on the second-floor corner. He always sent me a fat check for Christmas, and would tease me saying he was leaving me the condo in his will. He was into clocks and went on special river cruises in Europe with other clock lovers. He swam way out in the ocean each morning, and I always wondered if one day he wouldn't return, but he always did. He usually came with his girlfriend, who was actually his cousin. They were referred to as the kissing cousins. She was often drunk and would stand in front of my desk weaving from side to side, conjuring up the words she wanted to express. She was upset when I told her their condo needed an upgrade to be on par with the other rental units. She defended a silly white globe they had hanging over the dining room table. She insisted it was trendy, when in reality it resembled a science project from the 1950s.

I looked forward to some of the return guests with whom I'd buddy up while they were on Maui, and we'd frequent some of the less-touristy bars like the Sly Mongoose. One was a retired detective from Michigan, who always boasted that anyone who wanted to purchase a gun in his state had to first go through him. He was a big black guy, as sweet as chocolate cream pie. He was married to a white woman, a schoolteacher. They had two beautiful kids. Whenever I'd ask how his wife was, he'd correct me and say, "You mean the mother of my children?" God, we had some laughs.

There was an older woman who always stayed in the same condo on the second floor for a month each winter. She went through vodka like it was cold lemonade on a hot afternoon. One morning, she walked into the office claiming that the garbage disposal wasn't working in her condo. She was weaving from side to side, carrying a jug-sized plastic bottle of Smirnoff, and had her brassiere on over her T-shirt. I assured her I'd come to the condo and check it out. I had a special tool that I used to release stuck garbage disposals. Some guests insisted on using sink garbage disposals as trashcans, and threw anything down there that didn't bite back.

Repeat guests rented out the same condo each winter. They often showed up in groups, renting a number of condos, and rarely needed my attention. I called them the Whale Watchers. They knew their way around the island and acted like local residents. These are just a sprinkling of the many wonderful characters who inhabited the Kohola Look-Out. It became a second home to me, and I am still in touch with some of these people.

I was often asked the most ridiculous questions by visitors who weren't familiar with the islands—the first-timers, some of whom would probably never visit Hawaii again. A confused man came into the office asking if that island visible out there was Japan.

I stared at him. "No, that's the island of Molokai across the channel." Then he asked if he could drive there.

"No sir, you will have to take a boat to the other island."

A woman asked me what time the whales came out.

I said, "Any time they feel like it."

But my favorite was a guest who asked me if I really lived on Maui. My snarky reply was, "No, I fly in from California every day just to work here!"

I wouldn't want to overlook Volkswagen, the huge turtle that hung around our reef offshore. The turtle must have been more than a hundred years old. Return guests looked for him each year, and he was the topic of many a conversation.

Locals often came onto the property with fishing poles. In Hawaii all the beaches are public, even if they are in front of someone's residence. A turtle (not Volkswagen) became entangled in fishing line and was struggling off the rocks. Gus Matzumura, who was spearfishing out in the water, spotted the turtle in distress. He swam out to free the turtle from the rocks while guests were standing on shore cheering. Volkswagen was too smart to get caught up in fishing line. How else would he have survived all those years?

I maintained a vendor list of outside contractors and handymen, and some became close friends of mine. Like Gary Walker, who had hopes of someday getting in my panties. We went through a few cleaning companies until I hired a young man, Gael Rivera, from Mexico. He took over the cleaning contract at Kohola Look-Out. He became like a brother to me over the years we worked together. We remain close friends.

Then there were the plumbers, electricians, tour operators, and computer techs. I depended upon these vendors to keep the place running smoothly. And lest I forget, there was an endless supply of realtors who constantly swooped in for the kill on any condo that came up for sale. Roberta Vargas was one of the realtors with whom I became friends.

Spring arrived with a scratchy throat from the mango trees in bloom.

It was a Sunday, my only day off. I was sitting on the couch with a cup of coffee, contemplating whether I was cooking breakfast or going out for bloody Marys and eggs Benedict with Veronica Dove and Annie Hughes, when the phone rang. It was Cheyenne Bremmer. He was almost incoherent, and I struggled to make out what he was saying.

"Ricki's dead," I thought I heard him say.

"Cheyenne, what are you saying?"

"She was at my house last night to drop off our son, Donny. She was begging me to let her stay, saying that she wanted us to be like a real family. Maybe if I'd let her stay she'd still be alive."

"Chey, how is she dead? I don't understand."

He went on with the sad saga. "I told her to grab some beers out of the fridge and go home. I said we'd talk when I dropped Donny off at her house the next day. She left but she didn't want to. The next day when I went to her house to drop Donny off, I found her dead in a chair. She was slumped over with a small knife in one hand and a mango in the other. It was so fucked up, the way I found her. She'd just eaten a mango," he said, his voice cracking. "Her parents are coming to Maui. They think I had something to do with it."

"Oh my God, Cheyenne. What are you going to do?"

"I don't know. I'm totally freaked out. I can't believe they'd even think I would do something to her. The police interrogated me for a long time. Ricki's parents will be in town in a couple of days. There will be an investigation."

I was at a loss for words. I knew instinctively that Cheyenne wouldn't hurt her, and that he had nothing to do with her death. The irony of the situation didn't escape me though. Man leaves older woman for a young thing, wanting a baby; ends up with a baby, and the young twenty-two-year-old dies. So much for the age thing!

He was understandably upset and whimpered a bit, but he did have his son, which is what he'd wanted in the first place. I hung up the phone after we talked for a while. I told him I was sorry, and to keep me informed as to what was happening. I sympathized and felt bad for him, but I wasn't getting involved. I had already put him on a shelf in my past. I met Vero and Annie at a restaurant in Kaanapali for breakfast.

Annie told us the story of her twin sister who was on a cruise ship around the Hawaiian Islands. "She came to visit me at my apartment, and I took her to the Yacht Club for lunch," Annie said.

"Annie, what's she like?" I asked.

"She's nothing like me at all. She's a little old biddy, set in her ways. When she started talking about all the medications she took, and complained about being constipated, I drove her back to the cruise ship docked in Kahului Harbor.

My job at Kohola Look-Out ate up most of my time, and the months flew by. That fall my friend Cathy Rubia showed up on Maui. I took a few days off to spend time with her. She was on a Hawaiian vacation package tour, and was staying at a hotel in Kaanapali. I had a great time showing her around the island, and took her to all my favorite restaurants and bars. She thought Annie Hughes was a riot when we met her for lunch at the Yacht Club. Cathy still smoked like a chimney—Kools, I think. I remember sitting on the lanai of her hotel room whisking away the smoke.

We kept in touch after she went home, but eventually her emails stopped. I sent her a final email in a last-ditch effort to communicate. Weeks later I received an email from her brother. It said simply that Cathy had died of advanced lung cancer, and that she'd been in a nursing facility for a while. It crossed my mind that she'd already had it while I visited her in the slanted funhouse on Staten Island. Maybe even when we were on the Italy tour. We'd talked at length about so many things, yet she never mentioned a word about having cancer.

It was a week before Christmas. I bought a huge Christmas tree, lugged it up the stairs to my apartment, and left it tied up in a bucket of water in the corner of the living room, its top just skimming the ceiling. I planned on decorating it on Sunday. The holidays sometimes just reminded me of lost joys and the people I loved and missed.

I was awakened during the night by the sound of fluttering feathers, which was not uncommon. I often stirred during the night spooking Pua, who would fly off his perch on the nightstand next to my bed. I got out of bed, fetched the flashlight and the fish net, and walked into the living room intending to catch him. I heard a strange squeaking sound. I thought maybe Pua had flown into the Christmas tree and gotten tangled in the branches. I shone the flashlight all over the living room looking for him. The light skimmed the floor, and I saw him lying on the tile next to the bucket. When I reached to pick him up he was lifeless. I feared that he'd flown into the glass sliding door and broke his neck. I cupped him between my hands, his head hanging limp over my fingers. I sat on the couch staring at him on my lap, too stunned to even cry.

"Pua, Pua," I said, softly.

I tried all the things I saw Cheyenne do as the bird whisperer, but nothing worked.

I must have sat there for an hour in denial. I stood up and wrapped him in a cloth and began to cry. When the sun came up I took Pua and walked outside to the top of the gulch. I dug a large hole next to the fichus tree, the one that used to be on my lanai, and I buried him there. I was filled with such deep sorrow. I had a difficult time decorating that Christmas tree. I called Cheyenne Bremmer to let him know about Pua, and to find out how things were going with the police investigation. He told me that he'd been cleared of any wrongdoing. The autopsy showed that his young girlfriend Ricki had died of a brain aneurism.

A few days later Cheyenne showed up at Kohola Look-Out carrying his son in his arms. I saw the back of him through the office window—his long, straight, reddish-brown hair in a ponytail. He turned and walked toward the office, so I went out to meet him. We stood outside in the parking lot talking for a while. I made a conscious effort not to get lost in the ocean of his eyes. From his demeanor, and the things he was saying, I got the impression he wanted to get back with me. All I could think of was the time that Lucas Garzetti, strongest man in the Catskills, showed up at Deer Creek with his two-year-old son in his arms, informing me that he'd left his wife Connie. The similarities of the scenes were uncanny, and so was my reaction. It wasn't the ending I had anticipated or wanted.

Cheyenne seemed lost in disappointment at my indifference. I walked back to the office, and he got in his truck and drove off. I figured in time he'd just find another young thing. Eventually Cheyenne Bremmer moved back to Tucson, Arizona.

"Goodbye, sayonara, aloha," I murmured, when I heard the news. I was emotionally drained. I was sick of love, like the words in that Bob Dylan song.

Abby rented Silver Cloud Ranch for New Year's to ring in the year 2000. That was the last time we were up there before Oprah Winfrey bought the estate. Abby had special plates and champagne flutes etched with the year 2000 for us to take home as keepsakes. (They sit in my china cabinet today). Televisions were placed in strategic locations around the main house so we could watch the fireworks ring in the New Year as it happened all over the world. Each time another country hit midnight, we'd all stop what we were doing, grab our drinks, and toast the New Year in that city. God, I miss that place. I hope Oprah's happy there, and enjoys it as much as we did.

Y2K came and went without Armageddon. The financial markets survived with a mere blip on a computer screen, and life went on as before.

My realtor friend Roberta Vargas was going on a cruise to Tahiti. She'd been there before and assured me I'd love it. "It's like Hawaii was a hundred years ago," she said.

"Robbi"—I liked to call her that—"I'm not into cruises."

"Adriana, this is a small ship with not a lot of people."

"I don't know," I whined.

"By boat is the only way to see French Polynesia, the Marquesas, the Society and Cook Islands of the South Pacific. There are thousands of islands in the chain, only accessible by boat," Robbi said.

"What are some of the islands we'd go to?" I asked.

"Tahiti, Bora Bora, Fakarava, Aitutaki, Moorea, Hiva Oa," she read from the brochure.

I interrupted her. "Isn't Hiva Oa the island where the artist Paul Gauguin lived?"

"I don't know," Robbi said.

My interest was piqued, and I told Robbi I'd think about it. I did have vacation time coming, and this sounded like just what I needed. I did some research about the island of Hiva Oa, and indeed, it was where Paul Gaugin lived, painted, and was buried. I felt a thrill just thinking about walking in his footsteps. *Is fate drawing me farther into the South Pacific to spark a rebirth of creativity in me?* I wondered. I put a deposit on a cabin on the ship going to Tahiti, hoping the universe had a plan for me.

When the day arrived we were packed and ready. We flew on Hawaiian Airlines directly to Papeete, the capital of French Polynesia., where we boarded the ship.

"You're going to love the fact that you won't have to pack and unpack. You'll have the same cabin for the whole three weeks," Robbi said, walking up the plank to the ship, her long red ponytail swinging.

I think I counted almost as many staff as there were passengers. A bowl of fruit greeted me on a small table next to a large window when I entered my cabin.

I barely got settled in when there was a knock at my cabin door. It was Robbi. "Let's go straight to the bar. I want to say hello to everyone," she said, with excitement.

Robbi, a very attractive outgoing woman, owned her own real estate business. She seemed to know the entire staff, and they knew her. Everything on the ship was inclusive—food and liquor, and there was a lot of it.

That first night, the ship stayed in port until all passengers were accounted for. During the middle of the night, I was woken up by the engine starting and the movement of the ship leaving the dock. Once we were out at sea it was like being in a suspended world.

The island of Aitutaki in the Cook Islands was the first island we docked at. After our passports were checked on board, a small tender took us to shore. The different islands were governed by different countries, like in the Caribbean. Some were British, some were French, and so on. We took an open-air truck to the interior of the island. We passed houses where men dressed in lava-lavas were in their yards banging coconuts open on pointed sticks and drinking the juice. Others were picking papayas off trees and eating them. I wouldn't call it primitive, but it definitely was living off the land. There was a sense of community and sharing, but houses and farms were fenced off as private.

All the islands we visited had a heavy influence of Christianity. Churches were either stark white or very colorful. The interiors had very ornately carved wooden altars, and the statues all looked pagan. Some had stained glass, most had clear glass, and a handful had no glass at all. One church had a tall stand outside the entrance with a large shell at the top holding holy water. The French islands had a wonderful selection of wines from France for very cheap, and kids rode around on bicycles with loaves of French bread under their arms. Markets were mostly general stores that carried everything from clothing to pineapples.

In Aitutaki we paid a local guy to take us out on his boat to explore the atolls—a string of tiny uninhabited islands with nothing but white sand and palm trees. The water was a pale green, and so shallow that you could walk from one island to another. We loved swimming there and collecting seashells. It was like being deserted with no large landmass as far as the eye could see. I was lost in a world of the present and feeling content.

Aitutaki Atoll, Cook Islands

I woke up the next morning just as it began to get light. I put a sweatshirt on and walked out of the cabin to the railing to watch the sunrise—that is, until I flashed on those stories about women who were lost at sea, mysteriously tossed overboard, and reported as missing persons when the ship docked in port. I had a panic attack, and rushed back to my cabin as fast as I could.

Once we reached French Polynesia, the boat docked off the island of Fakarava in the Tuamotu Archipelago. We noticed a few new crew members come aboard. After breakfast we took the tender to shore. We had to go through a detection center before leaving or returning to the ship. Everyone had to be accounted for. Robbi got it in her head that we should bicycle around the small island. I wasn't so keen, not having ridden a bike in years. We rented bikes, but I failed to notice that they were all men's bikes. I was fine once I got going, but starting and stopping was perilous with my short legs. I was going along at a good clip when Robbi stopped to look in a shop. There were no brakes, and my legs couldn't reach the ground to slow the bike down, so I just stopped peddling. The bike fell over in slow motion with me on it. I didn't go down too hard, but I did hurt my tailbone. Robbi was in a fit of hysterics. There was no way I was getting back on that torture trap. I walked the bike back to the rental hut. I had to sit on an angle for days until my tailbone healed. Robbi and I still shake our heads and say *Fakarava* whenever something is fucked up.

I was excited when we dropped anchor in Bora Bora. We'd heard there was an extensive Tahitian pearl market. The streets were awash with tables of Tahitian pearl necklaces, bracelets, rings and loose pearls. The selection was overwhelming, and nothing stood out. I couldn't tell the difference between the real pearls and the fake ones. I was told that if the pearls were real, you were given a certificate of authenticity with the purchase.

I saw a ring in the window of a traditional jewelry store in town. It was the one that caught my eye—a large gray pearl set in a high silver setting. I had no problem dishing out two hundred dollars for it. I slipped it on my finger, got the certificate of authenticity, and left the store. I heard my mother Vita say, "Now that's an impressive ring," and I smiled. Perhaps she was watching me from above; maybe she even directed me to that particular store.

We had a day completely at sea. The ocean was rough and the water in the small pool on deck sloshed around and flowed over the sides. There wasn't much to do so passengers hung around the bars like flies on rotten fruit. Every time we sat at a bar, the same local Polynesian guy would show up. He was one of the crew additions that came on board from the island of Fakarava. He told us that's where he lived. He had a thing for Roberta Vargas; he had it bad. He followed her around like a lovesick puppy. If we came across him somewhere in town he'd hang out with us. I told her I thought she should go for it with him.

"You mean screw him?"

"That's what I'm saying."

"Are you crazy? He'll lose his job on the ship."

"Robbi, I doubt you're his first ride in this rodeo."

"I could never do that," she insisted.

"Someday when your old, and no one looks at you anymore, you'll regret this," I said.

"No, I won't," she insisted.

"It's your life. Do what you want with it. I'm just sayin'."

This guy had handsome Polynesian features, light-brown eyes, and creamy caramel skin. He was very respectful, and took time to escort us around town. He was a lot younger than Robbi, but who the hell would care? On our way back to the ship on the tender, Robbi's paramour was sitting next to her, serenading her with his ukulele.

"I'm telling you the guy is hot for you," I whispered. She rolled her eyes and looked away, ignoring me.

I hung out in my cabin that night dismayed that nothing artistic was happening to me, at least not that I was aware of. I thought of a quote I'd heard by one of my favorite authors—to me, he was a philosopher—Joseph Campbell: "The goal of life is rapture. Art is the way we experience it." I so needed art back in my life!

On a rainy day we docked at a private island the tour company used for special events. I walked around the island in my rain jacket taking photos of palm trees and native birds. The staff was busy opening coconuts and getting food ready on grills for a big Polynesian feast. I spied Robbi's paramour standing in the shallow water with his ukulele, serenading one of the female cruise passengers, and laughed to myself. I saw a table with hand crafted jewelry, and was attracted to a necklace of shells with knotted chords holding the design together. There was so much intricate work involved. The necklace was unique.

"How much?" I asked the Polynesian woman seated behind the table.

"Forty dollars."

I walked away thinking, *That is way too much for a shell necklace.*

"Twenty dollars!" she shouted after me.

I turned around handing her a twenty dollar bill, and she fastened the shell necklace around my neck with a smile. It became one of my go-to adornments on that Polynesian voyage.

Shell necklace

Each day I waited for a creative surge to infuse my being, but nothing like that was happening. There were a few days completely at sea. I attend lectures about the notable people who settled the South Pacific. *Mutiny on the Bounty* with Marlon Brando was playing in the auditorium. We had the option to visit the obscure island owned by Brando, but the tour was very expensive. Often, when we were moored off an island, Polynesian dancers would come aboard with music and a whole Tahitian review. I searched for similarities to the Hawaiian hula, but the music was mostly drums, and the dance movements were very fast, with a lot of shaking and sharp gyrations. The dancers wore huge headdresses of feathers and shells, with similar trim around their arms and legs, almost akin to Native American adornment.

I heard an early morning announcement over the ship's intercom that we were approaching the island of Mo'orea in the Society Islands. We were told it would be an impressive sight. I quickly got dressed and rushed to the rail. The scene of the steep volcanic mountains rising out of the sea as the sun was coming up, and the dense palm trees and primitive huts along the shoreline had the *wow* factor. We were greeted on shore with drums, dancing, and chants. I thought of Captain Cook's ships landing in the islands being greeted with leis, and bare-breasted beauties wading out in the water. Then I remembered how that all ended for him. Mo'orea was filled with interesting sights, hiking trails, sculptures, and rainforests to explore.

When we landed on the island of Hiva Oa in the Marquesas Islands, I was like a private detective searching for traces of Gauguin. He was the artist who most inspired my own art. I visited the Gauguin art center where copies of his paintings hung on the walls. I read some information on Eugene Henri Paul Gauguin, the Postimpressionist Painter. He died in 1903 at the age of fifty-four, and like many artists didn't become famous until after his death. We were directed to the house where he lived. I felt tiny chills walking up the stairs and into the primitive structure. The sign over the doorway read MAISON DE JOUIR (House of Pleasure). It was two floors, very spacious but sparse. Woven-grass mats lined the walls and floors. I tried to picture him lying on a bed with the young Tahitian girl he lived with, or standing at an easel painting, which wasn't easy in a totally empty space. He was forty-three and she was thirteen when he married her. She was called his Teha'amana (native wife). He already had a legal wife back in France.

I left the others and walked up a winding road to the top of a mountain, to the cemetery where Gauguin is buried. It overlooks a spectacular bay. I walked around looking for his gravestone. It took a while, but then I spotted it only yards away from the grave of the famous Belgian singer and actor Jacques Brel. My feeling as I stood in front of his grave was similar to how I felt in front of my parents' grave. I felt nothing, as if there wasn't a life spirit present at all. Perhaps their spirits drifted into the sky upon their deaths. I felt no artistic energy surging within me, no creative spark. I was disappointed and felt abandoned by the universe. Still, I was glad I paid my respects to Paul Gauguin.

Gauguin's grave on Hiva Oa

A frantic knock at my cabin door woke me up. I opened it to Robbi who was standing there in tears.

"My mother passed away. I don't know exactly what happened, but my sister just called me on my cell phone

"What are you going to do?" I asked.

"I've already spoken to the powers that be on the ship, and they will have a tender take me to shore in the morning. They've arranged for transport to an airport on a prop plane. I have connecting flights to Ohio. Who knows how many hours or days it will take me to get to Ohio from the middle of nowhere in the South Seas."

"Robbi, I wish I could do something to help you," I said, hugging her.

"What can you do? I just wanted you to know what was happening, and not to be surprised if I'm gone when you wake up tomorrow."

I asked Robbi if she wanted me to hang out with her, but she wanted to be alone. The whole thing was a sad and shocking turn of events.

We had reserved a stay at an inexpensive hotel in Papeete, Tahiti after the cruise ended, because there was only one flight a week to Hawaii, and it wasn't until the weekend. I wandered around town by myself. Papeete is a bustling city with people, scooters, and tiny cars rushing everywhere. I loved the Municipal Market in the center of downtown, where you could find crafts, jewelry, fresh produce, and clothing. There was a selection of food counters, French pastries, and a fish market in the back; the odor permeating that area of the market. The side streets were filled with interesting old buildings and churches. I took photos of a baptism in a cathedral. I spent some time in a store filled with Dolly Parton–type extravagant gowns and dresses, which the store owner claimed people all over the world ordered online. I would have liked to spend more time in Papeete. It was scary alone at night, so I just hung out in my hotel room after dark.

I did have one memorable dinner at a restaurant outside of town that someone strongly recommended. It was called the Blue Banana. I got out of the taxi and looked at the entrance under a long blue canopy—the place looked like a dive bar that no woman should enter alone. But I swallowed hard and walked in. The place was empty, but I could smell French food cooking. I sat at the bar and ordered a glass of French white wine. I asked if I could have dinner at a table on the water, but was told that no tables were available. My eyes scoped the restaurant, and there wasn't a soul in the whole place.

"You can sit at a table in the bar area," the bartender said.

I was slightly annoyed and felt that I was being neglected because I was a woman alone. I was handed a menu, and ordered the fresh fish of the day a la meunière, with potatoes au gratin. No sooner had I handed the menu back, than people began flooding in. Within the next fifteen minutes the place was filled to capacity. An oversized plate was set on the table in front of me with a whole fish dripping in butter, and potatoes au gratin in a small casserole dish with even more butter. I ate with gusto, not stopping until only the skeleton of the fish was left on the plate.

The next morning I took a taxi to the airport for my direct flight back to Maui. I had hopes that the universe had set this trip in my path to reconnect me with Gauguin (art), but all I found was his grave. My trip to the South Pacific was a trip I definitely wanted to repeat. I did just that two years later, also with Roberta Vargas, but to different islands in the Polynesian chain. On our second Tahiti voyage, Robbi's Polynesian paramour hooked up with a female passenger and wouldn't give her the time of day.

That February of 2001 Adam Hirschfeld came to Maui for a visit. He slept on the couch in my Livingroom. I brought him along to the Monday night pu pu party on the ocean side of Kohola Look-Out. He got a big kick out of the blowing of the conch shell at sunset. We saw whales pretty close to shore—it was peak whale season.

"Let's go on a whale watch," Adam said.

"I haven't been on one for a few years. I guess I just know they're out there in the ocean. Like living in New York and never going to the top of the Empire State Building. I think I was thirty years old the first time I took the elevator up one hundred and two floors to the observation deck. And I didn't even live in New York anymore.

Adam laughed. "I know what you mean. We take such local treasures for granted."

"I can get us a free concierge passage with the Pacific Whale Foundation."

"Let's go tomorrow," he said.

I picked up Adam after work the next day. We drove to the harbor and waited on the dock at the Pacific Whale Foundation booth with a line of other people. Our free tickets were waiting for us. The boat wasn't leaving for forty minutes, so we walked into the Pioneer Inn for bloody Marys.

"Ever hear from Dominick French?" Adam asked, noticing a piano in the corner.

"Once in a while he'll telephone me when he's in town, and maybe we'll have lunch. I never go the Missionaries Hotel anymore since he moved off island. The Mission Bar isn't the same without Dominick French at the piano. You know, the jerk stood me up in Venice a couple of years ago, although I had a fantastic time without him."

"He probably met a hot guy in Switzerland," Adam said, and we both laughed.

"I don't know Adam. I have such memories everywhere on this island, yet it never prompts me to want to leave. I don't get *rock fever* like some do."

"Look at your surroundings! How could anyone ever tire of this?"

I smiled at Adam. He paid the tab, and we walked out of the Inn toward the dock. The sun was waning as the boat pulled away from the harbor. I could tell we were in for one of those epic tropical island sunsets.

"Adam, how can the whales forget? They were hunted for hundreds of years in these waters. They can live over a hundred years. Don't they have a race memory?"

"I don't know the answer to that."

"It's as if they know this is a whale sanctuary now."

"I think I see a blowhole in the distance," Adam said, with excitement.

Just then, the captain shouted that whales were seen off the starboard side. Everyone rushed to that side of the boat. Sure enough, whales were in a heat following each other. Males will compete for a female. We saw a few tails and fin slaps, and way in the distance I saw a whale breach, but it was too far away to really enjoy. The sun was setting, and the sky turned shades of pink and red as the sun dipped below the horizon. We slipped our sweatshirts on because it was chilly as the trade winds kicked up. The captain cut the motor, and we drifted for a while. That's when whales came close to the boat, and we had a front-row seat for whale action.

On Saturday, I only worked till noon at Kohola Look-Out. Adam and I drove toward Hana and stopped at a botanical garden I'd never been to. There was an endless variety of exotic trees and plants. We wandered around for hours. I took a photo of Adam in a clump of bamboo, and another one feeding the ducks. I began singing that old song by The Incredible String Band, "Ducks On a Pond," and Adam giggled. On the way back to West Maui we stopped at a Budget Rental Car lot in Kahului, where I had my eye on a champagne-gold 2000 Nissan Pathfinder. The Cherokee Chief was getting old, and I wanted a new car. Adam told me to wait until later in the year when the new cars come out, and buy it cheaper."

That evening we hung around my apartment. Adam was in the kitchen cooking us something for dinner. I'd gotten rid of the big glass table that Cheyenne Bremmer snapped up at the Sands of Nirvana, so we sat on the couch with the plates on our laps, watching TV.

"Didn't you keep journals from our old commune days?" Adam asked.

"Yeah, actually, I still have them."

"I'd love to go through them," he said.

"Adam that seems as if it was all a dream."

"Still, I would love to read some of it with you."

I went to the bedroom closet where I had a stack of journals tied together in a box. I took them out and handed one journal to Adam, and fetched one for myself. We sat on opposite ends of the couch, our feet entwined, and took turns reading from the pages of my journals. "I'll begin, if you want," I said.

From my journal:

A farewell to Giant Hamburgers in Berkeley at 3 a.m., and he's grinning at me. On the ride to San Francisco International he does all the talking. "You'll be visiting me in a few months, right? My friend will freak out when I walk into his bookstore. We had a great summer together, so we should enjoy our independence after being together every day." Me, I'm too choked up to utter a word. We say goodbye in the sterile atmosphere of the airport. There's a brief embrace and a kiss. "Goodbye baby, pretty baby, see you in a few short months," he says. "No, not goodbye, au revoir!" he adds, blowing me a kiss as he walks to the gate. The old Jeep burned oil all the way back to Berkeley while cars passed us left and right over the Bay Bridge. Me in a numb delusional fog.

"Wasn't that the day we drove that guy Dean to the airport, the one you were screwing around with that summer? We were in Berkeley for summer vacation," Adam said.

"Yes. You know I did visit him on the campus at Syracuse University, but it wasn't the same. When that summer was over so was our romance. Your turn. You read one."

Adam picked a different journal and fished through the pages. He settled on this entry—from my journal, 1972:

The look of condescension, the kind that makes you want to vomit.
The kind that makes you feel threatened by your sister.
The kind that denies your existence with a clever little smirk.
The kind that makes you feel you're crazy, imagining things
You're just a fuck-up and will never get anything right.
You want to forget about the things you've observed
The looks, the stares, the loss of outward affection for days
The put-downs and the general sourness
So, it's all inside my head huh?
I've been through this movie before

"Adriana, I'll bet this was when you were at the university on Staten Island. You were really into women's politics."

"Yeah, and I was living with Troy Bloom in that Victorian on Waverly Street. God, I sounded angry! I'll read another one," I said.

From my journal 1971:

> Refreshing cool rain again
> Feeding the earth from the heavens
> The fruit trees will be much sweeter
> In our Garden of Eden
> Do you hear that Eve?
> Sound the trumpets
> Run around feet bare in the wet grass
> Sin Ropas (without clothes)
> It's the best way
> Let the rain feed and refresh you too
> For you Eve are the fruit in the Garden of Eden

"That's beautiful Adriana."

"That was when we were staying at the House of El Capitan Morales in Colombia, South America. Crystal, Ivy, and I were sunbathing nude outside. I wrote that for Crystal. You and Aiden weren't around. I think you'd gone to Bogota for a few days."

"Here's another one from our time at the finca (ranch). Ross Grant was always chastising Crystal about something and threatening to leave her. He really pissed me off."

From my journal 1971:

> Is this a joke?
> Is he asking you to leave your throne?
> What the fuck!
> You stupid woman.
> Don't give up your throne
> Be a queen
> You're a queen bee
> Wait a while
> It will get better
> He'll be better
> He'll come back for the honey
> Queen bee

Adam smiled and nodded his head in approval. It was Adam's turn to read;

From my journal 1969:

> Sunlight coming through the window
> Sparkling in your hair so golden
> Tenderness and love I feel
> For the sun, through the leaves, and for you
> It comes in coloring all the darkness
> Glowing on your face
> Your eyes, they are the sun
> All my sadness fades with the yellow of the room
> Sunlight filling the darkness of my heart
> And once again, I am you

Adam's eyes began tearing, but he didn't say anything; he just stared at me.

"Adam, it's about you, when I was in love with you."

"I know," he said, putting the journal down and rubbing my fingers.

We both were getting a little weepy and nostalgic, but he picked another entry from the same journal and read.

From my journal 1969:

> Green, green it was, so alive, so vibrant
> Rustling and swaying in the cold wind
> Sunlight is filtering through the pines
> Smells fresh in colors of green, yellow, and gold
> Warm wood. A tree is alive, it moves, its breathing
> It feels like me
> It comes apart like me
> Will become earth again like me

"I remember that day," Adam said. "We were tripping on mescaline in the woods behind our friend's commune in Aliceville. We had just left the others at the river."

"Adam, those were such magical days," I said. "We were all so young, so innocent, and open to anything. Our lives were still ahead of us."

"Adriana, these journal entries are art! They are not only beautiful, they tell a story of that time, not just our time in it. Have you ever thought about writing a book?"

"Not really, although I was a journalism major when I was in junior high. I always liked writing. I have a stack of papers filled with poetry and rambles besides these journals. I always felt the need to record my thoughts and feelings."

"Do it Adriana, write a book. Tell those who don't know that it was a special time, spiritual, organic, and thrilling. And yours was not an ordinary life. It was a life filled with art, love, and beauty."

And there it was—the universe sending me a message through Adam. Gauguin wasn't missing at all. The fountain of creativity I'd been searching for was right under my nose. Writing! It came to light in the simplest yet most profound way. That's when I realized that a supernatural power had directed me to keep those journals in a safe place all those years. It's why I carried them from place to place wherever I went. They were my redemption. It was the tale I wanted to tell the world all along. How rich, artistic, spiritual, and exciting it all was.

> It is because the reality I experienced exists no longer, and although its memories are the most precious and vivid ones that I possess, they seem so far away, they are composed of such a different kind of fabric, that it seems as if it originated on other stars in other millennia, or as if they were *hallucinations*.
> —Hermann Hesse, *Journey to the East*

I suppose the islands seduced me in a way a man never could. The tropics possessed infinite visual beauty and excitement, which was always important to me as an artist. In Hawaii I enjoyed these qualities without fear of disappointment or desertion. The islands offered me a life of peace. As a young girl I'd fall in love with a man with unabashed, delicious, total abandon, searching in him for something I already possessed within myself. It always resulted in the loss of the self. When I became a woman I saw turmoil and disappointment in relationships with men, even betrayal, as the price one paid for love. But as I grew older, all I wanted was peace, and that I found on a tropical island.

Adam stayed for another week on Maui, and each night we would read a little from my journals. Even though he and I took different paths in our lives and lived an ocean apart, we still had a special bond, a history, just as I had with others who were part of my life. After Adam went back to New York I made up my mind to write a memoir based on my journal entries, rambles, poetry, my artwork, and photos from my darkroom. I wanted to tell my story, and share the wonderful characters who colored my life—in a way, I was telling their stories as well—and about the people I fell deeply in love with along the way, who still remain part of me.

As I often did on a given evening, I walked down to the ocean to watch the sunset. I gazed out over the channel to the island of Molokai watching the sun dip below the horizon. A chill was in the evening trade winds coming off the surf. I delighted in the sound of the waves as they broke on the shore. I dug my feet in the sand, still warm from the day's sun. I thanked God for putting me in this magical place, this tropical paradise, this land of aloha!

Maui sunset

AFTERTHOUGHTS

I am of the baby boomer generation that came about due to a baby boom after the Second World War. A very large group of people fit in this category, born between 1946 and 1964. We all share some crazy things— nuclear-attack drills in elementary school, where we were told to hide under our desks, as if that would save us from the radiation effects of an H-bomb. (In reality all you could do was grab your ankles and kiss your ass goodbye!) If Johnny down the street came down with the measles, mumps, or chicken pox, your mom took you to his house so you could get it too. Everyone developed natural immunity to childhood diseases, which we were told could have deadly consequences if contracted as adults. We played outside in the streets after school until it got dark without fear, and were called home when dinner was ready. We grew up wild on the streets and in the country. We played in the dirt, and often took care of ourselves. I do remember a polio outbreak in 1955. Kids were kept home that summer, and there was no swimming at the beach or in public pools.

Those same boomer years witnessed the sexual revolution. Actually, it was the advent of the birth control pill that sparked a sexual-freedom revolution for women. I certainly did some experimenting in my youth, and am happy for it. My childhood friend Robby's mother often said regarding that subject, "You wouldn't even buy a pair of shoes without trying them on first."

My young life took a detour and changed dramatically when my mother enrolled me in the High School of Art and Design in Manhattan instead of my district high school, Henry Hudson, in the Bronx. I broke from my childhood friends, and a whole new world opened up. There were no racial, status, or gender issues, with different political ideologies thrown in the mix. Whatever our backgrounds as students were, *art* was the common denominator that united us. Suddenly my neighborhood seemed so *yesterday*, lacking and uninteresting. I was orbited into the unknown, mysterious cosmos.

After high school, I spent two years at the Fashion Institute of Technology. When I graduated, I worked as an assistant to a fur-coat designer in Manhattan's garment district. Then I took a long break to experience the real world.. I was somewhat sheltered as a child, which made me rebellious in my twenties. I hopped on the love bus and headed to Berkeley, California, to live on a commune during the summer of love in 1967. I traveled all over the United States and Canada, and spent three months in Colombia, South America in the summer of 1971. A different way of life seduced me, and as a result I chose an unconventional, freewheeling life path in the counterculture.

I went back to finish my second two years of college on Staten Island at Richmond College, majoring in women's studies, which is a derivative of the social sciences. The suppression of women's talents, and textbooks that omitted women's contributions throughout history, was disturbing and thought provoking. Mae West said, "Well behaved women do not make history." At first I was saddened, then angry, at how women were often relegated to making the coffee, and were told not to worry their pretty little heads about things. The pill put an end to the popular saying, "Keep her barefoot, pregnant, and down on the farm."

In my twenties I began keeping a journal. I suppose it was part of the introspection phase that began when I was a hippie, recording my experiences and feelings in the pages. I continued the practice of journaling for many years. At some point I stopped recording and stashed my journals under a pile of documents and family papers in my parents' apartment. I didn't see them again until my mother passed away, and I was dismantling the apartment they'd lived in for thirty-two years. That is when I came across letters I'd written to my parents, which my mother had saved. There were stacks of ramblings and poetry, portfolios of sketches I'd done, and my journals, on which my memoir is based. I had a lot of material in those pages, more than I could possibly put in a book.

When I wrote my first book, I thought it was the only book. A memoir trilogy was not on my radar. My three books in the memoir series are divided by different eras.

The first book in the memoir series takes place in the late '60s and early '70s, *Confessions of a Hippie: Always Searching for Love*. "Make love, not war" was a popular phrase during the hippie era. It's about peace, the antiwar movement, free love, and living in the politics of the counterculture. Although each book can stand alone, some of the characters introduced in book one make appearances in all three books.

My second book in the series, *Love and Loathing in the Islands: Searching for Gauguin*, is about breaking away from the security of the commune, falling in love with Hawaii, and experiencing a rebirth in my art.

In this third book in the series, *Redemption in the Tropics: Missing Gauguin*, I deal with the harsh realities of life, personal tragedies, love and loss, and how the resilience of art carries me through it all.

When I finished my first book I saw a painting by an artist on social media that I thought was perfect for *Confessions of a Hippie*. I contacted the artist to see if I could use her image for the cover. We agreed on a price, but after some time passed I began to think it was incongruous to use someone else's artwork when I had so much of my own. That is when I realized that I wanted to use my own artwork on the cover, and that I had more story to tell than was in that first book.

I made use of author quotes and quips from famous people to drive home the fact that many life events and emotions are universal, timeless, and shared by us all. I'd often record an interesting passage in my journals from a book I was reading, or the words from a song I'd heard that pertained to something I was going through in my own life. Such words do not have a specific time frame; they transcend time. I made a conscious effort to weave current events of the years I was writing about into my story to give the reader insight to what was happening around me during the time I was living in and writing about. Somehow I managed to conjure up humor, even during times of tragedy and great loss. I attempted to present the saga as the adventure story of a woman navigating her way through each era, and how she experiences it all through a woman's lens.

Art was always at the center of my universe. It took many different forms throughout the years. It was an inborn talent that offered me an outlet for expression, and gave me confidence, joy, and fulfillment. It was a *need*, not a pastime when I was bored. It was an anchor during times of turmoil and uncertainty, like a vessel I rode through troubled waters. Artists are very visual, and I was inspired by beauty—in people, my surroundings, color, even fabric. Inner beauty didn't escape me, but visual beauty inspired me. Writing was also an art form I used all along with poetry and ramblings in the journals I kept. The French writer Voltaire said, "Writing is the painting of the voice." For me it all fit together beautifully.

As to the characters in my story, the people in my life—those I loved and those who loved me-- became part of my being. They added to me in so many ways. They are forever thought of, loved, and missed. I never overcame my Alone Script, which plagued my romantic relationships with men. Looking back, I imagine I craved romantic love, which fades with the mundane existence of everyday life. I had a need for constant emotional validation from my partners. Or perhaps it was just the artist in me that thrived on attention and creative adoration, as if seeking to be the perpetual subject of a lover's painting.

I want to thank those friends who helped me with this memoir project, giving me encouragement along the way. Then there were those who were part of my life's story, who contributed memories for which I'd forgotten the details. To those of you who are dead now, I hope our paths cross again in another time and space. I have mentioned in my books that I often met people on my journey who I felt I'd known in another life. I believe the body dies, but the spirit, the soul, lives on.

Some interesting but unexplainable facts—I have no idea why each of the three books in my memoir series has twenty chapters. Perhaps it was a way of dividing the sections and stories in a similar manner to make the books fit together. I can't explain what motivated me to pack certain items in three boxes and mail them to myself, when I cleared out my parents' apartment after my mother's death. Perhaps a higher power was guiding me. They included family photos and the most precious sentimental items. Also in those boxes were my journals, letters, a portfolio of sketches, stacks of poems I had written, and the photographs I created in my dark room. The thirteen boxes professionally packed by a moving company and shipped to Hawaii were lost. The shipping company was a fraud, and I never saw those items again. I also cannot explain how a friend found my binder of photographs from my dark room in an abandoned storage locker, recognized me, and returned them to me. Coincidences? I think *not*! I did eventually sell my mother's 2.5-karat diamond solitaire engagement ring set in platinum, and used the money for a down payment on a piece of paradise, just like she told me I would. My mother was right. Damn it, she was always right! I live on the very hill where I bartended a real estate function with a catering company when it was just vacant land. I remember looking at the sun setting over the ocean thinking, *God, I'd love to have a place up here.*

What have I learned on my unconventional path? Truth is stranger than fiction. Angels and ghosts do exist. The universe will guide you if you let it. Youth is the time to experiment and be crazy. Nothing that happens in life is just a coincidence. Everything that occurred in my life seemed to be the result of a perfect storm of events.

I wouldn't call these comments advice, just my observed impressions over the years according to my own experiences:

Don't wait to live your life. Throw yourself out there into the cosmos. Do the things you crave, and follow your dreams while you are young. I've known too many people with bucket lists of things they wanted to do when it was the right time, or when they retired, only to be saddled with all the things that come with age, like responsibilities, and health or financial issues. You don't want to look back on your life feeling like you've missed it all. You want to look back and say, "Wasn't it all remarkable, beautiful, crazy, and wonderful?" Be glad that you were there for the ride.

A parting quote from Dr. Seuss:

"Don't cry because it's over; smile because it happened!"

Printed in the United States
by Baker & Taylor Publisher Services